THE ONTOLOGY OF THE ANALYTIC TRADITION AND ITS ORIGINS

DANVILLE
PUBLIC
LIBRARY

THE ONTOLOGY OF THE ANALYTIC TRADITION AND ITS ORIGINS

REALISM AND IDENTITY IN FREGE, RUSSELL, WITTGENSTEIN, AND QUINE

Jan Dejnožka

LITTLEFIELD ADAMS BOOKS

LITTLEFIELD ADAMS BOOKS

Published in the United States of America
by Rowman & Littlefield Publishers, Inc.
4720 Boston Way, Lanham, Maryland 20706

3 Henrietta Street
London WC2E 8LU, England

British Cataloging in Publication Information Available

Library of Congress Cataloging-in-Publication Data

Dejnožka, Jan.
The ontology of the analytic tradition and its origins: realism and identity in
Frege, Russell, Wittgenstein, and Quine / by Jan Dejnožka.
p. cm.
Includes bibliographical references and indexes.
1. Analysis (Philosophy). 2. Ontology. I. Title.
B808.5.D45 1996 111'.09'04–dc20 95–39426 CIP

ISBN 0–8226–3052–4 (cloth: alk. paper)
ISBN 0–8226–3053–2 (pbk.: alk. paper)

Printed in the United States of America

♾™ The paper used in this publication meets the minimum requirements of
American National Standard for Information Sciences–Permanence of Paper
for Printed Library Materials, ANSI Z39.48–1984.

Dedicated to
Panayot Butchvarov

with Honor
and
in Friendship

One cannot step twice into the same river, nor...grasp any mortal substance in a stable condition, but it scatters and again gathers...

—Heraclitus

The one...is now, all together, one, continuous....Nor is it divided, since it all exists alike; nor is it more here and less there, which would prevent it from holding together, but it is all full of being.

—Parmenides, *Truth*

Then may we not sum up the argument in a word and say truly: If one is not, then nothing is?

—Plato, *Parmenides* 166

That "unity" has in some sense the same meaning as that of "being" is clear...

—Aristotle, *Metaphysics* 1054a10-15

If we are to use the symbol *a* to signify an object, we must have a criterion for deciding in all cases whether *b* is the same as *a*, even if it is not always in our power to apply this criterion.

—Frege, *The Foundations of Arithmetic*

[T]he scholastics used to say '*One* and *Being* are convertible terms'. It now appears that 'one' is a predicate of concepts....And...'being' applies only to certain descriptions....These distinctions...put an end to many arguments of metaphysicians from Parmenides and Plato to the present day.

—Russell, "Logical Positivism"

But we forget that what should interest us is the question: how do we compare these experiences; what criterion of identity do we fix for their occurrence?

—Wittgenstein, *Philosophical Investigations* #322

Identity is...thus of a piece with ontology. Accordingly it is involved in the same relativity...

—Quine, "Ontological Relativity"

Contents

Preface

I treasure memories of my mentors, Larry Hardin and Murray Miron of Syracuse University and Panayot Butchvarov of the University of Iowa, and many old teachers and friends. Words cannot express my gratitude to my wife, Chung Wha, and to our family for their love and support.

I am deeply grateful to Panayot Butchvarov and Stewart Umphrey for their thoughtful comments (including Butchvarov 1988; Umphrey 1988). I am grateful to Willard Van Orman Quine, Ivor Grattan-Guinness, Gregory Landini, Kenneth Blackwell, Nicholas Rescher, Hector-Neri Castañeda, Guenter Zoeller, John McDowell, José Benardete, Evan Fales, Daniel Flage, Layman Allen, and Wyatt Benner for brief but important guidance. I am grateful to Ivan Boh, Leonard Carrier, Chip Sills, and Susan Hale for sending me material. Several anonymous reviewers kindly provided excellent help. Any errors, of course, are mine.

I thank the United States Naval Academy Research Council for research grants in 1987 and 1988. Mrs. Connie Grigor of the History Department and Mrs. Katherine Dickson of Nimitz Library were exceptionally helpful. My views do not reflect those of the United States Navy, the Department of Defense, or the Federal Government of the United States.

Some of my articles appear in chapters by kind permission of the editors of several journals. "Frege on Identity," *International Studies in Philosophy* 13 (Dejnožka 1981: 31–41) is much of chapter 2, section 1. "Frege: Existence Defined as Identifiability," *International Studies in Philosophy* 14 (Dejnožka 1982: 1–17) is most of chapter 3. "Russell's Robust Sense of Reality: A Reply to Butchvarov," *Grazer Philosophische Studien* 32 (Dejnožka 1988b: 155–64), and material from "Reply to Butchvarov's 'Russell's Views on Reality'," *Grazer Philosophische Studien* 32 (Dejnožka 1988: 181–84) and from "The Ontological Foundation of Russell's Theory of Modality," *Erkenntnis* (Dejnožka 1990: 383–418), are most of chapter 4. All are rewritten here. Permission to quote from correspondence has been very kindly granted by Willard Van Orman Quine, Ivor Grattan-Guinness, Gregory Landini, and Albert Casullo. Permission to quote texts has been kindly granted by Northwestern University Press for Frege, *The Foundations of Arithmetic*, and also by the Bertrand Russell Peace Foundation and Routledge for Russell, *The Analysis of Matter* (Dover), *Human Knowledge: Its Scope and Limits* (Simon and Schuster), *Logic and Knowledge* (Capricorn), and *The Principles of Mathematics* (W. W. Norton).

I proceed to state the limitations, aims, principal argument, and likely main objections to the book. I shall begin with the book's five main limitations.

First, much like its worthy predecessors, Michael Dummett's *Origins of Analytical Philosophy* and Benardete's *Metaphysics: The Logical Approach*, the present book is not a historical study in that there is almost no discussion of causal influences of earlier philosophers on the analysts, or of the analysts on each other. If you please, the book is a *proto*-historical study. It is not history of philosophy, but something that must be done prior to that. For the book identifies and analyzes the many different existence-identity connections in the different periods of Frege's and Russell's thought, so that others can then inquire after their causal antecedents and influences. If I had done a historical study of the causal relations of these connections, the book would have been far longer than it is, and would have taken many more years to write. Here I can only briefly state the obvious: Russell read Frege, Wittgenstein read Frege and Russell, and Quine read Frege, Russell, and Wittgenstein. As to influences of the ancients, I shall cite at the moment only Wittgenstein's admission that his objects and Russell's individuals were Plato's primary elements (PI #46; see *Theaetetus* 201–2). I do, of course, intend the book to be a historically accurate or at least reasonable account of the analysts. But in any case I hope that my helpful glosses and charitable interpretations result at least in a philosophically interesting book.

Johannes Herder defined the ambiguous term "origin" as meaning either cause, source (antecedent), or beginning (first of its kind). This book seeks the *beginnings* of the ontology of the analytic tradition. I seek to show that the 'no entity without identity' ontologies of the four analysts I discuss are far from the first of their kind. It is hard to make Herder's definition precise. It is not always clear when antecedents end and things of a kind begin. But everything I describe as an origin is a source at the very least.

A second limitation is that I discuss only four analysts. I could not discuss the whole analytic movement in this book.

Third, I treat only Frege and Russell in depth. I hope to supplement and deepen, not compete with, the huge literatures on Wittgenstein and Quine. Even so, my strict concern with the theme of 'no entity without identity' precludes my giving a full ontological portrait of Russell. To see the full portrait, sandwich my "The Ontological Foundation of Russell's Theory of Modality" (Dejnožka 1990) between chapters 4 and 5 and my "Russell's Seventeen Private-Language Arguments" (Dejnožka 1991) between chapters 5 and 6.

Fourth, I may not cite enough literature on Russell to satisfy some specialists. But that is because my book covers virgin territory. I had to devote most of my time to primary Russell literature—nineteen books and many papers by Russell. Still, my *Bibliographical References* show that I have read more secondary literature than some others who have written on Russell—or on Frege.

Fifth, it may seem odd that in a book on the origins of analytic philosophy, I do not discuss the pre-1900 Russell. I had enough to do discussing 'no entity without identity' in every major published work by the post-1900 Russell. The book would have been far longer had I repeated the fine work Nicholas Griffin did in *Russell's Idealist Apprenticeship* on identity and difference in the pre-1900 Russell. My book aims to supplement and deepen, rather than compete with, his work.

The recent renaissance in Frege-Russell studies, though including some excellent work, has confined its quest for the origins of analytic philosophy to the nineteenth century. My book goes well beyond Frege-Husserl comparisons and historical studies of Russell's idealistic upbringing to give a philosophical evaluation of what the analytic movement really amounts to. My thesis is that a single *kind* of ontology, 'no entity without identity' ontology, is fundamental to all of Russell's major works from 1900 to 1948, to the work of Frege, Wittenstein, and Quine—and also to substance metaphysics, its origin over two thousand years ago. Thus my aim is to show that the analysts, far from ending traditional ontology, at bottom continued and even developed it. I cannot see how our understanding of the pluralistic, diverse analytic movement, not to mention the pluralistic, diverse history of Western philosophy, could be more deeply transformed or unified, if I am right.

My methodology was to read the major books of the analysts, many of their lesser works, and a great deal of the secondary literature, gleaning like Rachel in the field of wheat for anything I could find on 'no entity without identity', then to create from scratch new portraits of Frege and Russell as the true analytic progenitors of this kind of ontology.

The specific thesis of my book is that there is a general kind of ontology, modified realism, which the great analysts share not only with each other, but with most great Western philosophers. Modified realism is the view that in some sense there are both real and rational (or linguistic) identities. In more familiar language, it is roughly the view that there are both real distinctions and distinctions in reason (or in language). More precisely, it is the view that there is *at least one* real being which is the basis for accommodating possibly huge amounts of conceptual relativity, or objectual identities' "shifting" as sortal concepts or sortal terms "shift." Therefore I hold that on the fundamental level of ontology, the linguistic turn was not a radical break from traditional substance metaphysics. I also hold that the seeming conflict in the analysts between private language arguments, which imply various sorts of realism, and the conceptual "shiftability" of objects, which suggests a deep ontological relativity, is best resolved by, and is in fact implicitly resolved by, their respective kinds of modified realism. There are many different sorts of modified realism, but all of them share a common general form.

I present Frege as a modified realist with fourteen 'no entity without identity' theories. Then I present Russell as a modified realist with forty-four 'no entity without identity' theories. Last, I briefly sketch Wittgenstein and Quine as modified realists, to show that modified realism best merits the title, the ontology of the analytic tradition.

My principal argument is: (1) While in the analytic tradition ontology and philosophy in general are held to be supervenient on language or, more deeply, on logical and conceptual theses, there is enough reformulation and presupposition of ontological themes, and even enough express pursuit of metaphysics through analysis, to allow analogies to some basic theses of the substance tradition. (2) The sufficiency of the analogy to traditional modified realism is ensured by seven criteria of modified realism. Any one criterion establishes a kind of modified realism, and the analysts satisfy most of these criteria as well as substance metaphysicians do. Here I assimilate the analysts' views to Aristotle's metaphysics as the paradigm of modified realism. (3) Therefore the analysts are modified realists. The argument may appear to attack the analytic lion in its own den. For example, did not Russell deride substances as confused and at best a mere linguistic convenience?

Three clarifications are in order.

First, much of stage (1) of my principal argument is familiar ground. That analytic philosophy reformulates ontological insights was argued by Gustav Bergmann (Bergmann 1967: 1–77). That arguments against metaphysics presuppose metaphysics was noted by F. H. Bradley. Either point satisfies stage (1). Thus when I argue in this book that all four analysts admit express vehicles for referring to extra-linguistic reality, I go far beyond what stage (1) requires.

Second, while Quine uses the phrase "'No entity without identity'" (OR 23), many very different kinds of thesis might be appropriately so described, some of which are not only incompatible with each other, but even with Quine's thesis. Throughout this book, when I use that phrase, I do not mean Quine's thesis in particular, but any theory on which some expression, conception, or property of existence is defined, explained, understood, or applied in terms of some expression, conception, or property (or relation) of identity. For instance, I argue that from 1905 on, Russell progressively divorces his 'not always false' existential quantifier from existence, reserving existence for any simple things which may constitute an ultimate interpretation of true existentially quantified sentences. If I am right, then Russell's 'no existential quantification without identity conditions' theory applies to logical fictions as well as to simples. Such a nominal "existence"-identity connection is incompatible with Quine's thesis, since so to speak, it takes the entity out of 'no entity without identity'. Yet on my liberal usage, it counts as a 'no entity without identity' thesis.

I base this liberal usage on my liberal definition of ontology in chapter 1. But while I think that the definition is intrinsically plausible, and justified by the single unifying theme of ontological interest, others may perceive it as so inclusive and eclectic that it sweeps all differences between traditional and analytic ontology under the rug, and the difference between the later Wittgenstein and the other analysts as well. Therefore I now further explain and argue for my liberal usage by modifying Peter Geach's succinct and excellent analysis of ontological analysis. I believe this applies to all four great analysts:

> On the face of it, we are committed to recognizing *A*s as a kind of object when we use the logical apparatus [or a criterion] of identity....I further hold that this commitment is only a defeasible one; a thinker may in fact defeat his commitment if he can show, or at least sketch, a method of paraphrasing away the ostensibly identifying...language he uses about *A*s... (Geach 1969: 66). For, as Quine has said, no entity without identity; he and I agree in regarding as *entia non grata* those philosophically postulated entities for which there is simply no telling whether men are talking about the same thing or not. And again Quine and I would both say: No identity without entity. Nonentities are not there to be the same or different... (Geach 1972: 288)

Geach speaks of the apparatus of identity *and quantification*, and of identifying *and quantifying* language; dropping quantification is my modification. I think that if *A*s are identifiable and talk of them cannot be paraphrased away, that alone constitutes their existence. Quantification is a useful but formalistic rubber stamp. Identity is what counts in the practice of all the analysts; and I suspect that this is because at bottom they agree with my analysis of analysis. Anyway, Russell's purely nominal "existence"-identity connection clearly is a 'no entity without identity' connection, on my analysis of 'no entity without identity' analysis. Russell holds that logical fictions are *not* entities; their ontological status is nil. He paraphrases logical fictions away in terms of classes, which he paraphrases away in turn through a contextual definition in *Principia*. In all this, Russell strictly conforms to 'no entity without identity' analysis as I just explained it, and just as much as Quine does, even though Quine admits classes and Russell rejects them, and both quantify over them. Thus my analysis of analysis is quite general. Even the later Wittgenstein is a 'no entity without identity' analyst, on my analysis of analysis. Whenever there is any puzzlement about admitting entities, he compares talk of such entities to paradigms of ordinary talk about ordinary phenomena using ordinary criteria of identity. He aims to discover whether talk of the putative entities is sufficiently analogous to paradigmatically correct talk for the putative entities to have sufficiently coherent identity conditions to be said to exist. In general, of course, he rejects talk of philosophically posited entities as so bewitched by simplistic conceptions of grammar that the identity conditions involved are not sufficiently coherent. And surely he would reject nonexistent objects as due to just such a bewitchment of grammar. The second stage of analysis, paraphrase, would consist of any cases where he does find an ordinary use that some talk of philosophical entities might have, to that extent reducing such talk to ordinary talk of ordinary things. While he admits only ordinary things, it must be realized that it is his profound and subtle *ontological theory* that only ordinary things exist and are identifiable. What makes it an ontological theory is the philosophical argumentation he gives for it. Thus, in my sense of "analysis," he is just as much an ontological analyst as anyone, due to the great ontological interest of his work.

Third, not only must we examine the intrinsic content of a 'no entity without identity' thesis, but we must also consider the role it plays in a philosophy. Russell illustrates this well. Concerning the intrinsic content of 'no entity without identity', Russell seems closer in 1903 to Quine, and to the Frege of *Basic Laws*, than at any other time. For the 1903 Russell, Quine, and the *Basic Laws* Frege alike, cardinal numbers are defined as classes of classes which preserve the identity conditions numbers ought to have, but are merely *reduced* to classes. Numbers are dropped as a special category, but classes are admitted. The 1910–59 Russell sharply differs from Quine by *eliminating* numbers. Russell continues to define numbers as classes of classes, but now rejects classes as strictly nothing. Yet from 1927 to 1959, Russell ever more closely anticipates Quine on the *role* 'no entity without identity' plays in philosophy. For during this period Russell questions and then weakens the analytic-synthetic distinction, adopts a holistic, social, and pragmatic theory of knowledge (if not theory of truth), and assimilates philosophy to science. Thus the 1927–59 Russell is closest to Quine on the role identity conditions play in defining physical events, space, and time. This book explores both the intrinsic contents of 'no entity without identity' theses and their roles in analyzing many specific topics, especially in chapters 3 and 5. I should add that my use of 'no entity without identity' is often better read as 'entity if and only if identity'; I am merely conforming to popular usage.

I expect my argument that the four great analysts are modified realists will encounter tremendous resistance from, and will sow confusion among, orthodox Anglo-American analysts. In fact, it has already done so. That is good, because the ironic point of the book is to achieve a double Copernican revolution: disinverting and setting right what many analysts mistakenly believe is their Copernican revolution from hopelessly Ptolemaic substance metaphysics.

The principal objection offered is that any comparison of two philosophical traditions must be based on an accurate understanding of each tradition in its own right. Otherwise one will find oneself distorting the explained tradition by imposing on it the categories, theses, approaches, methods, and tools of the other. In particular, claiming to find a distinction between real distinction and distinction in reason in any of these four analysts is just such a distortion and just such an imposition. For the analytic tradition understands itself, and these four analysts understand themselves, as holding that philosophy of language is the foundation of *all* philosophy. In particular, for these philosophers, *ontology is supervenient on language*. Thus they are anti-ontological in the sense that the *entire content* of any ontological thesis is exhausted by linguistic considerations.

Or, if you please, the analysts rest all philosophy on logical and conceptual considerations; and for *humans*, such considerations must be understood in terms of our capacity to use language. (I should perhaps retitle my book more exactly as *The Ontology of the Linguistic Turn and Its Origins*.) Thus even to consider the analysts' philosophies in terms of the many sorts of concrete entities, abstract entities, fictions, or phenomena they admit, in abstraction from their meta-philosophical view of ontology as a function of linguistic or, more deeply, logical and conceptual considerations, exhibits a pervasive misunderstanding of their philosophies.

Now, this principal objection is just the principal myth my book aims to explode. One fallacy in it is to assume that the best place to use a category, thesis, approach, method, or tool is necessarily its original home. Indeed, in interdisciplinary cross-fertilizations, the last place such things are used may be the best. It is an experimental question which the principal objection prejudges. Off-hand, we should have better luck understanding two consecutive traditions of Western philosophy in terms of each other then we would applying a car manual or socket wrench to either. Another fallacy is to assume that theses and methods cannot be adapted. A third fallacy is to assume that I am applying the categories, theses, approaches, methods, or tools of either tradition to the other at all. I am simply comparing them. In particular, Kahn and Hintikka argue that modern quantification should not be imposed as a tool to interpret the ancient Greeks. While I do note that Kahn and Hintikka do not seem to understand the modest aims and claims of modern paraphrase, my chief point in chapter 6 is that *even accepting* Kahn's and Hintikka's own anti-Fregean, anti-Russellian portrait of the ancient Greeks, Frege and Russell have far more in common with Aristotle than Kahn or Hintikka suppose. And on the analytic side of the house, consider Russell's thesis that in respect of their brief duration, his "particulars [sense-data] differ from the old substances but in their logical position they do not" (PLA 204). Are not momentary two-dimensional sense-data wildly different from Aristotle's material substances? Is not the slim resemblance they do have merely supervenient on the logical position Russell assigns them in language, and not due to any intrinsic nature of their own? —Things look a little different when we learn that Russell's sense-data are mind-independent and physically real, and have "that sort of self-subsistence that used to belong to substance" (PLA 202). Sense-data look even more like the old substances when we learn that Aristotle's substances are just as supervenient on logico-linguistic position as Russell's sense-data are, without any derogation of Aristotle's physical realism (*Categories* 1*a*–4*b*). In terms of the seven themes characterizing substance with which this book begins, it turns out that only theme (6), persistence through changes, fails to apply to sense-data. And it is widely admitted that mere duration is the least important traditional theme.

In fact the chief problem with the principal objection is that it ignores my principal argument. No flaw has been detected in my principal argument. The objection may seem wise. Yet it is also wise not to criticize comparisons of traditions until these comparisons are understood in *their* own right. In particular, my argument is analogical, and my admission of varieties of modified realism is as liberal as my admission of kinds of 'no entity without identity'. Even those who reject substances in any traditional sense count as modified realists if, according to my seven criteria, they admit sufficient substance analogues or can be interpreted as admitting sufficient analogues to real distinctions and distinctions in reason. Even if it were the case that the ontology of every analyst is arrived at through linguistic, logical, or conceptual considerations, and that the ontology of no traditional ontologist is, this would only make such analogies to traditional ontology deeper and more exciting, since they would persist through such seemingly great differences. Indeed, I agree with Butchvarov that analogy is the deepest form of philosophical understanding.

Thus the principal objection to my book seems a *non sequitur*. In particular, consider the many realisms of the four analysts as supervenient on their private language arguments. These arguments aim at establishing some minimal extramental and extra-linguistic realism of public objects. But they are based on premises purporting to assert common-sense facts which obtain regardless of what we may say or think about them. Now, consider the relativism involved in objectual identities' shifting as sortal concepts or sortal terms shift. Throughout this book, I use "shift" strictly as a metaphor. Viewing a card deck under the concept *card* does not literally chop the deck into fifty-two cards as if it were some nonresistant nullity. Sortal concepts simply individuate *different* but overlapping objects. Nor does an object literally change into a concept when we "shift" logical subject and predicate. Still, objects may seem never given independently of the concepts through which we conceptualize or view them. This relativism may be presented as a linguistic (or conceptual) thesis about objects. Yet the thesis is based on a common sense fact about our sortal terms or concepts, a fact which obtains regardless of what we think or say about it. Now, this realism and this relativism are just the two basic elements of the general modified realism common to the four analysts. Viewing the relativist thesis radically, as precluding realism by making it impossible or meaningless to speak or think about things as they really are, is self-defeating. Piercing the linguistic or conceptual veil reveals a host of assumed facts about language or concepts, facts which are assumed as objective in their own right—and on which the supposedly "supervenient" thesis is based. Thus the supervenience goes in the other direction. Linguistic or conceptual relativism is determined by the facts, not the other way around. All four great analysts, I shall argue, were well aware of this; it was many of their followers who inverted the insight.

Similarly for assertions that two things can exist independently of each other, and that one kind of thing is more real than another. Such assertions can be reconstructed as linguistic or conceptual proposals. Yet the proposals would be reformulations, admittedly often drastic reformulations, of what can only be called ontological considerations. To illustrate, let me reformulate these two kinds of assertion as they would apply to Frege.

First, then, Frege admits no modal operators in his notation. So how can he define real distinction as a capacity for independent existence? The short answer is that for Frege, being really distinct amounts to being *wholly* distinct. More deeply, Bergmann reformulates "categorially impossible" as whatever is ill-formed in the canonical notation (Bergmann 1967a: 23–24). As Bergmann well knows, this only hides a core aspect of traditional essence under a linguistic disguise. For Frege, this core aspect of essence is hidden under the disguise of an expression's semantic role or function. For Frege an object or function, and likewise a complete or incomplete sense, can be identified only in terms of an expression's logical role in sentences. It is precisely because of this "supervenience" that Frege can and does describe essential characteristics of objects and functions. This is the whole approach of Aristotle's *Categories*, which is most charitably paraphrased as metalinguistic. For Frege, essence is *shown*, not said, in his canonical notation. This reformulation of essence arguably applies even to Quine's canonical notation. Further, I admit *four* senses of "real distinction," and I mainly rely on sense (2), the only one which does not require substances or substance analogues. The deepest point is that even traditional ontologists recognized that defining real distinction and distinction in reason in terms of what can or cannot exist independently of each other is not yet philosophically illuminating. The whole problem is to explain this capacity for independent existence, not just rename or reformulate it. The explanation will consist in showing why we admit the metaphysical categories we do, how they interrelate, and why we assign to each category the ontological status we do, such as real being or mutedly real conceptual being. Only then can we fully explain Frege's or Bergmann's approach to such modal distinctions. Though the explanation will be traditional in general form, it may be quite contemporary in content, and may be eliminative of the modal aspects of the distinctions. All this is transparent insofar as Frege's and Bergmann's canonical notations are both intended as ideal languages which reflect the true classification of things. And even outside an ideal language, "wholly distinct" is said in different senses, or is at least explained in different ways, for different categories of entities. So too for the term it glosses, "capable of mutually independent existence."

Second, Frege calls his concrete objects more *wirklich* than his abstract objects. Some say that J. L. Austin translated "wirklich" as 'actual' rather than 'real' because he felt that Frege did not intend the term to have any ontological significance, but only to mark the presence of causal aspects among concrete objects. Now if this is so, one may suspect that Austin was overly scrupulous. Why did Frege choose *that* term? Is it not because people naturally feel that, as Plato put it, in some sense existence is power, and that therefore causal relations *do* mark reality in some sense? Using the word "actual" does not hide this intimation of the substantive. And what about Frege's *reeller, wirklicher, greifbarer*, which Austin himself translates as 'more real or more actual or more palpable'?

Russell was, if anything, even more explicit than Frege in his pursuit of metaphysics through analysis as a vehicle. Just think of his ending "The Philosophy of Logical Atomism" with an *Excursus into Metaphysics*. Russell rejected most traditional metaphysics. But he did not reject metaphysics. Rather, he tied metaphysics very closely to logical analysis. In fact he required that every analysis preserve a robust sense of reality.

My own way of making Russell's point against the principal objection would be this. Suppose that I make the logical, conceptual, and linguistic proposal in my metalanguage that in my object-language, only certain undefined expressions are to name items having all the characteristics of Aristotelian substances. Far from being some sort of relativistic barrier or hindrance to my realism, my metalinguistic proposal is precisely the vehicle by which I explain how I *can* denote Aristotelian substances. This metalinguistic rigmarole will never prevent me from being exactly the same kind of realist as Aristotle himself. Indeed, it will guarantee that I am, and as soon as I start using the expressions in question.

Jumping through metalinguistic hoops is like moving in Ptolemaic epicycles. Thus I hope I may be forgiven if I follow Frege and Russell themselves in so often using the "material mode" of speech. I am, of course, as aware as anyone that the heart of the linguistic turn is the reconstruction of meanings (or concepts or notions) as linguistic *uses*. In fact, I criticize others for forgetting this point in chapter 6.

Ideal language proposals for reconstructing substantive theses resemble metaphysical systems: "methodological" monism, nominalism, phenomenalism, physicalism. Any test of the adequacy of such reconstructions would seem to beg the question against some substantive thesis. As to ordinary language analysis, I need not repeat the criticisms made by the later Russell or recall Dummett's observation that the later Wittgenstein had a theory of his own about the nature of language. But I will repeat Richard Rorty's carefully understated point in *The Linguistic Turn* that there is much interplay between substantive philosophy and meta-philosophy (Rorty 1967: 39).

The principal objection is merely a reformulation of what I call the second revolt against the primacy of metaphysics in chapter 1. Correspondingly, my argument against that revolt is a version of the principal argument of this book.

A determined holder of the principal objection may reply that my daring to criticize the characterization of the analysts leading to the principal objection, and my offering criteria of modified realism as applicable to the analysts, beg the question against the principal objection. But if my argument and criteria are rejected by assuming that the principal objection is correct, who is begging the question? Surely the burden of proof lies with those who make the principal objection. For my principal argument already handles so-called supervenience. Specifically, objectors have to meet three conditions: they must destroy the analogical argument of this book, they must offer an anti-analogical argument that succeeds where my principal argument fails, and they must develop criteria of the *mere* supervenience of ontology on language or logic, applications of which overrule my applications of my seven criteria of modified realism in much detail to the analysts. Needless to say, they have not met these conditions. Who then is misunderstanding whom? Ironically, the very supervenience of ontology on language or logic is itself a rather substantive thesis about the relationship of ontology to language or logic.

Thus it is not clear to me that the four analysts I discuss would accept the characterization of their work that leads to the principal objection. Their work seems too subtle, too complex, and too thoughtful for that. There seems to be something that is really the case about language and logic, and even the world, in their work.

I shall also argue that identity is not always under a sortal concept for the analysts. A principle of charity calls out for this in light of (i) the vicious regress of classifications implied by the theory that identity is always under a sortal concept; and (ii) the need to explain how we acquire sortal concepts in the first place, i.e. in terms of prior identifications (Butchvarov 1979: 78–81). Russell expressly gives the regress argument (HK 423–24). Quine expressly acknowledges the need to explain how we acquire sortal terms, or "terms of divided reference." Quine says that to learn verbal responses at all, a child "must have...a prior tendency to weight qualitative differences unequally....In effect therefore we must credit the child with a sort of pre-linguistic quality space" (WO 83). Here Frege and Wittgenstein are the principal charity cases. However, all four analysts actually admit some items which arguably have and must have *given*, though, I admit, not always phenomenologically presented, objectual identities. These include Frege's phenomena, Russell's earlier sense-data and later noticed events, Wittgenstein's phenomena, and Quine's sensory stimulus patterns, if not also his initially posited physical objects. All these items have sortal *properties* which may be called the *basis* of our identifying them (see Butchvarov 1979: 122–23). My argument is only that we may single such items out prior to acquiring any sortal *concepts* or sortal *terms*. The exception to the rule that to be given is to be phenomenologically presented is, of course, Quine's neural stimulus patterns (and initially posited objects), which Quine presents as strictly physical. As Evan Fales observes, "Those who reject the given or its foundational role are not like sailors attempting plank by plank their leaky boat, but rather like sailors who do not even know they are at sea; nor what can serve as a plank" (Fales 1990: xix). Concerning stimulus patterns, Quine says, "...I do indeed combine foundationalism with coherentism, as I should think it evident that one must" (Quine 1990: 128). In the case of initially posited objects, my charitable gloss that their objectual identities are given to observers applies on pain of Quine's holistic science boiling down to sheer circularity (WO 3, 21–23). As we shall see in chapter 7, Frege admits phenomena which one can single out without using their sortal properties *as* sortal concepts, and prior to language acquisition. I wholly grant that for Frege concepts *are* properties. This is only a terminological difficulty for my argument. The question is whether we have to use properties *as* concepts in order to single out phenomena.

Even when we do use sortal concepts or sortal terms to identify things, I shall argue that no serious relativity is implied. Again, far from being barriers between us and the world, Frege's senses, Russell's acquaintance and knowledge by description, the later Wittgenstein's criteria, and Quine's theories are all intended precisely as the vehicles by which we learn all we can of a mind-independent, language-independent reality.

Realism *versus* relativism has seemed to many the issue that most characterizes this "rootless and alienated" analytical century. Radical relativity is "above all ignorant of itself" and its need for a robust realism deeper than itself. We "post-philosophers" need to understand our realist roots in the analysts and in earlier ages. The recent reports of the death of philosophy have been greatly exagerrated.

In 1989, Longwood Academic/Hollowbrook Publishing accepted an early version of this book for publication under the title *Being Qua Identity: The Ontology of the Analytic Tradition*. I bought back all rights to the book in early 1993 after I learned of Longwood's financial and legal difficulties, and dismal publication record, from a group of some thirty unhappy authors. That seems to be why Longwood sat on my book for three years despite what was called "unusually strong" pre-publication orders for the book. Longwood got as far as running galley proofs. But not one page of my book was printed; the book was never published. The book was advertised in the January 1993 *Proceedings and Addresses of the American Philosophical Association* and elsewhere. I must apologize to anyone who ordered it from Longwood. Since Longwood and its people had some half a million dollars in court-awarded debts already, according to a detective's report, you will probably never see your money again. I myself lost almost a thousand dollars in book orders, the repurchase of rights, and the legal fee. On the bright side, I consider myself lucky to be one of the authors who escaped, and I am deeply grateful to Rowman & Littlefield for publishing the book now. It has been almost continuously revised and updated from 1990 to 1995. It is a much better book, though there has been no change in views.

On August 11, 1995, as I was about to send the book to press, A. D. Irvine and G. A. Wedeking, eds., *Russell and the Analytic Tradition* (1993) arrived from California through interlibrary loan. A quick scan showed me that Nicholas Griffin apparently had arrived independently at some of my major ideas, and some other authors came close to some of my other ideas as well. I decided not to attempt to alter my book at the last minute—no views of mine would change in any case—but I shall offer some comments in the next four paragraphs.

Griffin sees unity, one of my glosses for identity, as the one topic that unifies all of Russell's philosophical phases. However, he says he cannot carry out the project of showing that to be so in a brief paper, and confines himself to a discussion of Russell's early phases. In contrast, not only have I carried out the project completely, but I extended it to Frege, Wittgenstein and Quine—and to the substance tradition as well. So there is overlap only concerning the early Russell. And even there the detail of our approaches differs. Also, while we both use the very same term, "modified realist," to describe Russell, we use it differently. For me, a modified realist is one who admits both real things and less than fully real things. For Griffin, an absolute realist holds that every word denotes some entity, while a modified realist holds that not every word denotes some entity. The result is that Griffin deems *Principles of Mathematics* a work of absolute realism, and sees Russell as moving to a modified realism in "On Denoting," while I deem *Principles* a work of modified realism, and see Russell as merely moving to a different sort of modified realism. Both of us are right, in our respective senses of "modified realism." In fact, Griffin's modified realists can include my *radical* realists, i.e., philosophers who admit only real identities and fictitious identities, which are not even mutedly real and lack all ontological status. Still, my compliments on a fine paper. Griffin reports that Francisco Rodríguez-Consuegra has been working along similar lines (Griffin 1993: 185 n.4). It seems that the idea of finding unity in Russell's different philosophical phases, at least, is in the air.

Two other authors in *Russell and Analytic Philosophy*, R. M. Sainsbury and Bernard Linsky, come close to my views on Russell on modality. "Sainsbury finds a surprising resemblance between Russell's theory of communication and recent theories of rigid designation" (Irvine 1993: x). Bernard Linsky reports that David Kaplan uses Russellian Propositions to explain direct reference, which is circuitously connected to possible worlds as "circumstances of evaluation" (B. Linsky 1993: 193). They might be interested in my more direct arguments that Russell's logically proper names *are* rigid designators (Dejnožka 1990: 395). However, I am glad for some confirmations of my general view that Russell is more like Kripke than Kripke seems to think.

Finally, "According to Landini, the doctrine of the unrestricted variable, a doctrine which he says entails that there are no types or orders of entities, was never abandoned by Russell—not even in *Principia*" (Irvine 1993: xiv; see Landini 1993a: 387). Landini says that in *Principia* individuals within the scope of the individual quantifier include all entities: particular objects (including complex entities), qualities, and relations alike. He observes that individuals included all entities in *Principles of Mathematics* Appendix B (there individuals also included classes as one, which are rejected in *Principia*). Note that from 1903 to 1911, Russell held that universals can be indicated by both subjects ("redness") and predicates ("is red") (POM 43–44; RUP 109, 123–24; in 1918 Russell rejects this view, PLA 205–6). Much of Landini's paper is devoted to showing that in *Principia* individual variables *can* be viewed as unrestricted in this sense; that is of course no argument that they *are* unrestricted in this sense, but only that such an interpretation is technically possible. I hold the more traditional view that in *Principia* individuals include only objects, since universals are of different types, or at least of different categories. But I think Landini is very close to the truth: namely, for the 1903–12 Russell, qualities and relations are complete entities in themselves, much like individuals. They subsist timelessly and independently of individuals. They are independent of each other too, except for certain *a priori* connections such as that red is a color. If I am right that Russell's particulars (sense-data) are quality-instances, then one might say that the difference between qualities and individuals is *merely* that qualities are not individuals, but universals. But while most ordinary dictionary words name universals (PP 93), I suggest that in *Principia* universals appear only as determinate constituents of propositional functions. I have four reasons: (i) Russell seems to imply in *Principia* that all variables, even so-called unrestricted variables, are type-restricted or at least categorially restricted (PM 4). (ii) On the very same page Russell gives variables whose values are restricted to men as his example of restricted variables, whereas if Landini were right one would expect the example to be variables whose values are more generally restricted, e.g. to particulars (PM 4). (iii) That universals are determinate constituents of propositional functions is the express doctrine of the 1911 Russell (MAL 216, 220–21). Universals should not have two semantic roles, a subject-role and a predicate-role, in the formal notation; and being determinate constituents of propositional functions is a special sort of predicate-role. (iv) The 1910 Russell wants logic to minimize kinds of entities assumed. Logic without metaphysics is his aim, even aside from epistemic caution. I hold that in *Principia* quantification over propositional functions themselves is purely nominal, since Russell states that propositional functions are not entities themselves. I hold that while Russell admits universals in his metaphysics, he finds he does not need to name them or quantify over them in his formal logic (PM 24, 72, 74 on not needing classes in his logic is somewhat different because Russell does reject classes in his metaphysics). That seems enough to preserve most of Landini's paper despite our disagreement on whether *Principia* uses unrestricted variables. I might add that Landini's view that the individual variables are unrestricted is compatible with my view that those variables imply no ontological commitment. I discuss Landini's views on Russell on ontological commitment in chapter 5, section 2. It is a measure of the broadness of modified realism that different theories of ontological commitment can be held by modified realists.

Also, in *Principles of Mathematics* Russell's variables were "absolutely unrestricted" and "any conceivable entity" could be substituted for them, including nonexistent entities such as the Homeric gods (POM 7, 14, 36, 40, 43–44, 89, 91. The variables in *Principia* can hardly be unrestricted in that sense because Russell no longer admits nonexistent entities. Of course, if there is no such thing as a merely possible entity, then in a certain sense the only possible entities are actual entities; and in that sense *Principia* variables would range over all possible entities (if not all conceivable entities) if Landini is right. But that is not quite the same thing as absolutely unrestricted variables in the *Principles* sense. Perhaps that may cast more doubt on Landini's view.

On August 12, 1995, I acquired Francis Jeffry Pelletier, *Parmenides, Plato, and the Semantics of Not-Being* (1990). Pelletier notes a widespread agreement that the ancient Greeks used a "fused" sense of "is," fusing existential, predicative, and veridical uses, if not also the identitative use, of "is" (Pelletier 1990: 19–20). Pelletier "find[s] it implausible to say that Plato did actually make conscious distinctions among an 'is' of predication, an 'is' of existence, and an 'is' of identity. For one thing, he nowhere says he was making such distinctions. For another it is not presupposed by anything he does say" (Pelletier 1990: 94). I find this close enough to Kahn and Hintikka that I need not change anything in chapter 6. Again, suppose we concede for the sake of argument that very much unlike the ancients, Frege and Russell make conscious distinctions among such uses of "is." That does not really matter to my argument. What counts for my analogical argument is the existence of fusion, not the awareness of it. Frege and Russell fuse the distinct uses of "is" together too. They do it consciously. The concepts of existence, predication, truth, and identity are distinct only in reason for Frege, as are the corresponding meanings-in-use for Russell. For Frege and Russell, logic is a package deal, and so is ontology. That the Frege-Russell fusion differs from that of the ancients by simultaneously preserving the differences only deepens the analogy. That their fusions are deliberate, even formal, looks like the very sort of philosophical progress the analysts claimed to be making.

An ontology is a theory of what there is, or more deeply, of what it is to be. A theory of ontological commitment is a theory of what we say or imply there is, or more deeply, of what we say or imply it is to be. The relationship between the two kinds of theory is different for different theorists. The more you take theory of ontological commitment as a guide to answering ontological questions, the more of an analytic ontologist you are. On my own view, ontology is prior to ontological commitment. We must have some conception of what there is before we can have any conception of what it is to say or imply what there is. Therefore I am not an analytic ontologist. But I retain an analytic orientation in that I find that notations which perspicuously articulate ontological commitments are very helpful in articulating ontologies. Theoretically that is trivial, but in practice it is good dialectical discipline.

From the purely logical point of view, different canonical notations are possible. In particular, not all such notations need treat quantification the same way. Whether the 'existential' (individual) quantifier expresses ontological commitment, in my view, should depend only on whether that helps articulate your ontology. Since Frege is a reductionist who reduces numbers to logical objects which objectively exist, it makes sense that his individual quantifier expresses ontological commitment. Since the 1918 Russell is an eliminativist who analyzes bodies as series of classes and eliminates series and classes as fictions, it makes sense that his individual quantifier does not express ontological commitment. He reserves ontological commitment for logically proper names and quantifications *in a theoretically ultimate interpretation.* Ordinary bodies would be quantified over in his initial interpretation of our talk of bodies, but certainly not in his final interpretation. While the later Wittgenstein makes existence a second-level quantifier, his discussion is too brief and nondescript to tell us whether he holds it expresses ontological commitment. Probably it does express ontological commitment, at least insofar as he would find taking ordinary talk of "some" nonexistent things as expressing ontological commitment a bewitchment of grammar. Like Frege, Quine insists on the ontological commitment of the individual quantifier, since like Frege, he is a reductionist as opposed to an eliminativist. Butchvarov's individual quantifier expresses no ontological commitment because he allows it to range over neo-Meinongian nonexistent objects. I myself use the individual quantifier to express ontological commitment because what Butchvarov deems nonexistent objects I deem existent objects of perception or thought (these are my "qualified objects"), and because where others reduce the logically complex to the logically simple, I build the logically complex out of the logically simple and admit both as real. But while we all differ, both in our ontologies and in our theories of ontological commitment, the point I wish to make is that all of us have chosen theories of ontological commitment which are both logically acceptable in themselves and appropriate to our respective ontologies. That is the easy part; the hard part is coming by the ontologies. However, we do best when we understand both ontology and ontological commitment in terms of identity.

I so conceive the relation of ontology to metaphysics that two philosophers might admit the very same metaphysical categories but differ in ontology by each assigning a different ontological status to the same category. For instance, both might admit bodies and minds, while one deems bodies more real than minds and the other deems bodies and minds equally real. Even if you admit only one category and one ontological status, say minds and substantial reality, these are, or ought to be, two different admissions. Categories concern what things are; ontological status concerns how real things are. Categories are contentually differentiated ultimate kinds of things; an ontological status is not a kind of thing but a kind of reality. But while ontology and metaphysics are distinct in concept, they are also intimately related. To deny any ontological status to things of a certain category is to reject that category. And to admit things of a certain category is to require of them the minimal ontological status of not being nothing, though it is not to fix their ontological status fully. Due to this relationship, identity is basic to metaphysics as well.

1

Introduction

What is it to be? In Aristotle's *Metaphysics*, to be is primarily to be a substance. Aristotle emphasizes seven themes: (1) the mind-independence of substances, (2) the forms or natures of substances, (3) the role of substances as ultimate subjects of predication, (4) the logical independence of substances (substances are those things which can exist even if nothing else exists), (5) the primary cognitive identity of substance, or the view that we primarily grasp real things, (6) the persistence of substantival identity through change, and (7) the unity or oneness of substances. Theme (7) is transcategorial; beings of every kind have unity. Unity seems to be identity in a sense more basic than those of cognitive identity or persistence through change.

I am concerned with what may be ironically called the ontologies affirmed by the four great analytic philosophers in their reductions or eliminations of traditional metaphysics. While the ontologies of Frege, Russell, Wittgenstein, and Quine are all different, all hold in one way or another that to exist is to be identifiable. This seems to reduce Aristotle's seven themes to one: theme (7). Even themes (5) and (6) seem to disappear. Theme (5) seems to vanish in Russell's view that we know bodies only as logical constructs, and in his later view that bodies are probably real at best and their qualities are unknowable. Theme (6) seems to vanish in Russell's constructing bodies out of momentary sensible events, and in his later theory of four-dimensional events. None of the great analysts admits traditional substances as a category. They reject theology and anything like Aristotle's immovable, immaterial divine substance which is the final cause of all motion. Even Wittgenstein rejects theology, despite his mysticism and ideal of Christian love (Pitcher 1964: 6, 11). The great analysts also reject Aristotle's view that ordinary things such as rocks, trees, and human beings are substances. Thus it seems they radically break from Aristotle.

Certain well-known issues arise in the new analytic ontologies:

(i) *The Problem of Nonexistents*

Are all existents (apples, people, muons) and no nonexistents (hallucinated or dreamed pink rats, fictional characters) identifiable?

(ii) *The Problem of Ontological Reduction*

When we define or analyze a thing in terms of identifiable elements, are we eliminating it, merely reducing it to another kind of thing, or establishing that it does exist as a structure?

(iii) *The Problem of Ontological Relativity*

Is every reference to objects intelligible only relative to the identity conditions embedded in some language or conceptual framework? Does the world divide into real objects, or is all talk of objects just a matter of our words or concepts?

(iv) *The Private Language Problem*

How can other people or I myself communicate about my private inner life in a public language? Do minds, thoughts, and feelings have public identity conditions?

(v) *Problems of Physical Entities*

If we do not directly perceive bodies, how can we identify them? What identity conditions for physical events are possible in general relativity theory or in quantum mechanics?

The three main contributions of this book are these. First, I show that Frege and Russell were the basic analytic progenitors of 'no entity without identity'. There are immense literatures on Wittgenstein's and Quine's existence-identity connections. Frege and Russell pioneered such connections, but there is virtually no literature to show it. Frege and Russell gave between them no fewer than twenty-nine private language arguments and fifty-eight 'no entity without identity' theories. Second, I therefore make all four analysts comparable on existence-identity connections (not: theories of identity) for the first time. In particular, I show that Frege and Russell are even more fundamental to the later analytic developments than has been supposed. This is so even though their influence is already rightly supposed to be tremendous and without parallel.

Third, I show that all four analysts give private language arguments ensuring that there are mind-independent real things which admit of slicing up conceptually or in language. Thus none of the four is a radical relativist; none makes a radical break from traditional modified realism. Indeed, Frege begins the linguistic turn with a core realist private language argument which the later analysts bedeck with further doctrines. These three contributions collectively change our understanding of the analytic movement and constitute a comprehensive, unified philosophical interpretation of it, and of its deepest origins.

It has long been noticed that Frege influenced Wittgenstein and Quine on 'no entity without identity'. Michael Dummett, in his 1967 "Frege," says,

In *Grundlagen* [Frege]...said that there has to be associated with every object—and therefore with every expression for an object—a "criterion of identity," a criterion for "recognizing the object as the same again"....This doctrine reappeared in the *Investigations* as a cornerstone of Wittgenstein's whole later philosophy. (Dummett 1967: 3/229)

Donald Davidson, in his 1969 "The Individuation of Events," says,

Quine has quipped: 'No entity without identity' in support of the Fregean thesis that we ought not to countenance entities unless we are prepared to make sense of sentences affirming and denying identity of such entities. (Davidson 1985a: 164)

Herbert Hochberg, in his 1978 *Thought, Fact, and Reference,* concurs:

Following Frege, Quine emphasizes the role of the law of identity in ontological issues. Just as satisfying the predicate "self-identical" was the criterion for *being an object* for Frege, it is the criterion for *being an entity* for Quine. (Hochberg 1978: 268)

In my 1982 "Frege: Existence Defined as Identifiability," I said:

The thesis (T) of this paper is that in Frege's philosophy existence may be and is best defined as identifiability....If thesis (T) is well substantiated, then we will be rewarded not only with a new understanding of Frege on the most fundamental level, but also with a more secure foundation of his place in history as the forerunner of Wittgenstein, Quine, Dummett, Geach, Castañeda, Butchvarov, and others with respect to discussions of connections between identity conditions and existential quantification or reference. (Dejnožka 1982: 1)

And José Benardete, in his 1989 *Metaphysics: The Logical Approach,* says:

...if one's very life depended on successfully summing up in four words the underlying rationale of the new essentialism, one could only be urged to reply,...'*No* entity without identity'. That that slogan has been patented by Quine to serve his own ends, among which his anti-essentialism is not negligible, undermines the reply not at all.... Devised in effect by Frege, the maxim is tacitly invoked by Wittgenstein at a key point in his famous private language argument, and if it is only Quine who expressly celebrates it as normative for the whole enterprise of ontology, Kripke is to be credited with pressing its modal version, 'No entity without trans-world identity'. Invoking these august names of analytic philosophy, we can safely say that the maxim expresses the fundamental principle of being as such, or being *qua* being, as regards the entire movement. (Benardete 1989: 155)

Benardete's fine statement about the entire analytic movement is immeasurably strengthened by adding the name of *Russell* to the list. Indeed Russell, not Kripke, is to be credited with pressing the modal version, 'No entity without trans-world identity'. But all these quotations, good as they are, need much developing. By way of preparation, I shall explain my own basic perspective and concepts in the two sections of this chapter.

Before beginning, I must explain why I do not discuss G. E. Moore, who is surely a fifth great analyst. Moore is a 'no entity without identity' ontologist. His *Principia Ethica* opens with an epigram from Bishop Butler: "Every thing is what it is, and not another thing." This reflects not only his theory that you can say of goodness only that it is goodness, but his rich jungle of categories. Moore finds almost nothing wrong with Russell's definite descriptions, in which identity and the existential quantifier work together (Moore 1989; see Russell 1989a: 690), and he uses that theory in his own way to speak of his imaginary objects (Moore 1966: 110–12). Moore understands problems of particulars and universals as problems of identity and individuation, and admits that all entities are self-identical (Moore 1966c: 51, 67, 69, 78, 349, 363, 375). His theory of perception basically concerns whether sense-data are ever identical with anything physical, whether this identical sense-datum ever recurs, and whether this very sense-datum might not have existed. He is also what I call a modified realist, since he admits a distinction between real distinction and distinction in reason (Moore 1968: 659; see Ducasse 1968: 226–27; compare Moore 1901). I do not discuss Moore only because I already discuss such topics concerning Russell. Indeed, Moore greatly influenced Russell. Moore converted Russell to realism, specifically to a pluralism of mind-independent sense-data and mind-independent universals; and Moore's 1901 paper, "Identity," influenced Russell on identity (Moore 1901; POM 44n, 51n).

1. Ontology and Metaphysics

I agree both with those who say the analytic tradition cannot be precisely defined and with those who divide it into three broad phases: the ideal or formal language approach (Frege, Russell, the early Wittgenstein, Quine), the ordinary language approach (the later Wittgenstein), and the present phase of consolidation and diffusion. I define the analytic movement by the very vague thesis that analyzing language is basic to understanding the world. I am not an analyst, since I make ontology and metaphysics prior to philosophy of language.

It is debatable whether Frege and Russell are analysts. Frege seems to some to be an epistemologist first and foremost, and anyway he largely limits his results to mathematics. Russell makes events prior to words, then constructs words out of events, then finds words but a small part of the world. But I count Frege and Russell as analysts because they make paraphrase into their respective canonical notations basic to ontology and metaphysics, as may be ironically implied in Russell's constructing words from events.

How can there be an ontology of the "anti-metaphysical" analytic tradition? And how can there be a single ontology in such a variegated "tradition"? Such general questions admit of four easy general answers.

First, Rudolf Goclenius introduced the word "ontology" to mean the study of being (Burkhardt 1988: 183). But today this meaning is too restrictive. One may call any study of being, the concept of being, or the meaning or use of the word "being" or its cognates "reality," "existence," and "actuality" ontological if it retains sufficient relevance to ontological issues. Clearly many analytic philosophers are ontologists in this broad sense. Similar broad senses have been useful in this century for "metaphysics," "ethics," and so on. This is not a definition (it would be circular if it were), but an explanation.

Second, the theory that there is an ontology of the analytic tradition is a *pros hen* theory of interpretation. Just as we may speak of a healthy human, healthy food, and healthy urine, so we may speak of the 1903 Russell's entity, being, Quine's referential apparatus, and even Wittgenstein's criteria of identity as ontological. The comparison is as follows. Humans are literally healthy. Food which produces healthy humans and urine which is produced by healthy humans are called healthy in virtue of those significant relationships. Russell's 1903 being is literally ontological. Quine's referential apparatus and Wittgenstein's criteria are aimed at producing true existential statements, and are rightly called ontological in virtue of their significant philosophical relationships to the 1903 Russell's being. If there is a highly generic identity among such things beyond their *pros hen* relationships, so much the better. As Panayot Butchvarov says, any resemblance at all is a generic identity (Butchvarov 1989: 75, 100).

Third, what I call the ontology of being *qua* identity, that existence (or the word "exists") is best understood in terms of identity (or the expression "is identical with"), seems to be the explanatory posit that provides the best philosophical illumination of what each great analyst is really trying to show us.

Fourth, showing how things are is the teleological end of all great philosophies. For each great analyst, 'no entity without identity' is the means to this end. It serves as a strategy that provides comprehensive unity to each of their respective outlooks.

Those are the four easy answers to the question, How can we responsibly speak of Frege, Russell, Wittgenstein, and Quine as having the same ontology, or of the later Wittgenstein as having an ontology at all? The long answer is the present book. But many texts provide quick support. For instance, Frege says in his "Dialogue with Pünjer on Existence":

> 'There are men' means the same as 'Some men are identical with themselves' or 'Something identical with itself is a man'. (PW 62)

In *Principia Mathematica*, Russell defines membership in the universal class of existents as being self-identical (PM *24.01). In *Quiddities*, Quine demurs from Hume's suggestion that existence is not different from identity on the ground that a universally enjoyed property of existence would take (x) as argument-place, while (self-)identity takes (x,x) instead (Quine 1987a: 89–90; contrast WO 116). Quine, the world's leading advocate of contextual definition, forgets that we can contextually define "x exists" as '$x = x$' (compare *Principia* *24.01; if a does not exist, then "$a = a$" is neither true nor even a proper instantiation of "$(x)(x = x)$"). Quine also forgets that the admittedly less perspicuous 'is self-identical' takes only (x). He even forgets that if we judge that existence is identical with identity, we *enforce* their indiscernibility with respect to argument-places (Butchvarov 1979: 37, 66–68). But this is only a minor mistake, easily fixed.[1] Quine definitely considers identity a "fundamental idea" (Quine: 1987: 89–90; 1983: 134ff.; 1980: 9–15; 1959: 208ff.; 1961b: 125; 1961c: 85, 95); WO sect. 24). Going deeper than values of variables, Quine says:

> The accessibility of a term to identity contexts was urged by Frege as the standard by which to judge whether that term is being used as a name. Whether or not a term is being used as naming an entity is to be decided, in any given context, by whether or not the term is viewed as subject in that context to the algorithm of identity... (FLPV 75–76)

As for Wittgenstein, one may cite *Philosophical Investigations* as connecting reference with criteria of identity (PI #253, #288, #290, #404). To be sure, such isolated texts, impressive as they are, cannot replace carefully thinking through the analysts' philosophies. But it seems wise to note even now that all of them accept some form of quantificational logic. Even the later Wittgenstein makes existence a second-level predicate (RFM 186/V #35).

Ontology is intimately related to metaphysics, the theory of ultimate categories of things. Andronicus of Rhodes coined *meta ta physica* as meaning the writings coming "after the physics" in his collation of Aristotle, but metaphysics is really the study with which those writings deal. Some might say that the categories are ultimate differentiations of being and that ontology is the study of undifferentiated being. Now insofar as metaphysics is the study of the nature and existence of broad categories of things, ontology is a branch of metaphysics by logical courtesy. It deals, paradoxically, with the nature and existence of the "category" of undifferentiated being. But strictly speaking, ontology is transcategorial. Of course, if we say, "To be is to be material," we do equate the study of being with the study of matter. But the equation is transcategorial in its very elimination of all categories other than matter. Of course, some ontologists admit different kinds or degrees of being. But even if every metaphysical category is also a kind of being and *vice versa*, so that the words "metaphysics" and "ontology" are co-extensive, those words are still not synonymous. Certainly when they are used as I have explained them, they are not intersubstitutable *salva veritate* in every context of discussion.

What does the objective world include? Common-sensically, it divides into many objects: the Sun, the Moon, stars, trees, people, and so on. We also speak and think about thoughts, smiles, numbers, and many other things. There are many similarities and differences among all these things, and this makes hierarchies of classifications possible. Leo the lion and Felix the cat are both feline, and so on. Insofar as our classificatory purposes may vary, the genera of one system may be the differentia of another. Humans compared to cats are generically animal and differentially rational; humans compared to angels are generically rational and differentially animal. This has led philosophers like Butchvarov to deny that there is any "true" classification (Butchvarov 1970: 6–11; see Butchvarov 1989: 75–79, 99–100, 118–19).

Any system of classifications, on pain of admitting an infinite series of classifications, will end with *summa genera* or ultimate classifications. This is the level of metaphysical categories. Where change consists of something of a given kind losing old properties and acquiring new ones, nothing can conceivably change in its metaphysical category. It is conceivable that Socrates can fall asleep, learn things, or even change into a rock or tree. But it is not conceivable that Socrates can change into time or into a number. We are not able to describe such transitions because we find nothing generically underlying them to persist through or undergo the transition. Perhaps that is only because such logico-metaphysical substrata have not been found yet in any plausible classificatory system. But I suspect the reason is that our most fundamental classifications are, at least in part, correct.

Frege divides entities on four levels. Each level is of metaphysical interest. The lowest divides physical from mental objects (ideas, and perhaps minds, can be "taken as" objects). The second divides concrete from abstract objects. The third divides objects (particulars) from functions, including "concepts" (i.e. properties) and relations. The highest divides references of names from: *senses*, which are roughly connotations of names; *forces*, which sentence forms "contain," and which include assertion, question, and command; and emotive *tones*, which we may express when we use sentences to communicate.

Frege's highest level is of ontological interest as well. As we shall see in chapters 2 and 3, every entity can be "represented" as an object with properties and relations, that is, represented as an object which is nameable by names which express senses and occur in asserted statements. I shall argue in those chapters that "the sense of expression A" ought to refer to an object for the same reason that Frege says "the concept *horse*" refers to an object. Similarly for "the force of sentence *S*" and "the tone of *S*."

For Frege identity, determinacy, and essence might seem equally deep ontological studies. For identity and determinacy arguably presuppose each other in Frege's principle of the identity of indiscernibles. And if references are not to be arbitrarily fixed in the matricial manner Frege's *The Basic Laws of Arithmetic* gives (BL vol. 1, sect. 29), that is, if a *principle* of identity is to determine identity for each kind of entity, then essence seems equally implicated. But the notion of identity is really the most illuminating one in ontology both for Frege and in general. The identity of an entity fixes its essence, and also its determinacy, and even its existence. (I mean the essence of an *existent's* existence; I am not suggesting an "ontological argument" that to have an essence is to exist. Frege derides such arguments.) A comparison to Aristotle will help show this.

Aristotle's five requirements for adequate definition by genus and differentia are helpful here, even if all the definitions I shall consider in a moment are contextual or implicit definitions of the existential quantifier. Several kinds of definitions of existence arguably satisfy most of Aristotle's requirements equally well. These formulations of them are perhaps as good as any:

(1) $(\exists x) = Df \ \neg[(F)\neg Fx]$ Property Possession Definition
(2) $(\exists x) = Df \ (F)(Fx \lor \neg Fx)$ Determinacy Definition
(3) $(\exists x) = Df \ (F)\neg(Fx \ \& \ \neg Fx)$ Consistency Definition
(4) $(\exists x) = Df \ (y)[(x = y) \lor \neg(x = y)]$ Identity Definition

(We may insert modal operators in (1)–(4) to form myriad Essence Definitions.) It seems that definitions (1)–(4) are neither too broad nor too narrow, are noncircular, are not negative where they could be affirmative (though each contains at least one negation sign), and do not use ambiguous, obscure, or figurative language (Copi 1978: 154–58). But Aristotle's most important requirement, best considered last, is whether any of (1)–(4) state what it is to exist. That is a difficult question, since (1)–(4) arguably all state essential attributes of existence, and arguably presuppose each other.

Aristotle held that the most general description of a thing gives the best explanation. For instance, two lines intersecting a third line at right angles in the same plane are parallel not because the angles are both 90°, but because the angles are the same. One might therefore hold that (2) is better than (4), since (4) is an instance of the law of excluded middle as expressed in (2). But in this case I would overrule Aristotle. For (4), which is a modern version of theme (7) of unity, is more illuminating than the others of what it is to cognize something that exists. What seems most important to our understanding of a thing as existing is its capacity to be singled out indefinitely many times in indefinitely many contexts. And (4) expresses that feature. This is not to infer what is basic to things from what is basic to our cognizing and understanding them, but to acknowledge that the unity of a thing is basic to our understanding of its existence. Frege expressly reasons in much the same way. Frege says in *The Foundations of Arithmetic*, "If we are to use the symbol *a* to signify an object, we must have a criterion for deciding in all cases whether *b* is the same as *a...*" (FA 73). This is not to infer what is basic to things from what is basic to our naming them, but to acknowledge that the identity of a thing is basic to our understanding of its existence. I shall elaborate this thesis in chapter 3. But there is a second reason for the priority of identity to essence in Aristotle and Frege.

In the Aristotelian tradition, identity is prior to essence insofar as essence is determined by a process of division of features into genera and differences, features presupposed as having identities (*Posterior Analytics* II 13; *Topics* I 5). For Frege, identity is prior to essence in much the same way. For Frege, essence is determined by fixing the sense of an identity, by establishing a principle of identity. This is done by specifying mappings of arguments by functions onto values, a process that always presupposes the identification of some entities (BL vol. 1 sects. 29–30). And Fregean identifiability can in principle always be fixed directly by consistently assigning a truth-value to each relevant individual identity statement. In this manner, even totally arbitrary functions can be defined as sets of individual mappings of level *v* values onto level *a* arguments.

Quine rejects traditional essences (WO 199–20). Nonetheless Quine says, "We cannot know what something is without knowing how it is marked off from other things" (OR 55). Quine's point is not epistemic ("know...knowing") so much as ontological ("what...how"). Thus Quine too makes identity prior to what things are, and in that sense to essence. There is every reason to believe that Russell and Wittgenstein would agree with Frege and Quine in this priority.

Third, definitions (1)–(3) presuppose the identity of properties, and definition (4) presupposes the identity of the identity relation. Definitions (1)–(4) also presuppose the identity of brackets and logical operators as signs at the very least. But (1)–(4) scarcely presuppose our understanding the *essential nature* of properties, identity, or negation, or our understanding them *in their full determinacy*. This sets identity apart as basic.

Frege's and Russell's definitions of existence respectively as denial of the number zero and as not always being unsatisfied do not expressly construe existence as identifiability. Likewise for Quine's view that the existential quantifier expresses existence. Nonetheless, 'no entity without identity' is at the bottom of the connection Frege and Russell pioneered between the numbers zero and one (more accurately, "at least one") and the purely logical quantifiers none and some respectively. This is also a helpful gloss on Quine.

The later Wittgenstein arguably would have rejected the whole approach of definitions (1)–(4) on the grounds that there is no necessary or sufficient condition of any expression's reference, and that there is no one use of words like "exist" or "refer." However, there seems to be an analogous view in Wittgenstein's equation of a satisfied criterion of identity with "warranted reference" in some sense (the term is not Wittgenstein's). Call it a warranted reference-identity criterion connection. And even the later Wittgenstein makes existence essentially a second-level predicate in *Remarks on the Foundations of Mathematics* (RFM 186/V #35).

What, then, is identity? David Wiggins argues that it is indefinable because there is no one way to count things as the same or to "assemble aggregates" into unities (Wiggins 1970: 310–11). This is a *non sequitur*. There is nothing inconsistent about Quine's view that identity is a very general relation, and that the real work of individuation is done instead by the many different sortal terms (TT 12; WO 91, 116). And the mere fact that identity is a very general relation does not entail that it is indefinable. There is as yet no unified theory in physics of the strong unity of the nucleus, the weak unity of the atom, the electromagnetic unity of a field, and the gravitational unity of the Earth. Yet all these have something definable in common: being physical unities. This is not to mention the possible identity of identity with some equally general property such as indiscernibility. What do the various colors have in common, besides being kinds of color? Yet color is easily defined as a general sort of wavelength. Frege's argument that identity is indefinable is better: since every definition expresses an identity, identity itself cannot be defined. I accept a similar argument: 'no entity without identity' requires existing definitions to have identities themselves. Perhaps Wiggins meant that a very general relation of identity cannot be *found*, and therefore cannot be defined. But that conclusion would be a *non sequitur* too, and for much the same reasons.

One might object that definitions define beings, and being is prior to identity, since the identity relation itself needs being. But the being of the identity relation is its identity. It is the identity of identity.

One might object that in this century we have learned that there can be several logically necessary and sufficient conditions of a thing which mutually imply each other, so that they are interdefinable; none seems more primitive than the others. Being identifiable, being determinate, and being capable of being a value of a variable might seem to be just such conditions of existence.

Russell says, "The whole theory of definition, of identity, of classes, of symbolism, and of the variable is wrapped up in the theory of denoting" (POM 54). Quine says, "The whole apparatus [of "objective reference: our articles and pronouns, our singular and plural, our copula, our identity predicate"] is interdependent" (WO 53). Quine says that a child's learning how to refer to objects is like scrambling up "an intellectual chimney, supporting himself against each side by pressure against the others" (WO 93). If that is so, I would argue that order of logical priority as such is not the order at issue here. What is at issue is philosophical understanding. Thus the order at issue is the order of explanation.

My contention is really that among the many ostensibly necessary and sufficient conditions of existence, identity is the one which best illuminates what it is to exist. Identity conditions are the decisive consideration even for Quine. Just look at his most famous arguments. Why are there no meanings?—Because there is no clear notion of sameness of meaning (OR 20–32). Variables are not even mentioned until Quine moves on to discuss Rudolf Carnap's artificial language (OR 33). Why are there no attributes?—Because there is no clear notion of sameness of attribute (WO 244; TT 100–1). Why are there no possible fat men in the doorway?—Because they have no identity conditions (WO 245, OR 4). On the other hand, why *are* there physical objects and classes?—Because they *do* have clear identity conditions, and cannot be paraphrased away (TT 100). Variables are not even mentioned. I am not saying that variables play no role in formalizing some of these arguments; sometimes they do. I am saying that all the arguments *turn on* identity conditions. Variables may help clarify the issues but they rarely if ever decide the issues, even for Quine.

Time and again, Quine's official 'pronominal' test of being the value of a variable is never actually used. Time and again, ontological decisions are based on identity conditions, and variables are never even mentioned. Thus it would appear that the pronominal test is a mere rubber stamp for identity conditions in Quine's actual practice of ontology. If items of a certain kind have identity conditions and if talk of them cannot be paraphrased as talk of items of some more basic kind, then everything else Quine officially requires for ontological commitment to them just seems to fall into place. Now, I suggest that the *reason* identity conditions emerge as the determining factor, the secret power behind the throne of variables, is that existence is best understood in terms of identity—and Quine is aware of that. Certainly the rubber stamp has a clarificatory and thus even a genuine confirmatory value. But Quine is no mere logician. He almost always cuts through the red tape of variables when ontological decisions must be made. And that is how it should be. I endorse Quine's sense of perspective on the matter completely.

In fact, as we shall see in chapter 6, even variables are best understood in terms of identity. Similarly for sortal concepts, which Russell argues involve a vicious regress of classifications if taken as needed for every identification (HK

423–24). Sortal concepts or sortal terms cannot even be acquired unless identity is already understood (Butchvarov 1979: 76–81). That is why objectual identity is not and cannot be always "under a sortal concept" (*pace* Wiggins' Thesis of the Sortal Dependency of Individuation, 1980: 16). That is why charity frowns on our saddling the great analysts with a thesis of sortal dependence, and smiles on our finding that they admit "primary identifications" which do not depend on our use of sortal terms of concepts. I do not deny that objects must have sortal properties, but only that we must always use sortal concepts to identify objects.

I can now return to the order of logical priority and argue that insofar as logical priority is explanatory priority, explanatory priority is logical priority. I am saying only that if the notions of, e.g., existence, essence, and accident must be understood in terms of identity, but the converse is not so (following Butchvarov 1979: 40–41, 123), then identity must be assigned logical priority over those other notions as well. However, so far as interpreting the great analysts is concerned, I shall be content if identity is merely first in the order of explaining their various ontologies.

I am told that I make ontology prior to logic for Quine; I make it sound as if Quine first identifies entities, and only then sets up his logic so that variables range over these entities. It should be clear from the last three paragraphs that this is a misunderstanding. I make identification prior in the order of explanation to both employment of variables *and* ontological commitment. I merely infer that insofar as explanatory priority is logical priority, identification is also logically prior to both. Even as we scramble up the chimney, all the sides being necessary and sufficient conditions of learning reference, one side, identity, illuminates all the other sides and therefore the whole chimney as well.

Who would explain identity in terms of existence, or illuminate identity in terms of variables? Bringing technical sharpness to a formal notation is one thing. Asking which notions really need explaining the most is quite another (see Butchvarov 1979: 40–41).

Due to its fundamental character, identity seems indefinable in any case. But I wholly agree with Wiggins that much can be said to elucidate it. Specifically, I agree with him that the most basic use of "to identify" is to single out; the secondary use is to single out again, that is, to re-identify. I agree that the most basic form of 'no entity without identity' is that "if there were no singling out by anyone at any time, it seems there could be no referring" (Wiggins 1980: 5). I agree again with Wiggins that one may distinguish between direct and indirect identifications, where direct identifications are of perceived things, and indirect identifications are of unperceived things if I know which thing I am thinking of (Wiggins 1970: 315–16; Wiggins 1980: 5). This gives us a four-part matrix: direct singling out, direct re-identification, indirect singling out, and indirect re-identification. The matrix enlarges on Aristotle's themes (5)–(7) about substance.

Besides the identity of things, there are thoughts and judgments of identity, and also statements of identity in language. The subject-terms of identity statements may be either referring ("this cat") or denoting ("the cat on the mat, whichever cat it may be"). But I do consider reference prior to denoting, since on pain of vicious regress, reference to some attribute must be possible before any description can be used attributively. That is, "naming is a preparation for description" (PI #49). Descriptions simply *are* referring general terms that are used to describe. (This does not make properties prior to the objects that have them.) Identity conditions are the truth-conditions of identity judgments and statements. Identity criteria are the criteria warranting the making or assertion of identity judgments or statements. I use the word "criterion" casually; the notion of a nonlogically sufficient condition seems confused (Butchvarov 1970: part 4).

Enriching the matrix, there are at least ten senses of the word "identifiable." "Identifiable" may mean: (1) capable of being singled out by conscious beings (the cognitive sense); (2) recognizable as the same item singled out before (the memorial sense); (3) knowable as a certain individual (the epistemic sense); (4) being an item of a certain kind or species (the essential sense); (5) having a criterion of individuation (the criterial sense); (6) being such that every identity statement about it has a determinate truth value (the identitative sense); (7) being self-identical (the reflexive sense); (8) having unity (the unitative sense); (9) being factually based (the factually informative sense); and (10) being able to be given to us in a new way (the novelly or phenomenologically informative sense). Senses (1) and (2) are from Wiggins; both admit of direct and indirect variants. But when I discuss 'no entity without identity' or "To be is to be identifiable," I shall be mainly concerned with sense (6), the identitative sense. Perhaps all ten sorts of identifiability are necessary and sufficient conditions of existence assertions. But I hold that sense (6) is philosophically the most illuminating necessary and sufficient condition of existence, and that all four great analysts presuppose that fact if they do not state it outright. This includes the early Wittgenstein; but the later Wittgenstein makes the criterial sense basic. Senses (7) and (8) might be even more fundamental. But sense (7) is included in sense (6), so that sense (6) gives a more general or full condition. And the traditional Aristotelian sense (8) is vague. Sense (8) needs explication in terms of a more precise sense such as (6) or (7). Sense (7) is the logical complement of sense (9), since factual identity is just nonreflexive identity.

Factually informative identity is a precondition of novelly informative identifiability. Even in a chaotic world or a mystically experienced world where everything is new, nothing can be novelly informatively identified if it cannot be factually informatively identified.

The identitative sense captures and reflects both senses (7) and (9) in language. The totality of identity statements about a thing is just all the reflexive (self-identical) and nonreflexive (factual) identity statements about that thing. The essential and criterial senses of "identifiable" provide guidance. They make the totalities of identity statements intelligible outlines of things instead of indefinitely long mere lists. That in turn allows feasible accounts of the cognitive, epistemic, and memorial identifiability of things.[2] One qualification of the identitative sense: on the face of it, totalities of identity *statements* need not exist for things to exist. Indeed, since statements need identities themselves, that would lead to a vicious regress of totalities of identity statements. Such totalities are just a pedagogic device: if there were such totalities, they would capture what I mean by identitative identifiability.

But a list of ten senses of "identifiable," even with some main relationships sketched out, scarcely constitutes an adequate ontology. That is because ontology has at least three fundamental levels concerning the implications of identity for realism, and these levels have not yet been explained.

First, existence is most primitively unitative or reflexive identifiability. For only the self-identity of a thing completely coincides with the thing's existence. That is because only self-identity is the complete coincidence of a thing with itself. To be self-identical is to be oneself, and that is to be something as opposed to nothing. Perhaps the argument is strictly a *non sequitur*, since as Wiggins says, coincidence is a metaphor. But the argument seems more convincing the more you think about it. It also identifies the actual with the possible, since it leaves no middle ground between being something that is and being nothing.

Self-identity seems identical with difference from (any) other (possible) things. But not so. How can either obtain without the other?—Difference is impossible without identity. If entities are different, then each must have its own identity. But identity is possible without difference. If there were only one entity having an identity, there would be nothing to be different from it. Difference is not identity. Difference is the negation of identity. If items are not identical, then they are different. In *Principles of Mathematics* section 429 Russell says, and I agree, that the being of an entity is not its difference from other entities, but "is simply its being," which is a precondition of its difference from other entities. Similarly for the self-identity of an entity. Those last two facts conjointly support the view that to be, in the most basic sense, is to be self-identical.

Many from Hegel to Butchvarov have held that the notion of self-identity is useless. Not so. Its basic uses are (i) pronominal, including pronouns, variables, and multiple places of variables, and (ii) repetitional, including nestings and iterations of names, and the forming of new sentences using old names. Uses (i) and (ii) are basic to formal inference as we understand it, and to sentential language as we understand it. Pronominal reference, which is given or stipulated noninformatively as reference to the very thing in question, is Quine's test of ontological commitment. There is a sense in which a pronominal reference in a complex sentence may be informative to some people, but that is a different sense which is nonstipulative, and which is relative to ability, alertness, and other factors affecting our detection of reference stipulations.

Here we already begin to see how variables are to be explained in terms of identity, specifically in terms of self-identity. Perhaps variables cast back some reflective technical light on the logical capacities of self-identity. But it should be clear which notion is more illuminative of the other.

Self-identity's two basic uses are basic to quantification for Frege, Russell, and Quine. Even Quine's "Variables Explained Away" merely reconstructs these two uses (Quine 1966a; FLPV 104). Ironically enough, Wittgenstein's diatribe against self-identity in *Investigations* #215–16 is bewitched by a picture of a thing's identity as its trivially fitting into its own spatial shape, and overlooks the basic uses. He forgets that the pronominal game can be very seriously played! In any case, it should be clear that variables and quantification must be understood in terms of identity, not the other way around.

Two classic difficulties with 'no self-identity without entity' are that many apples are the same as many apples, and nothing is the same as nothing; yet neither, so to speak, is an entity (see Plato, *Parmenides* 129, 162–64). Frege admits classes as objects; the *Principia* Russell assays them as fictions, literally not self-identical. Frege admits *not anything* as a representatively self-identical, second-level concept; the *Principia* Russell assays quantifiers as fictions. Frege seems right that the relevant truths are *about* something; at least that is the natural presumption about all truths.

A third difficulty is whether self-identity is realist or relativist, or simply indifferent to that debate. Benardete makes self-identity the basis of his realism. To understand an entity *qua* itself (e.g. Smith *qua* Smith) is the absolutist use of "*qua*," as opposed to its use relative to some concept (Smith *qua* citizen). But another philosopher might advocate a thesis of sortal dependence and reject the absolutist construal of "Smith *qua* Smith" by inferring that some sortal term or concept must be tacitly involved, leading to a thoroughgoing relativity. Yet a third philosopher might hold that self-identity is a precondition of real and relative items alike. If all things were real, they would be the same as themselves. Beauty would be beauty. And if, *per impossibile,* all things were relative, they would still be the same as themselves. Beauty in the eye of the beholder would be beauty in the eye of the beholder. Thus self-identity might seem logically prior to the realism-relativity dispute.

"The Eiffel Tower is itself" or "The Eiffel Tower is its own being" might be somewhat colloquially taken to mean the same as "The Eiffel Tower is real (nonrelative)." In that case, either of the first two sentences deductively implies the third. But here "itself" and "its own being" are only synonyms of "real." Such redundancies employing the merely copulative "is" are of no interest.

Still, I side with Benardete. Inferring realist entity from self-identity is a *non sequitur.* Following Moore, "X is self-identical, but is it real?" is an open question. But the inference remains reasonable, and seems more convincing the more you think about it. Benardete is extremely close to strict deductive validity; all he needs is the manifestly reasonable postulate that if "*a* is self-identical" is true, and if its predicate is an absolutist *qua*, then *a* itself is real (nonrelative). There is an interesting parallel in Quinean ontological relativity: Quine says, "if we choose as our translation manual the identity transformation,...the relativity is resolved" (PT 52).

Thus on the level of self-identity, I would eliminate relativity altogether as manifestly unreasonable. But relativity might be reformulated in a less radical but more intelligible way on a less basic level of ontology.

Second, existence is, on the next most basic level, factually informative identifiability, of which self-identity is a precondition. Existence connotes more coherence than does mere self-identity. It connotes being internally coherent as opposed to chimerical. More than that, it connotes being part of a stable, orderly world—the common-sense world of causally interacting things, as opposed to some isolated phantom or hallucination, however well-integrated with itself. The connotation is old. It leads to an existent's being 'intellectually visible', so to speak, in indefinitely many ways due to its relationships with other things, and also due to its own coherence as an item with different aspects. It also allows modality to enter ontology more fully in the form of combinatorial possibilities.

The inference from a stable, orderly world to a real world is strictly speaking another *non sequitur*. It raises the question of degree of coherence needed to be real, not to mention questions of logical constructionism. But the more you think about it, the more the inference seems to help explain what we mean by "real" (see Butchvarov 1979: 34–35, 40–43).

On this level, the realism-relativity question emerges again. One might argue that factually informative identity is incompatible with relativity because a true factually informative identity statement describes an objective relational fact. Or one might hold that every factually informative identity is relativist because every factually identified item must be viewed through at least one medium, such as a description. Or one might hold that this level is prior to the realism-relativity dispute, since both real and relative items seem to have factually informative identities. The real beauty of a certain sunrise may be factually identified with the first real beauty I see one morning. The relative beauty-in-my-eye of a sunrise may be just as easily factually identified with the first beauty-in-my-eye one morning. I believe that since a factually informative identification is an objective fact, we must seek a viable sense for the term "relative" at a still less basic level.

The third level concerns the logical structure of existence judgments and statements. All four analysts make the word "exists" a second-level predicate of predicates. Beings and their identities emerge as the truth-conditions for judgments and statements of existence and identity. So to speak, things must be sufficiently real and have sufficient identity to serve thus. For instance, if skyscrapers are only logical fictions, then one can truly say, "There are skyscrapers in New York City," only in a purely nominal sense. This level concerns realism as opposed to idealism, conceptualism, nominalism, and relativity. It is the level at which relativity finally may be admitted as a meaningful issue concerning what categories of things to admit, counterbalanced by how seriously one intends one's existential quantifier. Relativity may be admitted by admitting values of variables which overlap each other, and some of which are real in some sense and others of which are less than real in that sense. The real objects may be said to have real identities. And the less than real objects may be said to have identities relative to those of the real objects, in that their identities are just different conceptual or linguistic slicings of the real objects. Note that this is my first appeal to variables to illuminate something in a genuinely positive way. What they illuminate is not realism or ontological commitment, but how we can intelligibly and safely introduce a limited amount of ontological relativity. And this, on the lowest level of my ontology. Indeed, I need not have appealed to values of variables even here. I could have spoken directly of the overlapping of real and less than real objects. But I wanted to show how quantification figures into the issue of realism *versus* relativism. In fact, once again it is really variables which are being illuminated.

I shall argue shortly for a real-relative distinction that requires both self-identity and factually informative identifiability for each real and each relative item alike, but allows the introduction of a limited amount of ontological relativity in the way I just explained. Only such a modified realism (or modified relativity) will be coherent and stable, but it will be on this low third ontological level. I show in chapter 2, section 4 that Frege's and Russell's accounts of factually informative identities do not commit them to any significant ontological relativity. Similar arguments apply to Quine's account, which is virtually Russell's, and to the later Wittgenstein's account in terms of criteria. In chapter 7 I apply seven criteria to show that all four analysts are modified realists whose real and less-than-real categories surely all admit of both self-identity and factually informative identifiability.

All three levels help illuminate the respective ontologies of the great analysts one way or another. And all three have old origins. The origins of the first level are Parmenides, Plato, and Aristotle on connecting being and unity. The origins of the second level are Plato's conception of reality as stable and rational (*Theaetetus* 181*b*-183*c*), which goes back to Heraclitus's *logos*, and Plato's conception of existence as power (*Sophist* 247; see Butchvarov 1979: 34–35, 40–43, 109, 112). The origin of the third level is Thomas Aquinas (Geach 1969: 45–46), if not earlier traditional logic rightly understood (Angelelli 1967: 72–73, 124–25).

There were two great revolts against the primacy of ontology and metaphysics in philosophy. The first was the epistemological revolt started by René Descartes. The second was the linguistic revolt started by David Hume and rekindled by Frege. I shall now argue that both revolts were failures.

The epistemological revolt consisted of the claim that only metaphysics which we know to be true, or at least have some evidence for, is worthwhile, together with the claim that most or all metaphysics is not known to be true, or is beyond (a new sense of *meta*) any evidence we might have. The new first philosophy concerned the nature and existence of knowledge and evidence, and our nature and existence as human knowers. But such concerns are essentially metaphysical concerns. As Gustav Bergmann says, epistemology is "the ontology of the knowing situation" (Bergmann 1964: 126). And as F. H. Bradley says, "The man who is ready to prove that metaphysical knowledge is wholly impossible...is a brother metaphysician with a rival theory of first principles" (F. Bradley 1969: 1). At most, the epistemological revolt shows the primacy within metaphysics of metaphysical questions about knowledge and evidence and knowers. Ontology remains more fundamental than any metaphysics, concerning as it does what it is to be at all.

The linguistic revolt consisted of the claim that only metaphysics which is cognitively meaningful is worthwhile, together with empirical criteria of meaningfulness on which metaphysics on the whole is meaningless. This revolt may seem somewhat deeper than the first. For we cannot know a theory to be true or give evidence for it if we do not know what it means in the first place. The later Wittgenstein seems to find epistemological problems, like all philosophical problems, to be grammatical illusions. Frege rekindles the linguistic turn by answering Kant's epistemic question, How are numbers given to us?, with a definition of number-words (Dummett 1991: 111, 181; Dummett 1993: 5). But meanings and uses are worthless if we do not know them, or at least have evidence for them. Thus the meaning of "knowledge" and the knowledge of meaning may seem equally deep, if not mutually implicative, studies. But I suggest the following order of priority: language has epistemic presuppositions, and epistemology has cognitive presuppositions. Plato taught us that perception is not yet knowledge; I add only that knowledge is not yet verbalization.[3]

In any case, questions about the nature and existence of meanings or uses of words, or perhaps more deeply, questions about the nature and existence of logical or conceptual proposals, are by definition metaphysical questions. Therefore the linguistic revolt shows at most the primacy within metaphysics of questions about meanings or uses, or about logical or conceptual proposals. To echo Bergmann and Bradley, theory of meaning is the ontology of the meaning situation. And the man who is ready to prove that metaphysics is unmeaning is a brother metaphysician with a rival theory of first principles. Likewise for anyone who is ready to prove that metaphysics is supervenient on language or logic. I cannot repeat here Bergmann's long argument in *The Metaphysics of Logical Positivism* that ideal language and ordinary language methods alike merely reconstruct core aspects of metaphysics, and therefore are implicit metaphysics (Bergmann 1967: 1–77).

Thus both revolts showed inadequate self-reflection. For they did not see their own metaphysical presuppositions. They also showed this lack in a second sense. Descartes' theory of knowledge is unknowable on his own theory of knowledge. I do not mean only that Descartes' arguments for hypothetical doubt are themselves subject to hypothetical doubt. I mean that the very possibility of hypothetical doubt is itself subject to hypothetical doubt. Likewise, Hume's view that the meaning of a word is always an idea copied or derived from impressions is itself a metaphysical theory that cannot be confirmed by our sense-impressions. Similarly, logical positivism's principle of verifiability is cognitively meaningless on its own showing. The principle, stated "The meaning of a statement is the method of its (empirical) verification," is empirically unverifiable. Thirdly, the revolts failed in an ordinary professional sense. They failed to show in detail that metaphysics is unknowable or unintelligible. Indeed, such accusations are almost impossible to prove. On the face of it, subjects debated in great detail publicly for millennia are subjects we understand at least a little. But the skeptics and the logical positivists did not even attempt to analyze two thousand years of discussion to show its unknowability or unmeaning, or else its empty analyticity or tautologousness, in full detail.

Surely the burden of proof lies with the revolts. For the primacy of metaphysics over theories of knowledge and meaning is only common sense. That is because it is hard to picture how the world might have consisted only in epistemic or linguistic or, perhaps more deeply, logical or conceptual facts. On the face of it, the world includes some epistemic situations and languages, but mainly consists of nonepistemic and nonlinguistic facts. We do not even know of any epistemic or linguistic facts beyond our solar system. Russell carries the warfare even further into the enemy camp with a second common-sense argument:

> Language consists of sensible phenomena just as much as eating or walking, and if we can know nothing about facts we cannot know what other people say or even what we are saying ourselves. (MPD 110)

George D. Romanos added in 1983:

> ...the antimetaphysical stance of the positivists, and of many analytic philosophers of the succeeding generation, puts the greatest burden on this sort of linguistic absolutism. Conceding that there is no way the world really is, they continue to adhere to the view that there is a way we really say it is or conceive it to be, and that this absolute or determinate conceptual content or meaning of language may properly be subjected to something of the piercing philosophical vision usually associated with the efforts of metaphysicians....[T]heir...acceptance of the analytic conception of language involves assumptions about the nature of linguistic inquiry that parallel the pretensions of speculative

metaphysics regarding our access to extralinguistic reality. (Romanos 1983: 39–40)

I wholly agree with Bergmann, Bradley, Russell, and Romanos.

Later I go beyond talk of presuppositions and reconstructions to argue that Frege's senses, Russell's descriptions, Wittgenstein's criteria, and Quine's theories are positively intended as vehicles of reference to things in a physicalist world. If I am wrong, I can always fall back on Bergmann and Bradley to explain why the two revolts failed, and also to provide the basis of the principal argument of this book that the analysts are enough like substance metaphysicians to count as modified realists.

The failed revolts arguably establish at least a reorganization of priorities within metaphysics. Namely, within metaphysics it is advisable to pursue theory of knowledge and theory of meaning first, and only then categories such as space, time, matter, mind, number. At least one should do this as much as one can, since all these categories are dialectically related. Ontology remains prior to such metaphysical categories, though again there are dialectical relationships. Also, theories of verificationism which reduce "cognitive meanings" to methods of empirical knowing can find their proper task in regulating language use in the empirical sciences. Thus both revolts can enjoy at least some success.

In view of the two revolts' attempts to replace *ontology* with a new first philosophy, it is worth noting that both revolts took pains to preserve existence-identity connections appropriate to what they considered primary. The early modern philosophers made individuation, in the form of clear and distinct perceptions, or at least really distinct impressions, basic to their epistemologies. Following suit, phenomenologists found certain primitive identities to be presented. And devotion to 'no entity without identity' permeates the analytic tradition. Thus on the level of 'no entity without identity' ontology, the division of history of philosophy into traditional metaphysics, early modern epistemology, phenomenology, and the analytic tradition already seems artificial.

The failure of the two great revolts is in general the failure of theories of thoroughgoing relativity. For the first revolt in effect made our perception of the world relative to the nature of knowledge and to our nature as human knowers. The second revolt in effect made our discourse of the world relative to the nature of language and to our nature as human speakers.[4] Insofar as this is so, both revolts took the three great pratfalls of relativity. Namely, any kind of relativity presupposes as objective facts: (1) something to be viewed in a relative way, (2) someone to do the viewing, and (3) some medium or relation between (1) and (2) which constitutes or effects the relativity. (Even if Protagoras is right that man *is* the measure of things, presumably there are at least acts of judgment which effect the relativity.) For instance, for linguistic relativity to be the case, linguistic relativity must itself be an objective fact, and not merely a view relative to language. There must be (1) a world to be viewed relative to language, (2) people to view the world in such a way, and (3) languages through which such a relativity is achieved. All these must be objective facts. Even if people and the world are mere constructs, it must be an objective fact that such constructs are related as described by (1)–(3).

The two revolts also faced in effect the three questions concerning any rational case for relativity. (i) What is the rational case, or evidence? (ii) Is the rationality of the case, or the evidence for the case, itself an objective fact? (iii) Is the case any better or worse than the case for any objective facts concerning the matter in question? Questions (i)–(iii) show there must be an objective case for any theory of linguistic relativity if it is to merit our belief.

The three pratfalls and three questions alike show the self-defeating character of any thoroughgoing relativity. The three questions also undermine what may be called *almost* thoroughgoing relativities. For instance, suppose somebody holds that everything is relative *except* the existence of language-games, economic conditions, or Kuhnian scientific paradigm of the age to which everything (else) is relative, and except for the fact that the relativity obtains. Such a relativity is not self-defeating. But one may well question why such esoteric items *alone* might have the right to be called objective facts. For instance, is the evidence that Benjamin Lee Whorf's hypothesis of the linguistic relativity of Western substance *versus* Hopi process "metaphysics" describes an objective fact any better than the evidence that Western physics provides for objective physical facts? Or is it worse? I suggest that in general, if there is objective evidence that some kind of relativity is an objective fact about X, there is better evidence that there are instead (or at least also) objective facts about X.

Some dismiss the criticism that any thoroughgoing relativity is self-defeating as old and worthless. Such thinkers assert their own relativisms as if they were almost objectively true, and argue for them in an almost objective manner. Joseph Margolis's "robust relativism" replaces truth with "a weaker set of many-valued...truth-like values" in *The Truth About Relativism*. This would have, in Russell's phrase, all the advantage of theft over honest toil if no objective reasons for the replacement could be given. But Margolis gives some reasons:

> The *essential* insight is this: order does not require or entail uncondi-
> tional variance....The *inherent* discontinuities of history and method
> and rational policy cannot be overcome or rendered neutral by such
> formal strategies as clinging to excluded middle. (Margolis 1991: ix,
> 160, italics mine)

It seems Margolis is starting his own substance tradition, resplendent with essential insights, inherent discontinuities, and a whole parade of determinate assignments of determinate truth-like values. Any radical relativity worth its salt would preclude all of this—but of course this is a *robust* relativism. Likewise for

Peter Davson-Galle's imposition of Tarskian truth-levels on Protagoreanism (Davson-Galle 1991: 176). The idea is that relativity cannot defeat itself because *no* view can be *about* itself. I agree that since Protagoras says everything is relative, his view is best paraphrased as systematically ambiguous across all truth-levels. For any truth-level *t*, Protagoras will say on level *t* + 1 that all truths on level *t* are relative. But this approach presupposes that every truth determinately has some determinate truth-level. It also ignores the literature. Hartry Field has long warned of the presuppositions of Tarskian disquotation (Field 1972: 372–73), and Hilary Putnam has repeated the warning (Putnam 1991: 3–4). Tarski himself presents disquotation as a determinate function mapping determinate truth-conditions onto determinate sentences (Tarski 1956: 156 n.1, 161). And relativity is as self-defeating as ever, since for any truth-level *t*, the statement on level *t* + 1, "All truths on level *t* are relative," is itself condemned as relative by the statement on level *t* + 2, "All truths on level *t* + 1 are relative." By parity of reason, Quine cannot use his theory of truth as disquotation to safeguard his famous theses of translational indeterminacy, referential inscrutability, and underdetermination of theory from the charge that they are all self-refuting (and refute each other).

However, theory of truth is one thing, realism another. Quine would be the first to tell us not to question his robust realism on the basis of those three famous theses. Quine makes disquotation "an immanent standard of truth," but deems such immanence a "holophrastically" realist correspondence theory (Quine 1990a: 229; 1987d: 316; 1970: 10).[5] Wittgenstein too seems a holophrastic realist with a disquotational theory of truth as immanent in language-games. For Wittgenstein and Quine, private language arguments ensure the mind- and language-independence of things.

I follow Quine in speaking of relativity where many speak of relativism. I trust nobody will confuse philosophical theories of relativity with Einstein's theories of relativity, which is the usual reason offered for revising the meaning of "relativism." For many years *The Oxford English Dictionary* has defined "relativism" as "The doctrine that knowledge is only of relations." This remains the preferred meaning today. Relativism in this sense is not even an ontological doctrine, but an epistemological one on which knowledge, relations, or unknown things logically can be real.

The problem of realism *versus* relativity is perhaps *the* philosophical issue of the twentieth century. But ethical, cultural, and even "literary" relativity have taken the spotlight. Few today discuss the underlying ontological issues to which we now turn. In this dark night of the philosophical soul, few see that even supposing oneself lost in an abyss of irrealism presupposes an abyss, a self, and a relation, or that to be lost is in this sense to be found.

2. Modified Realism and Radical Relativity

Among problems (i)–(v) with which this introduction began, problem (iii), the problem of ontological relativity, may now be discussed in some detail. I shall discuss it in terms of what I call three main historical kinds of being *qua* identity theory. I use Butchvarov's definition of realism as a standard working definition of realism:

> Very roughly, I shall mean by...realism with respect to *x* the view that (1) *x* exists and has certain properties, a nature, and (2) that its existence and nature are independent of our awareness of it, (3) of the manner in which we think of (conceptualize) it, and (4) of the manner in which we speak of it. (Butchvarov 1989: 3)

Concerning the reality of persons, minds or ideas, clauses (2)–(4) must be restricted to the awareness, thoughts, and words of "other" minds. One's own mind arguably cannot exist independently of one's own awareness of it, or of the manner in which one thinks or speaks of it, yet should not be thought of as less real than other minds on that account. I reject Dummett's view that realism is a "truth-conditional theory of meaning resting on a...two-valued semantic theory" (Dummett 1981a: 441–42). As Quine rightly says, "The profound difference between Russell's atomism and my view is...that the rest of the truths are not compounded somehow of the observation sentences, in my view, or implied by them" (TT 181). And while what Quine calls his robust realism might not succeed due to some sort of relativity, it is wrong to condemn it as not realism merely because it is not truth-conditional.[6]

Four parameters or glosses are in order for our purposes. The three expressions we are concerned with are "being," "identity," and "*qua.*" First, then, being may be glossed as being-in-itself, reality, existence, actuality, substance. Second, identity may be glossed as unity or numerical oneness. Third, following Benardete, "*qua*" may be used in two senses, absolute or relative. Glosses of "*qua*" include "as," "conceived as," and "viewed as." Fourth, relativity may be relativity to a concept, conception, conceptual framework, context, description, formula, idea, linguistic convention, sense, or background theory. For instance, if every identity is *ontologically* relative to some sortal mental idea, then all things have being merely relative to our ideas.

While all four glosses are sets of verbal cues to help us interpret or assimilate technical philosophical theories to my own framework, they are based on common sense notions and ordinary ways of speaking. For instance, Hector-Neri Castañeda used to deride "*qua*" as obscurantist. But *The Oxford English Dictionary* defines "*qua*" as the perfectly ordinary "In so far as; in the capacity of." And whether a technical use is obscurantist depends on the care and skill of the individual philosopher. When I say that the present book is about being *qua* identity, I mean only that it is about being in so far as being can be understood, characterized, or defined in terms of identity.

Before stating the three main kinds of being *qua* identity theories, I must state three distinctions. In each case, the distinction is between one kind of identity common-sensically construed and metaphysically construed. Here one *may* appeal to a philosophical distinction between the ordinary language use and some special philosophical use of the word "identity" (and also "exists"). The special use may even have a common-sensical "core." But I shall explain the distinction between common sense and metaphysics as our ordinary distinction between seeming and reality. Common sense concerns what seems to be the case; metaphysics concerns what is the case. I can ground all three distinctions in such blatant metaphysics because the great revolts against metaphysics failed. In view of the common fact that we are sometimes mistaken as to what is the case, the burden is on those who wish to show that such distinctions are nonsensical or unknowable. For, to improve on Bernard Williams, knowing that a mistake has been made presupposes knowing both what seemed to be the case and what is the case, and also presupposes knowing that they are different (Williams 1967: 2/346). Let then one who is unaware of mistake cast the first stone.

The first distinction is between ordinary conceptual relativity and ontological relativity, or an ontological theory of *conceptual identity*. Conceptual relativity is a common sense datum. Frege's examples include the fact that one card deck is also fifty-two cards and the fact that one pair of boots is two boots. I think everybody would admit that conceptual relativity exists. It is another thing to admit an ontological theory of merely conceptual identity, and to assess which items have merely conceptual identities.

The second distinction is between the common sense datum that there are some objectual identities "out there" in the world independently of our concepts, for instance the identities of lions, and an ontological theory of *real identity*. Note that common sense conflicts with itself in ontology as much as elsewhere. Which items have real identities? Both cards and card decks common-sensically seem to have real identities. But cards and decks alike are subject to common sense conceptual relativity as well.

The third distinction is between the common sense datum that some identities are linguistic (as in Antoine Arnauld's examples of Augustus's finding Rome brick and leaving it marble, and the church that burned down ten years ago and is now rebuilt elsewhere), and an ontological theory of *linguistic identity*.

Insofar as we allow descriptions and concepts as glosses of each other, it is hard to distinguish conceptual identity from linguistic identity. This makes it correspondingly hard to tell whether an identity is real in a limited sense or literally fictitious. *Prima facie,* a conceptual identity is real in perhaps some very muted sense, while a fictitious identity (not: fictional identity, as for storybook heroes) is not real at all. Conceptual identity may be argued to be fictitious or unreal, and linguistic identity might *possibly* be argued to be real in a muted sense, say, "based" on reality. In that case, we may be forced back to a bald distinction between a "*fictitious* logical entity (ens rationis ratiocinantis)" and a "rational entity (ens rationis ratiocinatae)" (Kant 1982: 141; see Alanen 1986: 243 n.16 on Suárez). But a case that conceptual identity and linguistic identity are different, conceptual identity being real in a muted sense and linguistic identity being fictitious, might be made as follows.

Frege's verdict that a dog set upon by another dog as opposed to a pack is aware only of the "physical difference" (FA 42) is scarcely the last word in theory of animal cognition. Flying birds may single out a copse as one obstacle, while nesting birds have singled out individual trees in the copse. Birds can even be trained to correlate the number of spots on a box lid with the number of grains of corn in the box (Koehler 1956: 10–11). Surely such cognitive ability and concept formation ability make language learning possible, not the other way around. Thus, conceptual relativity is prelinguistic and even prehuman. It is this prelinguistic, prehuman relativity which is the main common-sense and *scientific* datum against the real identity of things. It is surely also the basis of the conceptual identities in traditional modified realism. Now birds are, in singling out trees, concerned with the real world. But birds are unconcerned with what are *prima facie* linguistic identities. At least it is hard to see why they would think of a building that burned down ten years ago and a new building on a distant site as the same church. The best explanation of this is that conceptual identities are real in some sense, while linguistic identities are not. Dogs become very experienced in classifying things that concern them. Language cannot explain that. But perhaps concepts can. Even if avian and canine image imprints and behavior-releasing mechanisms are not concepts, my argument remains a reasonable argument by analogy.

I shall now define three principal kinds of being *qua* identity theory. First, there is the theory of *radical relativity*, on which all identities are conceptual. Protagoras resembles a radical relativist. Second, there is *radical realism,* on which some identities are real and the rest are unreal or fictitious. Parmenides is a paradigm of radical realism if his One is real and his Many are unreal. This must not be confused with the recent "radical realism" of Edward Pols, which concerns the mind-independence of the directly known, and which would be at most a species of radical realism in my sense (Pols 1992). Third, there is *modified realism,* on which some identities are real and some identities are real in a muted sense. Historically, modified realism is a sort of golden mean. It may be called modified relativity with equal justice. Aristotle is a modified realist (see the preface to chapter 6).

Since these three theories are ontological theories, we may classify any entities admitted according to their kind of identity, e.g. real beings, conceptual beings, linguistic beings, beings in a muted sense, or fictitious or unreal beings.

(For me, all conceptual beings are beings in a muted sense, and all linguistic beings are fictitious beings.) Fictitious beings may be so called merely out of logical courtesy, or they may have an extremely low ontological status. They may also be mere objects beyond kinds of being, though they are not Meinongian nonexistents. The Rome Augustus turned from brick to marble is not nonexistent in the way Meinong's (Hume's) fabled golden mountain is.

What are the "muted" cases in modified realism? The answer would be more familiar if, instead of real identity, I spoke of real distinction. Then the muted cases would include distinctions in reason, modal distinctions, and even formal distinctions. That is, they would include identities in reason, modal identities, and formal identities. For convenience, I shall treat all these as conceptual identity.

There are other kinds of being *qua* identity theory. *Extreme realism* is the view that all identities are real identities. Perhaps some New Realists held such a view. *Extreme linguisticism* is the view that all identities are linguistic. Perhaps Carnap held such a view. *Common sense realism* is the view that there are some real, some conceptual, and some merely linguistic identities, roughly corresponding to the ordinary data, but adjudicating the conflicts internal to common sense. This is my own view. It is compatible with, and is a refinement of, modified realism. I see Quine as a common-sense realist, admitting both real physical objects and less real abstract classes, and paraphrasing away numbers, at least from his 1960 *Word and Object* (1975) to *Theories and Things* (1981).

Radical relativity is like Quine's ontological relativity in one way. Any medieval philosopher could have told you that Quine's rabbits are distinct in reason from their temporal stages and undetached rabbit parts. More accurately, if Quine is a relativist, then he would be an extreme linguist. He deals with words, not concepts, in "Ontological Relativity." But I allow either conceptual distinctions or linguistic distinctions as ontological assays of "distinctions in reason." And I shall argue in chapter 7 that Quine is a modified realist, and neither a radical relativist nor an extreme linguist in my sense. What he calls ontological relativity is merely what he calls inscrutability of reference, which is a thesis only about language and methodology, and not about the world (TT 19–21; PQ 459; PT 51–52).

Real distinction and the substance tradition go hand in hand. Radical relativists, however, must find the notion of a real distinction inapplicable. We may say that two entities are really distinct if and only if (1) either can exist independently of the other *and* (2) each has the ontological status of a real being. Many philosophers may think that requiring both conjuncts is needless. In a sense they are right. In traditional philosophy, the conjuncts would seem to imply each other. I emphasize conjunct (2) as a separate condition because without it the position of many earlier philosophers will be misunderstood. For them, many items which can exist independently of each other are not really distinct because they are not real things with real identities, but are merely parts or collections of real things. Their individuation consists merely of the concept we choose to "slice up" the real things before us. For instance, card decks can exist independently of each other as easily as individual cards can. But if cards are real things and card decks are mere collections, then many would hold that card decks are not really distinct from each other. Compare as theoretically susceptible to this kind of ontological analysis: Spinoza's water as one of extension's many modes, extension being in turn one of God's many aspects; Leibniz's body composed of many monads, Berkeley's city of many houses, and house of many walls and windows; Bolzano's, Reid's, and Hobbes's ship of many timbers (the rebuilt ship of Theseus); Hegel's book of many chapters and pages; Bradley's silk stockings reknitted with worsted; Husserl's melody of many tones; Heidegger's collection of many coins; Sartre's group of three men conversing; Frege's card deck; Russell's army of many regiments, and Russell's and Reid's regiment of many soldiers; Wittgenstein's composite broom and chessboard; Quine's rabbits, undetached rabbit parts, and temporal rabbit-stages; and Butchvarov's bicycle and amoeba.

There are at least three further senses of "real distinction." (2) Conjunct (1) may be used alone, and held not to imply conjunct (2). Now, really distinct things can have conceptual identities. This sense may correspond with contemporary usage better. (3) Conjunct (2) may be used alone. This has the merit of allowing things that cannot cease to exist to be real things. Here, conjunct (1) might be reintroduced in a *per impossibile* sense. Namely, if two things could, *per impossibile,* cease to exist at all, then if either could exist without the other, then they are really distinct. (4) One might add to conjunct (2) the proviso that a thing is real if and only if it can exist even if nothing else exists. I find this fourth sense of "real distinction" very hard to apply to cases. The reason is that the sense of "else" is too unclear. As John Stuart Mill noted in his *System of Logic*, a thing cannot exist without its properties, and a property seemingly cannot exist without belonging to a thing. And what about relations among things? Russell gives the clearest statement of the fourth sense I know: Each particular "does not in any way logically depend upon any other particular. Each one might happen to be the whole universe; it is a merely empirical fact that this is not the case" (PLA 202). But even such particulars might logically depend on properties. On the whole, I shall ignore this ancient and troubling fourth sense, which is best suited to God or a monistic One. The applicability of conjunct (1) alone is enough to ensure the existence of an objective fact. So that in insisting on conjunct (2), I am going beyond the call of realist duty to set up a safety margin. However, the *per impossibile* sense of "real distinction" is a valuable extension of that notion, and is defensible by being explicated in terms of the notion of independent content. E.g., the timeless Platonic forms *horse* and *dog* are, *per impossibile,* really distinct, because their conceptual contents are thinkable independently of each other. Another good explication is that those forms are really distinct if their respective instances would be. The four kinds of real distinction intimate four kinds of real identity.

All four kinds of real distinction are nonreflexive and nontransitive. For purity, they must also be symmetric. That is, *really* distinct items are really distinct *from each other*. All four kinds of real identity are reflexive, transitive, and symmetric. Thus all eight relations are equivalence relations.

Real beings can occur as real "parts" of a conceptual being. This would occur, for instance, if cards were real beings and card decks were conceptual beings. And conceptual beings can occur as conceptual "parts" of a real being. For instance, the round thing and the hard thing would be conceptually distinct but really one stone, if stones were real beings and round things and hard things were conceptual beings. This may be called the combinatorial interpenetrability of the real and the relative. Real things can still be simple in the sense of *real* indivisibility—or not, if you allow real things to compose real things, perhaps bricks and mortar to compose a wall. I am not concerned now with fine details. There are as many kinds of part-whole relation as there are pairs of overlapping categories.

A conceptual framework relativist such as the later Hilary Putnam might object, "We would only expect what you call real distinctions to occur among real things, once we determine within our framework what to call real things. That is not realism." My reply is that the mutual independence of really distinct things is framework-independent. Take two sticks and burn one. Does the remaining stick's ability to continue existing depend on our conceptual framework? If not, that gives us sense (2) of "really distinct." Our *assessment* of which level of the world's structure has the most real unities partly depends on our framework. Yet the strong unity of an atomic nucleus probably *is* more real, in *some* sense, than the gravitational unity of the Earth. That gives us senses (1) and (3) of "really distinct" as well. It is only common sense to hold that framework changes often yield real improvements in ontological analysis. Aristotle held that a tree with natural unity is more real than a chair with artificial unity. Trees held together better. But in the present era of superglue, the artificial unities are winning. This recalls Plato's suggestion that existence is power (*Sophist* 247; see Butchvarov 1979: 109).

Naturally, the substance tradition is full of modified realists. Aquinas says in *Summa Theologiae:*

> There is nothing to stop things being divided from one point of view and undivided from another (numerically divided, for example, yet divided in kind), and they will then be from one point of view one, and from another many. If a thing is simply speaking [un]divided (either because undivided in essentials although divided in non-essentials, as one substance having many accidents; or because actually undivided though potentially divisible, as one whole having many parts), then

such a thing will be simply speaking one, and many only in a certain respect. On the other hand, if things are simply speaking divided though in a certain respect undivided (as things divided in substance although undivided in species or in causal origin), then they will be simply speaking many, and one only in a certain respect... (Aquinas 1969: 159–60)

No subtle exegesis is needed to see that Aquinas is a modified realist. Aquinas even repeats the point (Aquinas 1969: 161; see 155–56).

Francisco Suárez, in his *Disputationes Metaphysicae,* accepts a distinction between real distinction, modal distinction, and mental distinction. He speaks expressly of "real identity" as the complement of real distinction. He also says that a real distinction can be made only between real entities, between thing and thing. This is conjunct (2) of our first kind of real distinction. Suárez follows Aristotle, *Posterior Analytics,* book 2, chapter 14 in making distinction (and identity) prior to grasping essence, as essence is determined by a process of division of features into genera and differences. Suárez follows Aristotle, *Metaphysics*, book 4, text 4 and text 5, and book 10, text 11 in finding that "whatever beings exist in the actual order prior to mental activity are either really identical or are really diverse, as otherwise there would be a middle ground between 'the same' and 'other'..." (Suárez 1947: 22). This is a *reductio ad absurdum* of radical relativity based on the law of excluded middle. Suárez is a modified realist, with both real identities and identities in modal and mental respects (Suárez 1947: 16–17, 20, 22, 31, 35).

Descartes, in *Principles of Philosophy,* may seem to be a radical relativist. He says that order and number "are only the modes under which we consider these things" (Descartes 1969: 241). But Descartes follows Suárez. Descartes says:

But as to *the number in things themselves* [italics mine], this proceeds from the distinction which exists between them; and *distinction* is of three sorts, viz. *real, modal,* and *of reason.* The *real* is properly speaking found between two or more substances... (Descartes 1969: 243)

Thus Descartes, too, is a modified realist. His real distinction is our first kind of real distinction, since his second sentence expresses conjunct (2).

Arnauld, in *The Art of Thinking*, may seem to be a radical relativist. For he considers Aristotle's categories to be "entirely arbitrary" and practically worthless classifications which often are a hindrance to science (Arnauld 1964: 42–45). But he also desires to find the "true classification" of things—and he does admit substances (Arnauld 1964: 39, 59). What is more, he says:

If two things succeed each other in one place, men tend to speak of these two things as if they were one. When speaking metaphysically, men may well distinguish the two things; but in ordinary discourse, especially when the two things in question are not perceptibly different, the two will be thought of as one. To refer to the two things as one is to emphasize their similarity but to obscure their differences. (Arnauld 1964: 144)

Arnauld proceeds to give several examples. We say the air that was cold (yesterday) is now warm, the river that was muddy is now clear, the animal's body that was composed ten years ago of certain particles is now composed of different ones. We say that Augustus found Rome brick and left it marble, but in fact there were two really distinct Romes with different substantival characteristics. We even say that this church which burned down ten years ago is now rebuilt. That this bread is really identical with the body of Christ, though it does not at all seem to be, shows that the reverse sort of confusion of identity may also occur. I classify Arnauld as a radical realist. He seems to treat identities other than real identities not merely as less real, but as literal mistakes or confusions (Arnauld 1964: 144-47).

Franz Brentano, in *Psychology from an Empirical Standpoint,* beautifully states what I call the meta-theoretical thesis of modified realism: that at some level of world structure there must be real things with real identities, even if it is beyond our power to know which level that is. He says:

It is impossible for something to be one real thing and a multiplicity of real things at the same time. This was asserted by Aristotle (*Metaphysics Z,* 16) and since then it has been insisted upon repeatedly, and rightly so. We can, of course, group together a multiplicity of objects and call their sum by one name, as when we say "herd" or "the plant world." The objects thus grouped, however, are not thereby one thing. What the name designates is not a thing, but what we might call a collective. A city, indeed each house in a city, each room in the house, the floor of each room, which is composed of many boards, are also examples of collectives. Perhaps the boards themselves are collectives composed of many elements, whether points, or invisible atoms or larger units. It is not our concern here to investigate this question. One thing, however, is certain: without some real unities there would be no multiplicities, without things there would be no collectives. (Brentano 1973: 156)

The last sentence implies a transcendental argument that there must be some real things, on pain of there being no pluralities. This is just my point that for conceptual slicing of the world into objects, there must be something to be sliced. Brentano does not specifically say at which level of structure we find the real unities. For instance, he does not say here that there are ultimate simple entities. But insofar as all multiplicities or complex items are collectives having conceptual identities, Brentano seems to imply that real things are simple, and in any case opposes conceptual identity to real identity, and is thus a modified realist (Brentano 1973: 157–62).

The later Brentano develops a "version of Aristotelian realism" (Nagel, 1956: 242) on which only things *(realia)* exist. *Entia rationis* are discarded for what are *entia linguae* at best. This suggests a radical realism not far from Arnauld's (Brentano 1971: 72–73, 84–85). This nominalistic version of Aristotelian realism is William of Occam's. Occam interpreted Aristotle as a radical realist with real substances and *entia linguae* in all other categories.

One must not confuse Geach's theory of relative identity with the theory of radical relativity defined above. Geach's theory is that logically complete identity statements are of the form, "*a* is the same *F* as *b*," where *F* is a sortal concept. That is, he holds that only such identity statements have determinate truth-values. Even if true, Geach's theory seems irrelevant to modified realism. Suppose that a statement of substantival identity must specify the *concept* of some substance. Now, the reality of substances simply outweighs the reality of all other categories of entities. Traditionally, the most paltry substance, even a grain of sand, is incomparably more real than everything in all the other categories put together. As Russell once said of his substantival particulars, "Each one might happen to be the whole universe" (PLA 202). Accordingly, just one true statement of substantival identity would be incomparably more *reflective* of reality than all true statements of nonsubstantival identity put together. Nor does this imply a single "true" classification of substances. It concerns only the bottom level of individual substances. That *a* is the same substantival whale as *b* leaves it entirely open whether whales are fish or mammals.[7]

Jonathan Lowe says "that an adherence to [Geach's] relativist conception of identity should carry with it an implicit commitment to a relativist conception of existence" (Lowe 1989: 57; see also Müller 1991: 189). This is correct but misleading. Geach's theory of relative identity is only about the logical structure of identity statements. It is the linguistic theory that identity statements are "incomplete" unless they specify some sortal term. But the theories of radical relativity and extreme linguisticism are ontological. They are not theories about the logical structure of identity statements, though they may be based on such theories. Likewise, rejection-of-Geach's-theory, which rejection I shall name "R," is also linguistic. An R-theorist, as such, is not a realist. An R-theorist may consistently accept any of the ontological theories I defined. The only "relative existence" Geach's theory implies is that there should be a plurality of category-restricted existential quantifiers corresponding one-one to the many relative identity relations (Geach, 1972: 144–58).

It is not even manifestly reasonable to infer "*a* is relative" from "*a* is the same *F* as *b*" on my third level of ontology. The very expression "*F*" provides an escape clause, in that *F* might be a substantival form implying the real being of *a*. If it is any consolation, it would be more probable than not that, *a* is relative, given that "*a* is the same *F* as *b*" is true, if more *F*'s than not were forms of conceptual beings. But "*F*" provides no converse escape clause in the inference of "*a* is real" from "*a* = *a*" on my first level of ontology, even where *F* would be a form of mere conceptual beings. "*F*" does not even occur in the Benardetean inference. The absolute use of "Smith *qua* Smith" carries over to "Smith *qua* Smith is Smith," or "Smith is the same Smith as Smith," bearding Geach's theory in its own den of logical form.

The distinction between theories of 'relative' and 'absolute' identity *statement forms* must in turn not be confused with the distinction between multivocal and univocal theories of the *sense* or *reference* of "is identical with" or even of "is the same *F* as." Nor must either of these distinctions be confused with the distinction between various ontological kinds of identity. For instance, a modified realist must admit two kinds of identity, real and conceptual, but may distinguish between the sense and the reference of the word "same," and be committed both to a multivocal reference theory and to a univocal sense theory of the word "identity." That is, a modified realist may hold that the word "identity" always expresses the same sense, but sometimes refers to real identity, sometimes to conceptual identity. (I do not speak specifically of Fregean senses or references.) Such a modified realist may or may not agree with Geach's theory of the logical structure of identity statements.

The basic argument for radical relativity is that if objectual identities shift as concepts shift, then every entity is both one and many; but a contradiction cannot exist in reality. A second argument is that whatever is is one and cannot be many; but every entity would (also) be many. Some might support the second argument by arguing that what is real cannot pass away; therefore it cannot be decomposed; therefore it cannot be many. But while so viewing reality as durability may have merit, there are deeper levels of realism. One better supports the second argument by arguing: Being an entity implies being one, and being one implies not being many. Neither argument can succeed because of radical relativity's self-defeating pratfalls. But this does not explain why the arguments go wrong. One might attempt to do that by showing that some things are one and real but not many (e.g. wholes *qua* wholes, simples, or actual infinitesimals), or that something can be one, many, and real after all. On the latter option one might argue that collectives or classes are one in a sense and many in another sense, and that they are real in some sense. But Russell simply inverts the argument when he argues that classes cannot exist because they would be both one and many (Russell's argument applies also to Brentano's collectives). Russell's resolution is:

The philosophy of arithmetic was wrongly conceived by every writer before Frege....They thought of numbers as resulting from counting, and got into hopeless puzzles because things that are counted as one can be equally counted as many....The number that you arrive at by counting is the number of some collection, and the collection has whatever number it does have before you count it. It is only *qua* many instances of something that the collection is many. The collection itself will be an instance of something else, and *qua* instance counts as one in enumeration. We are thus forced to face the question, 'What is a collection?' and 'What is an instance?' Neither of these is intelligible except by means of propositional functions. (MPD 53)

Thus number-predications become predicated of propositional functions as opposed to objects or collections. Frege gives a similar solution in *Foundations*, where *is a unit* is a second-level concept. Thus, far from "relativizing" numbers to concepts or propositional functions, Frege and Russell actually give number-predicates fixed and determinate logical subjects. The problem that a property, concept, or propositional function can in turn be viewed as one or as many, e.g. in the problem of universals or in definition by genus and difference, may seem only to postpone radical relativity. But for Frege, concepts and objects provide reciprocal identity conditions for each other, ironically in a way ensuring that many objects are really distinct from each other. And concerning determinacy of objectual identities, we need not know whether the concept *card of deck D* is a single complex universal, many simple universals, many complex particular properties, or many more simple particular properties, in order to know that exactly 52 objects fall under that concept.

But even granting this Frege-Russell logico-ontological sort of solution, (i) that we cannot *say* of objects that they are numerically one or many, since numbers belong to concepts, and (ii) that each object and each concept metaphysically *is* one, the arguments for radical relativity are scarcely defused. Even ignoring the seeming conflict between (i) and (ii), which Frege resolved by allowing the term "unit" both a numerical and a metaphysical sense (FA 42–43, 50–51, 62, 66–67), the problem is that objects in the world still overlap. Fifty-two cards still are, in some sense, one deck. That is the basic problem. I believe that the analysts were aware of it, and solved it by (iii) modified realism. I describe their different versions of modified realism, and explain the fallacies in the two basic arguments for radical relativity, in chapter 7.

A colleague criticizes the problem of radical relativity I raise as unreal, and my solution of it as therefore of no interest. I am pleased by this reaction because I take it as a sign that I am working on the right ontological level. For the two arguments for radical relativity I shall try to dismantle would be right at home in Plato's *Parmenides*. The problem of one and many which is central to the *Parmenides* is either the deepest puzzle in philosophy or it is nothing. For instance, George Pitcher is right that the *Parmenides* would appear to later Wittgensteinians as bewitched by a false picture of forms as "kinds of ghostly particulars" (Pitcher 1964: 203–11)—though with a little charity one might argue that Plato is pointing out the bewitchments. No doubt the problem of radical relativity would appear meaningless to verificationists as well. And long before such contemporary schools, even traditional scholars were hopelessly divided on the merits of Plato's *Parmenides*. Some regarded it as "Plato's profoundest philosophy" (Leibniz) or even as "the greatest masterpiece of ancient dialectic" (Hegel, Speiser), while others dismissed it as a joke—perhaps even a deliberate joke (Tenneman, Apelt, Wilamowitz) (see Cornford 1939: vi–ix).

The same colleague very kindly suggests that the logical clarity of Geach's relative identity thesis might be used to help explain and render my problem of radical relativity more intelligible. I am grateful for my colleague's helpful intent, but I am afraid that this suggestion will not work.

It should already be clear that the thesis of radical relativity is ontological, while Geach's thesis of relative identity is merely about the logical structure of identity statements. Geach is no radical relativist. He is a modified realist who admits mind-independent and language-independent entities including ordinary physical things, people, actual changes, actual mental acts, and God. He roughly follows Aquinas in admitting a real distinction between forms and individuals and also a logical distinction between subjects and predicates. He admits overlapping individuals following McTaggart and Polish mereology. He admits abstract entities such as numbers and linguistic entities such as predicables (Geach 1991: 253–57, 270; Geach 1969: 41, 61–64, 66–74). And Geach is justified in having a modified realist ontology. Broadly speaking, he accepts Quine's theory of ontological commitment and Frege's distinction between the actual and the objective (Geach 1969: 65–66). So that broadly speaking, he is as justified in being a modified realist as they are. Geach believes names refer to things as much as anyone; he merely differs on how to construe the associated identity criteria (Geach 1973: 295).

Geach's discussion of relative identity is always on the level of logical structure of language. (i) Geach's chief argument only concerns limiting predicables, or what most of us call predicates (Geach reserves the term "predicate" for actual occasions of use of a predicable) by a hierarchy of truth-levels to deal with semantic paradoxes. (The argument is weak; such paradoxes are only local problems not needing a big semantic regimentation.) (ii) Geach's discussion of "surmen" (men with the same surname count as the same surman) and other examples is on this level. (iii) When Geach connects his relative identity thesis with ontological relativity, he has only a version of Quinean ontological relativity in mind. And as I indicated earlier, that boils down to Quine's thesis of the inscrutability of reference (PQ 459; PT 51–52). The only "ontological relativity" Geach admits to is that within a language L, our ability to differentiate objects in the universe of discourse is limited by the number of predicables in L; a language allowing more differentiations could always be just around the corner. And this is the same modest relativity of identity Quine himself admits (Geach 1972: 238–49; Geach 1973: 287–302; Quine 1973: 59, 115–16). The only implication for metaphysics Geach finds in the relative identity thesis is that bare or featureless entities are precluded. Or more precisely, Geach believes that such entities are made possible only by the absolute identity thesis that things have self-identities "logically prior to having any characteristics" (Geach 1973: 289–90).—As if "*a* is the same *featureless entity* as *b*" did not conform perfectly to Geach's relative identity theory!

Let us try a daring way to apply Geach anyway. Pretend for the sake of the argument that Geach* (pronounced Geach-star) believes that the relative identity thesis logically entails that there is no single general identity relation which every entity has to itself, but instead many specific identity relations which different kinds of entities have (compare Geach 1972: 249). Statues have statue-identities; the materials they are made of have material-identities. Rivers have river-identities; the waters that pass down them have water-identities. We might object that the relative identity thesis ought to apply to all these specific identity relations as well. We might argue that there is a vicious regress of identity relations, and conclude that specific identity relations cannot have absolute existence or identity any more than statues or rivers can. We could surname these identity relations and make Geach*'s own surname argument. And there is no reason why the semantic paradoxes or the ontological relativity that figure so much into Geach*'s thinking should be affected as we move from the relative identity of statues to the relative identity of statue-identity. We might then conclude that Geach*'s relative identity thesis logically precludes him from saying how anything is in the world, since it commits him to a highly sophisti-cated form of radical relativity. (More accurately, since Geach* talks of predicables, not concepts, it commits him to a form of extreme linguisticism.) This argument could even be based on my own ontology as expounded earlier. Geach* would just be taking a typical relativist pratfall. I would not give this argument myself, since it is most uncharitable not to admit that there can be sorts of realist ontology other than my own. But we are only pretending Geach* has this problem so as to illuminate radical relativity.

Even more simply, one might pretend that Geach* believes that the relative identity thesis logically entails a form of extreme linguisticism on which the ontological locus of every identity relation is in relative identity statements. Perhaps Geach* doubts that (at least accidental) extralinguistic relations would have clear identity conditions (Geach 1969: 69).

However, not even the problem with Geach* is the problem of radical relativity this book is concerned with. Or more accurately, there is at most an overlap that backfires. To show this, consider how we might apply Geach, and then Geach*, to Frege.

Frege upholds the identity of indiscernibles. Now, Geach argues that indiscernibility is relative to the predicables of language L (Geach 1972: 240–41). And Wiggins argues that an absolutist identity of indiscernibles is incompatible with the relative identity thesis, given an innocuous assumption or two (Wiggins 1980: 18–20). This has been hotly disputed (Noonan 1980: 3). But let us pretend that the incompatibility exists for the sake of the argument.

Does Frege say anything committing him to the relative identity thesis, and therefore conflicting with his absolutist principle of the identity of indiscernibles? The test would be whether for Frege one and the same object *a* can be the same *F* as object *b* but not the same *G* as object *b*. It would appear that Frege passes this test. Frege says, "*One* pair of boots may be the same visible and tangible phenomenon as *two* boots" (FA 33). Thus one pair of boots is the same *phenomenon* as two boots, but surely not the same *boot(s)* as two boots. Wiggins tries to brush this off:

> [T]here is at least one really bad argument here *if* Frege really meant to suggest that, holding my gaze constant upon one external phenomenon, I can subsume the very same something first under the concept *copse* and then under the concept *trees*....Obviously a copse *is* trees. But the copse itself is not identical with any tree *or* with any aggregate of trees. (The copse tolerates replacement of all its trees...) (Wiggins 1980: 44)

Whether Frege really suggests this requires an interpretation of Frege's phenomena. Wiggins does not give one. My interpretation of Frege's phenomena, offered in chapter 7, is that they are indeed objects. Thus far our attempt to paraphrase the problem of radical relativity in terms of Geachian relative identity seems sharp and clear. It also makes the problem apply to all physical phenomena in Frege's metaphysics. The overlap of Geach*'s problem of ontological relativity and my problem of radical relativity is that both threaten to overwhelm all physical phenomena.

However, I shall argue in chapter 7 that phenomena are crucial to Frege precisely because they are objects which present their objectual identities to us independently of our using any sortal concepts at all. Their sortal properties cause us to grasp their metaphysical unities as objects even before we come to learn to use any such properties *as* concepts. Thus the objectual identity of a phenomenon is totally independent of our use of sortal concepts, much less of linguistic predicables. Phenomena are the basis of Frege's realism, not of any radical relativity. Therefore the overlap backfires. Presented real identities always trump radical relativity.

That leaves the pair of boots and the two boots. That is where Geach and Geach* must apply if they are to explain my problem of radical relativity. Crucial as I think phenomena are to Frege's realism, Frege's remarks on phenomena are few and far between. One might never miss them in his overall philosophy. Frege's objects as such are our true concern.

But here Geach and Geach* do not apply. Wiggins is right that for Frege a copse is *not* the same object as any tree, nor even the same object as the aggregate of trees constituting it at any given time. However, my problem of radical relativity does apply. As Wiggins himself admits and as anyone can see, in some sense a copse *is* trees after all. The problem is not whether "is" is ambiguous here, but explaining the ambiguity. I wholly grant Frege and Wiggins the sense of "is" in which a copse is *not* trees. The problem is to give an account of the sense in which a copse *is* trees. As to the intelligibility, nay clarity, of the problem, we just saw Wiggins himself call this latter sense of "is" obvious. There is even a problem with the identity of indiscernibles, since if a copse *is* trees, it is also both one and many. But the main point is that radical relativity threatens not because the copse is the same *F* as the trees in Geach's relative sense, but because it is *the same as* the trees in an absolute sense, "absolute" meaning 'not relative in Geach's sense'. The absolute sense in which the copse is not the trees is unable to trump radical relativity, since it is opposed to another absolute sense in which the copse is the trees. Thus the dilemma for realism arises on the level of two conflicting absolute senses of identity. This conflict cannot be analyzed in terms of relative identity.

We may call the absolute sense of identity in which a copse is not its trees the individuative sense, and the absolute sense of identity in which a copse is its trees the unitative sense. We may even say with Frege, "One pair of boots is not the same concrete object as two boots (individuative sense), but is the same physical phenomenon as two boots (unitative sense)." Despite the surface grammar of that sentence, it would be incorrect to analyze the sentence as a conjunction of two relative identity statements. That is because both uses of "is" express absolute senses of identity. Thus the sentence would be merely Frege's careful way of saying that though in a sense the objects are different, in a sense they are the same. Geach admits that Frege rejects the relative identity thesis since Frege says "it is inconceivable that various forms of [identity] should occur" (Geach 1972: 238). Worse, *concrete object* and *physical phenomenon* are not even sortal concepts. They are classificatory concepts, since it is logically possible either that some objects or that no objects fall under them. But they are not sortal concepts; we cannot directly associate determinate numbers of objects with them, since they lack individuative capacity. We cannot count how many concrete objects as such or how many physical phenomena as such there are in a room, only how many tables or chairs. Such mere classificatory concepts cannot generate the conflict, since they lack individuative capacity.

So here we finally find a logical formulation of the problem of radical relativity as threatening Frege. Namely, Frege must admit an absolute sense in which a copse is its trees. This seems to saddle him with two conflicting forms of absolute identity, the individuative and the unitative—and it is inconceivable that various forms of identity should occur. The two arguments for radical relativity arise not because of relative identity but because of a conflict of two senses of absolute identity. The arguments for radical relativity are purely negative: realism itself seems to be unraveling due to an internal conflict.

The arguments for radical relativity raised the problem of one and many. One necessary condition of the problem is two or more sortal concepts, say *copse* and *tree*, such that copses and trees overlap. Even then the problem will not arise if we apply only the individuative sense of absolute identity and say that copses and trees are different kinds of objects. I think that all commentators before me simply assumed that this *was* Frege's solution to any problem of radical relativity. And that is why they have seen no problem. But what they see as the solution is only the second necessary condition of the problem, which has not even arisen yet. The third and final necessary condition which ignites the conflict is the recognition of a second and conflicting sense of absolute identity in which the copse and trees *are* one and the same. As Wiggins says, "Obviously a copse *is* trees." Without that unitative second sense, the problem of one entity's being absolutely both one and many cannot arise.

Frege, speaking as he does of physical phenomena, ignites the conflict and faces the threat of radical relativity. I think all the great analysts were tacitly aware of the problem. At the end of this book, the reader must decide how much charity is really involved in thinking so.

Far from posing the problem, Geach arguably offers a solution. Geach aims to achieve a very conservative desert realism which avoids a proliferation of unwanted kinds of overlapping entities by reducing them to the ideology of language L (Geach 1972: 243–45). But if that is so, it is not Frege's solution but Geach's. And this is not a book about Geach. The solution I propose is modified realism. I propose that the individuative and unitative senses are not different and conflicting absolute identity relations. I propose that the "is" of identity always denotes the same identity relation, but that some true identity statements reflect real identities in the world while others do not. The question then becomes which true identity statements reflect real identities and which do not.

While the problem of radical relativity serves as a framework of this book, in fact most of the book would survive the problem's nonseriousness or even unintelligibility. Only this chapter and the last deal directly with it. The intervening chapters are preparatory in the sense of a grand tour of everything of interest in Frege and Russell as 'no entity without identity' ontologists, and they are contributions in their own right.

The general plan of the book is this. Chapters 2–5 explore Frege's and Russell's existence-identity philosophies in depth. Chapter 6 discusses Aristotle as a paradigm modified realist and begins to compare Frege and Russell to him. Chapter 7 uses seven criteria of modified realism to argue that all four analysts are analogous enough to Aristotle to be classified as modified realists too.

2

Is Frege a Radical Relativist?

There is a huge literature on Frege's realism. It has mainly concerned three issues: the ontological status of functions; idealism; and contextualism. William Marshall, Hans Sluga, and Michael Dummett cast doubt on Frege's realism due to these three issues respectively. First, Marshall argued that function-names do not refer. But his argument was overcome by a "smoking gun" letter from Frege to Edmund Husserl in which Frege extends the sense-reference distinction to concepts (Frege 1980: 63). Thus it is clear that concepts, and more generally functions, are objective references. Second, much of the debate since then has centered on Frege's views on objectivism in *The Foundations of Arithmetic*. Most would agree that Frege derides psychologism and idealism, and that in his later works he makes all logical subject and predicate terms into names that refer to existents. Most would agree that the mature Frege is an extreme realist with many affinities to his realist peers, Brentano, Meinong, Husserl, Moore, and the early Russell. But Sluga found that some key passages in *Foundations* seem like objective idealist texts. Sluga pointed out historic parallels in wording not noticed before—a contribution. But other texts in *Foundations* are inescapably realist. And Sluga's work, though good, is outweighed. Third, however, a key part of Sluga's case ironically survives in the view of his greatest critic, Dummett. Even Dummett admits the tension between contextualism and realism in *Foundations* to which Sluga drew attention. But I suggest that even this tension is not very serious. In my opinion, the most important issue of all concerning Frege's realism is a fourth one that so far has been ignored. Namely, for Frege objects shift as concepts shift. Identity is predicated not of objects, but of names expressing senses. Existence itself is predicated not of objects, but of concepts. These three facts suggest that Frege is a radical relativist in the sense I defined in chapter 1. And a radical relativist Frege is no realist at all. Thus even the debate on Frege's contextualism seems shallow in comparison. I shall now explain why radical relativity is a far more basic issue than contextualism.

Though almost the whole Western tradition saw the threat of Protagoreanism and adopted a modified realism to counter it, and though debates concerning Wittgenstein and Quine on relativity raged all about them, the Frege scholars have been embarrassingly silent on the question whether Frege was a radical relativist or a modified realist. Almost nothing in the literature on Frege shows much awareness of the great Western tradition of modified realism or seeks to determine Frege's place in it. I know of no major Frege scholar who mentions the fact that for Frege numbers, objectual identities, and objects shift as concepts shift as casting the slightest doubt on Frege's realism. And nobody compares Frege's views on identity to the great distinction between real distinction and distinction in reason which indicates modified realism. This includes Dummett (1981: 471–511; 1981a: 428–72), Sluga (1980: 105–24), Michael D. Resnick (1980: 125), Eike-Henner W. Kluge (1980: 115–16), Crispin Wright (1983: 3), Gregory Currie (1982: 43–44), and Gordon Baker (1988: 159). The short texts are discussions of number shifting which ignore realism; the long texts are discussions of realism which ignore number shifting. Nor do I see any such connection in Klemke, ed. (1968), Wright, ed. (1984), Baker and Hacker (1984), Mark Notturno (1985), or Nathan Salmon (1986). J. N. Mohanty sees the connection in Husserl, if not in Frege (Mohanty 1982: 40–41). Even Ignacio Angelelli, who shows such a deep awareness of the history of number shifting, confines his discussion to theory of classes (Angelelli 1967: 124–25, 57–58, 239–42). Hilary Putnam does oppose ontological relativity to "the ancient category of Object or Substance" (Putnam 1987: 36). But he does not mention Frege. And even Putnam fails to oppose realism to objectual identities' shifting as sortal concepts shift. Claire Ortiz Hill finds Frege's view that numbers are predicated of concepts "one of the major planks of his antipsychologism" (Hill 1991: 68). But Hill is mixing up two very different themes, and sets of sections, in *Foundations*. Frege agrees with Leibniz that number applies to everything, expressly including mental ideas (FA 31). Thus the fact that numbers shift as concepts shift applies to everything, including mental ideas. Thus the issue of relativistic irrealism *versus* determinacy of number and identity concerns everything, including mental ideas. Antipsychologism arises only from the private language argumentation of section 26; communicability applies only to objective entities, and not to ideas at all. Thus antipsychologism is a shallower, more limited issue for Frege.

To his great credit, Reinhardt Grossmann, in *Reflections on Frege's Philosophy*, sees the conflict between a Fregean radical relativity and Aristotle's category of substances (Grossmann 1969: 94–104). And to her great credit, Leila Haaparanta raises the spectre of relativity concerning Frege's senses as media through which we always must view objects (Haaparanta 1986b: 278–84). I discuss her argument in section 3. But even these two fail to connect realism *versus* relativity with real identity *versus* conceptual identity in Frege.

To be sure, everybody knows that objects are a far wider category than the old category of substances, and that the old category is ignored in the Fregean dispensation. But nobody has attempted to see what might remain analogous to real identity, or analogous to the old distinction between real distinction and distinction in reason, in Frege's philosophy. This basic question about Frege's ontology seems raised in the present book alone.

Contextualism and radical relativity do not entail each other. Contextualism is a linguistic theory. It is the linguistic theory that all words have meaning only in the context of sentences. Radical relativity is not a linguistic theory. It is the ontological theory that there is no more to objectual identity than our choice to apply one concept—or description, idea, or some other analogue—as opposed to another. Even if the analogue is descriptions, one may deny contextualism. A radical relativist may even accept Augustine's theory of names as described in Wittgenstein's *Investigations* #1. One may try to reinterpret radical relativity as some kind of contextualism. But saying that there are fifty-two objects on a certain table in the "context" of our application of the concept *card* adds nothing to saying that there are fifty-two objects on the table if we choose to apply that concept, and is on the face of it still no assertion about linguistic meaning. Conversely, a contextualist could accept Aristotle's theory of being and identity, that is, could be a modified realist for whom substances have real identities.

Peter Geach's theory of relative identity is compatible with contextualism and with radical relativity, but none entails either of the other two, and no two conjointly entail the third. I suggest that relative identity and contextualism are poor linguistic guises or substitutes for radical relativity. Geachian relative identity asserts only that identity statements must have a certain form. Contextualism asserts only that words have no meaning apart from their use in sentences. But radical relativity asserts that identities—the identities we ordinarily attribute to things—are conceptual identities. Only radical relativity is incompatible with real identity, and with realism. For only radical relativity (I momentarily include extreme linguisticism and the mixed theory that all identity is either conceptual identity or linguistic identity under this head) asserts that the ontological *locus* of identity itself is never in things, but only in our view of things. The question is begged as to the relation of identity to the world if one assumes that theories like contextualism or Geachian relative identity even *imply* that the ontological locus of identities is only in language.

This, then, is the true issue for realism: Is Frege a radical relativist? In the present chapter, I shall only defend Frege against the charge that he is a radical relativist. I give the positive case that Frege is a modified realist in chapter 7.

There is no doubt that for Frege, numbers shift as concepts shift. One card deck is four suits and fifty-two cards. But this may be only common sense conceptual relativity. Whether it is ontological radical relativity, on which all putative objectual identities are conceptual identities, is a problem of interpretation. I shall examine first Frege's concept of identity, and then his concept of existence. I shall then discuss some recent literature relevant to whether Frege is a radical relativist. Last, I shall discuss contextualism *versus* realism. Even though it has just been superseded as the most basic issue, it remains of great interest to 'no entity without identity' ontology.

1. The Concept of Identity

What is the identity relation? Is it a relation between names, denotations of names, or senses of names? Frege's answer has been the subject of much dispute, and this dispute is the main topic of the present section. But a section devoted to what identity is, according to Frege, would be incomplete if his view of senses, as well as his explanation of identity as indiscernibility, were not at least briefly discussed as well. I shall therefore also discuss those topics.

It is clear that in *Begriffsschrift* Frege held that identity is a relation between names, i.e., that the statement "$a = b$" has the same content as the statement "The names 'a' and 'b' stand for the same content" (BG 20–21). The question is whether or in what way Frege later changed this theory. Most philosophers seem to agree that Frege's major later statement of the topic begins with a rejection of the *Begriffsschrift* view. But what the rejection amounts to, and what other view Frege is led to, are far from clear. I am referring, of course, to the first two paragraphs of "On Sense and Reference." I shall state and defend my own interpretation of this passage first, and examine other interpretations later.

My view is that while identity remains a relation between names, now names are understood differently. In *Begriffsschrift*, names were mere labels. Now they are signs expressing senses. The statement "$a = b$" is now to be understood as expressing the thought expressed by "The names 'a' and 'b', which are understood to be signs expressing senses, *denote the same denotation.*" (This must not be confused with the absurd analysis that "$a = b$" means that the *names* "a" and "b" are identical!) In *Begriffsschrift* names, instead of expressing senses, correspond to ways of determining the contents they stand for (BG 21). A sense is a kind of unit of meaning in virtue of being all or part of a thought, where thoughts are what we express in sentences (SR 62). But a way of determining a content is not put forward by Frege as being the meaning of any name with which it is put in correspondence (BG 21). A way of determining a content seems best identified in "On Sense and Reference" not with a sense, but with the mode of presentation which is contained within a sense (SR 57). But even here there seems to be a difference: a way of determining a content is, as it were, on the side of the observer; it is a procedure one may employ, while a mode of presentation is on the side of what is observed: it is how something can present itself to us (Dejnožka 1979: 38; see Dummett 1993: 107, concurring).

That is my interpretation. I argue for it as follows. In the first part of the "On Sense and Reference" passage, Frege repeats the argument and position of *Begriffsschrift*. If identity were a relation between the objects named (technically between the object and itself), then an informative identity would be impossible. But informative identities are possible, as is proved by their being so often actual. Therefore identity is not a relation between the objects (SR 56–57). So far so good; what follows is what has been so hard to understand, beginning with the sentence, "But this is arbitrary."

I submit that Frege argues as follows. It is not enough merely that identity be a relation between names, for a difference between names considered as mere labels does not suffice to account for the possible informativeness of an identity. That is, the mere fact that the letters "*a*" and "*b*" are different, that they differ in shape, cannot explain the possible informativeness of "*a* = *b*" (SR 57). (In the language of the completed argument, the reason "*a* = *b*" need not be informative is that "*a*" and "*b*" can be easily assigned the same sense.) The trouble is that names considered merely as labels are arbitrarily assignable to any object. There is no reason to prefer assigning a mere label to any object as opposed to assigning it to some other object. So if names are mere labels, then any assertion made about names will have only an arbitrary connection with the objects they denote. And any statement using them to assert something about objects must take those objects as already known—as the objects to which the labels were assigned. It would then be impossible for an informative identity to be a statement either about such names or using such names. Frege therefore rejects the *Begriffsschrift* view. But it is important to realize what sort of rejection this is. The whole argument is based on the construal of names as mere labels; it is this construal that gives trouble. It should be precisely and only this construal of names that Frege wishes to change.

This is just what happens. We find in "On Sense and Reference" no hint of a return to the rejected view that identity is a relation between objects, nor do we find any hint of a theory that identity is a relation between senses, for example the relation of containing modes of presentation of the same object. What we find is a distinction between two construals of names, and this indicates that Frege finds one construal of names inadequate and substitutes another. The substitution is the sole improvement made on the *Begriffsschrift* theory, aside from replacing ways of determining contents with modes of presentation.

Now if on the earlier construal we could not explain how an informative identity is possible, how can we do so on the new construal? Specifically, how is the problem of arbitrariness avoided? A sign that expresses a sense designates in a certain manner, i.e., it relates *qua* linguistic expression to a definite way an object can be presented before consciousness. (With regard to names in ordinary language, the ostensibly named objects need not even exist.) Therefore names can no longer be arbitrarily assigned to any object. In fact, a name can now belong in principle to one object at best, even if we might not be sure in practice which object it is, or even whether it exists. As for the undeniable element of arbitrariness in language, this now appears at the level of assigning senses to names. Only in this way, Frege thinks, can pertinence to the subject matter be built into names, and it is this pertinence that ensures the possibility of an informative identity. Without it, we find ourselves once again viewing names as mere labels, and the assertion that two labels in our language denote the same object can hardly be a vehicle by which we learn anything factual about the world beyond our language.

The transformation of ways of determining the subject matter into senses containing modes of presentation is doubtless meant to enhance the pertinence we wish to build into names. A mere procedure on the side of the observer might 'determine', for all we know, two objects if we follow it, or none clearly. But a mode of presentation, being on the side of the object, belongs to one object only and belongs to it clearly, if it belongs to an object at all, thanks to the uniqueness (TW 80–81) and the determinacy (TW 33) of every object. There is still much room, of course, for difficulties in practice.

My interpretation is an interpretation of least change. *Begriffsschrift* makes identity a relation between names. The only change (I say again: the only change) in "On Sense and Reference" is that ways of determining contents evolve into modes of presentation contained in senses expressed by names. Why then assume that identity is no longer a relation between names? Why assume out of the blue that identity is now, say, a relation between objects? The burden of proof rests on other interpretations.

I have assumed that in *Begriffsschrift* names are mere labels. I do, however, admit the possibility that when Frege wrote *Begriffsschrift*, he had in his mind no clear opinion on whether names are mere labels of contents. The problem rests with the notion of content, which Frege later replaces with the two notions of sense and denotation (reference). In a sense, Frege should not arrive at the notion of a mere label until after he distinguishes sense from denotation, so that a mere label only denotes a denotation. In another sense, the very failure to distinguish sense from denotation makes names mere labels. In any case, if *Begriffsschrift* ways of determining contents were either meanings of names or were contained in such, Frege would have virtually given the "On Sense and Reference" theory in *Begriffsschrift*.

That concludes my basic argument for my interpretation. The argument occupied seven paragraphs. However, I wish to explain my argument further, since it has been misunderstood by early readers of this book, and others might fall prey to the same misunderstandings.

First, let me use a convenient new terminology to restate my interpretation. (1) The *name theory* is the theory that identity is the relation between names that they denote the same denotation, where names are signs expressing senses. (2) The *object theory* is the theory that identity is the relation between an object and itself that the object is the same as itself, where any named objects are named by signs expressing senses. (3) The *label theory* is the theory that identity is the relation between names that they denote the same denotation, where names are mere labels; observers may use different ways of determining contents, but such methods or procedures are not meanings of the names, and are wholly external to, i.e., are not, and do not contain features or aspects of, the objects named. (4) The *labeled object theory* is the theory that identity is the relation between an object and itself that the object is the same as itself, where any named objects are named by mere labels, and are only externally associated with any ways of determining contents. (5) My interpretation is that in *Begriffsschrift*, Frege rejected theory (4) and held theory (3), names definitely being externally associated with ways of determining contents. In "On Sense and Reference," I interpret Frege as first stating and rejecting theory (4), then stating and rejecting theory (3), then accepting theory (1). My interpretation may be called the *name interpretation*. (6) The interpretation prevailing today, which I seek to replace with my own, is the same as mine except that it holds that after Frege rejects theory (3) in "On Sense and Reference," Frege accepts theory (2). This may be called the *object interpretation*. Thus the sole difference between the name interpretation and the object interpretation is that the former sees Frege as adopting theory (1) as an improved version of theory (3), while the latter sees Frege as adopting theory (2). Theories (5) and (6) are, of course, by no means the only extant interpretations of "On Sense and Reference," as we shall soon see. (7) The *sense theory* is the theory that identity is the relation between senses that they are senses "of" the same denotation, in a very technical sense of "of" introduced by Montgomery Furth (1967: xix). (8) It is possible to hold that Frege accepts the sense theory in "On Sense and Reference." This may be called the *sense interpretation*. (9) The sense theory might be held to be an improvement on a hypothetical *Begriffsschrift*-style theory which Frege never held: that identity is the relation between ways of determining contents of determining the same content. This hypothetical theory may be called the *content theory*. (10) Since the content theory is merely a construction of my own from the resources available in *Begriffsschrift*, there is no *content interpretation* of *Begriffsschrift* to be discussed. My position, to be argued for below, is that the sense interpretation and the name interpretation both attribute workable theories to Frege but the object interpretation does not; and the name interpretation and the object interpretation enjoy some modicum of textual support but the sense interpretation does not. I endorse the name interpretation as the only one of the three which both attributes a workable theory to "On Sense and Reference" and enjoys a modicum of textual support.

I have been told I hold that in "On Sense and Reference," Frege's theory of identity is that (11) identity is the relation between names of *being the same name*. This is (12) the *same name interpretation*. I would like to assure everyone that I reject the same name interpretation, and accept the name interpretation instead. The whole point of the name interpretation is that the identity relation can obtain between different names—differently shaped physical signs which express different senses which contain different modes of presentation. Such names are as different as names can get in Frege's philosophy, but can still denote the same denotation. This is just what, on my interpretation, explains the possibility of informative identity statements for Frege. In contrast, the same name interpretation does not allow this explanation to Frege at all. The same name interpretation is just silly, both as a misreading of my name interpretation and as a misreading of Frege's problem of informative identity statements.

I am also told that I hold theory (8), the sense interpretation. I would like to assure everyone that I do not. I hold theory (5), the name interpretation. This is another silly misreading of my view, though not necessarily of Frege's.

I hope that explains what my interpretation is. I must also explain my argument's structure, since I have been viewed as giving a merely negative argument. My argument is in fact partly negative and positive. On the negative side, I argue against the object interpretation that the object theory it attributes to Frege is unworkable. Granted, it may appear to the unwary that there is nothing wrong with a true informative identity statement's describing that a certain object is identical with itself, since it is enough to account for the informativeness of that statement that the signs flanking the identity sign be different signs and that those signs express different senses. But this, unfortunately, is not the case. Even if the object is arrived at through different modes of presentation, because we approached it through different senses expressed by different subject-terms of the statement, the fact remains that what the statement actually describes is quite trivial, and to judge that the statement is to true is to judge something quite trivial. Specifically, if an identity statement describes some relation of an object to itself, then as soon as you grasp the thought expressed by the statement, and know which object(s) in the world the statement is about, you should be able to tell whether it is true or false. In fact, a corollary problem is that all identity statements would become *a priori*, since the traditional test of the *a priori* is that the truth or falsehood of the statement in question can be determined from its meaning alone. That the type of meaning from which we determine this would be denotative meaning instead of connotative meaning does not detract from this point. In contrast, if an identity statement describes a relation between its subject-names, then even if you grasp the thought it expresses and know which objects in the world the statement is about (in this case, its subject-names), you do not yet know whether it is true or false, at least if its subject-names are signs expressing senses. I should say, as a criticism of Frege's theory, at least if *at least one* of its subject-names is a sign expressing a sense. There is no reason why the other subject-term cannot be a mere label. Compare Russell, who allows an identity statement to be informative if *at least one* of its subject-expressions is a definite description. The other subject expression can be a mere label, i.e. logically proper name for Russell (PLA 247). And Russell's general point seems right.

Let me put my negative argument against the object interpretation another way. On the object theory, if "The Morning Star is the Evening Star" is informative and true, it is about one object perceived in two modes of presentation—or through the medium of two senses, if you like. Two key questions arise. (1) Are any objects denoted here? (2) If so, how many? The answer to (1) must be, "Yes." For Frege requires true or false statements to have denoting logical subject-terms. And the answer to (2) must be, "A single object." For otherwise the statement would be false. Therefore we denote here a single object through the media of two senses. Therefore a single object is denoted by us twice. Therefore the statement is that a certain object is identical with itself. Therefore, the statement is uninformative. The modes of presentation which ought to make it informative cannot be properly brought to bear, since they are not located on the level of denotative meaning. You could *relocate* them into the denotations, so that statement is not about the planet Venus, but about Venus *in the mode of morning presentation* and Venus *in the mode of evening presentation.* Call these latter objects "qualified objects." They are not identical with each other or with Venus, since they are distinct in reason from each other and from Venus. Thus the statement that they are identical would be false. To be sure, we could now give a workable theory of informative identity, which might be called the *qualified object theory*: "*a* = *b*" means the same as 'Qualified object *a* and qualified object *b* qualify the same object (which may or may not be itself qualified in turn)'. In fact it is my own theory, different from but owing much to Panayot Butchvarov's theory, and also to Antoine Arnauld's notion of a qualified thing, i.e. thing "as determined by a certain manner or mode" (Arnauld 1964: 39). But it should be clear that the qualified objects the statement is about are not Fregean objects. Frege does not admit qualified objects. Thus a qualified object interpretation of Frege's theory of identity is absurd, regardless of whether it brings modes of presentation properly to bear on the problem. For "The Morning Star is the Evening Star," if true, would be about, and its subject-terms would denote, not the object Venus, but two different qualified objects: Venus-in-the-mode-of-morning-presentation and Venus-in-the-mode-of-evening-presentation. Nor may qualified objects be equated to Frege's senses or to the modes of presentation senses contain, since these are not any sorts of objects at all, or so I shall argue later.

Again, the negative first stage of my argument is to reject the object theory as unworkable. Butchvarov gives the general form of this stage of my argument: Any theory of true informative identity statements on which the ostensibly identical object(s) are only apparently distinct objects, cannot account for the informativeness of such statements. To account for that, the identical object(s) must be, in some sense, genuinely different objects as well. I cannot describe Butchvarov's argument here (Butchvarov 1979: 9–28); Butchvarov endorses the object interpretation (Butchvarov 1979: 12, 21). Anyone against my view must refute not only my specific argument against the object interpretation of Frege, but must refute Butchvarov's general argument as well.

Note that on my qualified object theory, objects distinct in reason are genuinely different, and not just apparently distinct, since their properties differ, and continue to be judged to differ, even after "The Morning Star is the Evening Star" is judged to be true. And if we construe our two qualified objects as objects of perception or thought, i.e. phenomenologically, then they would even be *really* distinct as such, and would be judged distinct in reason only insofar as "The Morning Star is the Evening Star" is judged to be true, so that both would be judged to overlap Venus and each other. In fact, that construal is itself a qualification. And to be qualified is to be in some mode of presentation. My qualified objects differ from Butchvarov's objects mainly in that (i) mine are publicly available and (ii) Venus is not merely a construction of them.

That Butchvarov would undoubtedly reject the name theory as well is beside the point. That shows only that Frege did not approach theory of identity through Butchvarovian continental phenomenology. Frege is not concerned to describe what an expression or a statement appears to be about so much as to give a workable theory, however artificial. Frege never hesitates to impose highly artificial denotations to maximize determinacy. (In fact, in *The Basic Laws of Arithmetic* "The Morning Star = The Evening Star" would denote the truth-value, the True.) The vital point for interpreting Frege is that within Frege's system, i.e. using the resources Frege makes available, i.e., names, senses, and objects, the object theory does not work. This point is established by my negative argument in particular and Butchvarov's argument in general.

My negative argument relies on a certain principle of charity in interpreting Frege, namely that he would not have given such an unworkable theory as the object theory turns out to be. Since principles of charity will come up again in this book, I may as well now state my view that a principle of charity is not a mechanical or wooden rule to be applied automatically or blindly in every situation. The greater the philosopher the less likely he will be to hold a theory that does not work, as a rule of thumb. However, a principle of charity that "mistake-proofs" a great philosopher is, I think, itself a mistake. Great philosophers do make mistakes, and even paint themselves into corners from time to time. A principle of charity too strong to reflect any human fallibility is too blind and mechanical for me. I see a principle of charity instead in a very different way: as a matter of context, as a matter of all the facts, with no one factor being decisive in all situations. It is not a wooden rule but more of a "touchy-feely" kind of thing. Therefore I freely admit that as a weakness in my argument, reasonable people could differ on how to apply my own principle of charity to Frege. My response would only be that such a weakness is a double-edged sword. I am just as free to criticize the applications others make of the principle as they are to criticize mine. Thus the weakness is not specifically a weakness of my own argument, but simply a fact of life for all of us. Having considered the situation of Frege's theory of identity as well as I am able, I think my application of my principle of charity is as judicious as I can make it. Frege actually saw the problem of unworkability in the labeled object theory in *Begriffsschrift*, and it seems to take little charity on our part to say he realized in "On Sense and Reference" that the same problem continues on the improved version of that theory, the object theory. On the object theory, senses and modes of presentation are good enough smoke and mirrors to deceive those who do not try to look behind them, but for all that they are just smoke and mirrors. In contrast, on the name theory, they are internal and indeed essential to the very identity of a subject-term *qua* sign that expresses a sense, not only as subject-term, but as the *object* denoted by the subject-term. For on the name theory, the subject-terms of an identity statement denote themselves. That senses are arbitrarily assigned to signs in order to create names does not detract from this point. A sense is essential to the name it helps create, not to the physical sign.

If I had stopped the argument here, then my argument would have been an essentially negative one, specifically a proof by cases that considers two cases: the objectual interpretation and the name interpretation. My argument would have been merely that the name interpretation must be right because the objectual interpretation, invoking a principle of charity, must be wrong. It is a tacit assumption of my argument that there are only these two cases to consider in interpreting the beginning paragraphs of "On Sense and Reference." Again, I deem the sense interpretation to attribute a workable theory to Frege, but to be not called for or supported by the text. Again, I discuss this third option later, along with still other interpretations.

But I did not stop my argument there. It was vital that I go on to give a positive argument that the name interpretation of Frege's theory of identity *is* a workable theory. That is because it is no good to offer a proof by cases, arguing indirectly that case B must be right because case A is unworkable, if case B is as unworkable as case A. Therefore I had to argue that the name interpretation of Frege's theory of identity attributes to Frege a workable theory of informative identity statements. And this the name interpretation does, since on it the relata of the identity relation are genuinely different objects. Specifically these relata are different names; and in an informative identity statement they are as different as names can get for Frege. They are different physical signs, and they also express different senses.

Thus my argument here, properly understood, has two general parts. In the negative first part, I argue against the objectual interpretation as saddling Frege with an unworkable theory. In the positive second part, I argue that on the name interpretation, Frege has a workable theory. I rely on a situational principle of charity in interpretation. While I expressed this principle in a negative way, saying that surely Frege would not have held an unworkable theory, the more general principle I rely on is in fact positive: Surely Frege would have given the best argument he could within his system. We scholars use this positive principle of charity all the time, though admittedly with a grain of textual salt.

As an adjunct to the second, positive stage of my argument, I also invoked a principle of least change in interpreting Frege. The keynote of this principle is epistemic caution. The principle is: Where a philosopher states he is changing his theory, and our evidence is too close or too unavailable for us to make a call on how much he is changing his theory, it is best to assume as little change as possible, since then we will be as little mistaken as possible. This principle is not unrelated to Occam's razor as Russell understands it, and might even be stated, "Changes should not be multiplied or increased beyond necessity." I am not saying by any means this principle of least change is infallible, but merely that it describes the most natural and rational course of interpretation in the absence of a preponderance of evidence on either side.

Instead of a principle of least change, I might have spoken of a principle of greatest continuity. Such a principle would apply not only to Frege's transition from *Begriffsschrift* to "On Sense and Reference," but also to the development of the argument in "On Sense and Reference" considered by itself. In particular, in "On Sense and Reference," why would Frege jump all the way back to the labeled object theory he refuted first and attempt to revise it, when he could improve the label theory which he had just finished refuting? It strikes me that the burden of proof lies with those who claim that there is such a jump or gap. For the most natural and reasonable presumption is that there is no such gap.

I do not need to elaborate on how often our reasoning depends on assumptions of all kinds of continuities. We could hardly live without them. Other things being equal, our picture of the world would be far less inductively rational if we did not assume that things continue to behave as usual when their behavior is not perceived, or at least that their behavior would be perceived as usual if we did perceive it. This is exactly the situation we have here. We do not, so to speak, perceive Frege's theory of identity in "On Sense and Reference," either directly in an express statement or indirectly by means of a strictly deductive implication. Thus any interpretation must be based, broadly speaking, on inductive evidence. And here the most natural and reasonable assumption we can make is continuity.

I can now summarize the name interpretation as supported by three different inductive arguments. All three assume that the name interpretation and the object interpretation are the only two plausible candidates. (1) Assuming a principle of charity, Frege probably held the name theory because (he realized that) within his system, the name theory works, i.e. succeeds in explaining how informative identity statements are possible, and the object theory, at bottom, does not. (2) Assuming a principle of continuity, the name interpretation is probably right because it involves the greatest continuity from *Begriffsschrift* to "On Sense and Reference." (3) Again assuming a principle of continuity, the name interpretation is probably right because it involves the least jump or gap in Frege's argument within "On Sense and Reference." All three of these inductive arguments are, in general form, fairly straightforward and typically acceptable scholarly arguments. Of course, no inductive argument is logically decisive. It remains logically possible that the name interpretation is wrong. But weighing all three inductive arguments together, surely the preponderance of evidence favors the name interpretation. Note that these arguments are at least as much about how to reason as they are about what Frege says. This is a measure of the difficulty of interpreting Frege here.

I cheerfully admit that all three inductive arguments have a weakness: they all depend for much of their strength on assuming that the name interpretation and the object interpretation are the only two plausible ones. This means that I must show that all the other main possible interpretations are comparatively implausible in the end. Inevitably, this will be a matter of degree. I shall offer a critical survey of other interpretations in the literature shortly. But I cannot pretend to have surveyed all possible interpretations. Another one might always be just around the corner.

I proceed to consider seven objections to my argument. The first two are probably the ones most scholars endorsing the object interpretation would think of first. In fact, both were offered by an early reader of this book who endorses that interpretation.

First, my early reader tries to turn the tables on my interpretation by viewing the opening passage of "On Sense and Reference" as follows. Like me, he finds first a statement of the labeled object theory followed by a criticism of that theory, then secondly a statement of the label theory followed by a criticism of that second theory, and then finally a presumed but unstated resolution of the dilemma. Both of us view this resolution as involving a shift from construing names as mere labels to construing names as signs expressing senses. But while I view this shift as a revision of the label theory into the name theory, he views it as a revision of the labeled object theory into the object theory. He then argues that since our two views are mirror inversions of each other, he has at least denied me victory by achieving a stalemate.

My reply is that unfortunately this objection consists of merely stating that I might be wrong—that the object interpretation is equally *logically* possible. I have already admitted this fact. The objection detects no flaws in any of my three inductive arguments. In fact, it offers no criticism of my arguments at all. It simply ignores them altogether. Therefore, this objection seems to be no objection. All it does is observe that my arguments are inductive. All the probabilities remains on my side. Observe, for instance, that there is no attempt to invert my substantive principle of continuity into a principle of discontinuity. That is because a principle of discontinuity, in the present context, would appear preposterous as soon as it was articulated. Nor is there any attempt to show that the object interpretation is workable or that the name interpretation is unworkable. That, however, is attempted at least in part by my early reader's second objection.

The second objection is far more serious. It is an argument that the name theory is unworkable. If it had been coupled with a positive argument that the object theory does work after all, it would have aimed to turn the tables on my first inductive argument. Even as it is, it aims to destroy that argument by achieving a stalemate in which both the name interpretation and the object interpretation are unworkable, though for different reasons.

The second objection is this. Senses and many objects can be said to enjoy an existence apart from the existence of languages, while names cannot be said to do this, since what makes an object a name is its function in language. How then on my view could the Morning Star and the Evening Star have been for Frege the same planet before languages were invented? Twenty million years ago there simply were, I assume, no names to stand in the relation of denoting the same object. It is to no avail to say that today we can say that they were the same planet because today we have names.

In fact, to go well beyond my critic, Frege holds that there are metaphysical unities, or objectual identities, out there in the world. Frege sharply distinguishes these from arithmetical units, which he analyzes as second-level concepts predicated of first-level sortal concepts (FA 42–43, 50–51). But on my interpretation, objectual identities *cannot be talked about* in Frege's notation. Indeed, on my interpretation, objectual self-identities are *not even thinkable*, since all Fregean identity statements, on my interpretation, express thoughts about names as opposed to objects in the world. I mean that the senses which the subject-terms of such statements express are senses "of" the subject-terms themselves, in Furth's sense of "of" (Furth 1967: xix). They are not senses "of," say, the planet Venus.

One reply to this second objection might be that the name interpretation remains the interpretation of greatest continuity, and therefore the one most justified by the text, even if the name theory is no more workable than the object theory. But such a reply simply concedes the destruction of my first inductive argument and observes that my other two inductive arguments remain in force. A better reply can be made. The alleged ground of the object theory's superiority is really irrelevant to what Frege is doing. He is offering an analysis of the logical structures of sentences of the forms "$a = a$" and "$a = b$." What relevance to such an analysis has the question whether certain objects were identical before languages existed?

The very fact that Frege distinguishes the metaphysical unity of an object from the arithmetical notion of unit used in the equations, i.e. identity statements, of arithmetic, works in favor of the name interpretation, not against it. The reason the name theory does not capture pre-linguistic objectual identities is simply that it is not a theory about metaphysical unities, i.e. objectual identities, at all. It is instead a theory about the logical structure of identity statements. The situation is exactly parallel to that in arithmetic. Frege's theory of the number one, and of numerical units in general, is simply not a theory about metaphysical unities, i.e. objectual identities. That idea is one he sharply rejects early in *Foundations* (FA 27–32). Frege's theory of the number one is instead a theory about the logical structure of statements involving numbers. Nor is this a mere coincidence. To say that the Morning Star and the Evening Star are identical is to say that there is numerically one object they both are.

The dilemma for Frege interpreters, then, is this. Should we saddle Frege with the object theory, which is unworkable, or with the name theory, which implies a systematic ambiguity such that you can only show, but not say, an objectual identity? It seems to me that a principle of charity calls for the name interpretation as involving the lesser of evils. Frege can live with a systematic ambiguity of reference, but not with an unworkable object theory.

Our principle of continuity makes this decision even easier. The fact is that Frege already admits as a principal doctrine that there are things that cannot be stated in language, but only shown or represented. This concerns the famous problem of the concept *horse*, which I shall discuss later. Thus the name interpretation does not present a new or additional problem, but instead merely a problem of a kind Frege already treats as a mere paradox of the logical structure of language. If we cannot talk directly about objectual identities, well then, Frege already admits we cannot talk directly about concepts either. Frege probably would not allow us to talk directly about senses or forces or tones, either. So this would not be much of a problem to Frege. In fact, this might even help explain how Frege came to be a great influence on Wittgenstein, since it is a basic Tractarian doctrine that objectual identities cannot be said in language but only shown.

The principle of continuity makes our decision easier in a second way as well. Namely, Frege *had already admitted* the same systematic ambiguity in *Begriffsschrift*, thanks to his holding the label theory there. That is, Frege already allowed the reference of object-names to shift systematically from objects to object-names themselves in contexts of identity statements. He had already made objectual identities "shown, not said" in his canonical notation.

The principle of continuity makes our decision easier in a third way. Namely, in "On Sense and Reference" itself, Frege already allows systematic shifts from customary references to indirect references in contexts of belief, if not in contexts of what Russell calls propositional attitudes in general. The name interpretation merely assimilates identity statements (SR 56–57) to statements involving belief (SR 66–68), and surely also to statements involving modality.

To sum up, four arguments outweigh the second objection. First, the most it achieves is a dilemma between an unworkable theory and a systematic ambiguity Frege can live with; and charity favors saddling Frege with the latter. Second, third, and fourth, the name interpretation is far more continuous with Frege's philosophy in three basic ways.

A third objection is logical. The name interpretation implies a systematic ambiguity in object-names, specifically a use-mention ambiguity. Namely, they are used to denote objects in all statements except identity statements, in which they denote, i.e. mention, themselves. Quine, Dummett, and Sluga may be taken together as pointing out what they think are various technical difficulties in this. Quine says that such theories confuse use and mention (WO 116–17). Dummett says that the *Begriffsschrift* label theory "makes nonsense of the use of bound variables on either side of the sign of identity" (Dummett 1981: 544); presumably Dummett thinks this applies to the name theory as well. Sluga asks us to consider his statement (3):

(3) Object *a* has property *f* and *a* is identical with *b*; therefore *b* has the property *F*. (Sluga 1980: 152)

Sluga notes that on the label theory, '*a*' and '*b*' name themselves in "*a* is identical with *b*," but elsewhere within statement (3) name extralinguistic objects. Sluga says, "Consider now a substitution of two other terms '*n*' and '*m*' for '*a*' and '*b*'. Are we to make the substitutions for both occurrences of '*a*' and '*b*'or for only one of them? Either decision leads to awkward difficulties" (Sluga 1980: 152).

For several reasons, I am not persuaded that such objections are very serious. (i) Unlike Russell, Frege is noted for *not* confusing use and mention (Grattan-Guinness 1973: 112–13). In "On Sense and Reference" there seems to be no such confusion. Indeed, if I am right that senses are uses, then Quine is implying that Frege confuses mentions of names with the *senses* names express, which is absurd. On my own interpretation, "*a* = *b*" clearly *mentions* its subject-names. The name theory introduces a simple systematic ambiguity by making object-names name themselves in a single sentence-form, that of the identity statement in which the identity sign is flanked by two object-names. There should be no confusion. (ii) Logicians should be able to accommodate such merely technical problems as Dummett and Sluga raise. Sluga himself suggests that the difficulty he raises might be accommodated (Sluga 1980: 152). *Pace* Dummett, an identity sign flanked by two object-names is the *only* kind of identity statement whose informative identity Frege is trying to explain in "On Sense and Reference." Therefore any statement in which the identity sign is flanked by at least one bound variable will be interpreted exactly as it would be on the object theory. Therefore, so long as we strictly follow the use-mention distinction, any inference involving an identity statement will be valid on the name theory if and only if it would also be valid on the object theory. In fact, if anyone still sees a problem, I think we can simply stipulate that an inference is to count as valid on the name interpretation if and only if it is valid on the object interpretation. Frege is full of arbitrary stipulations maximizing rigor and fixing a determinate sense for indeterminate statements. Substituting terms á la

Sluga or quantifying *á la* Dummett can be handled simply by saying, Do what you would do on the object interpretation. If logical inference is not disturbed, but is on the contrary preserved, by systematic reference shifts in contexts of propositional attitude, then why not here too? (iii) Much the same systematic use-mention ambiguity exists in *Begriffsschrift*, since there Frege expressly asserts that identity is a relation between names. Yet Frege did not see this as destroying *Begriffsschrift* logic due to technical difficulties; so why should we think he perceives any such difficulties now? There is simply no evidence that Frege ever even saw the difficulties Sluga and Dummett specifically cite. (And that *might* be because the difficulties are not really there to be seen.) (iv) Most importantly, in "On Sense and Reference" Frege expressly tells us the one and only reason he is now rejecting the *Begriffsschrift* theory of informative identity statements. The exact nature of the reason has been subject to debate, but I think everyone can at least agree that the general nature of the reason Frege states is not that the *Begriffsschrift* theory of identity leads to ill-formed statements or inferences, but that it fails in its primary mission of explaining how an informative identity statement of the form "$a = b$" is possible. *Pace* Dummett, quantification and variables do not even occur in such statements. Dummett's objection is a total misreading of the text of "On Sense and Reference." It might seem a plausible objection to the name *theory*, but it is wildly irrelevant to the name *interpretation*. The name interpretation is of the first paragraphs of "On Sense and Reference," which do not even mention a problem about variables or quantification, but only a problem about informative identity statements whose logical subject-terms are both proper names.

A fourth objection is that in his 1884 *Foundations*, which occurs after the 1879 *Begriffsschrift* but before the 1892 "On Sense and Reference," Frege already seems to treat identity as a relation between objects (FA 73, 76–79). Geach believes that Frege holds the object theory in *Foundations* (Geach 1972: 218). Indeed, even if Frege does not expressly endorse the object theory in *Foundations*, he certainly does not use or mention the *Begriffsschrift* label theory there. And he does not hold the name theory in *Foundations*, since he has not yet differentiated sense from reference; objects in *Foundations* are undifferentiated objective 'contents'. The name theory is based on the differentiation of sense from reference. So from the evidence internal to *Foundations*, Geach has a strong case. Geach could also cite the dialogue between Frege and Pünjer on existence, which occurred even before 1884, to strengthen his case (PW 62–63).

I concede that this objection presents some evidence against my view. But what I think is happening is that Frege is casually omitting any use or mention of his *Begriffsschrift* label theory in these two works because presenting his theory of informative identity statements does not really matter in those works. It is also worth noting that these two works are not even mentioned in the "On Sense and Reference" passage I have been interpreting. Frege presents his new theory as a direct revision of *Begriffsschrift*, as if right up to this point in time he has been maintaining the *Begriffsschrift* theory.

A fifth objection offered by a colleague is that the name interpretation confuses the name theory with the fact that in an identity statement, the identity sign is flanked by two object-names. I would like to assure everyone that I have not confused them. For the record, the mentioned fact is merely syntactical, and obtains regardless of whether the name interpretation or the object interpretation is correct semantically.

A sixth objection is my own. Frege was not a continental phenomenologist, and cannot be expected have appreciated or to have even been able to formulate Butchvarov's general argument against all theories of informative identity statements on which the subject-terms do not designate genuinely distinct things. My reply is that Butchvarov's argument is a general one that applies across the board to all theories of informative identity. It is based on an ordinary apparent-genuine distinction common-sensically available to everyone. Far from giving the argument from the standpoint of his continental phenomenology, Butchvarov gives it prior to developing his phenomenology, as a general condition which any adequate theory—including his own phenomenology—must meet. In fact, I was able to formulate my own specific argument against the object theory as unworkable in strictly Fregean terms. I used only the resources Frege made available to himself in "On Sense and Reference."

A seventh and final objection is my own. If the name interpretation is correct, then we seem to lose the most natural gloss of the metaphysical unity of an object, which Frege sharply distinguishes both from numerical units and from the number one (FA 42–43, 48–49, 50–51, 58–59, 62, 66–67). The gloss is that metaphysical unity is self-identity. We seem to lose it because Frege says that "identity is...given to us in so specific a form that it is inconceivable that various kinds of it should occur" (BL 129). Thus it would seem that we cannot allow Frege any objectual self-identity if we already attribute to him identity as the relation between names of denoting the same denotation, since then he would have two kinds of identity. Of course, this problem might represent only a change of view going from *Foundations* to *Basic Laws*. But it seems to me that a deeper reconciliation is possible. Namely, the *Basic Laws* proscription seems against identity statements' having different logical structures where different kinds of objects are concerned. (The case at hand for Frege in *Basic Laws* is whether to accept "improper objects" as having their own form of identity.) This is a proscription against Geach's relative identity, just as Geach believes (Geach 1972: 238).

That concludes my discussion of seven objections to the name interpretation. I will be discussing further arguments for the object interpretation shortly.

Terrell Ward Bynum and Thomas V. Morris share my name interpretation.[1] It may be that Angelelli, who draws the same distinction between two construals of names that I do, does as well. But his main discussion is obscure on the point. The only definite difference between Angelelli and me concerns Frege's rejection of the view that identity is a relation between objects. Angelelli takes the uninformativeness of an identity on that theory to be the same as the contentlessness of predicates such as "is one" and "exists" when they are viewed as denoting first-level concepts (Angelelli 1967: 38–40, 43–44). This is not so: "is one," so viewed, is held by Frege to be contentless because all objects would fall under the concept it denotes (FA 40). But "is identical with" is not held to be contentless because it denotes a relation under which all pairs of objects fall. Far from contentless, identity on the rejected theory is uninformative precisely because it would be a relation a thing had only to itself, so that most (but not all) 'pairs' of objects would be mapped onto the False.

I am told that Sluga and Currie share my interpretation as well. I admire and accept Sluga's interpretation as far as it goes. And waiving my arguments against the object interpretation, I also admire and accept Currie's interpretation as far as it goes. But I do not see that either of them ever actually chooses the name interpretation over the object interpretation (Sluga 1980: 150–61; Currie 1982: 108–12).

I proceed to other interpretations, beginning with the object interpretation in more detail. The object interpretation is surely the most widely held one, and is quite plausible too. No doubt the reader will have noticed that I have already described (and discounted) some positive evidence in favor of it. I think that the name interpretation is better, but many readers may find it a close call. I do not expect to convince everyone. In fact, if I had not arrived at the arguments I did, I might well hold the object interpretation myself. I do hope at least to show that the object interpretation is far from clearly correct. But enough of preliminaries. Quine has very kindly written me,

> I have checked Frege's *Begriffsschrift* and "On Sense and Reference," as well as *Word and Object*, and all is in agreement with…[the object interpretation]. Frege thought in the *Begriffsschrift* that identity related the signs, but he thought better of it in "On Sense and Reference."
>
> In *Word and Object*, p. 117, I wrote only that Frege at first thought the one and later the other, without saying where. But the page in "On Sense and Reference" that I cited in my footnote [WO 117 n.6] is explicit. Frege there writes that in the *Begriffsschrift* he had thought that identity related the signs, but no longer thought so. (Quine 1995)

Quine is describing what I consider the best and simplest textual argument for the object interpretation. Namely, Frege seems to be *saying* that he used to think in *Begriffsschrift* that identity is a relation between names, but is abandoning that view now. The text in question is, "[Is identity a] relation between objects, or between names or signs of objects? In my *Begriffsschrift* I assumed the latter" (SR 56). I do not recall seeing Quine's argument anywhere else in the literature, but it is so natural and direct that I am willing to gloss everyone who holds the object interpretation as having been influenced by it merely by reading Frege. Quine's reading is very natural. But it is not the only natural reading. Frege does not say, "I assumed the latter, *but I was wrong.*" It is just as easy to take Frege as meaning, "I assumed the latter. But I now see that a modification is needed to uphold it." Thus Quine's argument, taken by itself, seems a fifty-fifty gamble. Thus interpreting Frege one way or the other must turn on other things.

Michael Dummett (1981: 544), Robert Ray (1977: 232), and P. D. Wienpahl (1950: 484) all hold that in "On Sense and Reference," identity is a relation between objects. I already discussed Dummett's argument concerning technical difficulties with quantifying into identity statements.

Ray sees the passage in the article after the sentence "But this is arbitrary" as giving an argument that identity is not a relation between names, and infers a return to the view that identity is a relation between objects. Ray thinks that Frege's argument is that "$a = a$" would express an identity fully as informative as the one expressed by "$a = b$" if identity were a relation between names, since each of the token-letters, "a" and "a," flanking the identity sign in "$a = a$," is an arbitrarily producible event and need not stand for the same object the 'other' letter stands for (Ray 1977: 230). But Frege gives no such argument. It is safe to assume that Frege thinks at least that the same letter always stands for the same object, at least in the same propositional context. This is so even though Frege accepts only tokens, not types (TW 194). Ray's citing the common fact that in English, "bank" can express different senses on different occasions is misguided, since even as early as *Begriffsschrift*, one of Frege's motives in having a formal notation at all was to avoid precisely such ambiguities of natural language in his object-names (BG 11). If anything, Ray has got the argument backwards. Frege is arguing not that "$a = a$" would be as informative as "$a = b$," but that "$a = b$" would be as *un*informative as "$a = a$," if identity were a relation between mere labels.

Ray argues that if Frege's view were that produced objects are the same sign only if they express the same sense, so that the difference in cognitive value between "$a = a$" and "$a = b$" might be restored, this view would be both false and odd. It would be false because the two subject-terms in "$a = a$" need not be the same sign; they can be assigned different senses, so that "$a = a$" remains as informative as "$a = b$" (Ray 1977: 231–32). This criticism would be right if Ray's interpretation were right, but we have seen that it is not.

Ray's argument that it would be odd if Frege's view were that produced objects are the same sign only if they express the same sense is that Frege's later theory of identity is that identity is a relation between objects (Ray 1977: 232). Ray's argument is a little odd itself. It does not appear to be logically valid. Treated as an inductive argument, he is saying that a philosopher must have held a certain opinion in an early work, since he held it in a later one. This temporally inverts the usual principle of continuity. Worse, Ray never argues for his argument's premise, which is that Frege later held that identity is a relation between objects. I presume that Ray has *The Basic Laws of Arithmetic* in mind. And as we shall see in a moment, the textual evidence is against him.

Montgomery Furth, while not taking sides on "On Sense and Reference," claims that by the time of the later *The Basic Laws of Arithmetic*, Frege did change from the *Begriffsschrift* view that identity is a relation between names to the view that it is a relation between objects (Furth 1967: xvii–xix). Furth offers no argument for his claim, but it is important and needs discussion.

My name interpretation concerns only two of Frege's writings, *Begriffsschrift* and "On Sense and Reference." I ascribe the label theory to the former and the name theory to the latter. *Basic Laws* is harder to fathom. Currie observes that one text in vol. 1 seems to endorse the object theory while another text in vol. 2 seems to endorse the name theory (Currie 1982: 112; compare Dejnožka 1981: 34; Dejnožka 1979: 49). Furth probably bases his claim on the vol. 1 text, sect. 7, which stipulates that "Γ = Δ" is to denote the True if and only if Γ is identical with Δ (BL 46). But this stipulation is not at all an attempt to state whether identity is a relation between names or between objects. Nor is it an attempt to define identity, since identity is indefinable for Frege (TW 80; Frege 1967c: 184; identity had been definable in *Foundations,* FA 76). It is an attempt to make the identity relation determinate, in accordance with vol. 1, sects. 29, 31. The vol. 2 text Currie cites is, "We use the equality sign to express that the reference of the group of signs on the left hand side coincides with the reference of that on the right hand side" (TW 201). Two years before Currie wrote, I found two other *Basic Laws* texts as well. Frege says, "Again, if I write '(2 + 3 = 5) = (2 = 2)', and took for granted that we know that 2 = 2 is the True, yet I should not thereby have asserted that the sum of 2 and 3 is 5, but only described the truth-value of '2 + 3 = 5' stands for the same as '2 = 2'" (TW 156). And Frege says, "If our sentence 'the sum of the Moon and the Moon is not one' were a scientific one, then it would assert that the words 'the sum of the Moon and the Moon' and the word 'one' did not coincide in reference" (TW 167). To sum up, we have three texts in *Basic Laws*, one from vol. 1 and two from vol. 2, which clearly describe identities as statements that two expressions refer to the same reference; and one text in *Basic Laws* vol. 1 which seems to Currie to support the object theory, but which does not even appear to describe the logical form of an identity statement, and which looks for all the world like an attempt merely to make the identity relation determinate. My conclusion is that in *Basic Laws*, Frege probably still holds the name theory of "On Sense and Reference."

Frege's correspondence from the time of *Basic Laws* may seem to cast some doubt on my conclusion. In an undated letter to Peano probably written between 1896 and 1902, Frege seems to assert the name theory; but in a letter to Russell dated August 2, 1902, Frege seems to assert the object theory (Frege 1980: 128, 143). These letters might even invert the timing of the two conflicting texts in

Basic Laws (vol. 1 is 1893 and vol. 2 is 1903). Here I appeal to my principles
of continuity and charity in interpretation, and suggest that Frege rightly thinks
that a strict adherence to the name theory does not really matter to the issues he
raises in that letter to Russell, much as he rightly thought that strictly insisting
on the label theory of *Begriffsschrift* did not really matter to the issues he raised
in *Foundations* or in the dialogue with Pünjer. For that matter, the reader of this
book may find that sometimes I myself casually write as if Frege held the object
theory, in contexts where it does not really matter. It is quite easy for any
author to do, as I can testify from personal experience.

P. D. Wienpahl's argument that in "On Sense and Reference" identity is a
relation between objects is an interesting one (Wienpahl 1950: 485). He
distinguishes three possibilities: identity is a relation between either modes of
presentation, names, or objects. He rejects the first possibility because to him
it means saying that "*a* = *b*" expresses the thought expressed by "The mode of
presentation associated with '*a*' is identical with the mode of presentation
associated with '*b*'," which of course entails that "*a* = *b*" is false whenever "*a*"
and "*b*" express different senses. Wienpahl does not see that "*a* = *b*" might be
understood as expressing the thought expressed by "The modes of presentation
contained in the senses of '*a*' and '*b*' are modes of presentation of the same
object." (I shall not discuss this variant of the sense interpretation further; my
rejection of the one as not being Frege's will apply equally to the other.)
Wienpahl sees Frege as finding problems with the two other possibilities. He
then claims that what Frege does is to go back to the view that identity is a
relation between objects, and concludes that the text must be incomplete because
it fails to mention this return. Wienpahl has no argument for this last claim of
his (Wienpahl 1950: 484–85).

The next interpretation I shall examine is offered by David Coder. Coder
holds that in "On Sense and Reference," Frege makes no explicit choice
between the view that identity is a relation between names and the view that it
is a relation between objects. While in *Begriffsschrift* Frege held the first view,
he now sees that both views, each in its own way, make an informative identity
impossible (Coder 1974: 340–41). Frege therefore chooses neither theory, but
merely insists that for an informative identity to be possible, its subject-terms
must not only (customarily) denote objects, but must express senses as well
(Coder 1974: 342). Coder's view seems a pleasingly moderate one. Frege does
not, indeed, pronounce either theory to be correct in so many words. My reason
for retaining my own interpretation is that Frege distinguishes between two
construals of names, and this distinction is clearly intended to be a refinement
of the *Begriffsschrift* view. Since in "On Sense and Reference" Frege openly
rejects the theory that identity is a relation between objects, and then finds a difficulty with the theory that identity is a relation between names, the offering of
a distinction between kinds of name can only mean that the second theory
survives in an altered form which aims to avoid the difficulty. Further, making

names express senses does not seem to help the first theory. If identity is a relation between each object and itself, and only between each object and itself, then senses will not teach us any more about the identity of any object than we already know, once its identity is given at all.

Leonard Linsky, if I understand him correctly, holds still another view. Unlike Coder, who says that Frege makes no choice between the two alternatives he discusses, Linsky sees Frege as definitely rejecting both in favor of a third view. This view is that names express senses as well as denoting denotations (L. Linsky 1967: 22–23). The trouble with this view is that it does not tell us what identity is a relation between. Now the task of explaining the possibility of an informative identity is not the same as the task of determining what identity is a relation between. But the whole problem of how an informative identity is possible arises precisely because this possibility seems incompatible with our *prima facie* belief as to what identity obtains between, namely, objects. The solution to this problem is not merely to introduce the sense-denotation distinction, but instead, if anything, to use that distinction to arrive at some view of what it is that identity obtains between that is compatible with the possibility of an informative identity. This is what the original problem is, and to see Frege as offering no solution to it is to accuse him of a gross oversight. This is just what both Linsky and Coder do.[2]

Nathan Salmon has a subtle view. For Frege an identity statement is not about names or senses, but about objects. But its cognitive value is due to the thought it expresses, and this thought does not contain the objects the statement is about. Salmon then criticizes Frege's criticism of the *Begriffsschrift* view that identity is a relation between names, saying that Frege ironically fails to see that he can now hold an informative identity statement asserts a relation between names taken as signs expressing different senses (N. Salmon 1986: 48–52). Salmon gives no argument for any of this. On my view, the irony is that Frege does hold the view Salmon perceptively says he now can hold. It is Salmon's hybrid which fails to explain how an identity statement can express a cognitively informative thought, if the statement asserts that a certain relation obtains between certain object(s). For then we already understand which object(s) the statement is about, e.g. "the massive physical object, the planet Venus" (Salmon 1986: 48). To be sure, if we understand the object(s) only *qua* presented in certain ways, then we have a beautiful explanation of informative identity statements. But the explanation is totally unFregean. Frege does not admit qualified objects. What we have is instead my own theory of informative identity. Nor is "Frege's puzzle" a wider puzzle about all predicates, with "nothing special to do with the identity relation" (Salmon 1986: 51). "The author of *Timon of Athens* wrote *Timon of Athens*" is not an identity statement (Salmon 1986: 12). But who can overlook that the identical expression "*Timon of Athens*" occurs twice in it? Thus Salmon's supposedly wider puzzle merely replaces "$a = a$" with the logically equivalent "The author of t wrote (i.e.

authored, i.e. is the author of) *t.*" Thus the "wider" puzzle is only about slightly disguised identity statements.

Haaparanta believes that Frege simultaneously holds four different accounts of identity. But if an identity statement is (2) "a metalinguistic statement" about two names' references and senses, then an identity statement is trivially (1) "a rule for substitutivity of names in different contexts." And if (2) is correct, then identity cannot be (3) "a relation between two objects" or (4) "a relation of an object to itself." For it is already a relation between names, as opposed to objects. To attribute accounts (3)–(4) to Frege after attributing (2) to him is to accuse Frege of the shabbiest inconsistency (Haaparanta 1986b: 280). The mutual logical inconsistency of three of these accounts, namely (2)–(4) as applied to cases, may be seen from their respective formalizations: $I("x," "y")$, Ixy, and Ixx. Account (2) alone is false for nameless identical objects. Account (3) alone is true of nonsymmetrically given nameless identical objects. Account (4) alone is false for nonsymmetrically given named identical objects. Frege himself gives a famous general warning against this very sort of multiple account. Frege says, "[I]dentity is...given to us in so specific a form that it is inconceivable that various kinds of it should occur" (BL 129). As we see, Haaparanta ignores this warning and attributes not only four forms of identity to Frege, but three of them are not even logically consistent with each other. Indeed, she makes Frege guilty of a quintuple inconsistency. Besides making Frege accept the triple inconsistency of (2)-(4), she makes Frege ignore his own warning against that sort of conflict. And fifth, Frege also gives a famous general warning against ambiguous symbols. Here Haaparanta makes Frege invalidate his project of introducing a rigorous notation. While my own name interpretation makes object-names systematically ambiguous, a systematic ambiguity is no ordinary ambiguity. If a name is systematically ambiguous, it always has exactly one sense and one reference in any given sentential context. If a name is ordinarily ambiguous, it has two senses in the very same sentential context. Frege is warning against ordinary ambiguities; he feels forced to accept some systematic ambiguities as a necessity of language. Haaparanta does not appear to be talking about systematic ambiguities, and certainly Frege admits no *fourfold* systematic ambiguity anywhere in his philosophy.

This criticism of Haaparanta assumes that her accounts (1)–(4) and Frege's two warnings all concern the logical structure of identity statements as opposed to the metaphysical unities of objects. I myself distinguish these two topics in Frege's philosophy. In the present chapter, I discuss the structure of identity statements. In chapter 7, I ask what might be analogous to a distinction between real identity and identity in reason among objects for Frege. Thus I hold that Frege has one specific form of identity statement just as he says, but in some cases it reflects real identities in the world, and in others identities in reason. Perhaps Haaparanta, too, distinguishes these two topics. But if so, she offers no indication of which topic she is discussing when.

Also, Frege's first warning might be only that different sorts of objects do not have different forms of identity. That would let Haaparanta off one hook. If anything, it would put me on the hook for distinguishing between real identities and identities in reason for objects. But I am off the hook. Frege is saying that identity statements can have only one logical form; I am distinguishing between two kinds of *objectual* identity. Frege's theory is about the logical structure of identity statements; my interpretation is about the ontological status of their objectual truth-conditions. And for all Frege's objects, identity remains indiscernibility *tout court.*

I grant Haaparanta that my criticism of her interpretation rests on a principle of charity in interpreting Frege. I am happy to leave it to the reader to judge whether I am being too charitable to Frege here. I admit that Frege *may* be multiply inconsistent concerning forms of identity. I am only saying that it seems very unlikely to me, and that Haaparanta does not seem aware of the problem.

Hill, too, saddles Frege with an inconsistent theory of identity:

> Frege had thought he could...show how analytic [sic] statements could be both true and informative. He attempted to do this by showing that both $a = b$ and $a \neq b$. To do this he split the identity statements of the *Begriffsschrift* §8 into senses and Meanings [references]....In other words, the statement "$a = b$" is true if we are talking about the extensions of "a" and "b," and "a" and "b" have the same extension. It is false if we are talking only about the intensions of "a" and "b" and there is the difference in sense the statement must have to have cognitive worth... (Hill 1991: 49)

But unlike Haaparanta, Hill is well aware that she (Hill) is saddling Frege with an inconsistent theory, and criticizes Frege's theory precisely for having the fatal weakness of inconsistency where "$a = b$" is true:

> [Frege's theory] of identity...is itself contradictory, and so leads to contradictions. The philosophical logic that admits "$a = b$" as a true statement in fact affirms both $a = b$ and $a \neq b$. Like the liar of the liar paradox (LK, p. 61) the statement "$a = b$," taken on the level of its signs or of the senses of its signs (and unless "a" and "b" designate the same object, on the level of objects too), would affirm something that is false. This opens the door to Russell's paradox... (Hill 1991: 169)

In our terms, Hill seems to hold that Frege's theory is that "$a = b$," taken as the statement about its different signs that they are identical, or taken as the statement about the different senses those signs express that they are identical, is false, while taken as a statement about the object(s) customarily referred to by the signs, may be true or false. It does not occur to Hill that a better interpretation would be that "$a = b$" is the statement about the different signs, taken as expressing different senses, that those signs *denote the same denotation*. Nor does she pay any more attention than Haaparanta does to Frege's famous general warnings that no ambiguous signs are to be admitted and that "it is inconceivable that various kinds of [identity] should occur." By the way, if Frege held that an identity statement can be taken in Hill's three different ways, then he would be scarcely guilty of inconsistency unless he held both $a = b$ and $a \neq b$ where he takes "$a = b$" the *same* way. But this is the least of Hill's problems. Hill makes Frege's "$a = b$" ambiguous and without even a determinate truth-value, which goes against Frege's whole project of a rigorous notation. Therefore her interpretation seems dubious, to say the least.

Bertrand Russell roughly holds that Frege's theory is that "$a = b$" expresses the thought expressed by "The senses of 'a' and 'b' contain modes of presentation of the same object."[3] This is what I called the *sense interpretation*. Peter Geach cautions that Russell unduly conflates his own theory of meaning in *Principles* with Frege's theory of senses (Geach 1972: 27–31). But even if that is true of Russell, the sense interpretation as I define it does not participate in any conflation of Russell's, since unlike Russell I am not taking Frege's senses as being very similar to the 1903 Russell's meanings. Herbert Hochberg presents the sense interpretation as an option in interpreting Frege (Hochberg 1978: 188), and Salmon attributes it to Linsky (Salmon 1986: 48).

Again, the sense interpretation shares with the object interpretation one advantage over my own view. Senses and many objects can be said to enjoy an existence apart from the existence of languages, while names cannot be said to do this, since what makes an object a name is its function in language. How then on my view could the Morning Star and the Evening Star have been for Frege the same planet before languages were invented? Twenty million years ago there simply were, I assume, no names to stand in the relation of denoting the same object. It is to no avail to say that today we can say that they were the same planet because today we have names. To put it another way, the name theory seems to entail that only named objects have identities; and if to exist is to be identifiable, it seems to entail that only named objects exist. The sense interpretation would also allow us to retain our interpretation of Frege's "On Sense and Reference" arguments as being arguments that identity is not a relation between objects and that it is not a relation between labels; the only difference from my view concerns which positive view Frege finally opts for.

Again, one response to this argument would be that ours is the interpretation of greatest continuity, and therefore the one most justified by the text, even if it is intrinsically a less plausible theory of identity. But I hope that a better response can be made. The alleged ground of superiority is really irrelevant to what Frege is doing. Again, he is offering an analysis of the logical structures of sentences of the forms "$a = a$" and "$a = b$." What relevance to such an analysis has the question whether certain objects were identical before languages existed? The truth is that Frege distinguishes the metaphysical unity of an object, i.e. objectual identity, from the arithmetical notion of unit used in the equations, i.e. identity statements, of arithmetic (FA 42–43, 50–51, 62, 66–67). So does Quine, since he fixes the identities of physical objects in terms of spatiotemporal regions. Perhaps this is part of what Quine has in mind when he says that the existence of objects long before the existence languages is no objection to his theory of the immanence of truth and fact. For Quine meaning is translation, and preservation of identity is fundamental to accurate translation.

One textual argument for the sense interpretation would be that Frege does allow a systematic shift to senses as references in contexts of belief (SR 65–68), and contexts of informative identity are sufficiently analogous. My reply is that Frege's theory of sense and reference is indeed a unified theory, and senses do play a very similar role in explaining both belief and informative identity. But as I shall explain shortly, the subject-terms of identity statements must denote objects, not senses (names, of course, are objects). Here the analogy falls short. Also, as a textual point, Frege presents the dilemma of informative identity as a choice between either names of some sort or extralinguistic objects as being what the subject-terms of an identity statement refer to. *Tertium non datur.*

Holding as I do that Frege's theory of identity is that "$a = b$" expresses the thought expressed by "The names 'a' and 'b', understood as signs expressing senses, denote the same denotation," my presentation of this theory would be incomplete if I did not discuss the question, What are Fregean senses? Frege does not tell us what they are. Frege tells us only that they are expressed by names, that they are abstract (noncausal) and timeless, and that they contain modes of presentation of objects, at least when they are senses expressed by object-names. But four ambitious answers are available in the literature. (i) the 1991 Dummett (1991: 225), Gustav Bergmann (1958: 447), Rulon S. Wells (1951: 442), and Howard Jackson (1960: 394) hold that all senses are objects.[4] (ii) Haaparanta holds that senses are functions (Haaparanta 1986b: 273). (iii) Furth holds that some senses are objects and the rest functions (Furth 1968: 9); the 1993 Dummett holds that some senses are objects and seems to hold that others are concepts (Dummett 1993: 61, 105, 129; a concept is "a component of a thought"). (iv) I hold that senses are intensions and are therefore neither objects nor functions, both of which are extensional (Dejnožka 1981: 36; 1979: 50). I praise Hill for attributing intensional identities to senses (Hill 1991).

View (i) is wrong for five reasons. First, some senses are complete and some are not (CO 54–55), while all objects are complete (Frege 1971b: 33). Second, "the sense of expression '$F( )$'" must denote a complete object, while "$F( )$" must express an incomplete sense. Thus if senses are objects, this sense must be both complete and incomplete. Third, Frege says right in "On Sense and Reference," "A truth-value cannot be a part of a thought, any more than, say, the Sun can, for it is not a sense but an object" (SR 64). Clearly, no senses are objects. Fourth, objects have extensional identities, while senses have intensional identities. Fifth, Frege's 'smoking gun' letter to Husserl dated May 24, 1891, making the sense-reference distinction for concept-names, features a diagram putting all senses on one line and all references on another, showing among other things that no sense is an object. Frege writes:

The following schema should make my view clear:

Proposition	proper name	concept word
↓	↓	↓
sense of the proposition (thought)	sense of the proper name	sense of the concept word
↓	↓	↓
meaning of the proposition (truth value)	meaning of the proper name (object)	meaning of the concept word (concept) → object falling under the con- cept

(Frege 1980: 63; brackets omitted)

The diagram also shows that no sense is a concept. This refutes view (ii). And since no sense is an object or a concept, the diagram also refutes view (iii) and establishes view (iv) as correct. The diagram also proves that concept words, and by extension function words in general, do have references (meanings) in addition to senses, *pace* Marshall (1956). Marshall wrote before this letter was widely publicized; today the diagram is in some half a dozen books on Frege.

Haaparanta has recently stated view (ii) as follows in "On Frege's Concept of Being": "I suggest that the Sinne [senses] are nothing but complexes of individual properties" (Haaparanta 1986b: 273).[5] This commits seven mistakes. First, it conflicts with the diagram in Frege's letter to Husserl, as we just saw. Second, Frege admits no individual properties. For Frege, concepts or properties are universals. This is plain from the fact that tokens of the same concept-name type never differ in sense or reference. If "$F(a)$ & $F(b)$" is true, then a and b have the very same property, $F(\ )$. (Strictly speaking, even the identity of $F(\ )$ with itself is representative; see chapter 3, section 3. But this does not detract from my point, since the "individual properties" of the resemblance theory of properties would not even be representatively identical.) What Haaparanta should cite from Frege is not individual properties, but uniquely satisfied complexes of universal properties, $[F_1(\ )\ \&\ F_2(\ )\ \&...F_n(\ )]$. Third, as Haaparanta herself admits, concepts (properties) have their own senses. Thus grasping the sense of an object-name would lead to a vicious regress of senses of senses, all of which are complexes of properties (concepts). Fourth, complexes of properties are incomplete because properties are incomplete. But senses of object-names are complete. The fourth mistake is compounded by the vicious regress, all of whose senses are incomplete. Fifth, an object-name would now denote an incomplete concept (its sense) in referentially opaque propositional contexts. Sixth, the thought expressed by any singular sentence "$F(a)$" would fail to be a complete thought. For Frege, concepts are properties. Falling under a concept is the very same as having a property, Frege explains in "On Concept and Object." This is the whole point of his logical assimilation of properties, understood as concepts, to functions in general. That assimilation is one of Frege's most famous theories. So that if Haaparanta means by "complex of properties" something other than 'conjunctive concept', the burden is on her to explain what she means, and why she thinks it is Fregean at all, much less saturated or complete, which is what any sense expressed by any object-name must be. Seventh, senses have intensional identities, while properties and complexes of properties, i.e. concepts, have extensional identities. If all and only red objects are round, then "x is red" and "x is round" refer to concepts that map the same truth-values onto the same arguments. Therefore, they refer to (representatively) the same concept, since a concept is a purely extensional mapping function. They do not refer to different concepts. Yet the senses they express (red, round) are quite different. Similarly for complete senses such as that expressed by "the red, round apple." All senses are intensional.

In contrast, consider Grossmann's *replacement* of senses with concepts (Grossmann 1969: 180; see 191). Grossmann offers the replacement not as a scholarly effort to gloss senses as concepts, but as the criticism that Frege ought to abolish senses because they are redundant: anything senses can do, concepts can do just as well. Grossmann's criticism is a brilliant and devastating use of Occam's razor. Of course, if we accept his replacement, we must be prepared to make accommodating changes as well, so as to avoid the seven mistakes found in Haaparanta's interpretation. For instance, we must consider whether concepts should now be assigned intensional identities, since the senses they are replacing have intensional identities.

According to view (iii), proper names express senses which are objects and function-names express senses which are functions. This view seems beautifully consistent with Frege's claim that names denote their customary senses when they occur in what Quine would call referentially opaque propositional contexts (SR 65–69; see FLPV 142), and is no doubt based on a tacit assumption that just like customary references, indirect references are objects and functions. But unfortunately, some of my twelve arguments against view (i) and view (ii) apply against view (iii). Notably, the tacit assumption contradicts Frege's express statement that a sense is not an object (SR 64), destroys Frege's diagram, and saddles Frege with objects and functions having intensional identities. Thus it seems that the tacit assumption is false. The singular definite article indicates an object if and only if it indicates a *customary* reference. And only the *customary* reference of an incomplete expression is a function—just as the diagram shows.

I have four arguments for view (iv). First, a sense "contains" a mode of presentation, and a mode of presentation is a mode of possible cognition. But a mode of cognition, as such, is not an object of cognition. An object of cognition would be in language a denotation, and would be either a Fregean object or a Fregean function. Now anything that is an object of cognition simply is not functioning as a mode of presentation. That is, if it is presented as an object, a way an entity is presented is no longer a way an entity is presented, but an object of presentation. A similar argument applies to the sense itself: a sense that is presented to us as an object is no longer a sense but an object. And as Dummett says so well, for Frege an item's role or function in language defines its metaphysical category. Thus if senses do not function as denotations, then they are a different category. Second, if senses were objects or functions, Frege probably would have said so. He has no qualms about telling us all about the different types of objects and functions anywhere else. His talk of senses has instead all the earmarks of an introduction of a category distinct from those of objects and functions (SR 56–61; see 64, "A truth value…is not a sense but an object"). Third, in the "smoking gun" letter to Husserl, Frege diagrams the senses and references associated with a statement and its logical subject and logical predicate by placing all the senses in one row under the statement and all the references in another (Frege 1980: 63). Fourth, senses cannot be objects or functions because senses have intensional identities, and objects and functions have extensional identities.

It would seem from the arguments just given that Frege is mistaken about his own senses in thinking that a sense can ever be denoted by a name. How then can we talk about senses? My answer is that if we use what Frege calls the form usual for asserting something of objects, then senses must be represented by objects much in the manner he says concepts are represented by objects (CO 45–46). Now, every mode of presentation contained by some sense is intimately associated with some sortal concept; for Frege, if an entity can be individuated at all, then there must be some such concept it falls under. This concept already has an object to represent it. But we cannot use this object to make, in addition to representative assertions about concepts, a second sort of representative assertion about senses. For concepts have extensional identities, while senses have intensional identities; many senses might be associated with one concept. But we might use a name, taken as denoting itself, to represent the sense it customarily expresses. Or we might simply 'take' senses 'as' objects, and more easily than Frege can take ideas as objects (SR 60), since senses are public.

What may be called the problem of the sense of expression *A* is really no more paradoxical than the celebrated problem of the concept *horse*. Frege says that "the concept *horse*" must denote not a concept but an object. And I say that for the very same reason of linguistic form, "the sense of expression *A*" must denote not a sense but an object. Indeed, it is hard to accept Frege's view while not accepting this view too.[6] The mutual representation of objects and senses is out of the question, since senses cannot be customarily denoted. Objects and concepts, of course, can represent each other, since both objects and concepts can be denoted (BL 92–94; here the object that represents a function is its course-of-values). But even if senses cannot be denoted and must be represented, they are still grasped directly by the mind, and are still the ways in which all objective denotable entities are objectively presented to the mind, as opposed to being barriers between us and the objective world.

But when I say that "the sense of expression A" must denote an object, that is both scholarship and criticism. For Frege does distinguish customary references from indirect references. When he says in "On Concept and Object" that "the singular definite article always indicates an object" (CO 45), even in the case of "the concept *horse*" (CO 45–46), this seems best glossed as 'always indicates an object if it indicates a *customary* reference'. For then "the sense of expression *A*" may refer to a sense as opposed to an object quite consistently with "On Concept and Object," since *that* expression indicates an *indirect* reference. If Frege meant that "the sense of expression *A*" refers to an object he surely would have said so, but he says instead it refers to a sense. My criticism is really this: Why should this one use of the singular definite article, totally unlike all others, provide a direct reference to a customarily indirect reference? The mere communication of intent to refer to a sense is not enough. It is a key tenet of Frege's that we cannot always refer to that to which we intend to refer (CO 46). The answer to the question just asked can only be that "the sense of expression *A*" must refer to a sense, if to anything, because its reference, if any, must fall under the first-level concept *sense of expression A*. But the answer is inadequate. For consider the first-level concepts *force of assertion A* and *tone of assertion A*. By parity of reason "the force of *A*" and "the tone of *A*," used in true or false statements, must refer to forces and tones. Indeed, we must admit as many shifts to customarily indirectly related items—as many exceptions to the sieve-like principle that the singular definite article always indicates an object—as there are kinds of entity which, like the sense of expression *A*, are not incomplete. Either that or we must discover subtle ways in which forces and tones *are* incomplete enough to assimilate them to the concept *horse* as opposed to the sense of expression *A*. If thoughts are complete senses which must have incomplete senses as constituents, then must assertoric force be incomplete, and be completed by thoughts, so as to yield complete *assertions*? Must emotive tones be incomplete, and be completed by assertions, so as to yield complete *joyous (or angry) assertions*? What is the difference between interrogative force and a thought conjoined to form a question, and not so conjoined? The problem of Bradley's Regress surely is not limited to relations among denotations and senses. Here the problem may be solved by primitive forms of completion which we may call *activation* by forces and *expression* by tones. A command-activating force or a joyous-question-expressing tone would resemble Russell's 'relating relations' quite closely in closing forms of Bradley's Regress. I regret that I cannot pursue this important puzzle further here, and can only indicate its existence and suggest a solution. My solution is that Frege would do better to stick to his principle that the singular definite article always indicates an object, and to speak only representatively about concepts, senses, forces, or tones by using that article marked with an asterisk. Even if forces and tones are enough like senses (connotations) to have intensional identities too, they can be spoken of representatively if senses can be.

What does Frege mean when he speaks of *informative* identity statements? Since modes of presentation and therefore also senses are on the side of the object, no matter how obviously true a certain identity proposition may be to a given observer in a given situation, the proposition is still informative if, as might easily be the case, the senses involved are different. This shows that Frege means by "informative" not novel but factual. He is explaining only the possibility that someone at some time might be informed by the identity proposition. We would not wish to commit Frege to the view that everyone is always surprised or informed whenever they hear a (true) identity proposition of the sort Frege would call informative. Thus Frege's theory of senses concerns sense (9), not sense (10), of "identifiable" as described in chapter 1.[7]

Yet another point helps clarify what senses are. I suggest in chapter 6 that senses can be contextually defined as certain *uses* of words, where uses are abstract, timeless kinds of use as opposed to concrete occasions of use. These uses are just what Dummett calls semantic *roles*. "The sense...of a singular term...is the way the object it refers to is given to someone in virtue of his knowing the language to which the term belongs" (Dummett 1993: 40; see 8–9). Dummett adds that Frege expressly deems thoughts (senses expressed by whole sentences) to be ways in which truth-values (references of whole sentences) are grasped (Dummett 1993: 11–12; BL 90). Thus to express a thought is to be "assessable by certain means as true or false" (Dummett 1993: 7).

I endorse Dummett's (and Geach's) identification of senses with uses, and Dummett's identification of them specifically with semantic roles. But I find three flaws in Dummett's account. First, Dummett says both that senses are ways references are presented and that senses are objects (or else objects and functions) in their own right. This seems inconsistent and categorially confused, unless Dummett is prepared to show the invalidity of my argument that senses are neither objects nor mapping functions because they are basically the modes of presentation they contain. Second, Dummett accuses Frege of having two conflicting ways of talking about senses (Dummett 1993: 6–11). On the first, senses are tied to language and semantics: since senses are ways references are presented, the notion of sense presupposes that of reference. On the second, senses are timeless entities in a "mythological" (Dummett's term) third realm and are theoretically "naked," i.e. graspable *sans* language use. I remove the tension by suggesting that senses are *use-types* and thus *are* timeless, but graspable even theoretically only in linguistic clothing. Third, Dummett says that the first way of talking removes the mystery of what senses are (Dummett 1993: 63). But even if senses are use-types, they remain a unique category unto themselves, and so almost as mysterious as ever.

I would go so far as to argue that concepts are not even parts or components of senses. If a gray pyramid looks blue and conical to distant public observers, then by hypothesis the concept *gray* is not a part of its mode of presentation to them. But neither is the concept *blue*. Like all concepts, the concept *blue* is just an extensional mapping function. But senses and the modes of presentation they contain are intensional. If all and only blue objects were round, then the concept *blue* would be (representatively) identical with the concept *round*, since both would map the same values onto the same arguments. But then if the pyramid's mode of presentation contained the concept *blue*, it would perforce also contain the concept *round*. But that is absurd, since the pyramid neither is nor is presented to the observers as round. Here none of the following four items in Frege's metaphysics must be confused with any of the other three: the abstract extensional concept *blue*, the abstract intensional mode of presentation of an object that seems blue, blue concrete objects in the physical world, and the private mental sensation of blue normally had by one when one perceives blue objects. My argument assumes that the content of a sense is exhausted by the mode of presentation it contains, and that modes of presentation can be illusory. But even if modes of presentation must be veridical, the modes of presentation contained in the senses expressed by "the gray thing in place *p* at time *t*" and "the pyramidal thing in place *p* at time *t*" surely would contain the same concept if they contained a concept at all. But then what would be the reason for their doing so? The concept's presence in them would be an idle wheel, so to speak. I suggest that all modes of presentation would be veridical in thoughts expressed in an ideal language, but not in every thought expressed in a natural language. Whether Frege considered the issue, I do not know.

One might now ask why senses should contain even modes of presentation. I am unhappy with the answer that senses are linguistico-semantic while modes of presentation are cognitive, since the whole question is why either cannot assume the duties of the other. The only plausible answer I have found is this: Some senses must be incomplete, so as to stop Bradley's Regress and to mesh with Frege's derivation of variables by removing smaller expressions from within larger ones. But all modes of presentation must be complete. Even incomplete functions need presentation *via* complete modes of presentation, or they will not be completely presented. Thus the picture of incomplete senses that emerges is much like that of propositional functions for Russell. Much as propositional functions have universals as determinate constituents and variables as undetermined constituents (MAL 165), I gloss Fregean incomplete senses as having modes of presentation as determinate constituents and variables as undetermined constituents that serve as the ties to bind thoughts together to stop Bradley's Regress. Of course, there is still no positive reason not to reduce complete senses to complete modes of presentation (or *vice versa*), except to maintain a general logico-metaphysical uniformity between senses and the modes of presentation they contain. But for Frege that would be a good reason.

I concede that the concept *horse* would be both (i) an incomplete concept and (ii) complete *qua* sortal concept in *Foundations*. But on my Russellian gloss, (i) is due to that concept's undetermined constituent, and (ii) is due to its determinate constituent. Also, if we allowed incomplete senses to contain incomplete modes of presentation in "On Sense and Reference," we would face a vicious regress of incomplete parts of incomplete parts, never arriving at a part which would be a complete mode of presentation.

My analysis of incomplete senses into constituents seems to advance our understanding of what senses are. It also brings Frege closer to Russell in a reasonable way. But it is only a speculation. And even if it is correct, merely parsing all modes of presentation as complete does not remove the mystery of what they and the senses which contain them really are.

Dummett further explains senses as criteria of identity (Dummett 1981: 498). This seems not only correct, but the most apt explanation we have of the importance of senses to 'no entity without identity' ontology. Still, this does not say much more than that the contained modes of presentation are ways to single out (and re-identify) the denotations, if any, the senses are senses "of" (Furth 1967: xix); and that is a trivial truth. Nor does it help that the 1991 Dummett also makes senses objects, as if criteria of identity were objects (Dummett 1991: 225), or that the 1993 Dummett seems to make some senses objects and others concepts, as if some criteria of identity were objects and others concepts (Dummett 1993: 61, 105, 129). Nor does it help that Dummett deems senses to be both linguistic roles or uses and objects (and/or concepts), as if linguistic roles or uses were objects (and/or concepts). Once again, senses remain as mysterious as ever.

My conclusion is that Frege's senses form a special, irreducible, indefinable category of entities, much as his functions and objects do (CO 42–43). I suspect that the mystery lies not in their containing modes or aspects so much as in their intensional identities. The notion of a thing's being given under different aspects is not only common-sensical, but "universally accepted in Western philosophy" (Angelelli 1967: 44). But the existence of meanings or intensions is highly suspect precisely because of the difficulty of describing intensional identity, as Quine explains in his famous paper "Two Dogmas of Empiricism" (FLPV 20–37). It seems one may defend intensional identity only as legitimately taken as given. Perhaps the best way to do so is to adapt Butchvarov's account of preconceptual, precriterial primary applications of the concept of identity, and his account of nonintentional consciousness of properties, to Frege's senses (Butchvarov 1979: 78–81, 139, 145–48; see 60–61). Such a defense is doubly ironic. First, Butchvarov is defending intensional properties. Properties for Frege are merely extensional mapping functions. Second, Butchvarov would reject Frege's senses on other grounds (Butchvarov 1979: 12–25), unless we assimilate (complete) senses to qualified objects much like my own publicly available ones (Butchvarov 1989: 72–74). And the latter suggestion is unworkable from the scholarly point of view. Senses are not qualified objects. If Frege were to admit qualified objects they would be not senses, but a special sort of objects. And he admits no such sort of intensional objects. But despite the ironies, such a defense of senses just might work.

If I am right that senses are an indefinable category, it would seem that there is little else to say about senses. It might seem that there is now little else to say about the identity relation either, since Frege says that it is indefinable (TW 80). But this is mistaken. Frege says that while identity cannot be defined (*Definition*), it can be explained (*Erklärung*) (TW 80).[8] What does he have in mind?

What may be called Frege's threefold distinction between definition, explanation, and explication (*Erläuterung*) is as follows. A definition stipulates the sense and denotation of the term defined (BL 82). As a stipulation it is neither true nor false (Frege 1971a: 7; Frege 1971b: 24). Not all names can be defined; to suppose that they can would involve us in a vicious regress of definitions (CO 42–43; BL 85). Therefore, Frege argues, there must be indefinable names. Their meaning is conveyed by explication, which consists of hints, metaphors, and suggestions (Frege 1971c: 59–60). While definitions are foundationally part of science, explications are a propaedeutic to science (Frege 1971a: 8; Frege 1971c: 59–61). Frege's definitions are intended to guarantee both sense and denotation for the defined term. Explications are not at all guaranteed to provide these (Frege 1971a: 8–9; Frege 1971c: 59). Thus scientific communications, i.e. communications seriously concerned with truth, always begin with an element of uncertainty.

What is an explanation? Frege says that Leibniz's "explanation" of identity (it was a definition for Leibniz, and identity had been definable in *Foundations*, FA 76) conveys something "fundamentally important" about identity to those who already possess that concept (TW 81). That distinguishes explanation from both definition and explication. But what does an explanation explain? While a definition provides a sign with a sense and a denotation, in an explanation the explained term is assumed to have a sense and denotation already. At the same time, an explanation seems to leave nothing to chance, as an explication would. I suggest that an explanation may be understood as the assertion that two names, both already assumed to have sense and denotation, denote the same entity. An explanation, if correct, is therefore a true statement. To call Frege's explanation of identity an axiom, as Frege does, is only to add that it cannot be derived from more fundamental truths (Frege 1971b: 23–25).[9] An explanation explains an entity that is presented to us in one way as being the same as an entity that is presented to us in another way. At bottom, it is simply an informative identity statement. In the case of explaining one relation as being another, a sufficient condition of an explanation's truth may be taken to be that the relations named always yield the same value for the same ordered set of arguments. This, as we know, is a sufficient condition for the fact that a pair of functions are interdefinable (relations are functions), in those cases where definition is allowed (TW 80),[10] and functions which are interdefinable as being each other can hardly be regarded as different functions. In this sense, Frege's explanation aims to state what identity is, just as a traditional definition would.

Frege's explanation that identity is indiscernibility, or intersubstitutability *salva veritate* (both relations relate names), commits him to both the indiscernibility of identicals and the identity of indiscernibles. The former principle is commonly viewed as trivial, but the latter is not. It is therefore surprising to learn that Frege officially defends the second principle in a trivial way. Frege argues that if *a* is not identical with *b*, then there is always at least one property *a* has which *b* does not have, namely, the property of being identical to *a* (BL 71). Technically this is a legitimate argument in Frege's notational system, since every well-formed predicate denotes a genuine property. But one wishes that Frege had given a more substantial argument. For example, it can be argued that if things could have all properties in common, then it would be impossible to identify or name anything. If there are one hundred oranges in a crate, having all properties in common, even spatiotemporal ones, how could I tell one apart from the rest? How could I tell that there are not ninety-nine but one hundred? This more serious sort of argument is in fact used by Frege elsewhere. He argues that since we cannot specify any property *x* has that is different from any property of *y*, we cannot conceive of variable numbers each in its individual being, and so cannot assign proper names to variable numbers or say that they exist (TW 109).

Now on the present interpretation, identity (including even self-identity as in *a* = *a*) may seem to be always and necessarily relative to the senses of the names between which it obtains, and to the sortal concepts with which those senses are intimately associated. I defer my verdict to the next section, so as to kill two relativist birds with one stone.

2. The Concept of Existence

Frege has two analyses of sentences of the form "*a* exists." First, they may mean "The sign '*a*', considered as expressing a sense, has a reference." And second, they may mean "$(\exists x)F(x)$," or waiving the famous problem of the concept *horse*, "Something falls under the concept *F*" (TW 104). Here the concept *F* must be such that "*a* exists" is true if and only if *a*, and only *a*, falls under *F*. The first analysis is parallel to Frege's theory of identity, on the present interpretation. This suggests a question: May there not be an analysis of identity parallel to the second analysis of existence? Frege does not give one himself. I suggest such an analysis in chapter 3, section 5.

In chapter 1, I described three ontological kinds of identity: linguistic identity, conceptual identity, and real identity. If Frege's theory is that identity is a relation between names understood as signs expressing senses, and if senses are intimately associated with sortal concepts, then is Frege's theory an ontological theory of linguistic or conceptual identity? And if Frege's theory that "*a* exists" is to be analyzed as "'*a*' denotes" or alternatively as "$(\exists x)F(x)$," *F* being the sortal concept intimately associated with the sense of "*a*," is Frege's theory of existence likewise an ontological theory of linguistic or conceptual being? The answer to our two questions is "No." Frege's theory of identity is not an ontological theory, but a linguistic theory of the logical structure of identity statements. And as such, it is a serious rival of Peter Geach's theory of relative identity. My argument is as follows.

The greatest issue concerning realism *versus* relativity in Frege, Russell, Wittgenstein, and Quine may seem to be the interpretation of the apparatus of their quantificational logic. For Frege, any quantified sentence has an n–level concept-name or relation-name as its logical subject-term, and an $n + 1$–level concept-name, which is the quantifier plus all occurrences of what we now call the variable it binds, as its logical predicate-name. Thus the concept *exists* is literally a property of concepts. Russell makes existence a property of propositional functions. Wittgenstein accepts that a number "is a property of a concept" (RFM 186/V #35). Quine quantifies. Now, equating existence with denial of the number zero as all four analysts do, and connecting numbers with identity, for fear of counting the same thing twice, radical relativity might seem essential to the nature of quantificational logic. That is, the fact that numbers shift and identities shift as concepts shift might seem to be the very basis of modern existential logic. Indeed, Frege's theory of identity, on my own interpretation, is that identity is the relation between two names of denoting the same denotation. And this only seems to confirm that Frege's definition of existence amounts to a form of radical relativity or extreme linguisticism.

But this is a misunderstanding of the motives for quantificational logic. Frege gives six explicit or implicit arguments why existence should be a property of concepts. (1) Existence assertions are informative. But a merely possible object is no object at all. So that to assert of an object that it exists would be uninformative, as all objects must exist. (2) A true or false statement always needs to be about something. But if "Object *a* exists" were false, there would *be* no object *a* of which to predicate existence. (3) Assertions of existence, "There is an *F*," are equivalent to denials of assertions of the form "All things are not-*F*." But the latter are not about things. For we know what such statements assert without knowing all things. (4) Assertions of existence are equivalent to denials of the number zero: "There are not zero *F*s." And assertions of number are assertions about concepts. By my own count there are eleven subarguments in *Foundations* that assertions of number are assertions about concepts (Dejnožka 1979: chapter 2). All of them are based on conceptual relativity. Next, Frege has two arguments about the numbers one and zero in particular. They correspond respectively to arguments (1) and (2) above. Namely: (5) Assertions of 1 are informative. But every object is one object, so that to say of an object that it is one would be uninformative. (6) Assertions that there are zero objects of some kind, if true, could not be about the objects of that kind, as there would be none.

The seventh basic motive for quantification, as Dummett notes at the beginning of *Frege: Philosophy of Language*, is that it is our only way to write statements involving multiple nested variables intelligibly (Dummett 1981: 8–9).

Out of seven basic motives for making existence a property of concepts, the conceptual relativity of objectual identity is only one motive, namely, argument (4). The other motives have nothing to do with conceptual relativity at all. I conclude, then, that conceptual relativity does not play an essential or even a very important role in the case for quantificational logic. It easily could have been totally ignored in the development of quantificational logic. And if mere common-sense conceptual relativity plays no great role, then ontological radical relativity scarcely can.

3. Some Relativist Interpretations of Frege

G. E. M. Anscombe and Geach, in their *Three Philosophers*, say:

Frege's own constructive theses are that a number attaches to a concept, and that to assign a number is to ascribe a 'property' to a concept. In spite of his clear explanations, he has been perversely taken to mean that an answer to the question 'how many' is always a conceptual i.e. an analytic statement: which is clearly absurd, and was never his intention. All obscurity vanishes from the first thesis if we say: A number is a number of a kind of things…[and] given the kind of things, the number is determinate, not a free creation of the mind.

As for the second thesis, it would indeed not do to call the number of a kind of things a 'property' of that kind of things: but what Frege explains as his meaning may be put as follows: it is incidental to or supervenient upon any given kind of things, how many things of the kind there are. (Anscombe 1961: 159)

Anscombe and Geach correctly note that numbers are not for Frege "a creation of the mind," and are in that sense not mere conceptual beings. That is due to Frege's anti-psychologism. But this has nothing to do with conceptual beings as

I explained them in chapter 1. For Frege, even a card deck is only conceptually distinct from its four suits and fifty-two cards. And the numbers concerned, one, four, and fifty-two, are distinct only in reason from each other if their definitions are successively interlinked (FA 87–96, BL 100–1). Far from eliminating conceptual beings, Frege might simply be locating such beings in the objective realm, making them public and communicable. Thus Frege might be a radical relativist; he is if all his denotations are conceptual beings. If they were, surely senses, forces, and tones would not lag far behind.

As William P. Alston and Jonathan Bennett note in their fine essay, "Identity and Cardinality: Geach and Frege," Geach says in *Reference and Generality*:

> Frege sees clearly that "one" cannot significantly stand as a predicate of objects unless it is (at least understood as) attached to a general term; I am surprised he did not see that the like holds for the closely allied expression "the same." (Geach 1980: 63)

Alston and Bennett also note that Geach says in "Ontological Relativity and Relative Identity:"

> the thesis that identity is always relative to…a criterion seems to me a truism, like Frege's connected thesis that a number is always relative to a *Begriff*. It is as nonsensical to speak of identification apart from identifying some kind of thing, as to speak of counting apart from counting some kind of thing. (Geach 1973: 289)

On my own interpretation, Fregean identity is a relation between names as signs expressing senses, where each sense is intimately associated with a concept (*Begriff*). Thus Geach's position seems especially powerful on my own interpretation. But Alston and Bennett make the decisive point:

> John Perry, in "Relative Identity and Number," points out that Frege most assuredly did not adopt what would have been an exact parallel of the Relative Identity Thesis, viz., a Relative Cardinality Thesis…. That is not Frege's doctrine. Instead of relativizing the numerical predicate, what Frege did was to shift the subject of numerical predication: he held that a statement of cardinality, rather than predicating anything of an object, individual, group, or heap, predicates "having n instances" of a concept. (Alston 1984: 555)

In fact there are six problems with imputing radical relativity to Frege. First, Frege does not relativize existence ("the numerical predicate" of not being 0), but shifts the subject of existence predication from objects to concepts. Second, even if Frege did relativize existence in this sense, this would yield only a Geachian theory of the logical structure of existence statements, i.e., a theory of restricted quantifiers. Recall that radical relativity is an ontological theory. Third, Frege does not relativize even identity in Geach's way, but shifts the subject(s) of identity statements from objects to names expressing senses. Fourth, even if Frege did relativize identity in Geach's way, this would yield only a theory of the logical structure of identity statements, not a theory that the ontological *locus* of identity is in our sortal terms or concepts. Fifth, even if the ordinary conceptual relativity of objectual identities is involved in one of the seven basic motives for quantification, the ontological theory of radical relativity need not be. Sixth, that single motive need never have existed for quantification to develop.

I proceed to Haaparanta's neo-Kantian theory that since Frege's objects are always presented through the medium of senses, they are therefore unknowable in themselves. Haaparanta (1986b: 273–85) argues:

A. Object-names "presuppose the existence of objects."
B. Existence is predicated of concepts.
C. Therefore "we cannot talk about objects and their existence directly, i.e., independently of the properties of objects."
D. "Between the name and the *Bedeutung* there is always the *Sinn*."
E. "...*Sinne* are nothing but complexes of individual properties...."
F. Therefore "An object is for us always an object that falls under some concept."
G. Therefore "objects exist for us only as subsumed under concepts."
H. Therefore "Frege's view is that we cannot reach the essence of an object by means of our concepts and our cognitive capacities....For Frege, it is impossible to know objects in themselves or to talk about them....According to Frege, we can say what an object is like, but we cannot say what it is....Frege did not regard it as possible to find out what objects really are in themselves."
I. But Frege sharply distinguishes predications (singular statements) from identity statements.
J. Identity "is a specific relation of an object to itself."
K. For Frege we can never know an object in itself since we cannot "know all its properties, which is not possible for
    <u>a finite human being.</u>"
L. Therefore, identity statements "claim more than our reason is able to grasp" and 'concern' "objects in themselves." This is in marked contrast to predications, which "approach objects from different points of view by means of the concepts that are available to us."
M. And this is why "an object is neither identical with any property nor with any combination of properties we can know it to have."[11]

According to Haaparanta's argument, Frege holds that identity statements have a mystic power to be about objects "in themselves" which mere predications such as "*a* is blue" sadly lack. This already seems strange. But arguments this complicated often go wrong at many points, and the present one is no exception. I have twelve criticisms.

(1) *Contra* (M), the reason why objects are not their properties is that objects are complete while properties are incomplete. Another reason is that otherwise some sentences such as "Blue(*a*)" would be analytically true or false, while Frege holds that they are synthetic.

(2) *Contra* (H), The reason why we cannot say what objects are is not that objects are unknowable, but that the term "object" is so fundamental for Frege that he considers it indefinable.

(3) *Contra* (H), For an object to fall under a concept *F* is for that object to have the property *F*. And if that object has the property *F*, then that object in itself has *F*, whether we regard that object as having *F* or not. It is *F* even if no humans exist. This is Frege's realism. Haaparanta seems to think "concept" means only something cognitive, merely because Frege uses the word *Begriff*. But Frege says:

> I call the concepts under which an object falls its properties; thus 'to be Φ is a property of Γ' is just another way of saying: 'Γ falls under the concept of a Φ'. (CO 51; compare Dummett 1981a: 169ff., and Wittgenstein, Z #704)

(4) Haaparanta's phrase "our concepts" in (H) is misleading. Concepts are emphatically not ours, as if we make or fashion them or as if they reflect a human viewpoint. Concepts are for Frege timeless, abstract existents. We can grasp them, but they are no more "ours" in some human sense than the Moon is.

(5) *Contra* (H), Frege repeatedly indicates that objects are essentially non-predicative in "On Concept and Object." Frege rather obviously thinks we can "reach the essence of an object" without knowing all the properties of the object.

(6) *Contra* (L), it is wrong to think that for Frege predications concern objects as conceptualized by us, while identity statements are special and somehow manage to concern objects in themselves. First, as we saw, it is crucial for Frege that the subject-names of identity statements express senses which contain modes of presentation. And senses are intimately involved with concepts. Thus, though Frege's identity statements are hardly of the Geachian form "*a* is the same *F* as *b*" (Frege always writes "*a* = *b*"), they are just as bound up with senses and concepts as are 'mere predications'. Second, the subject-names of identities are the very same expressions which are the subject-names in predications. Third, predications are even rewritable as

particular identity statements. "*F(a)*" becomes "(∃x)[*Fx* & (*x* = *a*)]." Fourth, whether an identity statement is an identity statement or a monadic predication depends on what you choose to regard as its logical subject-name(s). Fifth, for Frege every name in every sentence must express a sense. To sum up, I cannot imagine why level 1 predications for Frege would not be made about objects 'in themselves', if their propositional contexts are referentially transparent. Actually, Haaparanta has got things backwards. It is in identity statements that subject-names do *not* refer to the objects to which they *do* customarily refer in predications. For, at least on my interpretation, the subject-names of identity statements refer to themselves. Even then they refer to objects in themselves, since names are themselves such objects. The contrast Haaparanta wishes to draw does not occur even between Benardete's absolute and relativist senses of "*qua*," which respectively correspond to the "is" of identity and the "is" of predication. "Frege" in "Frege *qua* Frege" and "Frege *qua* mathematician" alike refers to Frege in himself. Thus the "*qua* mathematician" is logically posterior to the reference to Frege, and can indicate no more than ordinary conceptual relativity, unless Frege has *already* been shown to have merely a conceptual identity. Even Frege-*qua*-mathematician in "Frege-*qua*-mathematician *qua* qualified object" is logically posterior to Frege himself.

(6) *Contra* (L), an identity statement is itself a predicative statement. The identity predicate is a relational predicate no different, *qua* predicate, from "is larger than." In fact, it is no different, *qua* predicate, from "is blue." That is the whole point of Frege's famous assimilation of properties, taken as concepts, and relations, taken as relational concepts, to functions.

(8) *Contra* (C)–(F), concepts, senses, modes of presentation, and names expressing senses are not barriers or veils behind which objects in themselves hide, but vehicles by which reference to objects in themselves is achieved. At least this is the repeatedly stated view of the world's leading Frege scholar, which Haaparanta ignores (Dummett 1981a: 45–47, 53–55, 57–58, 104–5, 132, 250–51; and Dummett 1993: 51–52, 76). Dummett's point applies as much to identity statements as it does to monadic predications. Dummett's point is even more transparently correct in Russell's and Quine's explanation(s) of factually informative identity in terms of descriptions. In effect, Haaparanta is holding that veridical descriptions of objects are barriers to understanding them! For she herself proclaims that senses are complexes of properties, as we saw earlier. So much for knowledge by description. Even on my view, senses are at least intimately associated with sortal concepts. And concepts are "guarantors of objectivity" (Hill 1991: 130).

(9) The inference from (B) to (C) is formally and intuitively invalid. That existence is predicated of concepts does not entail that existence is somehow "relative" to concepts. Predicating existence of concepts simply is how Frege achieves ontological commitment to objects in themselves. Alston and Bennett explained this.

(10) (D), (F), and (G) are false. Haaparanta overlooks Frege's theory of the preconceptual, prelinguistic perception of objects. See chapter 7, section 1.

(11) *Contra* (K), knowledge of a complete object and complete knowledge of an object (knowledge of all its properties) are different things. Absence of the latter does not imply absence of the former. Knowledge of a single property of an object is genuine and objective, though partial, knowledge of the complete object.

(12) Even if objects were unknowable in themselves, that would not negate their real identities. But we do know that concrete objects have real identities, insofar as we know that concrete objects are real, i.e., have causal impacts or capacities, and are really distinct. We also know that all objects are objective, because we can follow Frege's private language arguments. There is nothing else we need to know about objects in themselves, in order to establish Frege's realism. And that is all we need to establish, in order to defeat radical relativity.

To sum up, Haaparanta's argument seems full of mistakes.

Last, I shall examine the Hintikka-Haaparanta theory that for Frege language is a "universal medium," meaning that "we cannot step outside the limits of our language in order to consider the semantical relations between language and reality" (Haaparanta 1986b: 276). In particular, any metalinguistic description of such relations is impossible. This is strange, for Haaparanta is aware that Frege says "*a* exists" may metalinguistically mean "'*a*' denotes." She tries to brush off that fact by simply insisting on her interpretation of Frege as holding that language is a 'universal medium', a begging of the question if there ever was one (Haaparanta 1986b: 280). It also rules out my interpretation of Fregean identity as a relation between names. And Haaparanta herself admits that Frege takes an identity statement "to be a metalinguistic statement concerning the number of senses and references of two names" (Haaparanta 1986b: 280). Third, it even rules out Frege's theory that names refer to their customary senses in referentially opaque contexts, and Frege's many discussions of names as referring to references. *Basic Laws* vol. 1, sect. 29, entitled "When does a name denote something?," is a metalinguistic doctrine if there ever was one. I hope that Hintikka and Haaparanta do not mean to rule out only formal metalanguages, since in *Foundations* and in general, Frege's metalanguage is just ordinary language.

The Hintikkas proclaim Jean van Heijenoort's observation that for Frege, formal notation is not just a *calculus ratiocinator* but a language, a *lingua characterica*, as proving that for Frege, 'language is a universal medium'. It seems to me that that observation proves just the opposite, since Frege talks metalinguistically a great deal about his *lingua characterica* in setting it up in *Basic Laws*, not to mention in his famous essays. And Heijenoort is a rather bizarre *deus ex machina* to be revealing Frege as a 'language as a universal medium' linguistic relativist. For Heijenoort's whole essay is based on Frege's objectivism, and discusses the deep antagonism between Frege's universal language, in which universal quantification concerns all objects, and the 1915 Löwenheim's notion of validity in selected limited domains of quantification. Heijenoort very explicitly says that it is the *Löwenheim* notion which is the one to which ontological commitments might be held relative. He says that it is only "[w]hen Frege has to deal with a special domain of objects, [that] he uses devices...equivalent to...relativization of quantifiers." Heijenoort does not say that for Frege there can be nothing metalinguistic, that is, beyond the scope of a particular language. He says that for Frege there can be nothing metasystematic, that is, beyond the universal scope of logic. That the two cannot coincide is shown by the semantic incompleteness theorem of Gödel, which Heijenoort cites (Heijenoort 1967: 324–30; contrast IW 1 and 27 n.1).[12]

Nor is the Hintikkas' critique only postponed to the level of logic. It is absurd to maintain that just because one's quantifiers range over all objects in the universe, one cannot say, "The name 'a' refers to object a," or even "There exists a relation R such that (R is referring, and for any x, (if x is a properly formed name in Frege's *Basic Laws*, then there exists a y such that (Rxy)))." Where object b is name "a," "Rba" is an instantiation. It does not occur to the Hintikkas that names might *be* among all the objects in the universe, or that the reference relation might *be* among all the level 1 dyadic relations in the universe, which one's appropriate quantifiers may range over. Semantical relations can not only be named, but can be very easily described by general statements which use quantifiers.

Fregean 'language as a universal medium' thus boils down to Frege's dry sarcasm that "As a general principle it is impossible to speak of an object [or, by parity of reason, of a relation, including semantic relations] without in some way designating or naming it"—itself an ostentatiously metalinguistic principle (FA 60). Frege's sarcastic statement of 'language as a universal medium' flagrantly and ironically violates that very view. Indeed, any statement of that view would. That is, the view is self-defeating, and Frege is well aware of that fact. The view also confuses '*considering*' semantic relations outside of language with *defining* semantic relations without using language that uses semantic relations we must already understand. For the view leaves ample room for naming indefinable semantic relations such as truth. Frege argues in *Kleine Schriften* that truth is indefinable because "in a definition certain characteristics would have to be specified. And...the question would always arise whether it were true that the characteristics were present." Haaparanta sees this as due to Frege's theory of 'language as a universal medium' (Haaparanta 1985: 41–44). But Frege says that the reason truth cannot be defined is that any attempt would be circular. Similarly for the reference relation. No doubt understanding any definition as such presupposes understanding reference as well as truth (and as noted before, identity). This is why truth and reference (and identity) are indefinable. The reason is a specific circularity in each case. No general theory of semantic relations is ever suggested. And if a general theory were built on these instances of the old fallacy of circularity, it would be just as trivial as they are.

To say that "We cannot step outside the limits of our language in order to consider the semantical relations between language and reality" implies that "We cannot consider the semantical relations between language and reality" is a gross *non sequitur.* Language is precisely what we use to succeed in describing the world, language, and semantic relations in an objective manner, as ensured by Frege's private language argumentation.

There may seem little point in discussing 'language as a universal medium' further. However, since the Hintikkas associate the view with some sort of linguistic relativity, I shall discuss it in more detail. My discussion will be of the Hintikkas' *Investigating Wittgenstein*, but will apply to Frege easily enough.

The Hintikkas hold that Wittgenstein held the fundamental view throughout his career that semantic relations, relations between language and the world, cannot be expressed: "One cannot as it were look at one's language from outside and describe it, as one can do to other objects" (IW 1). "This is the origin...of showing as distinguished from saying" (IW 2). The Hintikkas urge "the mutual dependence of linguistic relativity (impossibility of expressing reality as it is, considered independently of our language) and the ineffability of semantics [as just described]" (IW 5). Frege was another 'language as universal medium' theorist (IW 89–90). This is why he did not formally develop truth-function theory. The opposing view is that a metalanguage is possible in which one can describe one's language's semantic relations without presupposing them. Now as I noted earlier, Heijenoort finds quantifier relativization not in Frege, but in Löwenheim's limited domains of quantification. Thus the Hintikkas have it backwards. If metalanguages require limited domains, then it is metalinguistic quantifiers which must relativize. And even then the burden is on those who wish to show that quantifier 'relativization' entails radical relativity in our sense. In fact, all it seems to mean is quantifier *restriction;* see chapter 1 on Geach as a realist with restricted quantifiers. There are many other problems as well; I have twelve further comments.

(1) 'Showing' is a sort of ostension and involves language as much as 'saying' does. And Fregean explication of primitive words is explicitly verbal. But then showing and explication are both semantic relations. Thus the Hintikkas are obliged to show how either admits of linguistic relativity in any significant sense.

(2) It makes all the difference as to whether metalanguages for describing semantic relations seem possible, whether metalanguages are viewed as aiming ambitiously to define semantic relations, or modestly only to explain, describe, or identify them in an objective manner. This is related to my earlier point that semantic relations may be primitive. Following Bergmann's treatment of exemplification (not a semantic relation) in the ideal language literature on ineffability and 'showing' (Bergmann 1964: 45–63), I daresay that the word

"describe" is vague enough that the Hintikkas' distinction between saying and showing splits the hair of description too finely. If a semantic relation is shown, then it can be named, and the name can be used to describe.

(3) The existence of an expression is an objective fact. The existence of the object it names is an objective fact. Surely it is a fact, then, that the name refers to the object. Is it not an objective fact that millions of people have used names to refer to objects over the millennia? 'Language as a universal medium' itself, if it is an objective fact, is part of realism.

(4) 'Language as a universal medium', if correct, is a fact which has nothing to do with extreme linguisticism *versus* a realism of objective facts. That dispute concerns linguistic identity and real identity as explained in chapter 1. It has nothing to do with whether quantifiers range over all objects. The Hintikkas do not even use "linguistic relativity" to mean extreme linguisticism. They define linguistic relativity as the "impossibility of expressing reality as it is, considered independently of our language" (IW 5).

(5) Perhaps the Hintikkas mean '*logic* as a universal medium'. Peter Hylton says, "According to Russell's understanding of logic, all reasoning employs logic and is subject to logic. Logic can, therefore, have no meta-theory: we cannot reason about logic from the outside..." (Hylton 1980: 2–3). If logic applies to all things, is it because logic is like a pair of glasses we cannot take off, or because things themselves are determinate? Only the former alternative would suggest radical relativity. But Frege and Russell choose the latter, as Hylton is well aware. I praise Hylton for his clear and elegant statement of the 'universal medium' conception.

(6) The Hintikkas defeat their own thesis of the "mutual dependence" of "language as a universal medium" and "linguistic relativity" by giving an analogy which not only explains reference in terms of nonlinguistic items which have no semantic relations to each other, but even makes it possible for us to refer to facts which are independent of language. A pole used to probe a river bottom is likened to a name-object relation. The pole cannot be used to probe itself, but it can be used to tell whether there is a bottom and even what it is like (IW 50–51). The analogy seems excellent. The analogy compares the river bottom to objective things in general. But one needs no analogy to see that the fact that we cannot understand names, or the relation of a name naming an object, apart from understanding some language, does not even appear to imply that objects cannot be understood apart from understanding some language. In terms of the analogy, we can dive in the river and see the bottom. And without ever having seen mud or rock, we would not understand what poles 'tell' us at all. The pole might also be likened to a language. In that case the analogy is weaker because a language can be used to elucidate itself, as I shall explain.

(7) Frege argues that identity is indefinable because every definition is an identity, so that identity is always presupposed as already understood. This is very close to what the Hintikkas seem to have in mind by 'language as a

universal medium'. However, as we saw, Frege goes on to describe identity in some detail. He argues that it is a relation between names considered as signs expressing senses. He explains it as intersubstitutability *salva veritate*. I am unable to see how 'language is a universal medium' could preclude our giving a metaphysical theory concerning what reference and truth are properties of or relations between, just as Frege does for identity, or how it could preclude our explaining what reference and truth are, in Frege's sense of "explanation."

(8) Returning to the subtleties of the word "describe," is it not enough to describe reference to say, "It is the relation mentioned by Smith when he spoke about that Renoir in the Art Institute of Chicago as being called 'On the Terrace'"? And if the word "reference" is explained by examples, I doubt that presupposing an understanding of reference is much to worry about in describing reference well enough to children for them to learn how to use that word. After all, we presuppose they can see green when we teach them how to use "green."

(9) The Hintikkas call 'language as a universal medium' "fundamental," and then proceed to give a (more fundamental) reason for holding that view on the very same page. The reason is that all talk relies on "a given network of meaningful relations obtaining between language and the world" (IW 1). That being so, any attempt to describe the relations presupposes them (IW 2). So that this network presupposition is what is really fundamental. But by what right do the Hintikkas speak about such a network as if it were an objective fact? Is the linguistic relativity the Hintikkas profess to find in 'language as a universal medium' based by them on a purported objective fact about language?

(10) Grice and Strawson describe the phenomenon of a "family circle" of mutually definable terms in their famous essay "In Defense of a Dogma." This seems to be all that 'language as a universal medium' amounts to. Grice and Strawson show that distinctions made within a family circle may be well taken and quite objective. The burden is on the Hintikkas to show that and how Grice and Strawson go wrong concerning the family circle of terms referring to semantic relations (Grice 1965: 340–52).

(11) Dummett gives the most penetrating statement of 'language as a universal medium'. He says that Frege's context principle in *Foundations*

rules out as spurious all problems about what an expression stands for that cannot be expressed within the language, or, in other words, that cannot be stated as questions about the truth-value of some sentence... —about what its truth-value is, or at least how it is determined. We cannot, as it were, stand in thought outside our language and mentally apprehend the reference of the expression; and so it is no defect of a given manner of introducing the expression into the language that it does not enable us to establish such an extra-mental association of expression and referent. Grasping the reference of an expression just is grasping certain principles determining the determination of the truth-values of sentences of the language containing it. (Dummett 1991: 155–56)

Unfortunately for Dummett, the term "reference" is ambiguous. Does it mean references *qua* linguistic references or does it mean the objects referred to? Frege holds that dogs perceive objects, even though dogs have no language and so cannot understand what it means for a word to have a reference. The context principle makes it *possible* to refer to objects nobody can single out in sense perception. But it insists only that no *word* can be *understood* if it has no capacity ever to play a role in sentences. Even Dummett distinguishes between primary objects and secondary objects, such that we must single out concrete primary objects before we can refer by contextual means to abstract secondary objects. Indeed, *Foundations* is as metalinguistic as *Basic Laws*. It may not have the formal claptrap of a metalanguage handed to us on a silver platter, but it is as metalinguistic as any informal analytic paraphrase of natural language can be. As Quine would note, the mere use of quotation marks is a semantic ascent.

(12) Frege would not even accept Russell's 'epistemology as a universal medium', where we can never fully get outside our own subjectivity (PLA 179). Frege argues that we *can* break out of the world of our ideas, in "The Thought" and elsewhere. For Frege, our thoughts are totally objective.

4. Contextualism and Realism

Probably the view in Frege which has most seemed in the past to support irrealism is his contextualism. And in any case, we cannot avoid examining Frege's contextualism. For Frege argues as follows:

1. "Since it is only in the context of a proposition that words have any meaning, our problem becomes this: To define the sense of a proposition in which a number word occurs."
2. "If we are to use the symbol *a* to signify an object, we must have a criterion for deciding in all cases whether *b* is the same as *a*, even if it is not always in our power to apply this criterion."
3. "But we have already settled that number words are to be understood as standing for self-subsistent objects."
4. "And that is enough to give us a class of propositions which must have a sense, namely those which express our recognition of a number as the same again." (FA 73)

I have slightly changed the sentence order. Premise (1) states the context principle; premise (2) states what may be called Frege's 'no entity without identity' principle for objects. Premise (2) functions to narrow down the "very wide choice" of propositions left us by premise (1). Thus it seems that premise (1) does not entail premise (2) and that premise (2) does not entail premise (1), since otherwise both premises would present us the same narrow choice given in conclusion (4). Thus it seems that Frege is giving a definition by genus and difference of the sort of definition we must give whenever we wish to define a class of objects. Premise (1) states the genus: contextual. Premise (2) states the difference: identitative identifiability. Dummett goes on to adduce a further consequence for 'no entity without identity' theory:

> All legitimate questions about the reference of a newly introduced term 't' will therefore be ones that can be framed within the language....We can legitimately ask whether 't' has the same reference as some other term 's', because this is just to ask the question whether the sentence 't is the same as s' is true....If [such] questions can be asked successfully, then the term has a reference. There is no further test it can be required to pass, such as providing us with a means of imagining its referent, or a possibility of encountering or contacting it... (Dummett 1991: 156)

This is not quite right; later I shall show that to fix the sense of a numerical identity *is* to provide us with the means of encountering numbers. But the importance of the context principle to 'no entity without identity' theory is obvious. Our examination is also a test case of realism in all the analysts. Contextual definition is basic to the reductionist programs of Russell and Quine. Wittgenstein and Quine admit contextual accounts even broader than the sentential.

Some might argue that the context principle, if true, would be deeper than modified realism. For in that case we could speak of the identity of a thing only in terms of identity statements about that thing. My reply is that I already showed the mutual logical independence of modified realism and the context principle. And I showed that the linguistic revolt failed to dislodge traditional ontology and metaphysics from their philosophical primacy. We cannot tell whether the meaning of a word exists only in the context of a sentence unless we can identify words, meanings, and sentences in the first place.

Much of the interest in contextualism boils down to contextual definitions in ontological analyses. I argue in chapter 3 that Frege's explicit definitions are implicitly contextual "identity definitions." But contextual definitions concern only the logical structure of sentences. Their use does not entail radical relativity, which concerns the mutually independent existence of things. Much like the theory of contextualism, contextual definitions are too linguistic to amount to or even to imply radical relativity. And as Quine frequently observes, there is no Western tradition of contextual definition before Frege. There is only Jeremy Bentham's notion of paraphrasis (OR 72, 77, 101). This is in contrast to the offering of ontological theories to account for the common sense datum of conceptual relativity. Modified realism (modified relativity) has dominated the Western tradition from Aristotle on.

Sluga sees contextualism as originating with Kant's theory of judgments and passing with Sigwart and Lotze into mainstream nineteenth-century thought (Sluga 1980: 50, 90–95). Kant is no radical relativist, thanks to his things in themselves and his noumenal agents. But even if he were, his radical relativity would consist of his denial that things in themselves and noumenal agents have independent objectual identities. It would not stem directly from his theory of judgments. And even if there were a connection in Kant between judgment-contextualism and radical relativity, there is no necessary connection intrinsically or generally speaking.

Michael Dummett finds a "tension" between Frege's context principle and Frege's realism of abstract objects. Specifically, contextual definitions seem not to justify the defined terms' reference, but to be eliminative of reference. Dummett tries to associate this difficulty with the reason Frege gives for rejecting contextual definition in favor of "explicit definition" in *Foundations*. Frege's reason is that objects can be given in more than one way, while the sort of contextual definition he rejects allows objects to be given only in one way. For instance, on that sort of definition, directions of lines can be given only as directions of lines, and not, say, as the illustration Frege gives of a certain argument (Dummett 1981: 500–1; Dummett 1981a: 425–26, 452–53). For Dummett, *Foundations* is explicitly contextualist but questionable as to its realism, and the later *Basic Laws* is clearly realist but questionable as to its contextualism. I have twelve comments.

First, for Frege all definitions specify sense and reference in terms of the sense and reference of the defining expression. Thus Frege can give no eliminative definitions. All his adequate definitions provide references for their defined terms. There is no reason to suppose that contextual definitions, were they otherwise adequate, would be any different for Frege. Far from being eliminative of sense and reference, they too would fix a sense and a reference for the expressions they define. Frege does admit reduction, but reduction is not elimination. Numbers are not eliminated in the definition Frege accepts. They are merely reduced from mathematical objects to logical objects. There is no reason to suppose that the contextual definitions rejected by Frege would have been thought by him to achieve anything different if they had been successful.

Second, Dummett's tension follows neither formally nor intuitively from the reason Frege gives for rejecting the kind of definition he rejects. Even if that kind of definition is rejected for giving numbers only in one way, still it provides a determinate truth-value for indefinitely many identity statements concerning the defined objects as given in that one way. The definition Frege rejects is correct as far as it goes. For it states a true logical equivalence to which any adequate definition of number must conform: Numbers belonging to concepts are identical if and only if those concepts are equal. And the logical subjects of all these true or false statements must have (customary) references, for Frege, because this is his requirement for all true or false statements. That is just how the contextual definition Frege rejects is correct as far as it goes. And as far as it goes, it establishes reference to that which it attempts to define. In short, far from detracting from realism, it supports realism.

Third, Frege does not reject contextual definition. What Dummett calls explicit definition is really another kind of contextual definition (see chapter 3, section 1). Even Dummett would admit that this sort of definition establishes numbers as being identical with certain abstract objects, namely extensions.

Fourth, a context principle is not the same as the sort of definitions which it may or may not justify. It is neither a definition nor a sort of definition. The context principle in *Foundations* hardly entails the legitimacy of the single sort of contextual definition Frege rejects in *Foundations* so far as Frege is concerned, since Frege continues to accept that principle in that work. If it did, Frege would have had to reject it by *modus tollens*. Dummett himself admits as much. But Dummett misses that the fact that Frege keeps the context principle shows that he thinks that it is perfectly compatible with, and perfectly honored by, the definition of number which he does accept in *Foundations*. This amplifies the preceding comment.

Fifth, the reason why definitions fix sense and reference (or in the *Foundations* view, content) rather than eliminate them for Frege is simple. Thoughts, and also the references their component senses are senses "of"—I follow Furth's usage of "of" (Furth 1967: xix)—may be regarded in different ways, just as a pie may be sliced into different pieces. All the sliced sense- and reference-components for all contextually defined terms are justified as slicings of the whole defined expression they occur in, just as all new slicings of pie contain pie because they are slicings of a given whole pie. This is one of Frege's most famous doctrines. Even in *Begriffsschrift*, one can shift about the logical subject(s) and predicate of a single judgeable content as one pleases. In Frege's "On Concept and Object," "the concept *horse*" refers to an object, again allowing the inversion of logical subject and logical predicate. In *Basic Laws* Frege formalizes this inversion by means of the representation function. Thus in a contextual definition of the sort Frege rejects in *Foundations*, all that is attempted is the redrawing of the slicings of a certain pie. And this hardly affects the original pie (FA 100–1). Now, the context principle says in effect that slices of pie (names) exist only as (possible) slices of pies (sentences). If slices are removed from any pie tin, the removed slices denote objects. Any slices remaining in any tin denote functions; the empty parts of the tin are their argument-places. The context principle applies to any pie removed from or remaining in tins: nothing is a pie slice unless it can fit in as part of a pie in a tin. So that a contextually defined term, newly sliced, could hardly be a slicing of pie at all unless it had a sense and reference (or content) of its own as part of some already given whole pie. This is precisely how the context principle justifies realism for abstract objects, and how the definitions Frege rejects would justify realism if they did not have a problem of bad format (inadequate pie-slicing plan).

Thus in the definition of number Frege rejects, "'The number belonging to *F* is identical with the number belonging to *G*' is to mean the same as 'Concepts *F* and *G* are equal',", the content of "The number belonging to *F*" is presupposed as being some part of the whole content of "Concepts *F* and *G* are equal." But it is not presupposed which part it is. That could be discovered only by slicing the content of "Concepts *F* and *G* are equal" in a new way, namely into the identity relation as what in effect is now being left in the pie tin, and the number belonging to *F* as what in effect is now being taken out of the pie tin as a complete object. Where the concepts *F* and *G* are in fact equal, only one slice is taken out of the pie tin, since in that case that one slice is both the number belonging to *F* and the number belonging to *G*. Now since content was spread evenly throughout the original pie, Dummett is wrong when he says that the referent of the defined term is "simply bypassed altogether" (Dummett 1981a: 425). So to speak, that reference is made by the defining expression, though it is only by the defined expression that that reference is individuated as such. The specific reslicing just described has a problem only of bad, or more accurately, limited, format. On it, numbers are given only as numbers belonging to concepts. Frege's solution is to see that in two pie tins, one concerning numbers and one concerning extensions of concepts, where extensions are given as slices removed from pie tin *A*, numbers are slices removed from pie tin *B* in just the same way. Numbers, as removed slices of pie, are existent abstract objects. Pie tin contextualism, far from denying that, establishes that.

Concerning the later Frege, Dummett would object that the thoughts expressed by a defined sentence and a defining sentence cannot be the same if the constituent senses of each lead to our grasping different references. One might indeed understand the thought that two numbers are identical without understanding what it is for concepts to be equinumerous. Nor should we admit ways of grasping senses, as if senses needed second-order senses. But we need not admit Dummett's linguistic devices to shield the identity of the thoughts either (Dummett 1991: 168–76, 200–1). One way out is simply to equate the identity of thoughts with their logical equivalence for purposes of giving contextual definitions. Consider that mere co-extensiveness provides successful definitions in Frege's review of Husserl. Beyond that referential requirement, Fregean definition is just a stipulation or imposition of sense. The pie-slicing metaphor is, after all, only a metaphor, and this is one of its limitations. It provides only analogical illumination of Frege's contextualist realism. More accurately, we would have to speak of logically equivalent pies, or co-extensive parts of pairs of pies. And this is to mix the metaphor with more literal talk. But a better solution is to recognize that the context principle concerning senses makes thoughts logically prior to their constituent senses. Thus while some logical subject-sense and some logical-predicate sense must be grasped, there is no need to grasp every possible such internal division in order to grasp the thought *qua* whole thought. Indeed, in thinking otherwise, Dummett commits a plain fallacy of division. Dummett himself says of deductive inference, "Frege sought to explain its creative character as involving the recognition of patterns common to different thoughts—patterns there to be recognized, whose recognition was nevertheless not required for the thoughts to be grasped" (Dummett 1991: 305–6). This perfectly describes Frege's theory of contextual definition as well. It even assays different possible divisions of thoughts as actual patterns in them. *Mutatis mutandis* for splitting up contents in new ways by contextual definitions.

Sixth, if the context principle is true, then it is itself an objective fact. And how could any objective fact refute realism? It would be part of realism.

Seventh, I shall argue that the context principle is realist because its ontological basis and articulation are what may be called Frege's saturation principle, and the latter is realist. Dummett would sharply oppose this argument. In the beginning of *Foundations* Frege states three principles. The first is always to separate the psychological from the logical. The second is always to ask after the meaning of a word in the context of some sentence. The third is always to distinguish between concepts and objects. Dummett calls the third principle, which is an early version of the saturation principle, "unconnected," presumably with either of the other two, but certainly with the second, which he has just discussed (Dummett 1991: 22, 23). Dummett says that Frege did not "disentangle" the two principles until 1884; however, this amounts only to 'disentangling' the context principle from "the principle of the [*un*saturatedness] of concepts and relations" by adding the saturatedness of objects (Dummett 1981a: 370). To my mind this actually gives us the *full* saturation principle as the ontological basis and articulation of the context principle, insofar as the latter applies to *both* logical subjects and logical predicates. (Perhaps only the context principle would cover nonreferring indicators of assertion, question, or command.) In fairness, Frege does present them as two different principles in *Foundations*. But the two principles must be different, and 'disentangled', if one is to be the ontological articulation of the other in a philosophically interesting, informative way. If neither principle seems to entail the other, that may be simply because the saturation principle, which aims to resolve the famous problem of Bradley's Regress, is only one technically possible resolution of that problem. The problem is to explain how objects are related to their properties and relations without introducing a vicious infinite regress of relations. Frege's solution is to say that properties (concepts) and relations, indeed, all the entities he later calls functions, are inherently relating, i.e., in need of 'completion' by other entities, i.e., 'unsaturated'. If Frege's solution is true, it would be true *a priori*, and thus would be the only possible solution. Then presumably there would be a mutual logical entailment after all. In any case there is a mutual logical entailment on a more general level, namely, that words have meaning only in the contexts of sentences if and only if words, their senses (if any), and their references (if any) must be capable of relating together, respectively in sentences, the thoughts sentences express (if any), and the facts sentences and thoughts concern (if any), in certain ways if those sentences and thoughts are true, in which they are not related if those sentences and thoughts are false. I must admit two qualifications of these mutual entailments. First, Frege never expressly admits facts as a metaphysical category; and for the later Frege true sentences do not describe facts, but denote an object called "the True." Nonetheless, a sentence will not be true for Frege unless the entities denoted by its constituent logical subject(s) and logical predicate are in fact related as the sentence describes, and we may call their being so related a fact, in a perfectly ordinary sense of the word "fact" implying no ontological commitment to facts. Second, the context principle and saturation principle obviously both have application to thoughts expressed by false sentences as well as to thoughts expressed by true sentences.[13]

My eighth comment concerns Dummett's discussion of Crispin Wright's threefold distinction between austere reductionism, intermediate realism, and robust realism. All of these are characterized in terms of semantics. The austere reductionist holds that contextual definitions merely transform the surface syntax of defined sentences without revealing any genuine semantic structure. Dummett characterizes intermediate realism in terms of a "thin" notion of reference, and robust realism in terms of a "substantial" notion of reference. The thin sort of reference Dummett finds in *Foundations* is due to the fact that Frege used an undifferentiated notion of content and had no distinction between language and metalanguage there. The substantial sort of reference Dummett finds in *Basic Laws* is due to Frege's sense-reference distinction and language-metalanguage distinction there. Dummett admits that Frege *claims* to be a robust realist in both works, but Dummett uses these semantic distinctions to conclude that Frege *establishes* robust realism only in *Basic Laws*. Dummett says that in *Foundations*, Frege establishes at most the right to use the language of objects and existential quantification concerning numbers or directions, not the right to interpret such talk realistically. *Basic Laws* uses a substantial notion of reference because unlike *Foundations*, *Basic Laws* has a genuine semantic theory. Realist reference can be characterized only in terms of a semantic theory, and does not consist in a mental act of apprehending the item referred to. But in *Foundations*, any contextually defined terms would be "semantically idle," since grasping their specifically individuated contents "plays no role" in determining the truth-values of the sentences in which they occur. Thus in *Foundations* we do not really achieve even semantic reference to contextually defined objects, much less mental acts of apprehending them (Dummett 1991: 191–99, 205–6, 212).

My eighth comment is just this. Dummett's argument seems as remote from Frege scholarship as it seems from traditional theory of realism. The traditional theory is that there are things that exist and are what they are independently of what we think or say of them. It is captured by Butchvarov's definition of realism as described in chapter 1 of this book, and is completed by the traditional distinction between real distinction and other kinds of distinction as described in chapter 1. Realism concerns the ontological status of the items we admit, not whether we distinguish our language about those items from our language about our language about them. Who is more of a realist—a substance materialist who has no metalanguage, or a subjective idealist who has? Dummett would discard the substance tradition itself as irrealist for lack of a "substantial" notion of reference, and would embrace as realist idealists who happen to have metalanguages. Thus Dummett's notion of a realist is respectively too narrow and too broad.

The truth is that in *Foundations*, Frege establishes realism for numbers in sect. 26, long before he describes (!) his quasi-technical language for referring to them in sects. 62–69. He argues (not: "claims"), "The botanist means to assert something just as factual when he gives the number of a flower's petals as when he gives their colours. The one depends on our arbitrary choice just as little as the other. There does, therefore, exist a certain similarity between Number and colour; it consists...in their being both objective." The argument behind this analogical argument is his private language argument. Thus Dummett has got things backwards. What Frege claims but does not establish in *Foundations* is not his realism, but his *contextualism*.

Nor does it matter to realism whether we distinguish sense from reference. *Pace* Dummett, the notion of undifferentiated content in *Foundations* is exactly as objective as Frege's later notions of sense and reference, since Frege's private language arguments for objectivity do not significantly change, and apply across the board to content, sense, and reference alike. And we find the same division between real concrete objects and merely objective abstract objects in *Foundations* that we find in *Basic Laws*.

When Frege fully presents his realism, he distinguishes between the real and the merely objective within the domain of objects on the basis of causal considerations. To be real is to have causal impacts ("The Thought") or at least causal capacities (BL 16). This is a traditional metaphysical definition straight from Plato (*Sophist* 247; see Geach 1969: 65). Even the sophistical twist that imperceptible, merely objective thoughts can 'act' by being grasped and judged as true, and thus have at least a modicum of reality ("The Thought"), is from Plato (*Sophist* 248; see Geach 1969: 66). But on Dummett's late twentieth-century conception of realism, Frege should have used not causal considerations but metalinguistic considerations to define what it is to be real, or should have at least restricted his sense-reference distinction to concrete objects, so as to ensure that concrete objects alone are real. And that seems absurd.

Ninth, the "semantic idleness" of contextually defined terms ceases when we choose to actuate their potential contributions to determining truth-values of sentences containing them. *Contra* Dummett, sense must be construed in terms of potential contribution, on pain of robbing mere suppositions of all their sense.

Tenth, *pace* Dummett, reference, even to a contextually defined object, *is* a mental act for Frege, an act of apprehending a nonmental object. Dummett insists that thanks to the context principle, "There is no such thing as an immediate apprehension of an object" (Dummett 1991: 203). More specifically, he insists that for Frege, "abstract objects can be neither encountered nor presented" (Dummett 1991: 207; see 232). Dummett argues:

> As already noted, sect. 2 of *Grundlagen* opens with the question how numbers are given to us, seeing that we have neither ideas nor intuitions of them. It would...be a mistake to infer from his asking this question that his principle concerning criteria of identity...was intended to apply only to objects which we can neither perceive nor intuit....It would therefore also be a mistake to ascribe to Frege the view that some objects are 'given' to us in sense or in intuition, i.e. that sense-perception or intuition suffices for the awareness of them as discriminable objects with a persisting identity... (Dummett 1981a: 371)

Dummett goes on to say that for Frege the sense-perception of a concrete object requires the grasping of a thought. Thus he trips over his own interpretation, since he holds that thoughts, i.e. complete senses, are objects themselves (Dummett 1991: 225). But there is a worse problem.

Perhaps Dummett would explain why Frege says in *Foundations* that even a dog "certainly distinguishes individual objects" (FA 42). For Frege, dogs can grasp no concepts or thoughts because the use of words is a precondition of grasping anything imperceptible. See chapter 7, section 1 on Frege's theory of language as prior to concept formation, and on Frege's notion of a presented phenomenon.

Perhaps Dummett would also explain why Frege says, "In arithmetic we are not concerned with objects which we come to know as something alien from without through the medium of the senses, but with objects given directly to our reason and, as its nearest kin, utterly transparent to it" (FA 115). The whole idea of the linguistic turn in *Foundations* is to *answer* Kant's epistemological question, How are numbers given to us? (*pace* Dummett 1991: 111–12, 181). Frege's answer is that numbers are not given in sense-perception or by Kantian intuition, but to our reason (FA 114–15) with the *aid* of language. For Frege, thought is always garbed in language (CN 83–84; PW 269, 270), but *qua* reason finds the purely rational objects it apprehends "utterly transparent to it." We can grasp numbers through our reason because we speak. And reason is a mental faculty. Granted, it is hard to distinguish being directly given to our reason from having some sort of neo-Kantian intellectual intuition. But that is precisely what Frege tries to do by fixing the sense of a numerical identity.

Even with the sense-reference distinction, numbers arguably remain objects given to our reason through the most transparent of senses. Indeed, since every sense is intimately associated with a sortal concept which is a property its reference, if any, has, (e.g. "Aristotle" may express the sense 'the teacher of Alexander'), senses and references are not even wholly distinct from each other. Dummett himself speaks elsewhere of the "symbiosis" of sense and reference (Dummett 1991: 237). And Dummett holds that *senses*, at least some of which he deems to be objects, are grasped through reason. Dummett even admits of abstract objects that "as Frege held, they are given in thought, but not created by thought" (Dummett 1991: 240).

Admittedly, apprehension of numbers is very unlike sense-perception. As Dummett observes, "A physical complex apprehended by the senses may prove to have properties not apparent from our initial grasp of it. But whereas those of the physical system need in no way be implicit in our means of identifying it, those of the mathematical system must be" (Dummett 1991: 310-11). I think this is better expressed as a critique of numbers as entities rather than of our apprehension of them, though a critique of the latter is damaging enough to realism. The critique would be that to be an entity is to be identifiable in indefinitely many ways which are not implicit in our initial grasp of it." I have six replies to both critiques at once. First, this is Frege criticism, not Frege scholarship. Second, as Frege and Dummett well know, numbers are factually identifiable in my sense. Third, Frege insists that numbers *satisfy* Dummett's requirement. Frege says, "But the more fruitful type of definition is a matter of drawing boundary lines that were *not previously given at all*. What we shall be able to infer from it, cannot be expected in advance; here, we are not simply taking out of the box again what we have just put into it" (FA 100-1, italics mine). Dummett ignores this text. Fourth, to deny numbers or the apprehension of numbers on such grounds begs the question of what apprehension can be. In fact, Dummett has a narrow conception of what it is to be a mental act, leading him to ignore Frege's express and radical endorsements of mental acts of apprehending mind-independent concrete objects on the part of dogs (FA 42) and numbers on the part of mathematicians (FA 115). What better confession could there be that Frege admits mental acts of apprehending numbers? Fifth, if we accept rational mental apprehension of numbers, we need to demarcate it from sense-perception of concrete objects anyway. Dummett is better viewed as stating the demarcation than as destroying apprehension of numbers. In fact the latter conclusion is simply a *non sequitur*. My sixth reply occupies the next four paragraphs.

Dummett forgot three words: *mode of presentation*. For Frege, surely every sense without exception contains a mode of presentation. Certainly every *complete* sense does so, on pain of making informative identities impossible (SR 57). This includes the senses expressed by names of abstract objects. Thus abstract objects are presented to us after all. When we speak or think about abstract objects, they are presented to us through *modes of presentation*. And insofar as modes of presentation are modes of cognition (a leap over the narrowest of ditches), we cognize abstract objects. How can abstract objects fail to be presented if we grasp them through modes of presentation? This fact collapses the distinction between reference and attributive denotation altogether for Frege. Every sense is intimately associated with some sortal concept which the denoted object must attributively fall under; and every sense contains a mode of presentation by which the object is in principle singled out as a referent. And since every definition must provide both a sense and a reference for the defined term, and every sense must contain a mode of presentation, every contextual definition must provide a mode of presentation of a (presentable) objective entity, and thus must be a realist definition.

Some historical study might have helped Dummett grasp all this. Frege's notion of intension as "the way the extension is given" seems fairly common; it is shared, e.g., by Husserl and Carnap (Hill 1991: 108; senses are Frege's intensions).

Frege himself says in a letter to Russell, "But the question is, How do we apprehend logical objects?....We apprehend them as extensions of concepts...." (PMC 141). Dummett himself quotes the end of Frege's Appendix on Russell's paradox in *Basic Laws*: "We may regard as the fundamental problem of arithmetic the question: how do we apprehend logical objects...?" (Dummett 1991: 6).

Frege's statements might be interpreted as reducing to the determining of objects by functions (Hill 1991: 140). If so, then to "apprehend" a certain line would be only to determine it by the definitely descriptive concept *axis of the Earth*, and to "apprehend" a class may be only to determine it by its class-concept. But surely this Procrustean approach violates the realist letter and spirit of Frege's statements, as I just explained.

The issue of act theory is very important to realism. If the context principle were a *substitute* for singling out objects instead of the *vehicle* by which we single out objects, then there would be reason indeed to be suspicious of whether there are any abstract objects. For in that case none would be given to us. However, act theory is certainly not necessary to realism. Russell abandoned mental acts altogether for neutral monism in 1919 (LK 305–6), yet in the very same year he ardently championed the "robust sense of reality" perhaps more than ever (IMP 168–70). In 1927 Russell accepted a probabilistic physical realism, but he never returned to act theory. Quine is a robust realist who admits microphysical states and even abstract entities, namely classes, but he admits no mental acts. I do not see that Quine's physical objects, or even his abstract entities, are any less real for his rejecting mental acts. Russell and Quine are very interesting in this regard because they are largely empiricist in orientation. Broadly speaking, one would think that empirical realists would be the ones to want act theory, or at least our experience of the world, to yield realism, while rationalist realists, beginning with Parmenides, would be the ones to argue for their realism on the basis of logic alone. Even if Parmenides' view that you cannot think of nothing concerns acts of thinking, his deeper point is that nothing, so to speak, is not something *simpliciter*, not just not something *you cannot think about*. For Parmenides, it would not be mental acts as such that yield realism, but the ontological status of the *object* of the act. It seems to me that beyond Frege's radically wide conception of mental acts of apprehension, and radically wide linguistic theory that every true or false statement must have a denoting logical subject, i.e., must be about something, there lie deeper points reminiscent of Parmenides. Namely, there is no such thing as a merely possible, i.e. nonexistent, object (see TW 222); and there is no such thing as nothing. I completely agree with Sluga that Frege's philosophy of mathematics belongs to the "tradition of Western rationalism [of]...Parmenides..." (Sluga 1980: 58).

Eleventh, concerning *Basic Laws*, it makes no sense to admit that Frege has a context principle concerning senses, but no such principle concerning references. I have just urged that senses and references are not wholly distinct. Dummett himself says, "The references of the component expressions constitute their respective contributions to the determination of truth-value; and the sense of any one of them constitutes the particular way in which its reference is given to one who grasps the thought" (Dummett 1991: 193). Surely a reference is not wholly distinct from the ways in which it can be given.

My twelfth comment concerns the extensionalist character of Frege's formal program, specifically the problem of reconciling the context principle with defining extensions of concepts, or more generally, courses-of-values of functions (a function's course-of-values is best glossed as the class of ordered pairs of its arguments and values; another term for it is "value-range").

Dummett rightly sees that Frege upholds the context principle for senses in *Basic Laws* vol. 1 sect. 32. Dummett also agrees with Wright that Frege also upholds the context principle for references in *Basic Laws*, insofar as that in the formal notation, to have a reference is to have a properly introduced syntactic role in sentences as a saturated or as an unsaturated expression (Dummett 1991: 183–86). Wright's thesis may be called the syntax principle. Thus far all three of us agree; this is as close as Dummett comes to agreeing with me that the saturation principle simply is the context principle ontologically articulated. But Wright then adds that this syntax principle is expressed by the sort of contextual definition Frege rejected in *Foundations*. Call this the syntax* thesis. Wright sees the problem of bad format I raise for such definitions as trivial and able to be overcome by mere stipulations of truth-values. Dummett criticizes the syntax* thesis on two main grounds. (i) It allows Wright "to evade" the problem that Frege only postpones the question of identity criteria from numbers to extensions. (ii) The syntax* thesis would be equally applicable to defining identity statements about courses-of-values as meaning the same as statements of the equivalence of the concepts they represent, which is, "notoriously, not in order" (Dummett 1991: 188). Dummett concludes that we "have three options: to reject the context principle...; to maintain it, but declare that it does not vindicate [the sort of contextual definition Frege rejected in *Foundations*]; and to formulate a restriction on it that distinguishes the cardinality operator from the abstraction operator" (Dummett 1991: 189).

But there is a fourth option, which I call the Apollo option. It is a new application of one of the ideas in José Benardete's amazing book *Infinity* (Benardete 1964). Baffling to mathematicians but a delight to metaphysicians, the idea is that of a god who can traverse an infinite series. No doubt my application will be a bane to logicians but, hopefully, illuminating to ontologists. The idea has already shown its fertility by my recent application of it to show the invalidity of Aquinas' first cause and cosmological regress arguments (Dejnožka 1989). On this option, we seem able to maintain both the context principle and the sort of definition of number Frege rejects in *Foundations*, and to preserve the abstraction operator for extensions in general as well as the more specific numerical operator. Thus the Apollo option rescues Wright from Dummett, and rescues Frege from Russell's Paradox.

Benardete cites the merely predicative Grelling's Paradox as a version of Russell's to show that the actual infinite is not an essential condition of Russell's Paradox (Benardete 1964: 63). Indeed, as the 1910–19 Russell well knew, his paradox persists on the level of assigning truth-values to *sentences* about classes even if classes are logical fictions. The Apollo option does not make the actual infinite a necessary condition of the paradox's arising, but a sufficient condition of its solution. What will be actually infinite in number for us is not members of classes, but acts of Apollo.

Things are made easy for us by the fact that Frege's hierarchy of functions already constitutes the simple theory of types (Dummett 1991: 132). According to Hill, the concept-object distinction "led to" (Hill 1991: 138, 167), and the sense-reference distinction "is linked with" (Hill 1991: 3, 50–51, 169), Russell's Paradox.[14] But concepts and senses, as such, cannot create such a paradox. For Frege's simple theory of types eliminates the concept *concept that does not fall within itself* as ill-formed. It also eliminates the sense expressed by "concept of all concepts not falling within themselves," and eliminates senses impredicable of themselves. For senses have the same type-levels that objects and functions do. Now, concrete objects will not lead to such paradoxes (Dummett 1981: 530). Nor will anything else which is "not dependent on the notion of a class or extension of a concept" (Dummett 1991: 6). That includes forces, tones, selves, ideas, and surely many abstract objects such as the Earth's axis. Thus we have basically only classes to consider in Frege's metaphysics.

On the Apollo option, Goldbach's Conjecture is determinately true or false. Absent a proof, we can in principle run through all the even numbers to find out whether each one is the sum of two primes. In an analogous manner, Frege's program in *Basic Laws* I 29 renders it determinate whether the ostensible name "the class of classes not members of themselves," which gives rise to Russell's Paradox, has a denotation. *Basic Laws* I 29 lays down all the general sufficient conditions for names' having denotations. On the Apollo option, we simply run through all ostensible names to determine which of them genuinely denote. In effect we run through all objects and functions and assign which will fall under or within which. True, Benardete assigned Apollo simpler tasks, such as only going through the positive integers. But this task is worthy of a god of wisdom.

While we humans cannot carry out such a formal program, a god might do so in less than two minutes by making the first series of determinations in one minute, the second in half a minute, and so on, each series being similarly run through in its allotted time. Only *human* intuitionists would reject the option because "it is impossible to complete an infinite process" (Dummett 1991: 314). Why, Apollo himself might be a strong verificationist! Thus the problem with Frege's program seems not a problem of theory but a problem of practice, a problem of human limitations.

In fact there are two versions of the Apollo option, a moderate one which takes intensions into account, and a radically extensionalist one which runs roughshod over initially grasped intensions. Some may respectively call these versions extreme extensionalist realism and more extreme extensionalist realism. But either version will rescue Frege and Wright.

On the moderate version, the Apollo option detects and treats paradoxical classes as the merely local problems they are, but does so in the course of an active systematic approach, rather than passively waiting for problem cases to show up. Indeed, once Russell's Paradox is found out by this procedure, then if we wish to assign a denotation to "the class of all classes not members of themselves," we simply stipulate whether it yields the True when it is used to complete "( ) is a member of itself," and this will be part of the formal determination of that expression's sense and reference.

On the radically extensionalist version, we will simply *assign* the class of classes not members of themselves as falling under the concept *not a member of itself* (or not). We will pay no attention to any sense which that class's name may seem to express, since we are in the process of *assigning* it a sense. In fact the paradox need not even be *detected* for the Apollo option to work, since the paradox is intensional, while the Apollo option is purely extensional. (The paradox is logical as opposed to semantic, but is based on what the supposed intensional content of the problematic expression instructs us to do.) The heart of *Basic Laws* I 29 is that it makes the extensional prior to the intensional in determining whether an expression refers. In effect we are pounding round extensional pegs into seemingly round-and-not-round intensional holes without caring for any supposed damage we may cause, since we change the intensional holes into safe round ones by the very act of pounding. While a sense ought to contain the mode of presentation it seems to contain (for fear of vicious regress of senses of senses), even if that mode of presentation leads to Russell's

Paradox, in fact Frege must constantly regiment ordinary senses in the name of rigor. And a good thing, too, considering the problems with intensions. Intensions survive on the level of senses. Senses have intensional identities. Difference in reference implies difference in sense, but difference in sense does not imply difference in reference (Dummett 1993: 38). Different senses for the same reference are available on the Apollo option. Every sense "of" (Furth 1967: xix) an object is intimately associated with some sortal concept. But several senses may be senses "of" the same object or concept. Consider the senses expressed by "2^2" and "$2 + 2$" (BL vii, 6 n.3, 35), or even the senses expressed by "is red" and "is round," where all and only red objects are round. And whether or not Apollo can run through all the senses, they remain protected from paradox by Frege's simple theory of sense-types.

On either version, the Apollo option disposes of Frege's problem of bad pie-slicing format in the definition of number he rejects in *Foundations* by systematizing all stipulations of truth-values. It explains why in *Basic Laws* I 10, Frege's disposal of his own permutation argument against the truth of Axiom 5, in effect by appeal to the extensional conditions of names' denoting stated in *Basic Laws* I 29, is successful, *pace* Dummett (1991: 211). It even shows what is wrong with Dummett's accusation that these conditions are highly circular (Dummett 1991: 215, 233, 239, 318). For working the Apollo option is surely more like rebuilding Quine's Neurathian ship at sea than like committing a simple logical fallacy. In fact it is very much like planning how to cut the pieces for a jigsaw puzzle. It may be circular to say that the already-cut pieces must fit together. But there is nothing circular about assessing how cutting one piece affects how other pieces can be cut during the planning phase, and Fregean definition is just such a planning phase. Also, the Apollo option does not reject legions of innocent expressions in the manner of Russell's highly artificial "ramification" of classes into orders (POM Appendix B). The paradoxes simply come with the territory; and when they do, they are weeded out.

The Apollo option, as an extreme extensionalist realism, may or may not be good philosophy. It is not good scholarship in a narrow sense, since Frege actually takes another option in the appendix on Russell's Paradox in *Basic Laws* (he weakens Axiom V and admits "improper objects"), and later abandons logicism altogether. But the Apollo option provides deep philosophical illumination of Frege. If Frege had pressed his own obviously deep commitments toward extensionalism and realism just a little more deeply in response to Russell, or more interestingly, if he had shown just a little more faith in those commitments as they actually were, then it would have been most natural, if not inevitable, for him to have used the Apollo option to defuse Russell's Paradox, the problem with the abstraction operator, and the problem with bad pie-slicing format for fixing the identity of numbers. Thus the problem may have been not too much extensionalism, but rather not enough.

The Apollo option does not vitiate the intensionalist basic motive (3) for quantification, that we can know all whales are mammals without knowing any particular whale (FA 60), or what is the same, admitting the concept's "power of collecting together....the inhabitants of Germany..." even though we cannot perceive all of them (FA 61). For we are not gods, but finite humans. Motive (3) remains as a practical necessity for us. And as we saw in section 2, there are plenty of other motives for quantification.

These twelve comments show how Frege's contextualism, far from casting doubt on his realism, works together with it to establish abstract objects as identifiable and objective entities.

3

Frege: Existence Defined
as Identifiability

There is a huge literature on Frege's theory of identity. We reviewed the major interpretations in chapter 2. Much less has been written on Frege's 'no entity without identity' ontology. Most authors give only a perfunctory, even ritual, statement of the bare fact that Frege has such an ontology. They do not even attempt to state just what this ontology is. Thus they conveniently ignore all the difficulties which serious reflection would reveal.

The thesis (T) of this chapter is that in Frege's philosophy existence may be and is best defined as identifiability, where an object is identifiable if every identity statement about it has a determinate truth value. I shall use the term "identifiable" in this strict sense of identitative identifiability because I am concerned here with defining existence only within Frege's formal program, or within sufficiently similar formal programs. If we shifted our discussion from Frege's formal notation to ordinary language, then identifiability might be better viewed as admitting of degree. There, a minimal notion of identifiability would be that an object is identifiable if at least one identity statement about it has a determinate truth value. Between this minimal notion and the strict sense I will use, there is much room for degree.

If thesis (T) can be well substantiated, then we will be rewarded not only with a new understanding of Frege on the most fundamental level, but also with a more secure foundation of his place in history as the forerunner of Russell, Wittgenstein, Quine, Kripke, Dummett, Geach, Butchvarov, Castañeda, and others concerning connections between identity conditions and existential quantification or reference. But the serious student of Frege will find at least five basic difficulties with (T). First, when faced with an insurmountable logical difficulty in *The Foundations of Arithmetic*, Frege seems to abandon the requirement that for numbers to be named, a criterion for their identity must be provided. Second, what may be called Frege's private language argument seems to entail that subjective entities (minds, ideas) are not identifiable, so that identifiability can hardly be for Frege a necessary condition of existence. Third,

Frege's functions (or on my view that Fregean identity is a relation between names, function-names) cannot even stand in the identity relation, since "$F(\ )$ = $G(\ )$" is an incomplete sentence. So how can functions be identifiable? Fourth, even if identifiability were a necessary and sufficient condition of existence, why should we prefer our definition to Frege's own statement that "Affirming existence is in fact nothing but denial of the number nought" (FA 64)? Fifth, how could our definition be stated generally without violating Frege's type-hierarchy of discourse? I shall deal with these five difficulties in order. I end the chapter by stating what Frege's 'no entity without identity' ontology is in detail; it consists of at least fourteen 'no entity without identity' theories.

1. The Identity of Objects

In *The Foundations of Arithmetic*, does Frege reject the view stated there that if numbers are to be named, a criterion for their identity must be given? The world's leading Frege scholar says that he does. Now, there is no doubt that at first Frege tries to provide an identity criterion in the form of a contextual definition of "the number belonging to the concept *F*" (FA 73–74). But Michael Dummett holds that when this definition is thwarted by a logical difficulty, Frege abandons contextual definitions in favor of explicit definitions (Dummett 1991: 118–19; Dummett 1981: 500–1; Dummett 1973: 495–96; Dummett 1967: 3/235). To be sure, Dummett would admit, as everyone would, that even explicit definitions are contextual in the trivial sense that they tell us how to use the defined term in all sentential contexts (Dummett 1973: 6, 194, 501). Any criterion of identity provided by such a definition would, of course, be equally trivial. As Arthur Pap, for example, understands contextual definition, an explicit definition fails to be genuinely contextual by definition; an explicit definition does not show us how to get along writing sentences without using a term except in the trivial sense of providing a substitute term (Pap 1966: 425). Perhaps it is thinking of some such trivial sense of "contextual definition" that leads Dummett to say that Frege abandons contextual definitions in any substantive sense.

Pap's definition of "contextual definition" as 'definition that shows us how to write sentences without using the defined term' is needlessly syntactical in approach. My definition is different. I define a contextual definition as a definition whose aim is to fix the sense of, i.e., provide determinate truth values for, a particular, definite, proper subclass of the class of statements in which the defined term occurs, and which may provide determinate truth values for all other statements in which the defined term occurs only in an incidental manner. If that particular, definite, proper subclass is a class of identity statements, then the definition may also be called an Identity Definition. It is clear that an ordinary explicit definition, while it may be contextual and it may provide a criterion of identity in the trivial sense Dummett admits, is not contextual in the substantive sense I just defined, nor is it an identity definition in my substantive sense. Yet a syntactically explicit definition would be contextual in my sense if its intent were as described.

Why do I define contextual definition in terms of its intent? If there is one thing philosophers such as Wittgenstein and J. L. Austin have taught us, it is that our confronting a string of symbols, in the absence of accurate information as to how those symbols are being used, is not enough for our knowing what they mean. When it comes to strings of symbols that are definitions, it is crucial not to be taken in, as Dummett has been, by mere syntactical appearance. One must be wary even of assuming that the function of a given definition is what the function of definitions of its syntactical form usually is. Frege himself points out an instance of this very sort of mistake (FA 76). To determine the intent of a definition, the thing to look at is the context in which the definition is given. This fact is not based on some philosophical theory of contextual meaning. It is a point of common sense, of responsible scholarship. It shall guide my analysis of the definition of "the number belonging to the concept *F*" which Frege accepts.

I shall argue that Frege does not give up contextual definition, but rather substitutes one kind of identity definition for another, upholding the requirement of an identity criterion for introducing denoting expressions. The first definition Frege tries may be formulated as follows (Frege's actual discussion is of a definition of the direction of a line):

(I) "The number belonging to the concept *F* is identical with the number belonging to the concept *G*" is to mean the same as "*F* is equal to *G* (there is a one-one correlation between *F*'s and *G*'s)."

It is reasonable to interpret the difficulty Frege finds with this definition as follows. Definition (I) fails to provide a genuinely comprehensive criterion for the identity of numbers belonging to concepts. That is because (I) provides a determinate truth value for identity statements about such numbers only if the statements are of the form "The number belonging to *F* is identical with the number belonging to *G*." The general form we should be dealing with instead is, "The number belonging to *F* is identical with *q*," where "*q*" is any subject-term, say, "England." What statement, according to the lights of definition (I), is the statement "The number belonging to *F* is identical with England" to mean the same as: "*F* is equal to _____"? The sentence cannot be completed. "England" cannot occupy the open argument-place. The first occurrence of "*G*" in definition (I) is only a small part of what "England" would occupy there, namely, the whole of "the number belonging to the concept *G*." So we can hardly fit "England" into the place of the second occurrence of "*G*" in definition (I). This problem of bad pie-slicing format is hardly a reason for rejecting contextual definitions generally or as such. Dummett perceives this fact (Dummett 1973: 496). But instead of drawing the natural conclusion that Frege will simply use a different sort of contextual definition, Dummett has held exactly the opposite view for about thirty years.

Now we come to the definition Frege accepts:

(II) The Number which belongs to the concept *F* is the extension of the concept *equal to the concept F*. (FA 79–80)

Now definition (II) looks for all the world like a plain, ordinary explicit definition. No wonder Dummett was taken in. In the case of definition (I), at least we could see how it was an attempt to provide determinate truth values for identity statements about numbers. But (II) does not even appear to indicate in what sense its intent might be to fix the sense of an identity. The thing to look at, however, is not the definition itself, but the context in which it is given.

The best way to find out Frege's aim, I submit, is to look at the reason he gives for accepting definition (II). Frege did not pick the defining extension out of a hat. The beauty of definition (II) lies in Frege's having seen that numbers belonging to concepts, and the extensions in question, are basically identified and differentiated in the same way, in terms of the equality or non-equality of the concepts the numbers belong to. That is, not only do parallel completions of

(A) The number belonging to *F* is identical with the number belonging to *G*,
(B) *F* and *G* are equal, and
(C) The extension of the concept *equal to F* is identical with the extension of the concept *equal to G*

enjoy logical equivalence and carve up the same thought in different ways, but parallel completions of (A) and (C) each have three components, namely, identity and two subjects, such that identity of content can be very plausibly extended to the components as well. (By component contents I mean here the customary denotations of the subject-names and relation-names.) Once the component contents of (A) and (C) have been identified with each other, the mediation of (B) can be dropped, and the identification of numbers with certain extensions can take on a life of its own, as it does in definition (II), which does not mention equality.

Frege's reason for giving definition (II) is in effect that parallel completions of (A) and (B) are logically equivalent. Obviously Frege states his reason elliptically, since extensions, which are the basis of the definition, are not even mentioned in completions of (A) or (B). They are mentioned only in completions of (C). That is, the second logical equivalence, i.e., the one between parallel completions of (B) and (C), is unavoidably part of Frege's reason for giving definition (II). If this second equivalence had failed to obtain, definition (II) would have been incorrect. If this second equivalence had not been seen, definition (II) would never have been arrived at.

How, then, is definition (II) an identity definition? Its intent is to provide determinate truth values for the particular, definite class of identity statements about numbers, by identifying numbers with just those entities, given as already having a clear criterion of identity (FA 80 n.1), which are demonstrated as having just the identity conditions we want to provide for numbers. Once Frege is assured that the extensions in question have the right identity conditions for the numerical identities of arithmetic, he identifies numbers with them without further ado in a way that simply enforces by stipulation the truth values of all other identity statements about numbers, such as "The number belonging to *F* is identical with England," which is false because the extension of the concept *equal to F* is not England.

Dummett's criticism of definition (II) is that the problem of providing identity conditions for numbers is merely pushed back to the level of extensions (Dummett 1973: 501). But in light of the argument I gave in the preceding three paragraphs, this criticism is now revealed as a misunderstanding of Frege's intent. Frege's intent was to find some entities, given as already having clear identity conditions, such that these conditions were *substantively* the ones we want for numbers, and otherwise not inimical to what we want for numbers. Dummett gives the criticism because he sees definition (II) as merely explicit. But Frege's whole intent in picking the extensions he did was to provide arithmetically adequate and genuinely comprehensive conditions for the identity of numbers, as opposed to fixing identity conditions for numbers incidentally in the trivial sense in which a merely explicit definition provides truth values indiscriminately for all the statements in which the defined term occurs. If that were all Frege had in mind, we would indeed do well to wonder with Dummett as to what, in turn, were to be the identity conditions for these extensions. And this further question is about the identity conditions for these extensions in particular, since we are concerned with a specific proper subclass of extensions. It is not the deeper question what are the identity conditions for extensions in general. Nor is it about whether to define numbers as being classes of extensions. Frege says, "I attach no decisive importance even to bringing in the extensions of concepts at all" (FA 117). Dummett notes that in *Foundations*, a number is a class of first-level concepts. Only in *Basic Laws* is a number a class of classes resembling a Russellian number (Dummett 1991: 121–22).

So the immediate context of definition (II), on analysis, plainly shows Frege's intent to provide determinate truth values for a particular, definite, proper subclass of the class of all statements about numbers, in particular, for identity statements about numbers. All else is merely incidental, including the final syntactical form of the definition, which is simple and elegant. Frege did not, then, abandon the requirement that for numbers to be named, a criterion for their identity must be provided.

The larger context of definition (II), the whole of *Foundations*, abundantly supports our claim as to Frege's contextual intent. Frege states in the book as a fundamental principle that words have meaning only in the context of a proposition (FA X). This principle is never retracted later in the book. Nor should we expect it to be, since it is stated in the Introduction, presumably written or at least carefully considered as the author surveyed the completed work. With regard to defining numbers in particular, Frege states as a comment on this fundamental principle, "With numbers of all these types, it is a matter of fixing the sense of an identity" (FA X). This, too, is in the Introduction. Frege is telling us what to expect him to have done. And in the Analysis of Contents, Frege groups the sections concerning the definition of "the number belonging to the concept *F*" under the heading, "To obtain the concept of Number, we must fix the sense of a numerical identity." Frege even repeats this heading when the sections appear in the text (FA 73). Right after this repeated heading, Frege gives an argument that since words have meaning only in the context of a proposition, and since number words are to stand for objects, we must give a criterion for the identity of numbers if we are to assign them names (FA 73). Frege subsequently detects no flaw in this argument, nor does he later reject it. It is still in force when definition (II) is accepted. Nor is this all. At the end of the book, Frege recapitulates what he has done. He tells us three times that the issue is fixing the sense of a numerical identity (FA 115, 117, 119)!

By the year 1991 Dummett came to realize much of this, though resisting the natural conclusion I have drawn, that Frege's definition is substantively a contextual definition. In 1991 Dummett paraphrases my view, first published in 1979, when he says that Frege's context principle and requirement that the sense of an identity be fixed are neither definitions nor component clauses (i.e. formal parts) of definitions, but conditions "for the correctness of a definition" (Dummett 1991: 201; see also 1981a: 368). That is, an adequate definition must entail a criterion of identity, must provide determinate truth-values for every sentence containing the defined term, and must provide the "right" truth-values "for all sentences for which there are 'right' truth-conditions" (Dummett 1991: 201). Dummett is right, but has still not grasped the whole picture. I emphasize the role of identity criteria, and by extension the context principle, not merely in the context of *justification* of definitions, but also in the context of *discovery* of definitions. As I said, Frege did not pick his definition out of a hat. Secondly, I recognize Frege's definition *as* a contextual definition, due to Frege's openly stated *intent* to fix the sense of an identity for number. Thus, thirdly, the context principle and the requirement of an identity criterion, as background conditions of both the discovery and the justification of any adequate definition of number, constitute the genuine *logical form* of the definition Frege accepts, despite its surface form as an explicit definition. This is in the sharpest contrast to

Dummett, who narrowly insists that "an [explicit] definition would be forced to accept its apparent form as genuine" (Dummett 1991: 127). Dummett's argument, or more precisely its premise, is that the apparent form of the defined term is level 0, and for Frege, all names of this form do genuinely refer to entities of level 0, namely objects (Dummett 1991: 127). The premise is true, but the conclusion does not follow. For the genuine logical form of Frege's definition becomes visible only when we look at its full expression, and that is in parallel completions of (A), (B), and (C).

Under these circumstances, I think that any reasonable principle of charity would support my interpretation. Certainly a principle of greatest continuity (or least change) supports it. Why see Frege as abandoning contextual definition when we can see him as merely moving to another kind of contextual definition? I did not expressly use either principle in my arguments, but it is worth noting in retrospect that both of them strongly support my view against Dummett's.

My conclusion is that in *Foundations*, Frege holds that identifiability is a necessary condition of assigning denotations to expressions. It also seems a sufficient condition. Once the sense of an identity is fixed, there is no further ado about assigning denotations.

2. The Identity of Ideas

I turn now to the second difficulty with (T). That identifiability is a necessary and sufficient condition of denotation may be very well in *Foundations*, which treats of numbers, shapes, directions, and objects generally. Objects belong to Frege's objective realm, and therefore are already understood to be fully communicable in an ideal public language, hence interpersonally identifiable, hence identifiable. But what about entities in the subjective realm, such as our ideas? What may be called Frege's private language argument seems to entail that thanks to their essential privacy, ideas are not even minimally identifiable, much less identifiable in the strict, comprehensive sense of the term.

Frege gives at least twelve private language arguments.[1] The main one is this: An idea is essentially an item in the consciousness of a single person. Therefore even if an idea vanishes from one person's consciousness at the very moment an idea appears in another person's consciousness, the question whether the ideas are identical is unanswerable. Therefore it is impossible to bring together in one consciousness ideas belonging to different people. Therefore it is impossible to compare such ideas. Therefore a predicate supposed to state a property of an idea of a given person is applicable only within the sphere of that person's consciousness. Therefore, if a predicate is taken to stand for any property of any item that belongs to a given person's consciousness, all questions as to the applicability of that predicate to any item in another person's consciousness are (likewise) unanswerable and nonsensical. Now this applies to the predicates "is true" and "is false" as well as to any others. Therefore, if thoughts were ideas, then no one could dispute with his friends as to the truth or falsehood of any thought. Since the possibility of such dispute is a necessary condition of there being a science or body of thought common to many, there could then be no such science. But this is absurd. Hence thoughts are not ideas (Frege 1956: 299–302).

How does this argument, which concludes only that thoughts are not ideas, entail in any way that ideas are not even minimally identifiable? Even if the argument states that ideas are not interpersonally identifiable, so that they are not strictly identifiable, surely I can identify at least my own ideas in a 'specious present', so that they are minimally identifiable. Well, according to the argument, no predicate can be appointed to characterize an idea and still express a public sense. Therefore, since "is identifiable" is a predicate of a public language and expresses a public sense, ideas cannot be said to be identifiable. Similarly for the predicate "is minimally identifiable." So it seems that there are some entities, ideas, that are not even minimally identifiable, and (T) cannot be upheld. Similarly for minds.

The trouble with this objection to (T) is simply that "exists," too, is a predicate of a public language, so that Frege's private language argument entails not only that ideas cannot be said to be identifiable in any sense, but also that they cannot even be said to exist. Frege's argument is therefore actually an excellent argument in favor of (T), since it entails that a thing can be said to exist if and only if it can be said to be identifiable.

If items cannot be said to be the same, then they cannot be said to be anything, or even to be at all. Ontologically, if I cannot identify an item, then I cannot identify its properties (as its properties) either, or even determine that it exists. This ontological principle, I conjecture, is the mainspring of Frege's argument. It is implied in the very beginning of the argument, where Frege contends that because ideas are not interpersonally identifiable, they cannot be interpersonally compared or described. There is no difference between interpersonal describability and describability, any more than there is any difference between interpersonal identifiability and identifiability, since "is describable," too, is already a public predicate. This mainspring, by the way, makes identity prior to essence for Frege. If I cannot identify an item, then I cannot identify its essence (as its essence) either. That an essence is usually understood as a set of properties only confirms the priority of identity, since properties must have identities. Defining identity as indiscernibility (or having the same properties) reverses this priority. This is one reason why we should offer not a definition but an 'explanation' of identity as indiscernibility. Of course, 'no individual identity without properties' is a different issue. The identity of an individual may require properties as its 'basis', as Butchvarov has suggested.

Frege might have found these implications of his argument unwelcome, and perhaps even bizarre. He seems to show a tendency to avoid them. He seeks to show that perhaps an idea can be taken to be an object (SR 60). He also argues that different persons' ideas must have at least affinities if art is to be possible (SR 61). He seems to think that if ideas can be made out to be similar enough to objects, then somehow they can be spoken about after all. But this is nonsense. Not even the public predicates "can be taken as an object" or "has at least affinities with other ideas" can be appointed to characterize an idea. Thesis (T) therefore remains secure concerning the issue of subjective entities.

3. The Identity of Functions

The third problem with (T) is this. According to Frege, only objects can stand in the identity relation. Functions cannot stand in the identity relation (FA 89–90; TW 80n). Further, identity is given to us so specifically that there cannot be various forms of it (BL 129). Now if functions cannot even stand in the identity relation, how can they be identifiable?

Now we might use Frege's private language argument to dispose of the problem of functions. If functions cannot be said to be the same, then they cannot be said to be anything, or even to be at all. But as I mentioned early in chapter 2, a 'smoking gun' letter from Frege to Husserl reveals that for Frege, concepts (or more generally functions) are indeed the references of certain names. Nonetheless, it may be of interest to recall at least briefly the older dispute in the literature as to the ontological status of functions.

A strong doubt that function-expressions are to be understood as denoting may arise from Frege's paradoxical discussion of the concept *horse*. Frege says that the expression "the concept *horse*" denotes not a concept but an object, thanks to the role of the definite article "the" (CO 45–46). William Marshall uses three principles about names to bring out the paradoxical nature of this view. (i) An expression that one can quantify over is a name. (ii) Names of the same entity are intersubstitutable *salva veritate*. (iii) A name's denotation can always be described as the so-and-so. Now by (i), the function-expression "is a man" is a name. If Plato is a man, then there is something that Plato is. But then either (ii) or (iii) must fail to hold. If we try to describe the denotation of "is a man" as the concept *man*, then we have two names of the same entity that are not intersubstitutable *salva veritate*. "Plato is a man" is true, but "Plato the concept *man*" does not even express a thought. Marshall infers that a predicate or function-expression is not a name, and that quantification over a predicate is best seen as implying not denotation but rule-governed use (Marshall 1956: 359–60). Marshall's view makes it easy to defend (T) along the line I indicated, but Frege's 'smoking gun' letter shows that Marshall is wrong: functions are indeed references for Frege.

Like Montgomery Furth, I am in favor of ascribing denotation to function-expressions. I am not in favor of Furth's analogical approach, which is based on the paradigm of object-names' denoting. The problem is the lack of a clear criterion for the extent or type of formal similarity between object-names and function-expressions for our legitimately being able to say that function-expressions denote in some sense. That is, one can admit all the formal similarities Furth carefully draws and still question his conclusion. As a matter of fact, Furth's final definition of ascribing denotation to function-expressions is unfortunately close to Marshall's explication of quantification over predicates as merely meaning being well governed by rules. Both views seem inspired by the same passage in Frege (Furth 1968: 41–43; Marshall 1956: 357; BL 84, i.e., *Basic Laws* vol. 1, sect. 29, para. 2).

Dummett has the right idea for avoiding the quantificational problem of the concept *horse*. He paraphrases Frege's quantification over predicates into true ordinary sentences such as "There is such a thing as being a philosopher." Unlike "The concept *philosopher* exists," which seems to predicate a first-level concept of an object, Dummett's sentence predicates a second-level concept of a first-level concept (Dummett 1973: 216–18). (Observe that "being a philosopher" is the gerundial version of the obviously first-level "is a philosopher.") This bypasses Marshall's principle (iii) about names by a direct appeal to ordinary language type-levels.

Nicholas Measor rejects Dummett's paraphrase. For Frege, all first-level predicates in true or false statements denote concepts. This includes predicates which can apply to no object, such as "is round and not round." But there is, precisely because no object can be round and not round, no such thing as being round and not round (Measor 1978: 15). But while Measor has refuted Dummett's paraphrastic proposal, he has not refuted the fine general approach of Dummett's paraphrase. I myself regard the paraphrase "There is such a thing as being a philosopher" as incorrect because it asserts too much. It asserts the existence of the concept, but it also asserts that philosophers can exist. My paraphrase of "$(\exists F)[(x)(Fx = x$ is a philosopher)]" is instead, "There is something which perhaps nothing can be, namely, being a philosopher." Now in the problem case we can use "There is something which perhaps nothing can be, namely, being round and not round." This, I contend, is a true existential sentence in which the existence of a concept is asserted. All sentences of its form correspond in truth value to the formal statements they are intended to paraphrase. Moreover there is, beyond the mere difference in level, no detectable semantic difference between "There is (something, a thing such as...)" when it is completed by a proper name, and the same phrase when it is completed by a function-expression. My conclusion is that function-expressions denote in exactly the way proper names do.

My solution also takes care of Richard Gaskin's more recent version of Marshall's dilemma. Gaskin considers the sentence "The concept *horse* is not a concept." Gaskin tries two paraphrases for "The concept *horse*": "what the concept-word 'horse' stands for," and "is what the concept-word 'horse' stands for." He correctly finds that the former is a referring proper name and can be quantified over but is a level 0 object-name, and that the latter is a level 1 concept-expression, but is incomplete and therefore not a proper name and cannot be quantified over. Gaskin then infers that no paraphrase is possible, committing the fallacy of hasty generalization (Gaskin 1995: 164–65).

Using Frege's private language argument backwards, as it were, we might now infer that functions must be in some sense identifiable after all, since they exist and we can say truly that they exist. In any case it is certain that we must find some such sense if (T) is to be preserved. Now Frege writes that owing to the predicative nature of concepts, when one needs to assert something about concepts in the sentence form usually used to assert something about something, the reference of the subject-term cannot be the concept itself, but instead is an object that represents the concept (CO 46). Call this mode of assertion "representative assertion." I suggest that identity can be representatively asserted of concepts by means of the sentence "The concept *F* is identical with the concept *G*," where the subject-terms "The concept *F*" and "the concept *G*" denote objects that represent *F* and *G* themselves. (Actually, since I hold that for Frege identity is the relation between names of denoting the same denotation, I should say that the subject-terms customarily denote the representative objects.) This much already gives the main idea of the answer to the question in what sense functions can be said to be identical and can be said to be identifiable. Functions do not stand in the identity relation directly. The identity relation is predicated representatively of them instead.

Now in *The Basic Laws of Arithmetic* a function and its course-of-values represent each other (BL 92–94). Plainly, any assertion about either is a representative assertion about the other. Assertions that represent each other merely carve up the same thought in different ways.[2] So if the assertion that the courses-of-values of concepts *F* and *G* are the same, "$\acute{\epsilon}F(\epsilon) = \acute{\epsilon}G(\epsilon)$," representatively asserts that *F* and *G* themselves are identical, then there must be a relation *F* and *G* themselves do stand in, "corresponding to identity between objects" (TW 80). This relation is equivalence, or for Frege, "$(x)[Fx = Gx]$," where "*F*" and "*G*" mark the argument-places. Equivalence obtains between concepts if and only if identity obtains between their courses-of-values (BL 43–44).

I shall refer to equivalence as the relation of representative identity. This is not just for the reason that identity and equivalence correspond with each other in mutually representative assertions as described. It is not even for the reason that identity and equivalence can be technically shown to be first- and second-level representatives of each other in Frege's formal notation.[3] The reason I call equivalence representative identity, or if you will, an identity analogue, is instead best seen in the fact that for Frege, equivalent functions are interdefinable, that is, they are not, as it were, to be regarded as different functions (TW 80).

This does not mean that if all and only red objects are round, then the concepts *red* and *round* are the same concept, even though we seem to have here a single mapping-function with two modes of presentation. The concepts themselves would be not identical, but merely equivalent or representatively identical. Only their courses-of-values would directly stand in the identity relation (TW 80 and 80n). For strictly speaking, *red* ( ) is not even identical with *red* ( ); that is, *red* ( ) is not even self-identical.

Since mutual representation would be impossible if there were not a one-one correspondence between functions and their courses-of-values, we may say that the representative identity conditions for functions are exactly as sharp as the identity conditions of the objects that represent them. That this one-one correspondence obtains is the famed extensionality thesis, whose name we may honor by saying that for Frege, representative identity criteria are always extensional (Furth 1967: xl–xliv).

If, for all that, functions still cannot stand in the identity relation, then someone acquainted with our view of Frege's private language argument might object, "Functions are still not identifiable, since they still cannot stand in the identity relation. So how can the predicate 'is representatively identifiable' be appointed in the first place to characterize a function and still express a public sense? According to Frege's private language argument, this cannot be done." The objection is misguided. The representation function, $\xi \cap \zeta$, is well-defined in Frege's formal notation, and its use must be regarded as unexceptionable on the score of public communicability (BL 92). The said predicate would in any case be appointed to characterize not the function but the object that represents it, since "is representatively identifiable" is a first-level predicate. I therefore defend (T) by saying it is sufficient that functions exist if and only if they are representatively identifiable, where the criterion of sufficiency is that representatively identical entities are incorrectly regarded as different entities.

4. Is Existence Best Defined as Identifiability?

In the preceding sections of this chapter it has been made clear that it would have been very natural for Frege to have said that identifiability is a necessary condition of existence. That he would have held that it is also a sufficient condition is clear not only from the last paragraph of section 1, but also from the fact that for Frege, the logical subject-term of every true or false statement must have a denotation, so that if the statement "*a* is identifiable" is true, then "*a*" must denote some object (SR 62). Similar points hold for functions.[4] Let us concede, then, that identifiability is for Frege a necessary and sufficient condition of existence. Thus Frege would find it permissible to define existence as identifiability.

This brings us to the fourth difficulty with (T). Part of (T) was that existence may be defined as identifiability in Frege's philosophy, and this has now been well substantiated. But the rest of (T) was that existence is best so defined in Frege's philosophy, and this has not been shown. Besides the candidate definition Frege himself suggests, "denial of the number nought" (FA 65) and its early variants, definition of the existential quantifier using negation and the universal quantifier, and affirmation of at least the number one (BG 27 n.15; 28 n.16), there is also determinacy, i.e. conformance to the law of the excluded middle (TW 33, BL 84), and the property of having a property. Horses exist if and only if it is not the case that there are no (O) horses. Horses exist if and only if horses are determinate. Horses exist if and only if horses have properties. In fact there are as many legitimate Fregean definitions of existence as there are concepts equivalent to it. Compare the formal definitions of existence discussed in chapter 1. Why then should identifiability be preferred to the others?

The reason lies in what I called the ontological mainspring of Frege's private language argument. Our finding entities identifiable must be prior to our counting them, to our pronouncing them determinate, and indeed to our being able to say anything at all about them. Identifiability must be prior to counting for fear of counting the same thing twice. And we can hardly determine all or even any of the properties of a thing without being able to identify it in the first place. But this is just to state again the ontological mainspring of Frege's private language argument. On the other hand we can identify, say, people without counting them, without determining whether each person has or does not have each and every property, without determining essential human nature, and even without determining whether any person has any property in particular.

Now surely it is the case for Frege that an object exists if and only if at least one identity statement about it has a determinate truth value. Why then should we define existence as strict identifiability when we can define it as minimal identifiability? The reason is that it is legitimate to assert that an object exists not because we happen to find some identity statement about it to be true or false, nor even because the object is such that some identity statement about it has a determinate truth value, but because the object is such that no matter what its situation or condition, and no matter which identity statement about it we may be concerned with, that identity statement has a determinate truth value. This is the general ground for the legitimacy of existence assertions, constituting what existence assertions really amount to, and so telling us uniquely the sense of the word "exists," or what existence is, while the other features equivalent with existence merely constitute conditions that are necessary and sufficient for existence. That is why our definition is to be preferred over any of the others. That is why a genuinely comprehensive criterion of identity, showing strict identifiability, is Frege's correct theoretical requirement in *Foundations* for assigning objects number-expressions as proper names: "If we are to use the symbol *a* to signify an object, we must have a criterion for deciding in all cases whether *b* is the same as *a*, even if it is not always in our power to apply this criterion."

If Frege's suggestion that "Affirming existence is in fact nothing but denial of the number nought" is intended as a definition of existence, then it is a circular definition on his own showing (FA sects. 72–75; BL vol. I, sects. 38–40). Frege defines "0" as "the number belonging to the concept *not identical with itself*," and requires that zero belong to all and only concepts equal to that concept. Frege defines concepts as equal just in case there *exists* a relation which correlates one-one any objects which fall under them. It is the existence of this relation that introduces circularity into the series of definitions culminating in the definition of existence as denial of the number zero.

5. Defining Existence as Identifiability

The fifth difficulty is how to formulate a definition of existence as identifiability. One may define the existential quantifier, "$(\exists x)(Fx)$," "*F*" marking the argument-place, by saying that it is to mean the same as "$(Ix)(Fx)$," meaning "*F*'s are identifiable." Now someone might object to this definition, call it (D), that while, say, unicorns do not exist, surely all unicorns are identifiable if horses are, since there is not much difference between a unicorn and a horse. But this objection to (D) is ill-founded. First, I might stipulate concerning identity statements ostensibly about unicorns that each one of the form "$a = b$" is to be false while each one of the form "$a = a$" is to be true, so that every identity statement ostensibly about unicorns would have a truth-value and unicorns would be identifiable in my strict sense. But the stipulations would not amount to provisions of determinate truth-values in any meaningful sense. Second, an object that is not actual is not an object at all for Frege, and cannot be compared with anything to see if it is the same. Third, if, in "$a = b$," "a" has no customary denotation to be identical or not with the customary denotation of "b," then "a" in "$a = a$" has no customary denotation either. Both statements would be false, on my theory that identity for Frege is a relation between names. For it would be false that their subject-names denote the same denotation. Thus all identity statements about unicorns would be false.[5] (On the theory that identity is a relation between objects, no identity statements about unicorns would have a truth value at all for Frege in "On Sense and Reference," since their logical subject-terms would not be about anything. In *Basic Laws* the False is stipulated in any case.) But at least some identity statements about horses are true, since there are horses, and they are both self-identical and informatively identifiable. Identifiability thus needs two further conditions: the assignment of truth values to all the identity statements concerning an object must be nonarbitrary, i.e. nonstipulative; and the assignment of truth values to all the identity statements concerning an object, or to all the representative identity statements concerning a function, must include some assignments of the truth value, the True. Each condition distinguishes unicorns from horses on the score of identifiability (compare SR 62–63 and BL vol. 1, sect. 7).

Our definition (D) resembles Frege's definition (II) of the number belonging to the concept *F*. In both cases the syntactical form is that of an explicit definition. But also in both cases the entity defined is defined by being identified with an entity already given to us as having clear identity conditions, the defining entity being chosen for the sole intent of providing identity conditions for the defined entity that are substantially the correct ones and otherwise inconsequential (FA 65). I take the second-level concept *identifiable* as already having clear identity conditions, since its strict sense is quite clear. Beyond the mere difference in type-level, then, (D) and (II) are identity definitions of exactly the same sort, and satisfy (T) by securing the denotations of their defined terms in exactly the same way.

One may object to (D) that it defines only the second-level concept of existence, while (T) is concerned with existence in the broadest possible way. What about the existence of functions of all levels, not to mention the existence of senses and forces? I believe that much like functions, senses and forces can be denoted by means of the definite article only representationally, owing to the very same necessity of form of language that is the reason why "the concept *horse*" must denote an object (CO 45–46). And all of Frege's own categorial pronouncements, such as that functions are incomplete or that senses (complete and incomplete) are objective, are also best viewed as representations of, as it were, general features of the world that cannot be directly described in Frege's notation, thanks to the subject-predicate hierarchy. Similarly on the trans-categorial level: no broad definition of existence can be directly stated in the formal notation. Even the English formula, (F), "To exist is to be identifiable," must be regarded as a multilevel representation. Representation (F) is definition-al in character since identifiability really is a necessary and sufficient condition of existence in Frege's philosophy, even if this cannot be directly expressed in his notation or in ordinary language any more than his own express articulations of general metaphysical views can. Thus one may still advance (F) or even (D) as representations of something beyond the ability of language to denote. Indeed, this is the strategy of Whitehead and Russell in *Principia* *24.01, which is "systematically ambiguous" across types. *24.01 $V = \hat{x}(x = x)$ Df defines the "universal class" of all existents of all logical type-levels. Thus *24.01 is multiply representational. For *24.01 is strictly stated as ranging only over type 0 order 0 objects (PM 216; see 41–42, 55).

Somebody may object that the formula (F) does not represent a general feature of the world, insofar as Frege expressly derides views such as that existence is the concept superordinate to all other concepts (Frege 1979: 63), or that existence is absolute being (Frege 1979: 64). However, referring the problem of transcategoriality to a distinction between object languages and metalanguages, and making (D) and (F) metalinguistic sentences, or considering a representational definition as shorthand for an infinitely long conjunction of type-level definitions, may not be ultimately adequate. It is usually not best to view a metalanguage as an arena in which somehow one can say things that cannot be said in one's object language. Indeed, for Frege it is ordinary language, which roughly serves as his metalanguage, that gives rise to pitfalls or illusions such as the views about existence he derided (Frege 1979: 67). Nor does it seem best to think of (F) or (D) or of Frege's own general ontological statements (e.g. "Functions are incomplete") as mere shorthand for an infinitely long conjunction of statements concerning infinitely many type-levels.

Panayot Butchvarov rejects Russell's theory of types. But Frege's types are not Russell's; if they were, then Frege could have given Russell's answer to Russell's Paradox. (Frege has only a simple theory of types for concepts and senses.) Butchvarov might still solve Frege's type-hierarchy problem by widening the notion of generic identity. All of Frege's existential quantifiers may be said to share a generic identity. Formula (F) may be called a generic formula. However, this solution seems unavailable to Frege. For Frege, identity is given so specifically that there cannot be different forms of it (BL 129). Thus if identity is a relation between names of level 0 objects, then there is for Frege no second relation of 'generic identity' of existential quantifiers, which are certain concepts from level 2 on up. But perhaps a similar solution might succeed. Frege's concepts are universals, and some are generic universals. These may not have generic identities, but they do have representative identities. Perhaps a representational solution can even solve Alfred North Whitehead's objection to Russell that type-levels themselves (have identities and) are numerically different, presupposing numbers (Whitehead 1965; 15). For they too can be represented.

The question of how to say what it seems cannot be said remains, of course, one of the most fruitful issues of comparison of Frege to Wittgenstein. As the famous criticism of the *Tractatus Logico-Philosophicus* goes, if you cannot say it, you cannot whistle it either. But unlike Wittgenstein's obscure ladder metaphor, perhaps a responsible account of Frege's representation would prove to be an adequate whistle. My view is that *R1*, given as denotable, may represent *R2* if *R2* exists and can be put in one-one correspondence with *R1*, and our representing *R2* by denoting *R1* can be distinguished from our merely denoting *R1*. This is why a concept, which due to its predicative nature cannot be denoted by means of the definite article, may be represented by an object which can be so denoted. Our account also applies to forces and senses. Frege has good reason for asserting their existence. Forces ground the distinction between assertion, question, command, and supposition. Senses make informative identities, fiction, and false belief possible. Yet there are good reasons for saying that forces and senses, and probably also tones, cannot be denoted at all.[6] But all these can be identified and distinguished between, so they can be put in one-one correspondence with, and can be represented in language by, the names, punctuation, or behavior which customarily express, indicate, or convey them. We may indicate representation by various prefixing devices, since Frege's representation function, $\xi \cap \zeta$, can only represent functions or objects. Or else we can just 'take' all these 'as' objects (compare SR 60 on taking ideas as objects).

Let us now apply our account of representation to transcategorial entities. There is a tremendous intrinsic plausibility to saying that everything exists, is identifiable, and has at least one property. Even Frege, despite his having a type-hierarchy with a series of existential quantifiers, and his disbarring concepts under which all objects fall from having any content, seems to think at bottom of existence, logic, and determinateness as being the same for all entities. Perhaps, then, Frege is best seen not as denying that existence is a transcategorial, but as denying only that all the concepts of existence he admits, however similar, can be denoted by a single concept-name on a single type-level.

Now all functions of all levels are reciprocally represented by their courses-of-values. The expression "the function F" always denotes the course-of-values of function F. And this applies to the function on any level which is the existentially quantifying concept predicable of concepts on the next lower level, as well as to the concepts of which it is predicated. Similarly for the concept *identifiable* on any level. Let $E(\ )$ be the existentially quantifying concept on any level L. Let $I(\ )$ be the concept *identifiable* on level L. Let c be any concept of level $L - 1$. (I should use $C(\ )$, but this is easier.) And let the prefix "$*$" indicate systematic representation on all levels. Then:

$$(D1) \quad (*c)[*E(*c)] \quad =Df \ (*c)[*I(*c)]$$

(D1) contextually defines concept $E(\ )$ as being concept $I(\ )$. (D1) is based on those concepts' logical equivalence, which already entails that concepts $E(\ )$ and $I(\ )$ are not to be understood as different functions, thanks to Frege's extensionality thesis. Thus (D1) is our explanation of definition (D) and our analysis of formula (F). My conclusion is that thesis (T) is understandable, well-formed, and correct.

Is defining existence as identifiability circular? It might be argued that in *Basic Laws* vol. I, sect. 29, the determinacy and the existence of the identity relation presuppose the determinacy and the existence of its arguments and values. And identifiability presupposes the existence of the identity relation and the existence of truth-values. I grant that on the level of necessary and sufficient conditions of assigning references to expressions, identifiability and reference capability are necessary and sufficient conditions of each other. But identifiability is what illuminates reference, and, by extension, existence. Following Frege, I would speak of 'explanation' as opposed to definition.

Frege's own suggestion that affirming existence is equivalent to denial of the number zero is technically an explanation as well. Its level of circularity is not as immediate or fundamental as is that in my explanation. Its circularity concerns a series of defined names, not basic conditions of denoting. I showed this in the last paragraph of section 4. The series of defined names is more formally given in *Basic Laws*, vol. I, sects. 38–40. Thus Frege's explanation is not as deeply illuminating of existence as mine is. Frege's explanation does not illuminate the nature of existence as identifiability so much as the status of existence as a second-level concept.

Value, beauty, causation, God, and the thinking subject are not even minimally identifiable as denotable entities. I may identify a thing and fully describe it, and still ask whether it is good, beautiful, or causally efficient. I cannot identify myself as an object of introspection, and who has seen God? To be sure, in a fairly clear and ordinary sense I seem easily able to assert many true identity statements about values, beauties, causes, and thinkers, if not God. I mean that I cannot identify such things in the phenomenological sense in which such things are not objectually given to me. They are not denotable by contextual definition any more than they can be grasped in mental acts of objectual apprehension. Even the hints, metaphors, and suggestions Frege allows as explications of logically simple denotations (Frege 1971c: 59–60) do not help, as we still cannot denote these things. Wittgenstein was right that they are transcendental, at least so far as the denotable world is concerned (T 117, 141, 145, 147, 149). But we have seen that even the daily workings of language cannot be ontologically understood by means of denotation alone. If these things can in any sense still be distinguished from each other, and if they can be put in one-one correspondence *salva veritate* with what can be denoted, then our account of representation applies to them.[7] Perhaps those who found "that the sense of life became clear to them" did so by ceasing their search for denotable entities, and by letting things show themselves in their own way (T 6.521–T 6.54). But they need not pass them over in silence.

Last, I shall consider the being and unity of thoughts. The being and unity of a thought consist in the very same thing: the incompleteness of predicative senses. This is Frege's solution to the problem of Bradley's Regress. I discuss the regress in note 13, and in chapter 4, section 5. Richard Gaskin says, "Frege's solution can be seen as foreshadowed by Plato at *Sophist* 262a–c" (Gaskin 1995: 163 n.3).

Frege does not admit facts as entities, where a fact is a thing's having a property or standing in a relation. We cannot seriously deny that for Frege, objects have properties and stand in relations. The question is whether in so doing, they constitute new complex entities called facts. Frege's answer is "No." This answer must not be thought of as based on Frege's theory that sentences do not assert facts, but are instead proper names of certain objects, namely the truth-values. For one can consistently hold that theory and admit facts too. The argument we should use instead is that if Frege admitted facts, he would have said so; but he never says so. But if Frege *had* admitted facts (which he did not do), their being and unity would consist in the incompleteness of concepts (properties) and relations.

To sum up the book so far, Frege is the first 'no entity without identity' ontologist in the analytic tradition. Frege holds at least fourteen 'no entity without identity' theories, of which his theory of informative identity statements is but one:

(1) Every entity has a metaphysical unity.

(2) All objects are self-identical.

(3) $Fa \equiv (\exists x)(Fx \ \& \ (x = a))$.

(4) Objects are identical if and only if their names are intersubstitutable *salva veritate* in referentially transparent sentential contexts.

(5) For an expression "*a*" to name an object, there must be a criterion which tells us in all cases whether *b* is the same as *a*, even if we may be unable to apply this criterion. Thus objects are identitatively identifiable.

(6) An identity statement asserts that its subject-names refer to the same object; the statement is factually informative if the subject-names express different senses. This is the logical structure of identity statements.

(7) An entity is objective if and only if it has a public identity.

(8) Variable letters are not names, since any variable-entities would be indiscernible, and therefore would lack individual identities.

(9) Functions are representatively identical if and only if their courses-of-values are identical.

(10) A representative identity statement asserts that two functions are equal; the statement is factually informative if the subject-function-names express different senses.

(11) Senses have intensional identities. Difference in reference implies difference in sense, but the converse does not obtain.

(12) There is no *defined* entity without identity, since all definitions stipulate identities of sense and reference.

(13) The being and unity of a thought consist in the very same thing: the incompleteness of predicative senses.

(14) Objectual identities shift, in a perfectly ordinary sense, as concepts shift. But since objectual identities (metaphysical unities) are determinate, and numbers determinately belong to concepts, no radical relativity is involved.

4

Russell's Robust Sense of Reality

Panayot Butchvarov, in "Our Robust Sense of Reality," attacks Russell's ontology (Butchvarov 1986: 403–4). Butchvarov raises a deep ontological question concerning the Russellian critique of Alexius Meinong: Just what *is* the "robust sense of reality" Russell accuses Meinong of lacking when Meinong claims that "There are objects of which it is true to say that there are no such objects" (Meinong 1960: 83)? It is more fundamental than the standard semantic question: What is the meaning or proper use of Russell's existential quantifier? Asking that presupposes that we already have a robust sense of the reality of meanings or uses (compare Butchvarov 1986: 421). Butchvarov claims that: (i) Russell's existential quantifier needs a more fundamental conception of existence to determine its applicability in specific cases. (ii) For Russell this conception is that: CON. All objects exist. (iii) But CON begs the question against Meinong's theory of objects (compare Chisholm 1967: 5/261). (iv) And CON unravels because all genuine concepts (including existence) are classificatory. (v) A conception of existence as identifiability is a preferable, i.e. genuinely classificatory, alternative to Russell's CON. Here Butchvarov means by "identifiable," novelly informatively identifiable indefinitely many times. Thus what does not exist in this sense of "identifiable" may well exist in Frege's sense of "identifiable" as being such that every identity statement about it has a determinate truth value. Indeed, that is my first criticism of Butchvarov: Fregean factual identifiability is more fundamental (see chapter 1).

    I accept claim (i) but reject claims (ii)–(v). My rejection is largely based on three points: (1) Russell does not use the word "real" and its synonyms ("exists," "is actual," "has being") univocally, but in three senses. These senses are not rival theories or given at different times by Russell. They are related parts of one theory given in one broad period, 1905-19. They are best seen working together in "The Philosophy of Logical Atomism." (2) In one of these three senses Russell is a neglected major early proponent of much the same sort of 'no entity without informative identity' theory advocated by Butchvarov himself. (3) It is this sense, and not CON, which is Russell's conception of existence that governs the applicability of his existential quantifier. Thus claim (v)'s conception of existence as identifiability, far from being an alternative to Russell, is very close to Russell's own view.

It is understandable why Butchvarov does not notice the three points I just mentioned: they seem to be unnoticed in the whole literature on existence and identity. This is because identifiability has been associated at most with Russell's theory of sense-data and theory of logical fictions, and not with his theory of denoting. This has led to a neglect of how these three theories fit together. Indeed, admitting only what I call Russell's primary and tertiary senses of the word "real" may be called the standard interpretation of Russell's theory of denoting. Butchvarov is just giving a version of this standard interpretation. That is the real problem.

1. Russell's Three Senses of "Real"

What, then, is Russell's robust sense of reality? Russell says that "[the word 'real'] is a vague word, and most of its uses are improper" (PLA 224). But he writes of a "sense of" (IMP 170), "feeling of" (IMP 170), or "vivid instinct" (PLA 223) for reality which we have or ought to have. And other texts indicate that Russell admits no fewer than three fairly clear, quite distinct, and theoretically interrelated senses of the word "real."[1]

The primary (Parmenidean) sense is minimal. It is that to be real is not to be nothing. Russell says, "there is no such thing as the unreal" (LK 149). He says, "the unreal is simply nothing" (LK 150). This sense is more or less a negative survival of Russell's notion of being from *Principles of Mathematics*. As everything has being in this sense, it is anti-Meinongian, even though Russell considered it Meinongian in *Principles* (POM 449-53). The implied definition "To be is not to be nothing" is not circular. The first token or occurrence of "to be" is existential, but the second is copulative.

The secondary (Berkeleyan and Humean) sense is correlative. In the primary sense of "real," hallucinated or phantom particulars "have the same reality as ordinary sense-data. They have the most complete and perfect and absolute reality that anything can have" (PLA 274). Russell says that "they differ from ordinary sense-data only in the fact that they do not have the usual correlations with other things" (PLA 274). Thus the secondary sense is that to be real is to be correlated with (other) particulars (by which Russell means sense-data) in certain ordinary ways. I shall show shortly that to exist in this sense is also to be informatively identifiable. Real individuals in the secondary sense include other minds, bodies, and electrons. Particulars (sense-data) are not real in the secondary sense. Particulars are not themselves correlations.

The tertiary (Fregean) sense is formal. It concerns the logical structure of general and singular existence assertions. Russell's general conception of the tertiary sense is that "Existence is essentially a property of a propositional function" (PLA 232).

Russell not only describes these three senses of the word "real," but he describes their interrelationships as well. There are exactly three relations to describe: the primary sense's relation to the secondary sense, the primary sense's relation to the tertiary sense, and the secondary sense's relation to the tertiary sense. I shall describe these in order. This will show the unity of Russell's theories of sense-data, logical fictions, and denoting.

First, the relationship between the primary sense and the secondary sense is this. Hallucinations and phantoms are not nothing. Thus they have reality in the primary sense. So that if they are to be said to be unreal, it must be in another sense. And their being unreal in this second sense must be logically compatible with their being real in the primary sense. Being unreal in the sense of not being correlated with other particulars meets this requirement.

Second, the fundamental relation between the primary sense and the tertiary sense is this. Russell makes conformity to the primary sense a fundamental requirement of the adequacy of any analysis of the tertiary sense. He says, "In obedience to the feeling of reality, we shall insist that, in the analysis of propositions, nothing 'unreal' is to be admitted" (IMP 170). This refusal to admit anything unreal is just why existence would uninformatively apply to everything, if existence were a property of things. And that is precisely why he makes existence in the tertiary sense a property of propositional functions: so that existence assertions can be informative.

Third and last, what is the relationship between the secondary and the tertiary senses? For Russell, an ordinary thing (logical fiction) satisfies a propositional function if and only if the definite description we ordinarily use in effect indicates what correlations among particulars (sense-data) we should expect, and these correlations in fact obtain. Thus for ordinary things (logical fictions), the tertiary sense concerns the logical form of assertions that they exist, and the secondary sense concerns whether they exist.

Definitions of the different kinds of logical fiction proceed by identity conditions, that is, by defining what it is to have the same thing of that kind, at least for tables, persons, and numbers (PLA 273, 277). How can logical fictions be informatively identified for Russell? The very same particulars (sense-data) found to be correlated with an initially given particular confirm both informative existence and informative identity propositions about the logical fiction in question. In contrast, we know single particulars through acquaintance. And we know them so completely through acquaintance that all true identity statements whose subject-terms are logically proper names of particulars are tautologous and therefore uninformative (PLA 246; OD 46).

It is crucial to understand that these three senses of "exists," or three levels of Russell's theory of existence, are not three kinds of ontological status which things may have. More accurately, the primary sense does indicate a kind of ontological status, but the other two senses do not. I shall explain this for each sense in turn.

Russell believes things which exist in the primary sense "have the most complete and perfect and absolute reality that anything can have" (PLA 274). This is not only an ontological status, but it is arguably his highest (or his only) ontological status.

Russell believes that what we correctly say exists in the secondary sense is a mere logical construction or logical fiction, i.e. literally nothing. It is crucial to realize that the secondary sense is a merely conventional, or as some say nowadays, purely "nominal" sense of the word "exists." Its correct use implies no ontological commitment. In fact, its correct use implies exactly the opposite: ontological commitment is expressly denied. The most one could say is that what is correctly said to exist in the secondary sense has the negative ontological status of being nothing. This sense is meant to reflect Russell's metaphysical analyses of what ordinary people both think and call real—and Russell holds that what they believe in this regard is wrong (PLA 274). People believe that lions exist. Russell holds that their belief is false because a lion is not an entity, but a temporal series of classes of sensed and unsensed sensibilia (sense-data are sensed sensibilia). And series and classes are literally nothing. Therefore, to say truly that lions exist in the secondary sense is to deny ontological status to lions. However, Russell is willing to recognize it is *true* that, in a purely ordinary and conventional sense of "exists," lions, as opposed to unicorns, exist. And that is a very important dialectical consideration in Russell's ontology. Russell is not just paying lip service to a mere ordinary language use. He is accommodating our powerful common-sense belief in the existence of lions in a philosophically interesting way. That may be an influence of Moore's common-sense realism. But in any case it fully accords with my liberal definition of "ontology" in chapter 1. What is so interesting?—Russell analyzes this secondary sense of "exists" as purely *veridical*. That may seem anti-Parmenidean. But a lion is at least a fiction *bene fundata*, to borrow a phrase from Leibniz. Lions are cashed out in terms of lawful patterns of real sensed and unsensed sensibilia.

Existence in the tertiary sense is not an ontological status because it is not a property of things. In fact it is a property of propositional functions, and propositional functions are nothing (PLA 230–34), so it hardly confers any ontological status on them. Furthermore, the existential quantifier does not even confer ontological status on the values of the variables it binds in true statements. I believe that by the time of *Principia* Russell abandons the thesis that to be is to be the value of a variable. On my view, when we say, e.g.,

"Lions exist," the post-1910 Russell does not consider us to be ontologically committed to lions. He analyzes the "exist" as 'not always false', which has a veridical meaning-in-use, not an existential meaning-in-use. This complements the veridical secondary sense of "exists" as follows. Lions and unicorns alike have no ontological status and are nothing, but "Lions exist" is true and "Unicorns exist" is false in the common-sensical secondary sense of "exist." The tertiary sense of "exist" used in "Lions exist" merely reflects that fact. Even quantifying over sense-data in "Sense-data exist" does not ontologically commit us to sense-data, though sense-data are as real as anything can be. It is logically proper names which ontologically commit us to sense-data, since such names cannot name nothing. This is a highly controversial view of Russell's individual quantifier. Right now, I am merely explaining what my view is. I offer eight arguments for my view in chapter 5, section 2.

2. Against Meinong's Nonexistents

Butchvarov identifies Russell's *fundamental* understanding of existence as that of satisfying a propositional function. That is, Fs exist just in case the propositional function $F(x)$ is sometimes true (Butchvarov 1986: 404). This is the tertiary sense. Butchvarov then raises the question: Which objects are we to allow as arguments that satisfy propositional functions? If we wish to rule out Meinong's golden mountain, then there must be "a more fundamental notion of existence...that would allow us to tell what to count as arguments satisfying a propositional function...." (Butchvarov 1986: 405). Similarly for saying that for a simple object to exist is for it to be nameable by a logically proper name: what should we count as nameable by a logically proper name (Butchvarov 1986: 405)? May not a nonexistent simple object, a hallucinated white patch, be named by a proper name (Butchvarov 1986: 406)? Similarly for acquaintance as a criterion of existence. Similarly for other proposed definitions or criteria of existence (Butchvarov 1986: 405). What is this more fundamental notion of existence? Russell "did not even attempt to answer" this question (Butchvarov 1986: 405). I have three comments.

(1) It is important to distinguish two questions: (Q1) What is it to assert that something exists?, and (Q2) Which things exist? Russell is clearly answering (Q1) when he says that to exist is to satisfy a propositional function. Russell does not even appear to be answering (Q2). To think he does answer (Q2) when he says that is to confuse describing the logical form of existence assertions with determining the truth or falsehood of each individual assertion having that form.

(2) Russell *does* answer question (Q2). To tell *which* ordinary things to count as existing, the more fundamental sense we look to is the secondary sense.

An ordinary thing may be truly said to exist if certain correlations obtain. And all sense-data exist in the primary sense.

(3) What might Russell say about hallucinated golden mountains or nonexistent white patches? Russell has an analysis available for such cases. To see a golden mountain would be to be acquainted with a real particular, perhaps while thinking of that particular in connection with a definite description. For Russell, being acquainted with a particular (or "aspect") is the "only sense in which" even an existing mountain can be seen (KEW 74). We would see a certain nonexistent golden mountain, then, just in case the definite description in effect indicates what correlated particulars one might expect to be acquainted with in various situations, and these further particulars are not forthcoming. For Russell, to think of a golden mountain would be to think of a particular, perhaps in connection with a description. (Concepts should serve as well as descriptions do in this analysis; see PP 52ff.; IMP 168).) The hallucinated white patch is simply a "wild [uncorrelated] particular." For Russell, it is as real as anything can be. Butchvarov calls this a "primitive phenomenology" (Butchvarov 1986: 406), but this is a difficult issue. Nor need a particular be bare for us to be able to intend it apart from intending it "as" an aspect of a golden mountain (Butchvarov 1986: 414). Presumably it would have at least a golden color and a mountainous shape (KEW 64, PLA 179). In any case, a wild particular may be asserted to exist as a particular (i.e. sense-datum), if not as (an aspect of) a golden mountain (i.e. group of correlated particulars).

I return to Butchvarov. Butchvarov next criticizes Reinhardt Grossmann's suggestion that nonexistent objects cannot satisfy propositional functions because they cannot have properties. Butchvarov makes two points. First, he says this suggestion begs the question against Meinong, who would hold that the golden mountain is golden. Second, he says that the suggestion puts the cart before the horse. He says that we believe that the golden mountain lacks properties because we first believe that there is no such mountain. We do not judge that the golden mountain does not exist because we have determined that it lacks properties (Butchvarov 1986: 406). I have three comments.

(1) Butchvarov's two points do not apply to Russell's primary sense at all. The primary sense is that to exist is not to be nothing. This is the Parmenidean sense. It was Parmenides who said that you cannot say or think anything about what is not. It was Plato who asserted the contrapositive of this to say that if you can say or think anything about something, then it must be (Heath 1967: 5/524). Parmenides certainly would have agreed (Kirk 1985: 246). Nothing, so to speak, is not a thing that can have properties. Therefore, having properties is logically sufficient for being a thing which is real in the primary sense. Let me take each of Butchvarov's two points in turn for further discussion.

(2) Concerning Butchvarov's first point, it is Meinong who begs the question by assuming that there is a golden mountain in any sense beyond the

ordinary and trivial sense in which we so call or think of an object of thought or perception. This assumption may lead to a primitive phenomenology indeed! Now Meinong might argue as follows. Being an object that has properties and can be thought about is one thing. Being nothing is a second thing. And having some kind of being is a third thing. So that in between nothingness and the several kinds of being there is room, so to speak, for objects that are not nothing, yet have no specific kind of being (Meinong 1960: 79, 86). My reply to this is simply that the broadest kind of being *is* not being nothing. It is precisely with respect to the primary sense, and not at all to the secondary sense, that Meinong lacks Russell's robust sense of reality. Surely nobody claims that Meinong lacks the ability to tell hallucinations from reality, or to tell if golden mountains exist in the secondary sense (see Butchvarov 1986: 407).

In this connection, Meinong's three arguments against a third kind of being (besides his existence and subsistence) which all objects would have are surprisingly weak. They are as follows. (1) Being which is not opposed by nonbeing cannot be called being at all. (2) Such being is a mere postulate. (3) It is "the essence of assumption that it direct itself upon a being which itself does not need to be" (Meinong 1960: 85).

Concerning Meinong's first argument, the primary sense is the only sense which is genuinely and fully opposed by nonbeing. Call any kind of being an object cannot cease to have and still be an object at all, a *robust being*. Call any kind of being which is not a robust being, a *weak being*. Only a robust being is genuinely and fully opposed by nonbeing, since if an object loses a weak being, the object, which is not nothing, remains. Clearly Meinong's existence and subsistence are weak beings. Reality in the secondary sense is a weak being: particulars can gain or lose correlations. Reality in the tertiary sense is a weak being, at least if satisfaction of propositional functions can be gained or lost. Only reality in the primary sense is a robust being.[2] *Pace* Butchvarov, Russell's robust sense of reality does *not* consist in being able to tell unreal unicorns from robustly real horses. The 1918 Russell holds exactly the opposite. It is hallucinations which are robust beings. Correlatively "real" things are weak beings, and are real in a merely conventional sense. In fact, Russell deems them *logical fictions*. Russell would scarcely deem his own logical fictions robustly real. One must not be misled by Russell's *casual* example of unicorns as unreal and horses as real (IMP 168–70); I suspect it is just this text which misled Butchvarov (Butchvarov 1994: 42).

When Meinong speaks of requiring that being must be opposed by nonbeing, he does not really mean that. What he really wants is a *classificatory* sense of being which objects can have or not have. Without such a sense his theory of objects beyond being and nonbeing obviously would not have a chance. And this is just what limits Meinong to considering only weak beings. So for his theory of objects to succeed, Meinong must be *actively committed* to lacking a robust sense of being. After all, what kind of being is it that objects can cease to have, yet continue on their merry way? Could a weak being like that ever be the very being of an object? Then Russell was right. Meinong does lack a robust sense of reality.

Concerning Meinong's second argument, it is not a "postulate" but an *a priori* necessity that every object having any *Sosein* have being in Russell's primary sense as well. The famous independence of objects consists only in our being able to attend to their *Sosein* without attending to their primary being.

Concerning Meinong's third argument, the proper role of assumption is with respect to the secondary sense of the word "real." And this role is not even possible without the assumed object, A, minimally having reality in the primary sense, so that our assumption is not about nothing.

(3) I turn to Butchvarov's second point. Can we tell if something is real by telling if it has properties? Think of looking at an orange on your desk and telling whether it is real or hallucinated by determining whether it is really orange and round. It cannot be done! But this fact would pertain for Russell only to the secondary sense of reality. And to go on and question whether it is real in the *primary* sense of reality is self-defeating. Of course it must exist in the sense of not being nothing, if it has properties.

3. Is Existence a Classificatory Concept?

Butchvarov now moves to his deeper criticism of Russell.

Part One. Russell's more fundamental conception of existence seems to be: CON. All objects exist. Russellians take CON as beyond argument, and thus beg Meinong's question.

Part Two. If Russell's view, CON, is a substantive one, then the fundamental notion of existence which it uses must be a genuine concept (Butchvarov 1986: 409). But it is reasonable that "nothing can count as a genuine concept unless we can make sense of what it would be for it to *fail* to apply to something" (Butchvarov 1986: 410; compare Findlay 1963: 47). But then Russell's position simply unravels, for to admit this much is to admit that Meinong's view of existence as something which objects may or may not be said to have is correct. It is but a short step to employ our ordinary notion of reality to "the objects of our thought, imagination, dreams," and judge that many of them obviously do not exist (Butchvarov 1986: 411).

Part Three. CON appears to be obviously true to many philosophers because of a certain special feature of the concept of existence: it does not stand for anything, "real or unreal, individual or a property or a relation" (Butchvarov 1986: 412). That being so, "we do not understand how the concept of existence can be classificatory" (Butchvarov 1986: 412), and mistakenly considering it to be not classificatory, we believe it must apply to all objects. The only alternative would be to apply it to no objects, which is absurd.

Part Four. Butchvarov's claim that the concept of existence is transcendental, i.e., is classificatory but does not stand for anything, is "suggested" (Butchvarov 1986: 412) by Kant's argument that "being" is not a real predicate, since in thinking of 100 thalers, and in then thinking of the 100 thalers as existing, nothing is added to our first thought, not even a single coin. I have three comments.

(1) Neither Russell nor Butchvarov takes CON as beyond argument. Butchvarov himself argues against it in *Part Two*. Concerning reality in the primary sense, Russell takes CON as resting on the fact that "the unreal is simply nothing" (ONA 150) And Russell takes that fact as resting in turn on considerations about perception, description, property, and logical form (PLA 223–24, 233–44; compare IMP 172–73).

Concerning reality in the secondary sense, Russell would *reject* CON. Surely the concept of being correlated with other particulars *is* a classificatory concept. And existence in the secondary sense is not a non-property, but a relational property.

Concerning the tertiary sense of "real," Russell again clearly *rejects* CON. And it is this *rejection* of CON that leads Russell to hold that the word "exist" in the tertiary sense stands for no property of *things*, but for a property of *propositional functions*.

(2) Russell might well accept Kant's argument for each of Russell's three senses of the word "exists," since in none of them can the concept of existence be intelligibly added to the concept of a possible $100. (i) For Russell the concept of even an imaginary $100 already *is* a concept of something that exists in the primary sense, namely a wild particular. (ii) Concerning the secondary sense, the concept of an imaginary $100 essentially excludes, while the concept of a secondarily real $100 essentially includes, a correlativeness-content (perhaps in Kantian terms, a synthesis-of-appearances-content). Thus existence in the secondary sense is not addable to the concept of an imaginary $100, since doing so would *essentially change* the concept to that of an actual $100. (iii) Russell's only explicit discussion of possibility and actuality concerns the tertiary sense. Here the concept of a possible $100 is *the very same concept* as the concept of an actual $100. Namely, both are the concept of (the propositional function "x is $100" as) being sometimes true (PLA 231; compare IMT 37, 170, 182).

(3) The argument of *Part One* can be applied in turn to the concept of a classificatory concept. If Butchvarov's claim that the concept of existence is a classificatory concept is a substantive one, one that "*means* something" (Butchvarov 1986: 409) "a fact of philosophical importance, one that is worth arguing about" (Butchvarov 1986: 410), then Butchvarov's *concept of a classificatory concept* cannot count as a "genuine" concept "unless we can make sense of what it would be for it to *fail* to apply [to a concept]" (Butchvarov 1986: 410). But then, to continue Butchvarov's argument, this is as much as to admit that there may be concepts which are not classificatory concepts. Thus

Butchvarov's position simply unravels. Once this is admitted, it might be but a short step to finding concepts which in fact are not classificatory concepts. Perhaps the concept of primary existence is just such a concept, as well as Butchvarov's concept of "'there are' in its unrestricted sense" (Butchvarov 1986: 419). There is, of course, no difference between a genuine concept and a concept.

Butchvarov says in a later paper that the concept of a concept (call it *C*) is classificatory, since only some things are concepts (Butchvarov 1988: 166). I agree. This is an obvious fact. But I was concerned with the concept of a classificatory concept (call it *C**). Call Butchvarov's hypothesis that all concepts are classificatory, *H*. Now on *H*, *C** must be classificatory. And *C** is trivially classificatory in that not every thing is even a concept. But this feature more properly belongs instead to *C*. Call the view that the proper nature of *C** is to describe concepts as classificatory, *N*. Now on *N*, *H* logically entails that some concepts may be nonclassificatory. And this is a *reductio ad absurdum* of *H*.

What is our conception of a concept? Most basically a concept (or an ordinary concept) is something that can apply to more than one thing. It lets us understand things as being similar, as having something in common. A concept which does not even attempt to provide such understanding is simply unworthy of the name "concept." Now the feature of being classificatory, i.e., of possibly *not* applying to some thing, is obviously less fundamental. Having it does not even seem to be logically necessary to being a concept.

Even worse, as Frege implies, we cannot always tell in advance what the limits of applicability of a concept are (FA 1). Should we stop regarding as concepts what we always took to be concepts, or should we start regarding as concepts things which we never took to be concepts before, just because we now discover or destroy limits to the truth of some general proposition about, say, arithmetic? This is just what Butchvarov's regimentation (restriction of concepts to classificatory concepts) would require us to do.

Butchvarov's regimentation may be based on Spinoza's important dictum that to determine is to limit and negate. But I have seen no argument in Butchvarov or Spinoza even attempting to show that all concepts must be sortally determining. And it is unconvincing to base what purports to be a decisive refutation of Russell on a mere *ad hoc* regimentation.

How much should we regiment concepts and why? Frege and Russell require all concepts to be determinate, that is, to conform to the logical law of the excluded middle BL 84, PM 39; see PP 52, 72, 88). Why?—Because this ensures rigorous proofs and classifications. Butchvarov's restriction goes far beyond this, though proofs and classifications are already maximally rigorous on the Frege-Russell regimentation. What, then, is its purpose?

The Frege-Russell requirement also fulfills Spinoza's dictum. For every Fregean or Russellian concept which sortally determines also limits and negates.

That is, it is possible for their sortal concepts not to apply to anything. Again, what is the purpose of adding Butchvarov's restriction?

Are only classificatory concepts informative? Are all other concepts pointless? No. In "The Limits of Ontological Analysis," Butchvarov himself suggests that analogy is the deepest kind of understanding (Butchvarov 1974: 21–22). Merely assimilating two things, or finding that they fall under the same concept, tells us something positive about what they are, or at least what they are like. Surely this is the basic informative function of all concepts, whether classificatory or nonclassificatory. Classificatory concepts merely add the further information that not all things need fall under them. Now, saying positively what a thing is tells us far more about it than saying negatively what it is not. (That is why it is a principle of adequate definition that one should not define negatively what one can define positively.) And this fundamental kind of positive information is not given by classificatory concepts as such, but by *positive* concepts, which may be classificatory or nonclassificatory. Negative information is given by negative concepts as such, or better, Frege argues, by negated thoughts—and by classificatory concepts only in the indirect sense of implying that not all things need fall under them. Some nonclassificatory concepts give positive information, and others negative information. But none gives the merely indirect sort of negative information classificatory concepts do. That positive concepts can be hard to distinguish from negative ones—Frege cites *lives forever* and *nonmortal* in "Negation"—does not detract from my point. The concept *red* is paradigmatically positive, and the concept *nonred* paradigmatically negative.

Are kind-monisms, theories that all things (must) belong to one metaphysical category, uninformative? Hardly. Their informative content comes from opposing kind-polyadisms and also each other. Similarly for Spinozistic (necessitarian) thing-monisms.

Many know that Frege says in *Foundations*, "The content of a concept diminishes as its extension increases; if its extension becomes all-embracing, its content vanishes altogether." Few recall that Frege admits extensionless, uninstantiable concepts, such as *square circle* and *wooden iron*, right in *Foundations*. As Frege explains in *Posthumous Writings*, "there is nothing at all wrong with a concept's being empty" (FA 40, 87; PW 122). And Russell would allow the corresponding propositional functions in logic.

Frege's inverse relation of intension and extension makes sense if we construe extension as increasing in terms of logical classes of objects instead of individual objects. If all and only red objects are round, diminishing *red and round* to *red* does not increase the number of objects falling under the concept, but rather the logical extension (compare Stanley Jevons, quoted in Hill 1991: 110).

For Frege, there are many concepts under which only one object falls. And among these concepts, there are many under which only one object can fall, such as the concept of being identical with Plato. On Frege's persuasive view, a concept is a property that maps all items of a given type onto truth values in a specific way. Thus a concept, as such, is neither a classificatory property nor even something which more than one item can have in common. All objects are "identifiable" and "determinate." The two words inform by denoting representatively identical concepts which map objects onto truth values in a specific way. They even inform differently by expressing different senses. For Russell the words have different meanings-in-use. For one could believe that objects are identifiable, yet not believe they are determinate.

In chapters 1 and 2, I distinguished being factually informative from being novelly informative. (All Frege's informative identity statements remain factually informative even after they cease to be novelly informative for some or all of their audience.) Now A. J. Ayer points out in *Language, Truth and Logic* that even analytic statements (tautologies) can be novel (surprising). Thus it is clear that nonclassificatory concepts can yield novel informativeness. Frege would agree (FA 100–1). And as the Glossary at the end of Arthur Pap's *Semantics and Necessary Truth* well shows, "analytic" is said in many ways—and on some of them, statements whose logical predicates are nonclassificatory are *synthetic*, and therefore also factually informative. And for Quine, all statements, even ones with nonclassificatory predicates, have *empirical* content!

Daniel Barwick finds nonclassificatory concepts pointless (Barwick 1994: 10). Barwick overlooks the many arguments I gave over the last eleven paragraphs, showing that nonclassificatory concepts are "pointless" only for classifying things. Not every kind of genuine information is classificatory. Nonclassificatory concepts *are* informative. Indeed, only they *can* convey information about what all things must have in common. For *that* purpose, it is *classificatory* concepts which are pointless. Observe how point depends on purpose.

Suppose we admit that genuine concepts can be nonclassificatory. The issue is then whether in particular the concept of existence is classificatory. But there seems to be no reason why existence in the primary sense should (or even explanation of how it could) be classificatory. How, then, could Russell's position, CON, concerning this primary sense unravel?

I proceed to the last part of Butchvarov's 1986 article. Butchvarov asserts that the concept of identity is a transcendental concept more fundamental than that of existence (Butchvarov 1986: 416). He then gives this elucidation: For an object to exist is for it to be identifiable indefinitely many times (Butchvarov 1986: 417–18). And many objects do not exist, since they are not indefinitely identifiable.

I have two comments.

(1) Even accepting that many objects are nonexistent in the sense that they are not indefinitely identifiable, this would concern at most the secondary sense of the word "exist." There is no reason why it should, or explanation of how

it could, concern the primary sense. In the primary sense, such objects are as real as anything can be.

(2) On Butchvarov's own understanding of a genuine claim, the claim that to exist is to be informatively identifiable raises possibilities that (i) some things might be informatively identifiable but not exist, and (ii) some things that exist might not be informatively identifiable (compare Hamlyn 1984: 159). And from possibility (ii) it may be but a short step to finding such things, at least in the primary sense of "exists." Russell's particulars, of course, come immediately to mind. For informative identities are needed only for logical fictions.[3] Thus Butchvarov's position unravels again.

Russell's correlative sense of "real" resembles Hume's, and Russell's logical fictions resemble Hume's fictions (Hume 1973: 107–8, 193ff.). This correlative sense is also found in Berkeley for ordinary physical things (Berkeley 1965a: sects. 30–36). But surely Butchvarov's own entities, which "are" indefinitely many objects, are a variant as well (Butchvarov, 1979). Similarly for Hector-Neri Castañeda's "consubstantiations" of indefinitely many "guises" (Castañeda 1983; Castañeda 1974). In all five of these ontologies the very ideas, impressions, sense-data, objects, or guises which constitute "real" things in some correlative sense, providing them with all the positive content they have, are also the basis for their informative identifiability. *Pace* Butchvarov, ought we not to apply Russell's robust sense of reality to Butchvarov's own objects? Like guises and sense-data, they differ from each other, and are thus not nothing. And as to the whole "point" of Butchvarov's paper, which I supposedly "missed" (Barwick 1994: 3, quoting Butchvarov 1988: 166), that existence is "*'of course'*" a classificatory concept, both have missed *my* whole point: that it is unacceptable to treat Russell as having a single nonclassificatory concept of existence when he has a rich and sophisticated theory of at least *three* senses of the word "exists" such that existence in the most fundamental sense is "*'of course'*" *not* classificatory, and such that existence in the secondary sense *is* classificatory.

4. Russell and Parmenides

This book is not about Plato's *Parmenides* or, for that matter, Parmenides himself. Further, this book is concerned not with theological, neo-Platonic or mystical theories based on Plato or Parmenides, but with realist theories and logical theories based on their thoughts. I will only mention in passing that Russell discusses Plato and Parmenides concerning mysticism in "Mysticism and Logic" (MAL 9–16, 21–22). In 1914 Russell wrote, "It makes me realize more than ever the greatness of the pre-Socratic philosophers: Parmenides really invented metaphysical mysticism in the West" (Russell 1914; see MAL 13–14). Parmenides invented "the mysticism which may be called 'logical' because it is embodied in theories on logic. This form of mysticism, which appears, so far as the West is concerned, to have originated with Parmenides, dominates the reasoning of all the great mystical metaphysicians from his day to that of Hegel and his modern disciples" (MAL 13). But for our purposes, just substitute "monism" for "mysticism." Also, there is a definite resemblance between Parmenides' mysticism and the mysticism of Wittgenstein's *Tractatus*. For as has been known a long time, Parmenides' own thesis that you cannot speak or think about nothing condemns itself; and his philosophy largely consists of pronouncements on things which he himself deems unreal topics. As G. E. L. Owen says:

> So, to repeat that memorable image from Wittgenstein, Parmenides' argument is a ladder to be climbed up and thrown away....For it was just that cry of 'unthinkable, unsayable' that compelled Parmenides to treat his own arguments as stages to be passed and dismissed, since those arguments were compelled to use the very expressions branded unusable. (Owen 1974: 275, 278)

Indeed, saying "*a* exists," in the sense of predicating a property of existence of object *a*, would seem "unthinkable, unsayable" for all four analysts. Even the later Wittgenstein makes existence a second-level predicate (RFM 186/V #135). But I must proceed now to plain realist and logical theories.

The typical realist interpretation of Parmenides is that he is a monist. His One is the ultimate reality, Being itself. This attributes to him a monism based on considerations of language and thought, sometimes called logical monism. The typical logical interpretation of Parmenides, with which we are mainly concerned, is that he holds that one cannot speak or think of nothing, and that anything that is, is one. It too is based on considerations of language and thought. Both interpretations are compatible with each other. But the logical interpretation typically leads to some sort of metaphysical atomism, or to some logico-linguistic theory of how to talk of the existence and nonexistence of things, or to both. Parmenides led Plato both to an atomistic theory of elements in the *Theaetetus* and to a logico-linguistic theory in the *Sophist*, as well as to the world of forms in general, and to the most real form—the form of all forms, or idea of the Good—in particular. What we should keep in mind is that on both the realist and the logical interpretations of Parmenides, to be is to be one thing. I shall take Parmenides as the prototype of 'no entity without identity' ontology.

Nicholas Griffin says that Russell's three favorite pre-Socratic philosophers were Heraclitus, Parmenides, and Zeno (Griffin 1992: 477 n.3). Heraclitus was the chief philosophical opponent of Parmenides in antiquity; Zeno was the chief student and disciple of Parmenides. Russell is known to have read Plato's *Parmenides* in January-April 1899, and wrote that he found Plato's dialogues "really delightful" as early as December 1892 (Griffin 1991: 25, quoting a letter dated December 4, 1892 from Russell to his uncle Rollo Russell; and 335 n.16). Harold Joachim recommended John Burnet's *Early Greek Philosophy* to Russell probably in September 1892 (Griffin 1991: 26). Russell found Zeno's arguments "all immeasurably subtle and profound" (MAL 63).

A casual search reveals references to Parmenides scattered through Russell's post-1900 publications as follows: KEW 54, 131–32, 141; MAL 13, 15, 21, 22; HWP 32, 48–52, 53, 56, 58, 61, 63, 64, 65, 68, 69, 70, 71, 92, 105, 114, 119–20, 121, 127–28, 129, 149, 152, 233, 288, 476, 571, 595, 731, 732, 742, 758, 786; LK 370. References to Zeno include: POM 347–53, 355, 358; KEW 103, 107, 107n, 129–43; MAL 52, 63–64, 65–66, 69; OP 262; HWP 64, 92, 127, 804–6. There is even a reference to Plato's *Parmenides* (IMP 138). These references suggest that Parmenides is never far from Russell's thinking.

More important are the arguments and theories of Russell which may be justly called Parmenidean. Russell says, "What makes Parmenides historically important is that he invented a form of metaphysical argument that, in one form or another, is to be found in most subsequent metaphysicians down to and including Hegel. He is often said to have invented logic, but what he really invented was metaphysics based on logic" (HWP 48). Russell classifies Parmenides as the first philosopher to "infer properties of the world from properties of language," and counts himself, with appropriate qualifications, as being just such a philosopher (IMT 341–42).[4]

Russell subscribed to six Parmenidean theories of being in his post-1900 career: (1) being is an entity, 1903; (2) being is the world of universals, 1912; (3) being is general timelessness, 1914; (4) primary being is transcendentally necessary for logical atoms, 1918; (5) primary being is transcendentally necessary for object words, 1940–48; (6) qualities are substantive (atoms), 1940–59. I have described these theories in some detail elsewhere (Dejnožka 1990). They show a trend, moving from the realist Parmenidean understanding of being as an entity in its own right to various forms of Parmenidean atomism, or even to merely logico-linguistic theories of our talk of existence. While this is a trend in Russell's ontological thinking, it may also be fairly described as a trend in what he found of value in Parmenides.

In theories (4) and (5), Russell rejects literal being but accepts what may be called "transcendental being," which is literally nothing, since it is expressed by the existential quantifier, which is a second-level propositional function, and propositional functions are nothing. It is asserted in "$(\exists x)(x = a)$," which is always true where "a" is a logically proper name. The existence of a particular is transcendentally necessary with respect to thought and language. That is, it is logically necessary that for us to be acquainted with or to be able to name a particular, it exist in the primary sense. An acquaintance logically must be an acquaintance *with* something; a logically proper name logically must be a name *of* something. Russell gives at least twenty-three arguments for the transcendental Parmenideanism of theories (4) and (5) (Dejnožka 1990: 403–6). Perhaps his most penetrating argument is a twenty-fourth one, a vicious regress of mere appearances argument for the reality of that with which we are acquainted (HWP 129).

Russell quotes Parmenides as saying, "Thou canst not know what is not—that is impossible—nor utter it; for it is the same thing that can be thought and that can be....It needs must be that what can be thought and spoken of is; for it is possible for it to be, and it is not possible for what is nothing to be" (MAL 13–14; HWP 45). The 1945 Russell says:

> The essence of [Parmenides'] argument is: When you think, you think of something; when you use a name, it must be the name of something. Therefore both thought and language require objects outside themselves....This is the first example in philosophy of an argument from thought and language to the world at large. It cannot of course be accepted as valid, but it is worth while to see what element of truth it contains....[The element of truth is that] it is obvious that, in most cases, we are not speaking of words, but of what the words mean. And this brings us back to the argument of Parmenides, that if a word can be used significantly it must mean something, not nothing, and therefore what the word means must in some sense exist... (HWP 49)

Thus Russell sees Parmenides himself as the first transcendental Parmenidean. Russell sees the whole substance tradition as based on Parmenides' argument:

> What subsequent philosophy, down to quite modern times, accepted from Parmenides, was not the impossibility of all change, which was too violent a paradox, but the indestructibility of substance. (HWP 52)

Many ancient philosophers advanced forms of atomism to account for change in the face of Parmenides' argumentation. Russell himself can be quickly connected to this tradition. For his logical atomism in 1914–18, neutral monism in 1921, and theory of qualities in 1940 are all forms of substantival atomism. And Russell's sense-data (particulars) are explicit substance substitutes (PLA 201–4). To borrow a phrase from José Benardete, they are "tiny packets of Parmenidean being." Russell says, "The essence of a substance, from the symbolic point of view, is that it can only be named" (Russell 1971a: 337).

G. S. Kirk, J. E. Raven, and M. Schofield confirm that the thesis that you cannot talk or think about nothing is a genuine part of Parmenides' thought, and "has exercised a powerful influence on many philosophers, from Plato to Russell" (Kirk 1985: 246).

Now, Charles H. Kahn suggests that Parmenides was primarily concerned with the veridical use of "is," not with the existential use. Kahn thinks that probably the Islamic and medieval substance theorists, and certainly the substance theorists after Descartes, saw Parmenides as Russell does, as primarily concerned with the existential use of "is." But Kahn thinks that such a view is out of date:

> Summarizing our positive results so far, we can say: in Greek ontology, from Parmenides on, the question of Being is a question as to what reality must be like—or what the world must be like—in order for knowledge and true (or false) discourse to be possible. It is, in effect, the first question which Wittgenstein set out to answer in the *Tractatus*: How must the world be structured if logic and scientific language are to be possible?....[T]he veridical starting point for Greek theories of Being or reality anticipates in a rather striking way the contemporary standpoint which (following and developing certain ideas of Tarski) takes the notion of truth for sentences as basic in any theory of meaning or knowledge. (Kahn 1982: 14, 16)

This is the veridical message Kahn finds in Parmenides, which Kahn sharply separates from Russell's and Quine's quantificational logic, specifically from the existential quantifier, which Kahn seems to believe expresses the existential sense of "is." But on my interpretation of Russell, only the tertiary sense of "exists" is expressed by that quantifier. I called that sense Fregean. I did not call it Parmenidean. But perhaps I should have, if Kahn is right, since the so-called existential quantifier really expresses a veridical meaning-in-use, 'not always false'. I sharply distinguished that tertiary sense from the primary sense of "exists." It was only the primary sense that I called Parmenidean. That sense is existential. It implies that logically proper names have transcendentally necessary ontological commitments. But that sense also concerns the structure of the world. It concerns the logical atoms from which the world is constructed. Kahn's own description of Parmenides seems imbued with transcendental Parmenideanism of this very sort. Kahn himself is showing that on my interpretation of Russell, Russell's primary sense of "exists" is Parmenidean, just as Kirk, Raven, and Schofield said it was. Kahn depicts Russell as having only one existential use of "is," and finds it in Russell's individual quantifier. Kahn overlooks Russell's primary, Parmenidean sense of "exists," misses that Russell's individual quantifier is merely veridical, and also fails to see how Russell's tertiary quantificational sense of "is," while it is sharply distinguished from the primary sense, is intimately related to, and ultimately based on, that primary sense. In fact, all four great analysts are contextualists making the truth of sentences prior to the reference of their constituent expressions. Thus if Kahn is right, then he is actually bringing Russell and the other analysts closer to Parmenides than ever. See chapter 2, note 13 on Frege's contextualism, and chapter 6, note 8 on Russell's. Indeed, some of the analysts accept even wider holisms than that.[5]

The other great analysts seem to be neo-Parmenideans. None of the great analysts admits nonexistent objects. Significantly, "nothing" is analyzed away as 'not anything' by all four great analysts. Even the later Wittgenstein makes existence a second-level predicate (RFM 186/V #135). Frege requires that every true or false statement have a denoting logical subject (SR 62–63). This is the traditional principle that a proposition must say something about something. Quine's thesis that to be is to be the value of a variable smacks of the Parmenidean in a similar way. The *Tractatus* admits a neo-Parmenidean logical atomism. Wittgenstein says that his objects and Russell's individuals were Plato's primary elements (PI #46; see *Theaetetus* 201–2). And Plato's primary elements were a direct response to Parmenides. I suggest that even the later Wittgenstein has a theory about language and extralinguistic ordinary phenomena such that genuine reference, by expressions associated with paradigmatic criteria of identity, is not to nothing. Fiction is a language-game that is played, but it is a derivative game. Nonexistent objects would be a bewitchment of grammar.

But the analysts break ranks on admitting a Zenonian changeless world. I suspect that Frege's concrete objects are fairly traditional physical substances which change their accidental properties and move in three-dimensional space. Frege belongs to the world of classical physics. Indeed, he defines "concrete object" in terms of causal power or capacity to act. This is not to mention that Frege admits selves who act, hopefully in accordance with their duties, in "The Thought." I discuss Russell's changeless world in chapter 5, section 8. The post-Einstein worlds of Russell and Quine owe much to Hermann Minkowski's four-dimensional space-time. But Quine says, "Time as a fourth dimension is still time; and differences along the fourth dimension are still changes" (TT 10). Viewed as four-dimensional, all physical objects are processes, i.e., events (WO 171; Benardete 1993: 269). For Quine, what the fourth dimension calls for is not literal changelessness, but only speaking and "thinking tenselessly" (PQ 293). Quine rejects Zeno's paradoxes as fallacious (Quine 1976b: 3, 9, 16; see WO 172, TT 178), and assays actions such as walking and chewing gum at the same time as one event (TT 11–12). Last, the *Tractatus* might seem easily read as Zenonian because it rejects causation (T 6.37). But it does not really address the traditional problem of change. Changes or events might qualify as Tractarian objects. There is mention of velocities of particles (T 6.3751), but no discussion of how to analyze them into elementary states of affairs (see Black 1970: 347). There are remarks about time and processes, but no suggestion of how to analyze them either, except for "We cannot compare a process with 'the passage of time'—there is no such thing—but only with another process (such as the working of a chronometer" (T 6.3611; see Black 1970: 361). Richard M. McDonough argues that the Tractarian "Wittgenstein's account of the logical propositions can be used to resolve traditional paradoxes in the philosophy of logic [including] a logical version of the Paradox of Achilles and the Tortoise" (McDonough 1986: 91). But even if that is so, there is no evidence that

Wittgenstein even saw that he could resolve the Achilles. The later Wittgenstein would accept ordinary talk of change; and he accepts ordinary talk of our doing things. He undoubtedly views traditional theories of causation and agency as bewitchments of grammar, and also the traditional problem of change itself: What remains the same through change? Most tellingly, he probably would view Zeno (and to a large extent Parmenides) as bewitched by grammar (compare Pitcher 1964: 190 [Zeno], 201–3 [Heidegger and Sartre on nothingness as a kind of thing], 204–5 [Plato's *Parmenides*]). This breaking of ranks suggests that Parmenides influenced the great analysts more deeply than Zeno did.

As to the modal dimension of Parmenides' thought, I have already discussed Russell's elimination of modality elsewhere (Dejnožka 1990). Here I can give only a brief sketch of what I list as theories (13), (20), and (26) in chapter 5.

Russell accepts a form of logical fatalism. Just as the past cannot be other than it was, the present cannot be other than it is, and the future cannot be other than it will be. Otherwise they violate the law of noncontradiction (MAL 146–47). Nothing can be altered. This neo-Parmenidean existence-identity connection is theory (26) in chapter 5. It is eliminative of modality, since the law of noncontradiction involves no modal notions.

Russell has a sophisticated eliminative theory of modality with three levels corresponding to his three senses of "exists" or "is real."

In the primary, Parmenidean sense of "exists," sense-data (particulars) exist. They are not literally necessary beings. Their existence is logically contingent. There is only the transcendental necessity that acquaintance must be acquaintance *with* something, and that logically proper names must be names *of* something. I argue that logically proper names are Kripkean rigid designators (Dejnožka 1990: 395). If so, then sense-data have trans-world identities. This reference-rigid identity connection is a natural development of Parmenidean transcendental necessity. It is theory (20) in chapter 5.

In the secondary, Berkeleyan and Humean sense of "exists," logical fictions are truly said to exist. This is a purely conventional or nominal, yet common-sensical, sense of "exists." Ontological status is clearly and positively rejected. Logical fictions are nothing. In this sense we may conventionally say truly that ordinary bodies exist. But bodies are analyzed away as classes of correlated sensed and unsensed sensibilia. This gives rise to combinatorial possibilities. This is just neo-Parmenidean atomism. Again, the very same particulars found to be correlated with an initially given particular confirm both informative existence and informative identity propositions about the logical fiction in question.

In the tertiary, Fregean sense of "exists," existence is a second-level property of propositional functions. Existence is analyzed away as the veridical notion 'not always false' Here Russell analyzes possibility away as the very same veridical notion 'not always false'. Propositional function $F(x)$ is possible with respect to x =Df $F(x)$ is not always false. Propositional function $F(x)$

is impossible with respect to $x =$ Df $F(x)$ is always false. Call this theory MDL. The neo-Parmenidean idea is that since there are no merely possible objects, something true of all things is, for that reason alone, true of all possible things. MDL banishes modality from logic. Only veridical notions are used. Yet MDL *functions* as a modal logic. For Russell, a modal logic is as a modal logic does.

Russell uses possible-worlds-talk in many published works, and also describes MDL in many published works. These two sets of works overlap both in time period and in membership. Raymond Bradley sees MDL as contradicting Russell's use of possible-worlds-talk because if there are no merely possible objects, then no possible world can have 'alien objects', i.e. things not found in the actual world (R. Bradley 1992: 16–17, 25–28, 56–60). Bradley forgets that we can have *knowledge by description* of alien objects. With more charity than Bradley, I gloss Russell's possible-worlds-talk as a nonmodal combinatorial atomism (Dejnožka 1990: 395; modal combinatorial atomism was an *erratum*).

Russell's possible worlds have no ontological status. They are nothing. I gloss them as a special kind of logical fiction. Where Russell deems a vector of motion "doubly a fiction" because motions are fictions and vectors of motion are not even motions but mere creatures of analysis (POM 474), a vector of motion in a merely possible world is triply a fiction, lacking ontological status on three counts. To Russell, possible worlds are merely "Leibnizian phraseology" (IMP 192). This is theory (13) in chapter 5.

Since the propositional function $x = x$ is true for all values (PM *24.01), it is necessary in MDL. That is, self-identity is necessary in MDL.

MDL would be a very natural elimination of modality for many analytic philosophers. One need only accept quantification and reject merely possible objects. Quine has very kindly written me, "Certainly I have no objection to necessity and possibility when interpreted in Russell's way. But our colleagues in modal logic will not settle for anything so innocent" (Quine 1990b; compare Quine 1987b: 114; Quine 1987c: 292; PT 30, 73; FLPV 4). As to the logical howlers MDL may seem innocently to commit, see my *Erkenntnis* essay (1990).[6]

There are several other responses to Parmenides which are perhaps unique to Russell. In *Principles of Mathematics*, Russell says,

> It is plain that there is such a concept as *nothing*, and that in some sense nothing is something. In fact, the proposition "nothing is not nothing" is undoubtedly capable of an interpretation which makes it true—a point which gives rise to the contradictions discussed in Plato's *Sophist*. (POM 73, 75)

Russell is not admitting a Heideggerian *das Nicht* here. "*Nothing* is a denoting concept, which denotes nothing. The concept which denotes is of course not nothing, *i.e.* it is not denoted by itself. The proposition which looks so paradoxical means no more than this: *Nothing*, the denoting concept, is not nothing, *i.e.* is not what [it] itself denotes" (POM 75).

For the 1914–21 Russell, no doubt doughnut holes and other privations simply go the way of logical fictions trod by doughnuts themselves. Presumably privations' identity conditions are similarly logically smooth.

Russell's humorous anecdote, "The Metaphysician's Nightmare," tells of one soul's attempt to avoid the devilish power of the negative by saying everything in positive terms, i.e., without using words like "not" (Russell 1954a). This is a reference to Russell's "minimum vocabulary" approach to ontological commitment (HK 79, 257–66).

If we cannot do without a negation sign in our minimum vocabulary, there is Russell's effort to portray negation itself as, on the most basic level, a positive inhibitor of other positive forces (IMT 211–12; HK 121–25).

Russell himself regarded the most difficult issue to be the need to admit negative facts, such as the fact that the Empire State Building is not made of wood, in a complete description of the world (PLA 215). For the 1918 Russell, negative facts are just as real as any other kinds of facts (PLA 183–84, 211–16). This may sound anti-Parmenidean. But Russell admits no nonexistent facts described by false statements. The negative facts he admits are described by negative true statements, such as "The Empire State Building is not wooden." As Herbert Hochberg says, "'Negative' entities are one thing; nonexistents are another" (Hochberg 1978: 294). Thus when Russell speaks of "negative existence," he really means "the existence of negative facts" (PLA 215).

Russell holds that the only difference between a positive fact and a negative fact is not any constituent, but a feature of its form called a positive or negative *quality* (Russell 1971f: 287). Russell says little about the qualities of negative facts and how they relate to the constituents of such facts. In fact, he says that the difference between positive and negative facts is "ultimate and irreducible." (Russell 1971f: 287; PLA 216). The origin of this theory of positive and negative qualities is Plato's response to Parmenides (*Sophist* 263A).

Hochberg adds, "Russell held it to be obvious that we are not acquainted with negative facts," (Hochberg 1978: 296; see Russell 1971f: 317; IMT 81–83, 92–93, 162–64; HK 121–26, 132–37). But I am sure Hochberg would agree that Russell holds we can identify negative facts, and can identify their constituents, structure, and qualities, in thought and discourse. How else could Russell give examples or assert his own theory?

In 1940, Russell denies that there are nonmental negative facts, and restricts negative facts to the mental world, i.e., to our talk and thought about the world (IMT 92–93; see 73–76, 81–86). This is a further accommodation to Parmenides which perhaps only postpones the problem Parmenides raises. Russell discusses negative facts again in 1948 (HK 121–26, 131, 493, 133, 504).

5. Facts and Propositions

Our main ontological interest is not in negative facts, but in the existence and identity of facts and propositions generally. I shall begin with a quick sketch of facts. Russell admits facts as early as 1912 and as late as 1948 (PP 123, 129–30, 136–38; HK 133–34, 143, 498). I shall confine my remarks to facts in his 1918 "The Philosophy of Logical Atomism."

Facts are real; they are part of Russell's robust sense of reality. Russell says that "facts belong to the objective world....[Facts], just as much as particular tables and chairs, are part of the real world" (PLA 183). Russell's metaphor for the robust reality of particulars is famous: "Logic...must no more admit a unicorn than zoology can; for logic is concerned with the real world just as truly as zoology, though with its more abstract and general features....A robust sense of reality is very necessary in framing a correct analysis of propositions about unicorns..." (IMP 169–70). But few realize he uses the same metaphor for the robust reality of facts: "I am concerned with a 'zoo' containing all the different forms that facts may have....In accordance with the sort of realistic bias that I should put into all study of metaphysics, I should always wish to be engaged in the study of some actual fact or set of facts, and it seems to me that that is so in logic just as much as it is in zoology" (PLA 216). Nonetheless facts are not entities, i.e., complex particular existing things (Russell 1971a: 337; PLA 182). All facts are complex; but there are no complex entities (PLA 190–93, 202). Indeed, atomic facts (facts which have no constituent facts) are logically prior to particulars, which Russell defines as "terms of relations in atomic facts" (PLA 199). This is the metaphysical basis of Russell's context principle. Particulars are the substance substitutes (PLA 201–4). But facts, like particulars, are complete. Indeed, in a sense facts contribute even more completeness than particulars do, since the main argument for facts is that we cannot describe what the world is like without admitting them; a mere list of entities cannot tell us how the world is structured, i.e. how things are related (PLA 183, 191–92).

Throughout this book I shall follow popular usage in speaking of Russell's analyzing ordinary things such as chairs into temporal series of classes of sensed and unsensed sensibilia. This is the one time I shall point out that that popular usage is not strictly correct. Russell *defines* chairs as series of classes, and *analyzes* chairs as complicated facts. He sharply distinguishes definition from analysis. One defines symbols; one analyzes the world. Definition is logico-linguistic; analysis is ontological (PLA 194, 196). Thus while chairs have no ontological status as Russell *defines* them; they are real facts as Russell *analyzes* them. Russell thinks that complexity is not definable, but ultimately something we are just acquainted with (PLA 197).

For the record, I detect a tension in Russell in that there is surely a one-one correspondence between logical fictions and real facts. This is perhaps especially clear in the case of ordinary bodies. If bodies are facts, then they are not empty logical fictions. In fact, analyzing bodies as facts has the merit of coming much closer to the common-sense belief that bodies are real, and without sacrificing the main point of analyzing them as logical fictions: namely, the use of Occam's razor to shave away bodies as metaphysical things in themselves. As to whether numbers are real facts or logical fictions, this is just an old problem under a new guise: namely, that propositional functions are nothing, yet have universals as determinate constituents. I shall discuss that problem in chapter 5, section 2. Clearly Russell aims to defuse the tension by his distinction between definition and analysis—how successfully, I cannot say. Another tension is that defining bodies as series of classes allows some flexibility to account for the identity of bodies in counterfactual situations, since the memberships of the classes can fluctuate; but analyzing bodies as complex facts seems to permit only exact and determinate identities of bodies through their actual histories—though one might try complex general facts. Having mentioned the distinction, I shall now lapse back into popular usage of "analysis" to mean what is properly called definition for the remainder of the book.

The existence and the identity of any fact are the very same thing. Both consist of there being certain constituents in a certain ordering relationship. This is theory (32) in chapter 5. Arguably, atomic facts are slightly more real than molecular facts, and particular facts are slightly more real than general facts; their respective identity conditions would vary slightly as well. But Russell does not expressly say so (PLA 183, 270).

Further discussion of facts would be peripheral to this book. I discussed only part of Russell's views about facts in 1918. Ayer notes that in 1940, Russell replaces atomic facts with events which are bundles of qualities (Ayer 1972: 33, 113). This replacement is theory (15) in chapter 5.

I proceed to a quick sketch of propositions. Richard Gaskin observes that traditionally, the (existence and) unity of a proposition consists in its saying something about something (Gaskin 1995: 162). This is Parmenidean: you cannot say something about nothing, or say nothing about something, or say nothing about nothing, and have a true or false statement. The chief argument threatening this unity and existence is called Bradley's Regress, after F. H. Bradley's modern formulation. Gaskin finds the first clear statement of the regress in Peter Abelard, and finds similar regress arguments in Plato's *Parmenides* (Gaskin 1995: 161). I discussed Bradley's Regress in chapter 2, note 13; it is the problem of always needing further relations to relate relata to the relations that relate them.

Alan R. White warns that Russell is not always consistent in his use of the word "proposition" even within a single publication (White 1979: 23). White also warns that Russell uses the term propositional "constituent" in at least two ways: "in the ordinary sense of that which is contained in or occurs in something....[and] to be what the proposition is about....[This second] view of 'constituent' is, perhaps, analogous to the sense in which a person can be said

to be in or to appear in a book, newspaper, or list in which he is mentioned"
(White 1979: 26). White says:

> Russell, even within the same paper, sometimes identified the proposi-
> tion with a sentence as something whose components are words and
> sometimes identified it with something whose components are mean-
> ings, either in the sense of concepts or of images or in the sense of
> things, for instance, material objects and people which are what is
> meant by the words or the images. Since he sometimes called what is
> composed of the things meant by the words a 'fact', he therefore
> sometimes distinguished propositions from facts and the constituents of
> propositions from the constituents of facts, and sometimes identified
> them....
>
> The difficulty about the identification of propositions is that, on the
> one hand, they seem inseparably linked to some means of (verbal)
> expression—hence, the temptation to identify them with sentences—
> while, on the other hand, they both lack the linguistic characteristics of
> sentences...and possess non-linguistic characteristics...hence, the
> temptation to give them a separate existence of their own. Russell
> provides a salutary example of the difficulties inherent in either
> suggestion. (White 1979: 29–30)

Ayer finds four main theories of propositions in Russell. First, in his 1903
Principles of Mathematics, Russell views a proposition as a complete entity
toward which we may have a mental attitude of belief. Second, he abandons this
view in his 1906 "On the Nature of Truth and Falsehood," for he cannot explain
the distinction between truth and falsehood. Nor would making propositions into
facts help, since he would have to admit false facts to explain falsehoods (PE
149–53). Thus Russell abandons his quest for propositions which are complete
entities, and instead assays a proposition as propositional constituents bound into
a multiple relation by and with a mind (PE 149, 153–59; PM 43–44; PP
126–28; PLA 224). Third, in his 1919 "On Propositions," Russell abandons all
metaphysical selves including his own (Ayer says 1921, thinking of *The Analysis
of Mind*). Thus he must also abandon mental acts, including acts of judgment
that a proposition is true or false (LK 305; AMI 18). Thus he must abandon his
second theory of propositions. Russell accordingly returns to complete
propositions, admitting two kinds: image-propositions and word-propositions
(LK 308–9; AMI 240–42). Fourth, in his 1940 *Inquiry*, Russell refines the third
theory by allowing habitual response to play a defining role (IMT 184–89; see
Ayer 1972: 59–62). To these four theories, White adds a fifth: Russell
sometimes treats a proposition as a class of sentences (IMT 12, 166; see 313;
White 1979: 23). These five theories are in effect theories about the being and
unity of propositions, as I shall now show.

Russell's first theory of propositions is in his 1903 *Principles of Mathematics*. Propositions do not exist, since what exists is particular (POM 466–67). But propositions are entities (POM 49). They have being (POM 449) and an indefinable sort of unity (POM 51, 139–40). My gloss is that their being and unity amounts to the same thing: their saying something about something. To ensure propositional unity, the 1903 Russell offers a response to Bradley's Regress. This is his theory that a "relating relation," or verb *qua* verb, binds itself to a thing or things so as to yield a propositional unity (POM 35, 47–50, 52, 84, 100; see MPD 49). This is theory (33) in chapter 5.[7]

I shall discuss Russell's second theory of propositions only as it appears in "The Philosophy of Logical Atomism." In this work, the ontological status of propositions is very different from that of facts. Propositions are not real. Propositions are mere symbols (PLA 185). They lack ontological status. They are literally nothing. In *Principia* that is because propositions are incomplete symbols (PM 43–44). In contrast, facts are complete—and are not symbols. Propositions are true or false; facts are neither (PLA 184–85). ("False facts" would be nonexistent facts, which Russell rejects.) The identity conditions of propositions are very different from those of facts as well. For every fact there are two propositions, one asserting the fact and one denying it (PLA 187). Nonetheless, "in a logically correct symbolism there will always be a certain fundamental identity of structure between a fact and the symbol for it; and...the complexity of the symbol corresponds very closely with [but may be simpler than] the complexity of the facts symbolized by it" (PLA 197). This is theory (34) in chapter 5. It is a form of "picture theory" of meaning. Of course, as a string of written or spoken words, presumably a proposition may be "considered as a fact on its own account" (T xix).

Russell's second theory is that propositions are incomplete symbols and have no ontological status, but may be nominally said to exist and be the same if the same propositional constituents are ordered by a mind into a certain ordering relation. The 1918 Russell's approach to Bradley's Regress is similar to Frege's:

> [A] predicate can never occur except as a predicate. You may say "'Red' is a predicate", but then you must have 'red' in inverted commas because you are talking about the word 'red'....Exactly the same applies to relations....A relation can never occur except as a relation, never as a subject. (PLA 205–6)

This is theory (35) in chapter 5.[8]

Russell's third and fourth theories make propositions complete entities again. The third theory is that propositions have the being and unity of images or verbal expressions. The fourth is that propositions have the being and unity of habitual behavioral effects. On these theories, propositions are as robustly real as facts. These are respectively theories (36) and (37) in chapter 5.

Russell's fifth theory makes propositions incomplete, insofar as it makes them classes of sentences, since classes are incomplete symbols (PM 81; PLA 253, 262, 265–69; IMP 182). Propositions have the ontological status and identity conditions of classes: namely, they are nothing and are extensionally identical, i.e. identical if their memberships are identical. Nonetheless, propositions can be nominally said to exist insofar as that classes can be taken as apparent individuals and named by apparent names (PM 80–81). This is theory (38) in chapter 5. White's criticism is simple: classes are neither true nor false (White 1979: 23).

5

Russell's Forty-four 'No Entity
without Identity' Theories

It was Frege and Russell, not Wittgenstein or Quine, who began what may be called the ontology of the analytic tradition: to be is, in some sense, to be identifiable. I showed this in chapters 3 and 4. But it remains to be fully shown for Russell.

The neglect of Frege is understandable. As we saw in chapter 3, the world's leading Frege scholar, Michael Dummett, has long held that Frege abandoned his requirement that for objects to be named, conditions for their identity must be provided. But the neglect of Russell is incredible. Explicitly or implicitly, Russell held at least forty-four theories of 'no entity without identity' ontology over a period of fifty-seven years, in metaphysics as diverse as neo-Meinongian realism, logical constructionism, neutral monism, and representational realism. But I must recall my warning, stated in the preface to this book, that I use the expression 'no entity without identity' far more generously than Quine does. For brief and perhaps vague initial guidance, these theories may be stated as follows:

(1) All entities ("terms") have self-identity (1903).

(2) Individual identities and numbers shift, in a perfectly ordinary sense, as descriptions shift. But since individual identities (the metaphysical unity off an individual, as opposed to numerical unity) are determinate, and numbers determinately belong to descriptions, no radical relativity is involved (1903–59).

(3) Classes "exist" (class quantifier) if they have at least one member; members also fix a class's extensional identity (1910–59).

(4) Similarly for numbers, which are classes of classes (1910–59).

(5) Bodies "exist" in the secondary sense as temporal series of classes if they have sufficiently many lawful sensibilia as class members; the very same members also fix a body's extensional identity (1914–21).

(6) Similarly for other persons (1914–18) and even oneself (1921), who are (temporal series of) classes of lawful sensibilia.

(7) Similarly for causes, insofar as causes are series of ordered classes of events (1914).

(8) Similarly for spatiotemporal points, which are classes of overlapping events (1914).

(9) Similarly for changes, which are "continuous" series of events (1914).

(10) Similarly for ordinary things in general relativity theory, which are (series of) classes of events (1927).

(11) Similarly for quantum phenomena, considered as structures of events (1927).

(12) Similarly for possible worlds, considered as nonexistent complex entities which are structures of terms (1903).

(13) Similarly for possible worlds, considered as a special kind of logically fictitious structures of both actual and nonactual, i.e. merely described, sensibilia or events (1914–48).

(14) Events retain identity and existence until some change occurs (1914–18).

(15) Events are bundles of qualities very literally conforming to the principle of the identity of indiscernibles (1940–59).

(16) The common-sensical world of ordinary things which are "real" in the secondary sense is based on recognized similarities (1948).

(17) An ordinary thing exists as an identifiable "causal line" of events (1948).

(18) When a region is identified by causal lines' converging on it, probably an event exists in that region; a proper name probably denotes such an event in case of factually informative lineal identifications (1927–48).

(19) Simple existents have logically primitive identities, if not also a kind of ultimate reality nothing else has (1903–59).

(20) Sensed items, i.e. items given in acquaintance, have phenomenally given, rigid trans-world identities and are "as real as anything can be" in the primary sense of "real" (1914–18; [19] and [20] are compatible).

(21) Physical laws describe very general physical facts which remain the same in all frames of reference (1927).

(22) Two structures are identical if the relata of the relations involved are correlated one-one in order (1948).

(23) Diversity in effects implies diversity in causes (1912–59).

(24) Diversity in objects of perception implies diversity in real things (1912–59).

(25) Existence of causal relation is identity of differential equation (1913).

(26) Things cannot be different from what they are (1913).

(27) Distinctions among things are prior to distinctions among their properties (1903).

(28) A singular definite description implies an ontological commitment to a self-identical entity (1903).

(29) Definite descriptions are implicit existential quantifier-identity connections (1905–59).

(30) *Unum nomen, unum nominatum*; to change the meaning of a name is to change its denotation (1903–59).

(31) Variable expressions preserve identity (1903–11).

(32) The existence and the identity of any fact consist of the very same thing: there being certain constituents in a certain ordering relationship (1918).

(33) The being and unity of a proposition amount to the same thing: their saying something about something; propositional unity is ensured through a theory of "relating relations" (1903).

(34) "[I]n a logically correct symbolism there will always be a certain fundamental identity of structure between a fact and the symbol for it; and...the complexity of the symbol corresponds very closely with [but may be simpler than] the complexity of the facts symbolized by it" (PLA 197) (1918).

(35) Propositions are incomplete symbols and have no ontological status, but may be nominally said to exist and be the same if the same propositional constituents are ordered by a mind into a certain ordering relation; propositional unity is ensured by the theory that predicates can function only as predicates and relations can function only as relations (1918).

(36) Propositions are images or verbal expressions, and thus have the real being and unity of images or verbal expressions (1921).

(37) Propositions are defined in terms of behavioral effects, and thus have the real being and unity of habitual behavioral effects (1940).

(38) Propositions are classes of sentences, and thus have the ontological status and identity conditions of classes: namely, they are nothing and are extensionally identical, i.e. identical if their memberships are identical (1940).

(39) $(x = y) = (F)(F!x \supset F!y)$ Df (PM *13.01).

(40) $(Fa \vee \neg Fa) \supset [(Fx \vee \neg Fx) \equiv ((x = a) \vee \neg(x = a)]$ (PM *13.3).

(41) $V = \hat{x}(x = x)$ Df (PM *24.01; V is the systematically type-ambiguous "universal class.")

(42) Functions are formally equivalent if and only if their extensions are identical (see PM *12.1, *12.11; functions have intensional identities).

(43) $Fa \equiv (\exists x)(Fx \ \& \ (x = a)$ (see PM *13.195).

(44) Entities have metaphysical unity (1898–1959).

Gareth Evans says "Russell's Principle" is that "in order to be thinking about an object or to make a judgment about an object, one must *know which* object is in question," and cites Peter F. Strawson as admitting "an essentially Russellian bifurcation between 'demonstrative identification' (knowledge by acquaintance) and 'descriptive identification' (knowledge by description)" (Evans 1982: 65). My list confirms but goes far beyond these excellent observations.

Theories (39)–(42) are overarching logical principles. I believe they shape the logical outline of Russell's ontology, but there is no doubt that their primary missions are logical. Theory (39) implies both the identity of indiscernibles and the indiscernibility of identicals. Russell and Whitehead describe theory (40) as follows:

Its purpose is to show that, if a is any argument for which "Fa" is significant, i.e. for which we have Fa v ¬Fa, then "Fx" is significant when, and only when, x is either identical with a or not identical with a. (PM 171–72)

Since "significant" means 'true or false', theory (40) thus concerns the bivalence of logic as well as the law of excluded middle. More importantly to us, theory (40) implies that every object is logically determinate if and only if every identity statement about it has a determinate truth value. This is 'determinate entity if and only if identitative identifiability' (see chapter 1).

Theory (41) defines existence as self-identity. Russell admits, "Any other property possessed by everything would do as well" (PM 216). But the fact remains that he could and did choose to define existence as self-identity. Theory (41) is controversial, at least to those who admit self-identical nonexistents. Russell himself was a neo-Meinongian in his 1903 *Principles of Mathematics*, in which *24.01 would define a universal class of entities, if it were offered there.

Theory (42) is the axiom of reducibility (PM 166–67). Its purpose is to reduce all systematic ambiguities across the types of functions, and across the orders of functions within each type, down to talk on the lowest type-level of functions. It prevents there being "a hierarchy of different degrees of identity" (PM 57), thus honoring Frege's point that there is only one identity relation. Without it, an objectual identity statement could be true due to objectual indiscernibility with respect to first-order properties yet false due to discernibility with respect to second-order properties, leading to a series of orders of objectual identity. It solves the problem by reducing all properties of an object to first-order properties (PM 57). Russell concedes its "purely pragmatic" status (PM xiv, 55–60). Its pragmatic nature merely inverts that which the ramified theory of types had to begin with. The real problem is that it seems to take back everything the ramified theory of types gives, including protection against paradoxes.

The *Principia* concept of identity is neither the concept of singling out nor that of recognizing. It is not a epistemological or cognitive concept, but purely a matter of logic. However, the general concept of identity fixed by Russell's logic helps explain how factually informative identities are possible within the physics and psychology of perception. And this is closely tied to Russell's views on cognition and epistemology.

I shall be concerned with theories (1)–(38). Granting theories (39)–(42) as correct, a great question remains: How should we flesh out the logical skeleton they provide with specific identity conditions for each of the many metaphysical categories we may wish to admit? The existence of theories (1)–(38) shows that Russell made no bones about answering that question. It is in assessing which entities may be simple and then in achieving adequate definitions of complex entities that he goes beyond the general requirements of theories (39)–(42). In this sense theory (19) is a general, overarching principle implying that every definition fix identity conditions for what is logically complex in terms of the identity of what is logically simple. But insofar as we can never be sure we have found any ultimate simples, Russell must in fact settle for theory (20) to fix identities by description in terms of given identities of presented data, data which are *cognitively* simple. Thus it is not the principle of acquaintance as such, but the principle of 'no entity without identity', that is fundamental to Russell's sensed particulars, which emerge as primarily metaphysical and only secondarily epistemological. "Particulars = terms of relations in atomic facts. Df" (PLA 199). The later Russell defines particulars as ultimate constituents of physical structure, but ultimate "in relation to the whole of our knowledge," thus retaining this metaphysical primacy, though "particular" is now "not an *absolute* metaphysical term" (AMA 277–78, italics mine). The principle of acquaintance is only the cognitive vehicle we limited humans must use to conform to the principle of 'no entity without identity' in developing our categories of entities as best we can.

How then does Russell view or conceive theories (1)–(38)? The thesis of this chapter is that Russell thinks of theories (1)–(38) as fundamentally concerned with identity conditions. Many of theories (1)–(38) have been individually well-discussed. But everybody overlooks that theories (39)–(42) are overarching principles of 'no entity without identity' that in effect unify theories (1)–(38) as a class. That is why nobody has discussed theories (1)–(38) in light of their *collectively* being 'no entity without identity' theories in the same sense in which everybody admits that Frege's and Quine's theories of number and of physical objects are. Why have theories (1)–(38) not been brought together before to illuminate their general goal of achieving 'no entity without identity'? And if the philosophers with whose quotations I began chapter 1 really believed that Russell is a great proponent of 'no entity without identity', then why do they not even mention him with Frege, Wittgenstein, and Quine?

I am speaking of a new understanding of Russell on the most fundamental level, and of a deeper understanding of his place in history. The whole tradition of 'no entity without identity' must be reassessed as much richer than we thought, thanks to Russell's broadening it with forty-four theories.

Some may object: Russell's 'no entity without identity' is close enough to Frege's and Quine's, thanks to the common framework of predicate logic as a canonical notation. But what about the ordinary language identity criteria of the later Wittgenstein? The objection ignores two facts. (i) The later Russell largely makes both language and mind into game-like, rule-like habitual behavior (Russell 1971f; AMI; OP; HK). (ii) The Hintikkas show that *Investigations* admits objectual reference and even a simple sort of ordinary grammar picture theory for ordinary noninterjectional assertions, without any demand that there be Tractarian 'final analyses' (IW 225–27). Facts (i) and (ii) respectively make

Russell resemble the later Wittgenstein and the later Wittgenstein resemble Russell. And the later Wittgenstein makes existence a second-level predicate (RFM 186/V #35).

The chapter sections are: 1. Particulars and Universals, 2. Classes and Ontological Commitment, 3. Minds and Bodies, 4. General Relativity Theory, 5. Quantum Mechanics, 6. Common Sense Recognition, 7. Inference of Events, and 8. Space, Time, and Events.

I discuss: theory (2) in chapter 7, section 2; theories (13), (20), and (26) in chapter 4, section 4; and theories (33)–(38) in chapter 4, section 5. For further discussion of theories (13) and (20), please see Dejnožka (1990).

1. Particulars and Universals

I shall discuss Russell's four main phases on individuation: monism (1884), extreme pluralist realism (1903), particulars and universals (1912–40), and events as bundles of qualities (1940–59). To provide historical perspective, I shall begin with the later Russell's discussion of the traditional theory of substances.

Russell says that the problem of individuation of things was dominated by the theory of substances for two thousand years. Russell both characterizes and criticizes substances and the concomitant notions of essence and accident in terms of identity. Substances are that which remain identical over time. Essential properties are those a substance cannot lose without losing its identity; accidental properties are those it can lose without losing its identity. The later Russell gives three main criticisms of theory of substances. First, the notion of a thing as remaining identical over time is scientifically outmoded, since relativity theory's four-dimensional space-time continuum eliminates "persistent material units moving in a three-dimensional space" (AMA 152). Second:

A substance is supposed to be the subject of properties, and to be something distinct from all its properties. But when we take away the properties, and try to imagine the substance by itself, we find that there is nothing left. To put the matter in another way: What distinguishes one substance from another? Not difference of properties, for, according to the logic of substance, difference of properties presupposes numerical diversity between the substances concerned. Two substances, therefore, must be *just* two, without being, in themselves, in any way distinguishable. How, then, are we ever to find out that they *are* two? (HWP 201)

Third, the notion of substance is only a linguistic convenience:

Two percepts to which the same word applies are thought to be identical, unless both can be present at once; this characteristic distinguishes general names from proper names. The basis of this whole process is the ["pre-human"] emotion of recognition. When the process...is complete...identity of name is taken to indicate identity of substance... (AMA 152)

Likewise for the notions of essence and accident:

The "essence" of a thing appears to have meant "those of its properties which it cannot change without losing its identity"....In fact, however, this is a verbal convenience. The "essence" of Socrates thus consists of those properties in the absence of which we should not use the name "Socrates." The question is purely linguistic: a *word* may have an essence, but a *thing* cannot. (HWP 200–1)

All of Russell's criticisms concern substantival identity. Thus it should be no surprise that "when 'substance' is rejected we have to find some other way of defining the identity of a physical object at different times" (HK 316).

Russell's first phase is his admitting a Hegelian connection between reality and "identity in difference" (see Russell 1990: 537). Russell succumbed to Kant and Hegel in 1884. Bradley, Bosanquet, and McTaggart were the direct influences. The 1898 Russell says, "*Ens et unum convertuntur*" (Russell 1990: 228). Nicholas Griffin rightly takes that as a case of 'no entity without identity', but wrongly adds that Russell "could not have held" such a view when he moved to mind-independent realism, since such a view "is altogether too verificationist" (Griffin 1992–93: 193). There are many forms of 'no entity without identity', and not all of them are verificationist. Only rejecting *identity-in-difference* was part of Russell's later rejection of monism. Russell rejected monism due to there being asymmetric relations requiring different entities as relata, due to a confusion of subject and predicate he found basic to identity-in-difference, and due to problems with the monist theory of truth. Rejecting the substantival unity of the world as a whole, Russell moved to the analysis of the unity of a sentence and the analysis of the unity of limited but complex things—and to the theory that analysis is not falsification (PE 137–46; MPD 47–49). Griffin sees the main issues as logical, *pace* Herbert Hochberg, who sees them as metaphysical. But as Griffin virtually admits, both sorts of issue find a unified solution in Russell's theory of terms, which is primarily metaphysical: terms are Russell's first substance substitutes. I shall not repeat Griffin's otherwise superb discussions of this first phase (Griffin 1992–93; Griffin 1991).

Russell's second phase peaks in 1900–2 with the writing of *Principles of Mathematics*, a work of extreme Platonic and neo-Meinongian realism. Russell distinguishes being, had by substantival entities called terms, from existence, had only by those terms which exist (POM 43, 449). Everything has being, since being is opposed to nothing. Even nothing has being in a sense (POM 73-75). All beings have "numerical identity" (POM 44).

There are different views on whether the extreme realism of *Principles* extends to impossible objects. Quine does not see that Russell "faced" the question of impossible objects (Quine 1971: 5). But Alfred Jules Ayer argues:

> Anything that could be mentioned was said by him to be a term....It followed that in principle one could use names to refer...even to logically impossible entities like the greatest prime integer. (Ayer 1972: 48)

Ayer's argument is strong. Russell indeed says that "anything...that can be mentioned, is sure to be a term; and to deny that such and such a thing is a term must always be false" (POM 43). But terms do not include classes as many, since "every term is one" (POM 43, 523). And Russell openly *rejects* the class of classes not members of themselves as self-contradictory and impossible (POM 101-7). Since classes are objects (POM 55n, 523), this class would be an impossible object *par excellence*. Russell also rejects the null class because it cannot exist (POM 75). And he rejects at least eight other sorts of things as impossible.[1] This is why it is natural, even necessary, for Russell to give marks of termhood which, *pace* Ayer, do *not* apply to every seeming term. First and foremost, "every term is one" (POM 43). Also, terms are logical subjects and "immutable and indestructible" (POM 44):

> What a term is, it is, and no change can be conceived in it which would not destroy its identity and make it another term. Another mark which belongs to terms is numerical identity with themselves and numerical diversity from all other terms. (POM 44)[2]

Thus it seems to me that, besides the greatest prime integer (which is no term, but a class of classes), Russell must reject the term that is not, the plural term, the changed term, the destroyed term, the strictly predicative term, and the non-self-identical term as impossible. I am not begging the question against Ayer, since I say this in light of the nine sorts of things Russell himself rejects (see note 1). The first quoted sentence anticipates theory (14). The second quoted sentence states theory (1) for terms. While the mark of being one clearly fails to apply to classes as many, it is not clear which other marks fail to apply, if classes as many have logical being and are distinct from their overlapping and fluctuating memberships.

There are two reasons why Russell would not reject impossible classes yet admit impossible terms. First, the standard *reason* for rejection would be the same: self-contradiction. Russell would reject the plural term because it is both plural and (*qua* term) nonplural, and is both a term and (*qua* plural) not a term. Second, if anything, Russell would reject impossible terms *before* he rejected impossible classes. Classes as many are not even entities, and so to speak, have less to lose by being impossible than terms do.

In fact Russell does reject many terms as impossible, such as the particularized relation and various Fregean functions (POM 201, 508–10). These must be terms, since they are not classes.

The 1903 Russell upholds the identity of indiscernibles as applying to all terms (POM 39). He says, "Every term is the only instance of some class-concept" (POM 63). Thus just like Leibniz's version, Russell's version does not distinguish existent terms from merely possible terms. But Russell's version is weaker than Leibniz's, in that it does not entail that points or instants are unreal due to their being indiscernible from each other. Russell says:

> To be exactly alike can only mean—as in Leibniz's Identity of Indiscernibles—not to have different predicates. But when once it is recognised that there is no essential distinction between subjects and predicates, it is seen that any two simple terms simply differ immediately—they are two, and this is the sum-total of their differences....For before two subjects can differ as to predicates, they must already be two; and thus the immediate diversity is prior to that obtained from diversity of predicates....Two colours, or two simple smells, have no intrinsic difference save immediate diversity, but have, like points, different relations to other terms. (POM 451–52)

Here Russell bases theory (1) on theory (27). He seems to find the individuality of things—ultimate subjects—in their having no instances (POM 363; compare 249). I said that Russell's theory is weaker than Leibniz's. But Russell's argument for the immediate diversity of simple entities is precisely what allows him to admit the spatial, the temporal, and the material points of classical physics in *Principles* Part VII, Matter and Motion. Such points cannot be distinguished by their interrelationships without begging the question as to their identity, since they are empirically indistinguishable. But Russell can hold that all such simple points are immediately different from each other.

But since spatial, temporal, and material points comprise *three* different classes as many, at most only *one* of these classes could be a class of "bare particulars," i.e. of mere individuators. Recall that Russell would hold that the members of these classes cannot be distinguished by the relations they stand in, since that presupposes their being different individuals. Even granting that only material points are mobile (that only they stand in causal relations will not help, since that presupposes their individuality), how can Russell distinguish spatial points from instants unless the former have an intrinsic property of spatiality and the latter of temporality?—And then why not add intrinsic materiality for material points?

Russell does not speak in *Principles* of possible worlds in so many words, but he might as well have. Possible worlds would be identifiable in terms of the self-identities of their terms, including properties and relations. Indeed, possible worlds would themselves be complex terms. This is theory (12), which follows both Leibniz and Leibniz's hero, John Duns Scotus, in its 'no *possible* entity without identity' connection.[3]

What is the 1903 Russell's criterion of existence? He rejects Leibniz's two ways of distinguishing the actual world from all others—the specific form of the principle of sufficient reason, as well as the principle of metaphysical perfection (PL 34–38, 200). Russell can only fall back on Leibniz's principle that perception indicates the actual world. Russell accepts "the principle that knowledge as to what exists...is always and wholly empirical" (POM 488). Thus "a science of what exists...requires experiment and observation" (POM 488).

Russell's third phase begins in 1911. In "On the Relations of Universals and Particulars" (read in 1911 and published in 1912), Russell discusses three theories: (i) There are only particulars. (ii) There are only universals. (iii) There are both particulars and universals. Russell rejects (i), which he associates with Berkeley and Hume, due to his famous vicious regress of similarities argument—a generalization of Plato's Third Man, since Platonic participation is a sort of similarity, and Platonic forms are really particulars (see HWP 127). Russell rejects (ii) due to an argument which ends:

> Thus the fact that it is logically possible for precisely similar things to coexist in two different places, but that things in different places at the same time cannot be numerically identical, forces us to admit that it is particulars, i.e., *instances* of universals, that exist in places, not universals in themselves. (RUP 112–13)

No subtle exegesis is needed to see that it is the consideration of identity that leads Russell to admit particulars.

Of four senses of the word "particular," (a) percept, (b) entity existing in time, (c) nonrelation, and (d) object denoted by a substantive as opposed to a (predicative or relational) verb, (d) is the best because "[a] particular is naturally conceived as a *this* or something intrinsically analogous to a *this*" (RUP 109). Russell says,

> What is not a predicate or relation is, according to one traditional definition, a substance....As far as logical properties are concerned, our substances will be fairly analogous to traditional substances....In the world we know, substances are identical with particulars in our fourth sense, and predicates and relations with universals. (RUP 122–23)

Such particulars need not remain self-identical for long times; they can be and are momentary. Visual space

> is composed of a finite though constantly varying number of surfaces or volumes, continually breaking up or joining together according to the fluctuations of attention....A white sheet of paper, for example, may be seen as a single undivided object, or as an object consisting of two parts, an upper and a lower or a right hand and a left hand part...and so on." (RUP 114–15)

This assay of fluctuations of objectual identities as merely fluctuations of attention probably applies to Frege's phenomena (chapter 7, section 1) and to the later Wittgenstein's phenomena. In any case, Russell was still expressing this sort of objectual fluctuation in terms of Gestalt unities in 1940 (IMT 56, 59).

The 1911 Russell does not say whether his particulars (sense data) are "bare" particulars or "quality" particulars. He seems concerned only to show *that* there are both particulars and universals, which must be in *some* relationship of things' having properties. Such a generic position would be compatible either with Gustav Bergmann's bare particulars which "exemplify" universals or with Panayot Butchvarov's quality particulars ("objects") which in a special sense "are" universals ("entities"). But all of Russell's examples of sense-data, such as patches of color, suggest that his particulars are quality particulars. If Russell's instances were bare particulars, then patches of color would not be particulars but facts, e.g. the fact that particular *p* exemplifies universal *U*.

It might seem that the 1940 Russell's criticism of his own earlier particulars as unknowable instances underlying what is given to us suggests that these earlier particulars are bare particulars. Similarly for the 1959 Russell's criticism that the very argument he used in 1911 to establish particulars—the argument that two color patches can be exactly similar yet be numerically different—shows that the earlier particulars are unknowable substrata (MPD 119–20). But if so, both arguments are unsound. For the 1911 Russell's position is compatible with particulars' simply being the sense-data themselves, in the manner of Douglas C. Long's common-sensical assay (Long 1970). And as evidence of how the 1911 Russell thought of his particulars, the arguments seem outweighed by Russell's express equation of particulars with color patches and sounds in 1918: "Some [logical atoms] will be what I call "particulars'—such things as little patches of colour or sounds" (PLA 179). This is how Russell seems to think of sensed particulars from 1910 to 1927 (PM 174–75, AMA 180). Thus I agree with J. O. Urmson that Russell's particulars are color patches and the like (Urmson 1966: 17, 57). Indeed, I agree more specifically with Wilfrid Sellars and Ronald Jager that Russell's particulars are quality-instances of (perhaps small groups of) universals (Sellars 1974: 60, 66; Jager 1972: 76–77). This is just how Russell speaks of them (RUP 111, 113). In fact the two later criticisms are quite general in scope, and apply to bare particulars, to whole sense-data, and to any other sort of unknowable substratal instances. My suggestion is that the later criticisms probably were intended to apply to whole sense-data.

In fact, not only are color patches sense-data, but they are complex sense-data composed of simpler sense-data (PP 46). "Our judgment then analyzes the datum into colour and shape, and then recombines them by stating that the red colour is round in shape" (PP 114). This color and this shape are sense-data in their own right (PP 12, 46, 101). Russell says "the colour itself is a sense-datum" (PP 12). No bare particular seems involved in Russell's analysis of the color patch into a color that has a shape. Of course, not every particular is a sense-datum. Russell admits physical bodies as late as 1912 (PP; see MAL 206-7), and admits at least one's own mind as a "pin-point particular" as late as 1918 (see MPD 120). But these alone would not involve bare particulars.

The following distinctions lend perspective on Russell's particulars. Panayot Butchvarov correctly distinguishes his own neo-Hegelian view that objects truly and informatively said to be identical are really different objects of presentation from Russell's view that such objects only apparently differ, since for Russell their difference is only one of description (Butchvarov 1979: 10, 18). But William J. Greenberg mistakenly distinguishes his own neo-Hegelian view that objects truly and informatively said to be identical are "two-sided and multi-faceted" from Russell's view, which Greenberg believes is that such objects are "essentially bare" (Greenberg 1985: xiv, 59, 98, 120, 132). The 1911 Russell's particulars (sense-data) are essentially instances of qualities, and they are multi-faceted. Green particulars have shapes and sizes. "The green patch I now sense is the largest patch I now sense" may be both true and (factually and novelly) informative. The two descriptions differ, but the reason they can differ is that the simple, i.e., really undivided, particular they describe is a multi-faceted instance of several universals.

Concerning particulars (sense-data) and universals with which we are acquainted, Russell sees no need to give an identity definition. "We may have knowledge of a thing by acquaintance even if we know very few propositions about it—theoretically we need not know any propositions about it" (PP 144). Also, Russell says that each particular "stands entirely alone and is completely self-subsistent....When you are acquainted with [a] particular, you have a full, adequate, and complete understanding of the name [for it], and no further information is required" (PLA 201-2). Such a theory of "clear and distinct" percepts implies real identity in my fourth sense. The completeness of acquaintance implies that sense-data even have trans-world identities, which is theory (20). For the meaning of a logically proper name is its denotation; full acquaintance is obtained with meaning and denotation simultaneously. Thus there is no possible world in which a name can change its denotation without changing its meaning; nor can one fail to be aware of a change in meaning. This is theory (30); compare Recanati (1993: 10–19) and Peacocke (1975: 111). I have little to add to Urmson's fine distinction between an earlier and a later version of theory (30). Russell's early version is his 1903 neo-Meinongian view that "every noun must be the name of something having some sort of being" (Urmson 1966: 189). We saw that Russell admits only nine sorts of exception to this, including "class of all classes not members of themselves" (see note 1). Russell's later version is that logically proper names must be such names (Urmson 1966: 190).

The individual identity of presented universals seems presented. Concerning presented universals Russell says, "It may be that white is defined as the colour of 'this', or rather that the proposition 'This is white' means 'This is identical in colour with that', the colour of 'that' being, so to speak, the definition of white. That may be, but there is no special reason to think that it is" (PLA 202–3). Presented universals ought to have trans-world identities too, by parity of reason. But then all universals as such ought to have.

Presumably simple items would be logically prior to identity definitions as well. Russell holds that a sense-datum is replaced by a different sense-datum if and only if it alters its appearance enough (PLA 203). This implies theory (19). Simples may include particulars (sense-data), qualities, and relations. For Russell, "ultimate simples, out of which the world is built,...have a kind of reality not belonging to anything else" (PLA 270). Simples with which we are not acquainted would be knowable by description. The 1918 Russell admits simples, but concedes he might be wrong and that analysis might be endless (PLA 202; see POM 145; HK 252; MPD 164–65).

The fourth phase occurs when the 1940–59 Russell asserts theory (15): that ultimately every event is either a quality or a bundle of qualities. Russell gives two reasons: (1) Identity is definable as indiscernibility, and in this way the identity of indiscernibles is upheld and made analytic. This precludes the possibility of there being numerous indiscernible Eiffel Towers in Paris. (2) The bundle theory makes counting possible, since there will be just one Eiffel Tower. Reason (2) presupposes reason (1). For counting presupposes that we are not counting the same thing twice or counting different things as one thing (IMT 97, 102–3, 130).

Two further reasons for preferring the bundle to the instance theory are: (3) Bundles are simpler if instances are eliminated. This accords with Occam's razor. (4) Instances are unknowable things in themselves (IMT 265; see 98). If things were instances of qualities, then the concept of identity would be inapplicable to things. For we could have no evidence that this Eiffel Tower is identical with that one. Russell says, "A word must denote something that can be recognized, and space-time regions, apart from qualities, cannot be recognized, since they are all alike..." (HK 82). But mere instances have no qualities and are indistinguishable (HK 298). Thus Russell finally rejects his 1903 "immediate difference" version of the identity of indiscernibles in 1940.

Bergmann (1971a: 15), Hochberg (1971: 68, 74), William J. Winslade (1971: 99), Wilfrid Sellars (1974: 91), and Albert Casullo (1984; 1982; 1981) claim that the 1940 Russell's qualities are universals; Edwin B. Allaire's assertion that the 1940 Russell rejects particulars implies as much (Allaire 1970a: 236). They repeat Morris Weitz's mistake, which Russell himself corrected long ago in his "Reply to Criticisms": "Like most other people, Mr. Weitz has failed to understand the tentative theory, set forth in the *Inquiry*, according to which a given shade of colour is a particular, not a universal" (Russell 1989a: 685; see 714). Alan Donagan rightly deems these qualities "discontinuous particulars" (Donagan 1970: 148–50), and Long rightly deems them "repeatable particulars" (Long 1970: 267–68). One shade of red need not occur continuously across time or space. Russell says phenomenal "[r]edness may be to the right of redness, or above redness…; [physical] redness may be in America and in Europe" (IMT 100). A sense-datum, now a "complex of comprecent qualities," is repeatable. Indeed, if history is cyclic with respect to qualities, then each stage "is numerically identical with" the next (IMT 102). This repeatability explains why asymmetric spatiotemporal relations no longer imply diversity of relata. Repeatability is explained in turn by the identity of indiscernibles. For the very instances which would preclude literal repeatability are the instances which would also preclude counting the number of indiscernible Eiffel Towers in Paris. Qualities emerge as very unlike Quine's "scattered particulars," gold and water. The whole of gold does not recur in each piece of gold, the way the whole of a certain shade of red recurs in each spot of that shade. No doubt repeatability is what misled Bergmann and company. But there is powerful textual and systematic evidence that for the 1940 Russell, specific sensible qualities such as a specific shade of red are particulars, while relations and generic properties remain universals. Long states the main reason: qualities are syntactically particulars; they are ultimate logical subjects (Long 1970: 267; MPD 127). This goes well beyond the trivial sense in which we call different universals "individual" universals (Allaire 1970: 252).[4]

Timothy Sprigge criticizes the 1911 Russell's argument that asymmetric spatial relations imply different relata as a *non sequitur* without being aware that Russell himself does the same thing (Sprigge 1979: 151–54). The 1955 Russell says in a note appended to his 1911 paper, "I no longer think that there are any spatial or temporal relations which always and necessarily imply diversity. This does not prove that the theory which asserts particulars is wrong, but only that it cannot be proved to be right" (LK 124). By "particulars" he means his old instances of 1911, since he now admits qualities as particulars. Russell repeats this criticism in *My Philosophical Development* (MPD 119–20). Sprigge makes a fine effort to show that monism can accommodate asymmetric relations. But this can scarcely be the pluralist Russell's motive. Repeatability, the rejection of instances, and the identity of indiscernibles are Russell's motives in order of increasing priority.

I have six comments on Russell's critique of his 1911 theory.

First, by making qualities recurrent particulars, Russell can solve a problem of individuation Frege cannot: How many red objects are there? For Frege there can be "no finite number" of red objects because red is not a sortal concept (FA 66). But for Russell, each shade of red is one recurrent particular. We humans discern, and there may be, only finitely many (actual) red objects.

Second, the argument from asymmetry of relations for particulars was more generally Russell's main argument for pluralism. Thus in rejecting it, Russell weakens his own case for pluralism, and seems to need asymmetric relations among qualities (*brighter than*, *louder than*) to carry the ball. But it would be hard for Russell to convince us that such relations are not internal to the qualities they concern. And ensuring that bundles of qualities do not recur requires assigning them artificial spatiotemporal "qualities" (IMT 101–3).

Third, Russell's rejection of particular instances as unknowable destroys his argument in 1911 against position (ii) that only universals exist. Thus, though the 1940 Russell *says* qualities are particulars, he has not disproved that they are universals. Nor can the 1940 Russell use qualities to repeat his 1911 argument that particulars are needed to individuate exactly similar color patches. For Russell now admits only *generic* monadic universals, and no color patch could be a bundle of only such universals. But only if he has some other argument that qualities are particulars would he not *need* to repeat that argument. Merely *saying* that qualities are particulars begs the question against position (ii) that only universals exist. At most, qualities are made ultimate subjects.

Fourth, the 1940 Russell views even spatial and temporal relations as presented qualities of "complexes of compresence" (which replace his complex data of 1911–18). As William James would say, I can see that the book is on the table as easily as I can see the table. But in rejecting particulars as unknowable instances, Russell overlooks that the *numerical difference* of two exactly similar color patches is presented to us just as easily as the book on the box. This is not to admit bare particulars, but only to admit their intelligibility as "mere individuators." The problem with bare particulars is not their unintelligibility or unknowability so much as their superfluity, since the color patches themselves are already different (Long 1970: 280–82).

Fifth, Russell's reasons (1)–(4) for rejecting unknowable substratal instances are quite general in scope. Now according to the later Russell, all we can know about physical things is by description. We can know only their structures, not their qualities. Thus it seems that reasons (1)–(4) apply to the later Russell's own unknowable qualities of physical things. Thus the later Russell's physical structures are structures of nothing. For they are complex relations whose relata we must reject as unknowable substratal quality-instances.

Sixth, in much the same way, we must reject all of the later Russell's bundles of qualities as unknowable substratal instances. The 1940 Russell's reasons (1)–(4) all apply—e.g., How many bundles is the Eiffel Tower? The 1959 Russell's criticism applies as well. This criticism is that the old particular instances are unknowable substrata because "the statement that *x* has such and such a property is always significant, never analytic" (MPD 119–20). It is this premise which allows the identity of things to be prior to the identities of their properties, so that two things can intelligibly have the same properties. Now, the 1940 Russell makes each bundle a whole prior to the qualities in the bundle, so that the statement that bundle *b* has quality *q* is never analytic (IMT 128–29). On his own reasoning in 1959, this makes bundles unknowable substrata. My own view would be that the 1911 Russell's quality-instances are *not* unknowable substrata, since they are essentially identified in terms of the qualities they instantiate; to change a property is to change the particular (RUP 114–15; see PLA 203). Thus the particulars of 1911 have *all* their properties analytically, following Leibniz. Even bare particulars exemplify their qualities analytically, in that they can be identified only by means of the qualities they exemplify. They can scarcely be directly identified in themselves. No doubt bare particulars have their properties analytically in one sense and quality particulars have theirs in another. But it would beg the question to decide whether the particulars of 1911 are bare by imposing the former sense on them. I would apply the same reasoning to rescue bundles too. Bundles cannot be identified independently of the qualities they bundle. They can scarcely be directly identified in themselves. Even traditional substances have some properties analytically, in that they cannot be identified independently of their essential properties (compare Wiggins 1980: 4–5; Kenny 1980: 35). This is not to make having properties prior to having an identity, but to make properties the basis of many identifications.

What about the identity of the 1940 Russell's qualities? It seems to be just given in acquaintance for qualities with which we are acquainted. But the 1914 Russell admitted a problem with sense-data which surely applies to the new qualities as well:

When we are considering the actual data of sensation in this connection, it is important to realise that two sense-data may be, and must sometimes be, really different when we cannot perceive any difference between them. An old but conclusive reason for believing this was emphasized by Poincaré. In all cases of sense-data capable of gradual change, we may find one sense-datum indistinguishable from another, and that other indistinguishable from a third, while yet the first and third are easily distinguishable. (KEW 112–13)

Of course it seems easier to admit hidden differences in sense-data than in qualities, even though the 1912 Russell's sense-data included colors and the 1940 Russell's qualities are particulars. But the problem does emerge, namely as the question, Which quality does the second bundle really contain? The recurrence of the problem should be no surprise, since noticed qualities (and bundles) *are* the 1940 Russell's sense-data. But hidden qualities are indistinguishable from each other, and are therefore subject to the later Russell's own arguments (1)–(4) against instances. The 1940 Russell does not notice this dilemma.

2. Classes and Ontological Commitment

Russell's first major theory of classes is in *Principles of Mathematics*. Classes are intimately connected with problems of identity and existence from the very beginning. Here one subtlety must be discussed in some detail. Namely, Russell distinguishes between mathematical existence and empirical existence. He speaks of "the mathematical sense of existence" (POM 362). He also says that "mathematics is throughout indifferent to the question whether its entities exist" (POM 458). Thus he seems to admit two senses of the word "exists."

Mathematical existence might seem the same as being, since all things can be counted. But the existence-theorems "are almost all obtained from Arithmetic," i.e. concern only arithmetical entities (POM 21). Mathematical existence is involved when Russell speaks of "The existence-theorems of mathematics—i.e. the proofs that the various classes defined are not null" (POM 497). This reduces mathematical existence to class existence (POM 21), in keeping with the *Principles* program of reducing mathematics to logic and class theory. For mathematical existence essentially concerns an object's being shown to be a member of some class. This is "'existence' (in the logical sense)" (HK 276). Thus it seems that mathematical, or logical, existence is at bottom the object *some a*. For this is the object that Russell employs in proving the existence of numbers (POM 57–59). Only in "On Denoting," when *some a* is replaced by the existential quantifier meaning 'not always false', can objective truths replace objects in existence-proofs, paving the way for numbers' being fictions.

I shall call existence in the actual world "empirical existence." Russell means empirical existence when he implies that all existents are particulars. He says, "not colour, but only particular shades of colour, can exist" (POM 470). He also says that "we may define as a possible existent any term which has a causal relation to some other term" (POM 476). On this definition, mathematical existents such as numbers are not possible existents. He means by "possible existents," possible empirical existents. He also says that a necessary condition of existence is existence at some time (POM 476). Again, this rules out numbers and indicates empirical existence.

Now which of these two kinds of existence do classes have? Do they have mathematical existence or do they have empirical existence? The question is about classes not "as many," but "as one" (POM 68–69, 76, 104, 130–36). Russell says:

> What we called, in Chapter VI, the class as one, is an individual, provided its members are individuals: the objects of daily life, persons,

tables, chairs, apples, etc., are classes as one. (A person is a class of psychical existents, the others are classes of material points....) These objects, therefore, are of the same type as simple individuals. It would seem that all objects designated by single words, whether things or concepts, are of this type. (POM 523)

Our question now appears as: Do persons, tables, and chairs have mathematical existence or empirical existence for the 1903 Russell? Based on Russell's saying that sciences of what exists require observation, it would seem natural to say that tables and chairs have empirical existence. Persons, too, are particulars, stand in causal relations, and exist only at certain times. And the evidence we have for the existence of persons is wholly empirical. Thus some classes as one—people, tables, and chairs—seem to have empirical existence.

Also, tables, as classes as one, would seem to be empirical existents as pieces of matter. For they can scarcely belong to purely rational Dynamics (POM 467–68).

Thus Russell admits forerunners of theories (5) and (6) as early as 1903. But a problem arises. No class as many is an empirical existent or even a term. So can a person or table be both many and one, both a term and not a term, both an empirical existent and not an empirical existent? Russell says:

Now I am far from denying—indeed I strongly hold—that this opposition of identity and diversity in a collection constitutes a fundamental problem of Logic—perhaps even the fundamental problem of philosophy. (POM 346)

Russell and Whitehead state theory (3) in *Principia*. Theory (3) resolves this fundamental problem by rejecting both classes and one and classes as many. Theory (3) also underwrites the reductive nature of theories (4)-(13):

We do not assume that there is such a thing as an extension: we merely define the whole phrase "having the same extension."...Since extensional functions are many and important, it is natural to regard the extension as an object, called a class, which is supposed to be the subject of all the equivalent statements about various formally equivalent functions....This view is encouraged by the feeling that there is something which is identical in the case of two functions which "have the same extension." And if we take such simple problems as "how many combinations can be made of things?" it seems at first sight necessary that each "combination" should be a single object which can be counted as one. This, however, is certainly not necessary technically, and we see no reason to suppose that it is true philosophically. (PM 74; see 24)

Russell seems to be rejecting not only classes as one, but even classes as many, as objects. (Russell had already rejected the view that propositional functions define anything more than classes as many in *Principles*, Appendix A.) The text divorces objectivity and identifiability, on the one hand, from denoting an existent, an entity, or even a *Principles* "object," on the other. It implies that it is a *non sequitur* to infer the applicability of the latter notions merely from the applicability of the former. Only the former notions now seem needed for asserting the identity of classes. The divorce does not preclude there being an existential quantifier-identifiability connection for classes, if the existential quantifier for classes does not express genuine existence.

Russell announces his parting from Frege's object-identity connection in his 1914 *Our Knowledge of the External World*. Russell praises Frege's notion of objectivity: "Frege has the merit of...recognizing the world of logic, which is [objective but] neither mental nor physical" (KEW 156). Then Russell praises Frege for eliminating the need to assume numbers as "some new and mysterious class of metaphysical entities" (KEW 158). For Frege defines numbers as classes of classes. And Russell even sees, as the best Frege scholar of our own generation, Michael Dummett, has not, that the fundamental issue in Frege's definition of number is fixing the sense of an identity for numbers (KEW 157–58; MAL 68). The parting of ways occurs when Russell denies the existence of classes in turn, and asserts that "the doctrine that classes are fictions...is not destructive," i.e., not destructive of the objectivity of the world of logic and mathematics (KEW 160). What Russell proclaims for numbers and other classes is just *Principia* objectivity-without-objects. In short, he makes theories (3)–(4) of *Principia* even more openly fictionalist in *External World*.

Russell's argument for nondestructiveness uses the nonsubstitutability of class terms for individual terms in statements to show that "classes cannot have the same kind of reality as things have" (KEW 160). He shows how to rewrite statements ostensibly about classes so that "there is no longer any reference at all to a 'class'" (KEW 161). He concludes that "all the apparent objects of logic and mathematics" need not be assumed to exist as definite objects (KEW 161). The "propositions in which numbers verbally occur have not really any constituents corresponding to numbers, but only a certain logical form which is not a part of propositions having this form" (KEW 161). Occam's razor is supported by the 'not always false' individual quantifier, with identity statements about "classes" providing the backbone of coherence of ongoing discourse in logic and mathematics. By 1927 Russell says, "I mean by 'objective' not anything metaphysical, but merely 'agreeing with the testimony of others'" (AMA 150).

Russell's 1927 *The Analysis of Matter* provides his fullest explanation of ontological commitment. Here Russell categorically denies that the so-called existential quantifier has any ontological commitment. He begins by describing the logical structure of a science, "considered as a deductive system." First we define what may be called "initial entities." From these, along with some "initial propositions," we attempt to deduce the rest of the science. But there is no ontological commitment to these initial entities. In fact, "What we really have to begin with, in this treatment, is hypotheses containing variables." Each initial proposition is not an axiom supposed to be true, but a "hypothesis that a set of entities (otherwise undefined) has certain enumerated properties." For there may be several such sets of hypotheses from which the rest of the science may be adequately deduced. No doubt these remarks apply to logic and mathematics as well as to the natural sciences. Russell adds:

> ...the word "entities," which we have been using, is too narrow if used with any metaphysical implication. The "entities" concerned may, in a given application of a deductive system, be complicated logical structures. (AMA 1–2; compare POM 188, 211)

Logical structures may be said to exist, but evidently they do not qualify as actual existents. Thus the value of a variable for Russell may be an entity, but it may also be something quite different, a logical structure (see HK 140–41). In either case it may be equally well quantified over using the individual quantifier (AMA 8, 9).

Each science may have several workable sets of initial propositions, or sets of hypotheses, from which the rest of it may be deduced. And for each such set of hypotheses, there may be several sets of objects which fulfill the hypotheses. "The substitution of such a set for the undefined objects is 'interpretation'" (AMA 5). It seems, then, that for Russell ontological commitment is not made by propositions, variables, or quantifiers, but by interpretations of propositions. But even interpretations often substitute not genuine entities, but only further logical structures, for the variables of a set of hypotheses. The interpretation of numbers as classes of classes is a case in point (AMA 2, 4, 5).

Structures are complex relations. Thus they are identical if their relata are correlated one-one in order. This is theory (22). The notion of substructures allows structures to have degrees of identity, or more precisely, orders of identity, since higher orders of relations are involved. Corresponding structural statements about identical structures have the same truth-value, making "translation dictionaries" possible (HK 254–55).

Russell uses the term "ontological commitment" only once that I know of, in 1959 (Russell 1985b: 173). In *Principles* he uses expressions such as "entity," "absolute distinction," "absolute and metaphysical validity," "metaphysically true" (POM 187, 188, 221). In 1927 his usual expressions for ontological commitment seem to be "metaphysical implication" or "philosophical import" (AMA 2, 5). His 1927 vehicle for ontological commitment does seem to be an interpretation. But there may be interpretations of interpretations. And ontological commitment seems reserved for the ultimate interpretation, if any, in each series of interpretations. It is reserved for "primitive entities," for particulars that exist, i.e., for events (AMA 2, 8, 9). Objects which are "mathematically primitive" to a given science may in fact be "logically complex structures composed of entities which are metaphysically more primitive" (AMA 9). Thus for Russell, the ontological question is, "What are the ultimate existents in terms of which [the science] is true (assuming that there are such)?" (AMA 9) In "The Philosophy of Logical Atomism," "simples have a kind of reality not belonging to anything else" (PLA 270). Even in *Principles*, only simples have "absolute and metaphysical validity" (POM 221). And again, analysis, i.e. interpretation, may be endless (PLA 202, MPD 164–65). There might be no entities for propositions to be about at all.

Much the same picture is found in 1948 in Russell's *Human Knowledge*. There Russell expresses his theory of ontological commitment in terms of the notion of a *minimum vocabulary* into which all true talk about the world may be paraphrased (HK 79–81, 257–59, 302–3). This notion is just a linguistic stand-in for a list of the simplest things we can talk about. This concerns eliminative paraphrase in accordance with Occam's razor. Russell expressly speaks of "values of variables" which may be mere logical structures in interpretations (HK 140–41; see AMA 2–9). These texts are later than, but seem compatible with, *Principia* logic.

Much the same picture is found again in 1959 in Russell's *My Philosophical Development*. Russell says, "When we say 'there is' or 'there are', it does not follow from the truth of our statements that what we say there is or there are is part of the furniture of the world….Mathematics admits the statement 'there are numbers' and metalogic [metaphysics] admits the statement 'numbers are logical fictions or symbolic conveniences'" (MPD 173; see PLA 265–69). Once again there is not the slightest hint that *Principia* logic is being revised. And once again I must remind everyone that logical fictions have no ontological status; they are, in a word, nothing. Therefore when Russell takes them as values of bound variables, as he very clearly does in 1959, he is very clearly making no ontological commitment to them at all.

This picture of the later Russell contradicts Quine's thesis that to be is to be the value of a variable. Quine's thesis might suit Frege but it does not suit Russell, despite all those who have thought that "Russell is the source of Professor Quine's celebrated dictum" (Ayer 1972: 54).[5] Russell did hold that to be is to be the value of a variable in 1906 (Russell 1973b: 198). But we know that Russell abandoned this view because he tells us he abandoned it (MPD 53–54, 117–18). Thus the question is not whether he abandoned it but when. I suggest he abandoned it at least implicitly in *Principia*. I shall now offer eight arguments for this view.

My first argument concerns the meaning of the individual quantifier. Quine defines it as meaning 'there exists' (OR 94–95, 97, 99; WO 176, 184, 242; PQ

533–34). But Russell defines that quantifier as meaning only 'it is not always false that'. That is a veridical sense of "is," not an existential sense.

It might be objected that here *Principia* seems to speak in a Janus-faced way. The existential quantifier is said to express both existing and being 'not always false' (PM xx–xxi, 15–16, 19–20). And statements employing it are said to express "existence-theorems" (PM 20). Russell might well be read as simply making existence and being not always false intersubstitutable. But my gloss is that here Russell is eliminatively *defining* "exists" as 'not always false', just as in "On Denoting" (PM 19–20; OD 42). The latter is a technical notion and the former is an ordinary notion in need of paraphrase.

A second objection might be that 'not always false' is not intended to define the meaning of the individual quantifier but merely to specify the truth-conditions of its use. My reply is that in *Principia*, there *is* no difference between meaning and use for any incomplete expressions such as quantifiers. That is the whole point of the famous *Principia* doctrine of 'meaning in use'. Use means use in significant, i.e. true or false, statements. This includes specification of truth-conditions. Russell's meanings in use are in this respect very close to Frege's senses, following Dummett on Frege. I briefly discuss meaning in use in chapter 6. Furthermore, the truth-condition of a statement need not be the existence of the individual it is apparently about. The truth-condition of "Body *b* exists" might be a temporal series of classes of sensed and unsensed sensibilia; and in 1914–18 I think that is just what it was.

My second argument concerns what Russell allows as values of variables. Russell says, "The values may be any set of entities, propositions, functions, classes, or relations, according to circumstances" (PM 4). Is it not most curious that this laundry list *begins* with entities? Are the rest of the items on the list then *not* entities? They are *not* entities. To go down the list: (1) Entities, of course, are entities. (2) But a proposition "is a false abstraction" and "is not a single entity at all," but is instead merely an "incomplete symbol" (PM 44). (3) Functions are not entities. Function-expressions have no independent meaning, i.e., denotation, of their own, but merely "meaning in use" (PM 30, 66–67, 71). (4) Russell expressly denies that classes exist (PM 24, 71–72, 81, 83). Like propositions and functions, classes are incomplete. (Thus since numbers are classes of classes, Russell denies that numbers exist. Frege and Russell both allow numbers as values of variables, but only Frege admits numbers as entities.) (5) Relations here are a species of functions, since they too are incomplete (PM 81). To sum up, almost nothing on Russell's list of values of variables is an entity! Therefore, in *Principia*, to be is definitely not to be the value of a variable.

Gregory Landini objects to my second argument as follows: Only genuine variables require that to be is to be the value of a variable. And wherever Russell says he admits anything besides entities as values of his variables, he is not talking about his genuine variables, but about what are mere notational conveniences which merely appear to be variables. Landini fleshes this out by arguing that (i) Russell's class variables are eliminated by his contextual definitions of them, (ii) Russell's propositional variables are never quantified over, quantification being a condition of being a genuine variable, and (iii) Russell's propositional variables do not even occur in his formal logic (Landini 1995).

My reply to Landini has several parts. First, there is no difference between a variable and a genuine variable, just as there is no difference between a horse and a genuine horse. Second, even a genuine variable is a mere notational convenience with only a meaning in use, unless you admit a 'variable entity' it denotes, which Russell does not. Third, (therefore) any distinction between real and apparent variables should be a distinction in logical form only. That is what Russell's and Frege's own distinction between real and apparent variables concerns. In today's lexicon, Frege and Russell would call bound variables apparent and unbound variables real; this is their bow to the historical origin of the notion of a variable in mathematics. Of course, they have no notion of binding a variable, but arrive at variables as place-markers for smaller expressions within larger expressions. But in the present context, one would think that "apparent" variables should be a matter of surface grammar and "real" variables a matter of 'true' logical grammar, not a matter of what values they can take. Fourth, Landini offers no definition, criterion, or explanation of what a genuine variable is as opposed to a mere notational convenience. The only argument Landini appears to be using is that a genuine variable is one that takes only entities as values. Thus his objection begs the question. Lacking any independent criterion of genuine variables, Landini is arguing in a circle. And appearances are on my side, as I shall now explain.

Consider Panayot Butchvarov's neo-Meinongian–neo-Lejewskian logic with variables ranging over nonexistent mere objects. Is there anything wrong with Butchvarov's variables? Are they not genuine variables? Are they mere notational conveniences? Butchvarov thinks they are genuine enough to explain how he can assert that there are objects nobody is aware of (Butchvarov 1979: 97n, 253–54, 260 n.2). In effect, Landini is denying that anyone can have a logic with genuine variables ranging over nonexistent items. I deny that there are nonexistent items, but I would never deny my noneist colleagues genuine variables with which they can significantly express a realist position.

I reply to Landini's sub-arguments (i)–(iii) as follows. (i) All of Russell's variables without exception must be contextually introduced. Since they lack independent meanings of their own, and have only meanings in use, there is no other way to introduce them. (ii) The reason Russell does not quantify over his propositional variables is simply that they belong to his propositional calculus as opposed to his predicate calculus. What values they take has nothing to do with it. I see no reason why he could not quantify over them any time he wanted to. The reason he does not is merely expositional, even pedagogical. He *need* not quantify over them to explain the propositional calculus. (iii) Propositional variables do occur in Russell's formal logic. Landini is counting only Russell's predicate calculus as his formal logic. But Russell's propositional calculus is just as formal. And it could not get along without propositional variables.

Landini is but the sorcerer's apprentice. Quine chooses to call "schematic letters" what Frege and Russell call real variables, and "genuine variables" what Frege and Russell call apparent variables (Quine 1980: 9–10). Hey, presto! Only bound variables are genuine variables. This is verbal hocus pocus. The jargon is quicker than the mind. Pay no attention to the free variables behind that curtain! Thus Quine brushes aside centuries of mathematical variables as not "genuine." To be sure, one may discover with the progress of science that all kinds of things are not as they seemed. But "*x* is a free variable; therefore *x* is not a genuine variable" is a *non sequitur* on the face of it. So is "*x* occurs in matrices (open sentences), not in actual sentences; therefore *x* is not a genuine variable." Even "*x* is a 'schematic letter'; therefore *x* is not a genuine variable" is intuitively invalid. Quine's argument is instead:

> Such [bound] letters are called *variables*. Care must be taken, however, to divorce this traditional word of mathematics from its archaic connotations. The variable is not best thought of as somehow varying through time, and causing the sentence in which it occurs to vary with it. Neither is it to be thought of as an unknown quantity, discoverable by solving equations. The variables remain mere pronouns for cross-reference to quantifiers... (Quine 1959: 128)

Quine concludes, "This vague metaphor is best forgotten" (Quine 1983: 70). But this argument is simply more smoke and mirrors. Frege and Russell both admit free variables, which they both call the *real* variables; and both very easily reject all metaphoric talk of 'variable entities' (TW 84–85, 109; IMP 167–68). In fact, none of the metaphors Quine mentions is to be found in *Begriffsschrift*, *The Basic Laws of Arithmetic*, or *Principia*. Russell's theory of what a variable is avoids all such metaphors (PM 4–5). Nor must it be thought that only bound variables are pronominal. Consider riddles like two of the ones Gollum asked Bilbo in *The Hobbit* (Tolkien 1974: 81, 82). In them the free variable is not merely pronominal—it is an actual pronoun! Quine himself cheerfully admits that schematic letters are just free variables: "Note carefully the role of the schematic letters '*p*' and '*q*'....Similarly the schematic notation '*Fx*' may be conveniently used...when we want to direct attention to the presence therein of the variable '*x*' as a *free* or unquantified variable" (Quine 1970: 24).

My own view is that real, i.e. free, variables and apparent, i.e. bound, variables are just the same old variables in different contexts, respectively open sentences and complete sentences. The words "free" and "bound" just mark the difference in context. My argument is that Russell's theory of what a variable is applies to free variables and bound variables alike—Frege theory applies to both too, for that matter.

My third argument concerns the most basic question here: What is a variable? The answer is simple. Frege and Russell both take their variables to be historically a generalization of the mathematical notion of a variable (PM 4). They do not commit C. D. Broad's "genetic fallacy" of claiming that a later stage of a thing is just an earlier stage of the thing in disguised form, precisely because they are making a simple and direct generalization. The mathematical notion of a variable is that of a mere place-holder, and the Frege-Russell notion of a variable is basically the same notion applied more widely than just in mathematics. (Variables differ from zero as a place-holder in that zero is a determinate number, while variables are undetermined places where determinate items can be inserted. Waiving certain Fregean technicalities about defining zero for different sorts of numbers, there is only one number zero; but there can be many different variables in a sentence.) A variable is merely an abstraction from a determinate expression within a larger expression, arrived at by removing one or more occurrences of the determinate expression and replacing them with the same place-marker. Once you have acquired the notion, you can put a variable in an expression without bothering with the removal-replacement process, as when you write out an algebraic equation to be solved for x.

Right after describing the historical genesis of logical variables from mathematical variables, and giving his laundry list of values of variables, Russell states what appear to be his three necessary and sufficient conditions for an expression's being a variable:

> To sum up, the three salient facts connected with the use of the variable are: (1) that a variable is ambiguous in its denotation and accordingly undefined; (2) that a variable preserves a recognizable identity in various occurrences throughout the same context...; and (3) that either the range of possible determinations of two variables may be the same..., or the ranges of two variables may be different... (PM 4–5)

I submit that this is Russell's theory of what a variable is, and coming as it does on the heels of his anti-Quinean laundry list of variables, it goes completely against Landini's imposition of Quine on Russell. Taking only entities as values is not one of the three conditions. Nor is it implied by the three conditions taken together (PM 4). Not only does this definition of variables allow nonentities as values of variables, but Russell's laundry list shows that he does expressly allow many sorts of nonentities as just such values. Practically everything on the list is a nonentity!

This account of what variables are is important because it shows why variables are necessary to quantificational logic—and why quantification is not necessary to variables. A language L can be rich enough to include variables but not quantification, but not the other way round. For *L* can include only real, i.e. unbound, variables. Quantification is a necessary and sufficient condition of our permitting apparent variables, but is neither a necessary nor a sufficient condition of our permitting real variables, in *L*. In fact quantification is far from the only use variables have. Their most basic uses, which apply to alegebraic and logical puzzles even about *chimerae*, are pronominal and repetitional. Their usefulness is more logical, inquiry-related, or even epistemic than ontological. That is just why neo-Meinongian–neo-Lejewskian quantification over mere objects with no ontological status is intelligible, as Butchvarov well knows. It is also why to be is not to be the value of a variable.

Russell later repudiated his distinction between real and apparent variables, professing in effect to find a tacit universal generalization in every use of an ostensible real variable (PM xiii). But the distinction is very much part of historic *Principia*. And even its repudiation does not affect my arguments.

My fourth argument concerns Russell's description of all his specific sorts of variables in *Principia*. Right after giving his theory of what variables are, Russell explains all the specific sorts of variables he admits. He does not even appear to suggest that some are genuine variables and others are mere notational conveniences. He simply calls them all variables (PM 5).

My fifth argument concerns an important epistemic feature of Russell's individual variables, i.e. variables which may take individuals as values. Russell's principal explanation of how variable letters such as "*x*" are to be understood in *Principia* is:

> The values [of a variable] may be any set of entities, propositions, functions, classes, or relations....The small letters of the ordinary alphabet will all be used for variables, except *p* and *s* after *40....Of the remaining letters, *p*, *q*, *r* will be called propositional letters....*f*, *g*...will be called *functional letters*....Ordinary small letters other than *p*, *q*, *r*, *s*, *f*, *g*, will be used for variables whose values are not known to be functions, classes, or relations... (PM 4–5)

Thus *x, y,* and *z* "will be used for variables whose values are *not known* to be functions, classes, or relations." That is a far cry from variables whose values *are known* to be *individuals*. This applies to "(∃x)", and also to "E!(ιx(φx)". In fact Russell never mentions individuals when he explains such quantifiers; he talks about individuals only when defining "individual" or discussing types (see PM xix, 19–20, 51–55, 68–69, 129–33).

My sixth argument concerns *Principia* retrospectively in light of Russell's use of *Principia* logic in his 1914–18 analyses of bodies and other minds. For convenience, I shall discuss only bodies. I shall be arguing that Russell would properly use his individual quantifier to quantify over bodies even though bodies are logical fictions and therefore not entities, since bodies are at least apparent individual entities and the individual quantifier is best understood as ranging over both genuine individuals and apparent individuals. This is perhaps my most controversial argument, and if it does not succeed, I shall be content to rest on my other seven arguments. It is closely based on my fifth argument.

My fifth argument seems to imply that the 1914–18 Russell would properly use "(∃x)" to quantify over minds and bodies, even though he constructs these as temporal series of classes of sensed and unsensed sensibilia, and even though such series and classes are incomplete. The reason is that minds and bodies are *not known* to be metaphysical individuals over and above such constructions. Russell always takes pains to say that, e.g., metaphysical selves *may* exist. I suggest that since Russell's "(∃x)" expresses not an existential sense of "is" but only a veridical sense of "is" as 'not always false', *Principia* already leaves the door open for quantification over individuals which *may* "exist" only in the secondary sense as constructions. Granted, the constructions themselves *are* known to be incomplete, and cannot be quantified over using "(∃x)". What is not known is whether body *b* before us is merely a construction. Furthermore, quantifying over constructions using the class-quantifier leads to the bizarre result that phantoms and hallucinations, as classes with wild particulars as their single or few members, are just as real as constructed ordinary minds and bodies with their myriad lawful members, since a class exists even if it has only one member—and these have at least one member.

The dilemma for the 1914–18 Russell is this. "Body *b* exists" ought to be writable in the canonical notation. Bodies are analyzed as temporal series of classes of senses and unsensed sensibilia. Such series and classes are incomplete, hence strictly nothing. Thus such series and classes are said to exist only in a purely conventional sense. They are said to exist if they have even just one member. But then to say that bodies exist in this sense is to admit phantoms and hallucinations as existing bodies, since the classes these involve always have at least one member, namely a 'wild' particular. And a time-serial class of classes would exist if one class exists as its member. Thus a phantom, *qua* time-serial class, would exist in the secondary sense of "exist." (There could also be 'continuous phantoms' on the serial level; nobody would consider them to be bodies.) But this is absurd. Phantoms are not bodies. I call this the problem of the phantom body.

By default only the individual quantifier is left. There is no third option. The only other main sorts of quantifier Russell has are for propositions and relations, and these seem most inappropriate for phantom individual bodies. But can the individual quantifier be used, if bodies are not individuals? The only way out seems to be the one I provided: bodies can be quantified over as *apparent* individuals. In fact, Russell already admits much the same sort of solution in another context:

It seems obvious that, if we meet something which may be a man or may be an angel in disguise, it comes within the scope of 'all men are mortal' to assert 'if this is a man, it is mortal'....It is obvious that *always* includes some cases in which *x* is not a man, as we saw in the case of the disguised angel. If *x* were limited to the case when *x* is a man, we could infer that *x* is a mortal, since if *x* is a man, *x* is a mortal. Hence, with the same meaning of *always*, we should find 'it is always true that *x* is mortal'. But it is plain that, without altering the meaning of *always*, this new proposition is false, though the other was true. (LK 70–71)

By parity of reason, just as disguised angels are seeming men, bodies are *seeming individuals*. Russell admits bodies *seem* to be individuals to the ordinary person. Russell even admits they may *be* individuals. That is why the individual quantifier can be used to assert their existence. I concede that "is a man" is written as a type 1 order 0 predicate, say "*Mx*," while being an individual is shown by the shape of a type 0 constant letter, say "*a.*" But the same argument applies in both cases. Where *x* is a *disguised fiction*, we would not want to infer that *x* is an individual any more than we want to infer that a disguised angel is a man.

One objection to my sixth argument might be that there are five big disanalogies between seeming men and seeming individuals. First, "Men exist" is *false* if there are no men, but only angels in disguise, while I am arguing that "Men exist" is *true* in case there are no metaphysical selves, but only apparent individual men. Second, presumably angels in disguise have ontological status as angels, while apparent individuals are logical fictions and have no ontological status. Third, men are a subspecies, *homo sapiens sapiens*, while individuals are a metaphysical category. Fourth, both men and angels *are* individuals, while the same cannot be said of, say, both bodies and apparent bodies. Fifth, Russell's aim is to find some rational, "natural restriction upon the possible values of" *x* in "*x* is a man" such that they are "restricted within some legitimate totality," i.e. according to theory of types (LK 71). And allowing both genuine individuals and temporal series of classes to be values of the same variable scarcely yields a legitimate totality. But I do not think that such disanalogies really matter to my argument. The crucial respect of resemblance obtains: namely, in both cases Russell admits as values of the variable items which do not actually satisfy the description concerned, but which are sufficiently similar to items which would that we do not know the difference (compare LK 70–75). The crucial fact is that both logically fictitious men and angels disguised as men *seem* to be men; they are not known *not* to be men. Indeed, if the angels' disguises are not lifelong and perfect, then logically fictitious men will seem even more like genuinely individual men than disguised angels will, since the former are all men ever *are*, if men are logical fictions. That is what counts when Russell says in *Principia*:

"Ordinary small letters other than p, q, r, s, f, g, will be used for variables whose values are not known to be functions, classes, or relations" (PM 5).

The real objection to my sixth argument is that surely Russell would not use the individual quantifier in this way. Using the individual quantifier to assert the "existence" of a body would be a mere notational shorthand for a full analysis. If he were to use it at all in his analysis of a body, he would do so only in order to assert the existence of each unsensed sensibilium. And in fact, since he analyzes bodies as temporal series of classes, he should not be using the individual quantifier at all. He should be using the class quantifier instead. Otherwise, all perspicuity would seem lost: indefinitely many different sensibilia would be treated as if they were a single fictitious body.

My reply is that it is very tempting to think we know what Russell's analysis of a body would look like, since he openly states he analyzes a body as a temporal series of classes of sensed and unsensed sensibilia. But this statement is not itself an analysis of a body. Nobody has ever given such an analysis of a body. Rudolf Carnap tried but failed. Russell never even tried, but merely gave a sketch which Carnap filled out as best he could. So we do not know what a successful analysis would look like, because we have never seen one. Russell said of analyzing bodies in terms of sense-data alone, "I soon...became persuaded that this is an impossible programme" (MPD 79). But then he came to find analyzing bodies in terms of sensed and unsensed sensibilia possible, at least in 1914–18. Thus the question of workability was clearly on Russell's mind. And that invites using a principle of charity in interpretation.

Griffin says Russell never successfully constructed bodies out of sensibilia (Griffin 1991: 11). This is the general consensus, and I agree with it. I shall not attempt to assess the old debate whether such an analysis is impossible only in practice or is in principle impossible to complete due to the indefinitely many sensibilia involved, or whether Russell's device of dealing with sensibilia by the classful avoids the problem or only postpones it to the indefinitely many classes needed. (Even with the collective power of classes to capture infinitely many members, the merest flicker of a candle would involve indefinitely many classes of sensibilia in its actual history alone, not to mention all the situations it *might* have been in.) There was even a debate whether analyses need be complete propositions, so that "Body b exists" may retain a determinate truth-value upon analysis, or whether the complete analysis need only exist in reality, regardless of whether we finite humans could fully discover it, or express it in a finite sentence. I am merely adding to this quagmire that since a class exists if it only has one member, even a phantom would count as a body.

I have been speaking of specific analyses of specific bodies. Perhaps Russell was only concerned to give a general analysis of bodies in general. In that sense he definitely did give an analysis. To that extent the old debate is wholly avoided. The question is, How would we best represent Russell's analysis? Once again, it is tempting to think we know, because he says bodies are temporal series of classes of sensed and unsensed sensibilia. It is very tempting to say that only the class quantifier should be involved. But while the old debate is avoided, the problem of the phantom body remains, since it arises specifically from the class quantifier's use, and is avoided only by the individual quantifier's use.

Thus we are faced with a dilemma. Either we saddle Russell with an unworkable analysis of bodies using the class quantifier or with a workable analysis using the individual quantifier. It seems to me that a principle of charity calls for the latter. The only price we pay is to admit that those temporal series of classes of sensed and unsensed sensibilia which appear to be bodies, are apparent bodies, hence apparent individuals, hence can be quantified over as if they were individuals. Not only is this plausible, but we can assimilate it to a view of values of variables Russell himself endorses in the context of genuine and apparent men (LK 70–71). By 1927 Russell uses the individual quantifier to quantify over ordinary bodies as mere logical structures; and perspicuity is preserved by providing interpretations of interpretations (AMA 2–9).

My seventh argument supports the sixth. It is based on Russell's 1924 paper, "Logical Atomism," which does not even appear to be modifying the *Principia* definition of the individual quantifier as meaning 'not always false'. The argument is this. Whatever can be named by a logically proper name must be simple. If an item has any complexity, then it is a fact and ought to be asserted by a statement. "The way to mean a fact is to assert it; the way to mean a simple is to name it" (LK 336). But Russell adds, " When I speak of 'simples' I ought to explain that I am speaking of something not experienced as such, but known only inferentially as the limit of analysis....If what we take to be simple is really complex, we may get into trouble by naming it, when what we ought to do is to assert it....[And] we do not experience simples as such" because they may always turn out to be complex (LK 337–38). There might be no simples and analysis might be endless. But even if a complex experience logically must be composed of presented simples, we can never know if we are correctly singling out a simple *as* a simple (LK 337). Russell presents this as an obstacle to "the actual creation of a logically correct language," i.e., "an ideal logical language (which of course would be wholly useless for daily life)" (LK 338). All this is, of course, consistent with restricting the individual quantifiers to simples in *Principia* logic construed as an ideal logical language. My only point is that all this implies that human beings are never entitled to use the individual quantifier in serious discourse about the world unless we may use it to quantify over what *may* turn out to be merely apparent individuals. If to be is to be the value of a variable, then all values of variables must be simple; but we can never know what is simple. And if we allow quantification over apparent simples, then why not over apparent bodies? Indeed, this may be precisely why Russell says in *Principia* that variable letters bound by the individual quantifier "will be used for variables which are not *known* to be" nonindividuals (PM 5, italics mine).

Thus the argument hinges on whether Russell exclusively intended *Principia* logic to schematize an ideal logical language, or whether he intended it to be also capable of actual use by human beings. I do not believe that the pre-1927 Russell expressly answers this question. But it seems to me that his actions speak far louder than any words he said or might have said. The post-*Principia* Russell is constantly touting his logic as essential to framing his own analyses of bodies, minds, numbers, space, and time, and is constantly blaming earlier thinkers for using an inferior logic. It may look like window dressing at times, but the fact remains that Russell himself used *Principia* logic to analyze things more than anyone else. Charity suggests he must have come to know this meant that the individual quantifier can take merely apparent individuals as values of its variable. Indeed, he expressly admits it in his 1927 book, *The Analysis of Matter*, as we saw earlier (AMA 2–9). It is possible that such uses of the individual quantifier are 'tongue in cheek'. But charity also seems to call for not saddling Russell with any Tractarian quagmires about whistling what you cannot say, or using 'important kinds of nonsense' to expose nonsense. The question is really the same as in the sixth argument: Does Russell advocate a clearly unusable form of logical analysis—or an actually usable one?

My eighth argument supports the seventh and the sixth. It is that Russell openly states in *Principia* that classes can be named by apparent names. He says "we can dismiss the whole apparatus of functions and think only of classes as 'quasi-things', capable of immediate representation by a single name" (PM 81). Russell goes on to enumerate two advantages of doing so which need not detain us here. As for classes, so for temporal series. Russell does not get as far as expressly admitting classes as apparent individuals which can be values of variables bound by the individual quantifier. But the leap from admitting apparent names for classes to admitting classes as apparent individuals is a leap over the narrowest of ditches.

This concludes my eight arguments that implicitly in *Principia*, the individual quantifier is ontologically noncommittal, having a veridical meaning-in-use, not an existential meaning-in-use. I have not attempted to assess how well Russell was aware of that at the time. But charity and the first few pages of *The Analysis of Matter* suggest that at the least, he gradually became fully aware of it. In *The Analysis of Matter*, Russell does not even appear to present his view that the individual quantifier can range over logical structures—over *apparent individuals*—as a revision of *Principia* logic. If it were, one might expect some mention of such a huge revision in the preface to the second edition of *Principia* in 1927, published in the same year as *The Analysis of Matter*. But there is no such mention. This is not to mention that the problem of the phantom body begins in 1914. I myself might date his full awareness to about 1914.

My interpretation inverts that of Douglas Lackey. Lackey observes that in an unpublished note "in 1906, Russell wrote '...whatever can be an apparent variable must have some kind of being', and specifically applies this rule to quantification over predicate variables. This passage anticipates Quine's own slogan 'to be is to be the value of a bound variable' by some forty years" (Lackey 1973: 134). Lackey later reveals that Russell also published the view in 1906 (Lackey 1973: 190; Russell 1973b: 198). Lackey's account of the 1906 Russell is excellent. But Lackey also claims that because "the *Principia* system requires that propositional functions serve as variables of quantification,....*Principia* is committed to propositional functions *in re*" (Lackey 1973: 133). Lackey notes that properties have being in 1912 (in PP), and adds, "It is hardly credible that Russell could have been unaware of the ontological commitments inherent in a system on which he had been working for ten years" (Lackey 1973: 133). Lackey is repeating Quine's famous criticism that in *Principia*, Russell rejects classes only to reify propositional functions by quantifying over them (Quine 1971: 8). Lackey's later paper in *Russell* is even more excellent in describing the 1906 Russell's Quinean criterion of ontological commitment, but still imposes this criterion quite uncritically on *Principia* (Lackey 1974–75).

The Quine-Lackey-Landini position is dubious. Russell's logic is changing during these years, and not least with respect to its ontological commitments. He rejects nonexistent beings in 1905, then classes in 1910. So we should be quite cautious of finding in *Principia* a test of ontological commitment held four years earlier. We should look to *Principia* itself, and to Russell's retrospective comments on changes in his conception of ontological commitment. When we looked to *Principia* itself, we found that Russell allows entities as values of variables, but allows everything he denies is an entity as values of variables too: propositions, functions, classes, and (function-)relations. And the retrospective Russell openly confesses that he abandoned his *Principles* view that to be is to be the value of a variable, as having "had a kind of morning innocence" (MPD 53–54, 118–19). Again, the only question is not whether he abandoned it, but when. My eight arguments suggest he did so in *Principia*. Certainly to the 1927–59 Russell, Quine, Lackey, and Landini are just morning innocents. Curiously enough, they never mention the later Russell on ontological commitment.

Quine and Lackey conflate a propositional function with the universal which is its determinate constituent (see MAL 216, 220–21). A propositional function also has an undetermined constituent, indicated by a variable letter (see MAL 221.) Russell admits universals as higher type-level terms in *Principia* (taking PM xix as a retrospective gloss on PM 43–44). Universals are real; however, propositional functions are not. "[A]djectives...and verbs stand for universals" (PP 93). Russell also uses "denotes," implying that the verb "like" is a type 1 order 0 logically proper name (PP 93). Such words may "feel" incomplete and "seem to demand a context" (PP 94). But the universals they denote are real, and are surely complete beings (PP 100); the incompleteness devolves to the undetermined constituents of propositional functions. Nor does Quine lose the battle on propositional functions only to win the war on universals. Russell quantifies only over the former in *Principia*. He admits no variables that take universals as values in that work so far as I can see.

In fact, since the seed of the veridical quantifier is already in "On Denoting," Russell's 1906 position on ontological commitment seems a mere oddity, an aberration in his development from 1905 to 1948. Why base our whole picture of Russell's ontological journey on his only retrograde step?

My interpretation also controverts the extremely natural and plausible view of Ivor Grattan-Guinness that Russell admits several senses of "exists" in *Principia*, and that while, e.g., classes exist in a merely and purely conventional sense, the existential quantifier for individuals, "($\exists x$)," expresses an ontological sense. Grattan-Guinness is absolutely right that for Russell, all individuals exist, and that this is the right quantifier to use for individuals. Unfortunately, Grattan-Guinness overlooks my eight arguments. However, I retain great respect for Grattan-Guinness's interpretation. Not only is it the one I would accept if my own did not succeed, but it is the one I did accept for over twenty years, though without articulating it in anything like the detail Grattan-Guinness does. I see it as the standard interpretation, and as more plausible than Landini's, since all Grattan-Guinness does is carefully describe the senses of "exists" which seem to be in *Principia*, and never bases his interpretation of the individual quantifier as implying ontological commitment on the circular argument that individual variables are genuine, where a genuine variable is one that implies ontological commitment. Reasonable people can differ on ontological commitment in *Principia*; my own arguments repeatedly rely on charity in interpretation.

As Grattan-Guinness observes, Russell's class identity-class "existence" connection confers no ontological status on classes, but is merely verbal, in *Principia* if not in *Principles* (Grattan-Guinness 1973: 71–72). Theory (3) is that classes "exist" if they have members. And thanks to the extensionality of classes, the very members that define a class's "existence" also define its identity. *Principia* *20.071 defines class "existence"; *20.31 and *20.43 assert the extensional identity of classes. This "being" *qua* identity connection governs theories (4)–(13). One possible reason for the conventionality of classes' "existence" is to soften the fact that the null class, which appeared basic to logicizing mathematics, is the only class which does not exist. In *Principles* classes exist if they have members and are extensionally identifiable in terms of their members (POM 20–21); Russell dutifully infers that there is no null class, only a null class-concept (POM 75) But in 1910 the null class is on a par with other classes, since *no* classes exist. The null class alone cannot be quantified over using the class quantifier (PM 29, 190, *20.071), but then that quantifier is merely conventional.

Russell gives at least five formulations of the notion of a description from 1903 to 1918. (i) Denoting phrases stand for denoting concepts in 1903 (POM 53–56). (ii) Denoting phrases have no independent meaning in 1905 (OD 51). (iii) Descriptions are nothing and mean nothing, but only have meaning in use in 1910 (PM 30, 66–67). (iv) Descriptions have at least one determinate constituent (a universal) and at least one undetermined constituent (a variable) in 1911 (MAL 216, 220–21). (v) Descriptions are nothing, presumably because they have an undetermined constituent (a variable), in 1918 (PLA 230–32, 234, 253–54, 262). It is not clear that (ii)–(v) indicate significant differences in theory. But there is a deep difference between (i) and the rest which I shall now explain.

The theory of definite descriptions plays a pivotal role in the great change on ontological commitment from *Principles* to "On Denoting." In *Principles*, the mere use of the singular definite article is a neo-Meinongian general criterion of ontological commitment to a denoted entity; I have found only nine exceptions. Russell says about the notion of *the*, "The use of identity and the theory of definition are dependent on this notion, which thus has the very highest philosophical importance" (POM 62). Concerning definition Russell says:

> The word *the*, in the singular, is correctly employed only in relation to a class-concept of which there is only one instance....Every term is the only instance of *some* class-concept, and thus every term, theoretically, is capable of definition, provided we have not adopted a system in which the said term is one of our indefinables....[Even where we define a class] what is really defined is *the* class satisfying certain conditions....Thus the notion of *the* is always relevant in definitions... (POM 62–63)

Concerning identity he says:

> The connection of denoting with the nature of identity is important, and helps, I think, to solve some rather serious problems. The question whether identity is or is not a relation, or even whether there is such a concept at all, is not easy to answer. For, it may be said, identity cannot be a relation, since, where it is truly asserted, we have only one term, whereas two terms are required for a relation. And indeed identity, an objector may urge, cannot be anything at all: two terms plainly are not identical, and one term cannot be, for what is it identical with? Nevertheless identity must be something. (POM 63)

The second objection to identity appears eighteen years later in the *Tractatus*, where Wittgenstein succumbs to it and denies that identity is a relation (T 5.5301–T 5.5303). But Russell goes on to offer an indirect proof that identity is a relation. He adduces a vicious regress of relational identities against the opposing analysis that "two terms are identical in some respect when they have a given relation to a given term"—i.e. the *same* relation to the *same* term, and concludes by forfeit that we must make a "sheer denial that two different terms are necessary" for a relation to obtain (POM 63–64). Russell continues:

> But the question arises: Why is it ever worth while to affirm identity?...When a term is given, the assertion of its identity with itself, though true, is perfectly futile...but where denoting concepts are introduced, identity is at once seen to be significant. In this case there is involved, though not asserted, a relation of the denoting concept to the term, or of the two denoting concepts to each other. (POM 64)

This is theory (28), which is replaced by theory (29)) in "On Denoting."

Theory (29) in effect contextually defines "The *F* is *G*" as 'There *exists* an *x* which is *F*, and that *x* is *G*, and any *y* which is *F* is *identical* with *G*'. The 1959 Russell says that the theory of descriptions: eliminates Meinong's jungle of nonexistent referents of expressions like "the golden mountain"; shows that an expression can contribute to the meaning of a statement without having any "meaning in isolation," i.e., denotation; explains the possibility of factually informative identity statements; shows the great difference between logically proper names and descriptions; allows analyzing ordinary names as disguised definite descriptions; and illuminates the nature of existence by showing that significant existence assertions really predicate the property 'not always false' of descriptions, thus eliminating existence as a property of things or as a kind of thing itself. Theory (29) thus coordinates Russell's theory of existence with his definition of number, his solution of the problem of one and many in terms of classes, and his subsequent elimination of classes and analysis of ordinary things as classes, i.e., fictions (MPD 63–65).

But Russell had explained factually informative identities in terms of denoting concepts, and had described Frege's view that existence is second-level in *Principles* (POM sect. 64 and Appendix A). What is new is the contextual elimination of 'independent meaning' from definite descriptions. That is, the new thing is the elimination of ontological commitment from the use of the singular definite article. This is done by showing how to eliminate the singular definite article through a contextual definition. "The author of *Waverley* is Scott" is defined as, "There exists an *x* such that *x* wrote *Waverley* and anything which wrote *Waverley* is identical with *x*; and *x* is identical with Scott."

> Thus the identity [e.g. of Scott with the author of Waverley] is that of a variable, i.e. of an identifiable subject, 'someone'....Here the identity is between a variable, i.e. an indeterminate subject ('he'), and Scott; 'the author of Waverley' has been analyzed away, and no longer appears as a constituent of the proposition (MAL 220).

Indeed, "a variable preserves a recognizable identity in various occurrences throughout the same context, so that many variables can occur together in the same context each with its separate identity..." (PM 4-5). This is theory (31), first appearing in 1903 ("variables have a kind of individuality," POM 94) and resulting in the axiom of identification of real variables (PM 13, 97/*1.72). Russell admits no variable people in addition to the definite people there are (IMP 168-73). Thus he agrees with Frege's rejection of variable *entities*, presumably for Frege's reason that such entities would be indiscernible (TW 109). Following Frege, Russell rejects even partly indefinite particulars both in his theory of universals and in his logic.

Russell learned about connecting existence and identity some eight years before Quine was born. Russell published his own first such connection five years before Quine was born. Russell said, "The whole theory of definition, of identity, of classes, of symbolism, and of the variable is wrapped up in the theory of denoting" (POM 54) some fifty-seven years before Quine said, "The whole apparatus [of "objective reference: our articles and pronouns, our singular and plural, our copula, our identity predicate"] is interdependent" (WO 53), some nine years before Russell met Wittgenstein, and supposedly shortly before Russell read Frege with any genuine understanding.

But Russell's 'no entity without identity' has a root in the past. Frege and Russell alike were influenced by Leibniz. Russell's deepest lesson from Leibniz was the dictum, *Quodlibet ens est unum*, and the biconditional of which it is part, *Ens et unum convertuntur*. Russell says in *The Philosophy of Leibniz*:

> "Where there are only beings by aggregation," Leibniz says, "there are not even real beings. For every being by aggregation presupposes beings endowed with a true unity, since it only derives its reality from that of those of which it is composed, so that it will have none at all if every component is again a being by aggregation."...What is not truly one being, is not truly a being [for Leibniz]. (PL 103-5; see 71)

The dictum's influence may not be obvious. Russell does not include the dictum among Leibniz's five "principal premises," or even mention it in his account of Leibniz in *A History of Western Philosophy*. Thus Russell may appear not to consider the dictum important even to Leibniz. In his own philosophy, Russell sometimes denies that there must be simples if there are complexes, and affirms both that complexity is presented and that presentations must be real. These views come close respectively to denying that beings by aggregation derive their being from beings that are truly one, and affirming that beings by aggregation are real. Leibniz's dictum cannot even be significantly stated for Russell or Frege. For if every item is one ('is a unit' for Frege), then it cannot be informative to say that there is one such-and-such. I appeal, therefore, to *Principia* itself. Russell says:

In the case of descriptions, it was possible to prove that they are incomplete symbols. In the case of classes, we do not know of any equally definite proof, though arguments of more or less cogency can be elicited from the ancient problem of the One and the Many.*
*Briefly, these arguments reduce to the following: If there is such an object as a class, it must be in some sense one object. Yet it is...of classes that many can be predicated. Hence, if we admit classes as objects, we must suppose that the same object can be both one and many, which seems impossible. (PM 72)

This 'more or less cogent' argument's first premise openly states *Quodlibet ens est unum*: "If there is such an object as a class, it must in some sense be one object." I also cite Russell's letter of January 1, 1906 to Philip Jourdain. Russell says:

What was wrong was assuming individuals which have no being....I now extend this to all classes. The error seems to me to lie in supposing that many entities ever combine to form one new entity. (Russell 1973a: 68)

Here Russell endorses *Ens et unum convertuntur*. *Quodlibet ens est unum* is implied by the second sentence, and its converse is implied by the first sentence.

Ens et unum convertuntur is the ontological power behind the logical throne of Russell's atomism. It explains Russell's lifelong tendency to equate the real both with the simple and with what is empirically given as one thing. Conversely, it explains his rejection of classes as fictitious or unreal. In short, the dictum explains Russell's modified realism, on which some identities are real and others are conceptual. Where Occam's razor is the negative epistemic root, *Ens et unum convertuntur* is the positive ontological root of Russell's rejection of the old classes as many and classes as one. It is the positive reason for his eliminative solution of "perhaps even the fundamental problem of philosophy."

The lesson was not just from Leibniz. Leibniz found "Plato's profoundest philosophy...in the *Parmenides*" (Cornford 1939: vi). Again, Russell read Plato's *Parmenides* in early 1899 (Griffin 1991: 335 n.16), just a year before his book on Leibniz was published (Griffin 1995).

Geach says that in *Ens et unum convertuntur*, it makes no sense to view the two transcendental terms as logically convertible or intersubstitutable *salva veritate*, much less to define or explain being as one; what was meant is only that the two terms "turn together, like a train of gear wheels" (Geach 1973: 287–88). I wholly grant that Geach is right about the classical Latin meaning of *convertuntur*. But the real question is *why* the two terms turn together. Is it a mere coincidence? Is it, perhaps, some sort of a pre-established ontological harmony? Aristotle says, "That 'unity' has in some sense the same meaning as that of 'being' is clear" (*Metaphysics* 1054a10–15). I suggest that is why being and unity turn together. Besides, we are concerned with being and unity as they appear in the analytic tradition, and are scarcely restricted by classical Latin. Frege and Russell distinguish the metaphysical or objectual sense of unity from the numerical sense; Wittgenstein and Quine may be glossed as doing so as well. The problem of classes concerns metaphysical unity.

3. Minds and Bodies

In *Principles* bodies are classes-as-one of material points (POM 523). Material points would remain existents even if classes of them are no longer existents in *Principia*. Russell's 1912 *The Problems of Philosophy*, far from eliminating material points, speaks freely of bodies. Also in *Principles*, all minds are existent classes-as-one of psychical existents (POM 523); one's own mind remains an existent until the 1919 Russell (LK 299, 305–6).

In the 1914 *Our Knowledge of the External World*, Russell wishes to instantiate theory (3) to the physical world. This requires replacing bodies with classes of events, classes which do not exist as objects, but which can be said to be "real" in some appropriate sense. This sense is the secondary, or correlative, sense of "real" or "exist" described in chapter 4. Thus bodies cannot be quantified over using the class quantifier, even though they are (temporal series of) classes. For a class has class existence if it has but one member (PM 188, *20.071), while bodies need indefinitely many members to count as real. While "[o]bjects of sense [sense-data], even when they occur in dreams, are the most indubitably real objects known to us," what we call real are only appropriately correlated groups of such objects (KEW 71). Thus bodies require the individual quantifier, even though they are not individuals. And bodies are at least *apparent* individuals.

Russell constructs a model of the ordinary world as a system of perspectives, based on Leibniz's monadology. He says:

We can now define the...common-sense "thing," as opposed to its momentary appearances....Given an object in one perspective, form the system of all the objects correlated with it in all the perspectives; that system may be identified with the...common-sense thing....All the aspects of a thing are real, whereas the thing is a mere logical construction. It has, however, the merit of being neutral as between different points of view, and of being visible to more than one person, in the only sense in which it can ever be visible, namely, in the sense that each person sees one of its aspects. (KEW 73–74)

Russell's analysis logically commits him to holding that an alleged physical thing is considered real by us if and only if there are informative identities about it across perspectives. For the very sense-data in the various perspectives which constitute the correlative reality of Russell's logical constructions also provide, *ipso facto*, for informative identities across those perspectives concerning those constructions. It is only natural, then, that Russell finds that providing identity conditions for 'physical things' is the most serious difficulty his theory must face. Russell says, "The problem is: by what principles shall we select certain data from the chaos, and call them all appearances of the same thing?" (KEW 86; see HK 290). He explains:

> If it is to be unambiguous whether two appearances belong to the same thing or not, there must be only one way of grouping appearances so that the resulting things obey the laws of physics. It would be very difficult to prove that this is the case, but for our present purposes we may let this point pass, and assume that there is only one way. (KEW 88)

The indented quotation states theory (5). It concerns not just sense-data but unsensed sensibilia as well. Most physical things are constructions entirely or almost entirely of unsensed sensibilia. This means that the 1914 Russell was definitely no ontological idealist and definitely no phenomenalist. True, in *External World* Russell seems to construct possible sense-data out of sensed sense-data. But Russell makes it plain, in other works published in the same year, that sensibilia are physically real and exist independently of being sensed by anyone. Russell also says in retrospect that he had found phenomenalism, i.e. the use of only sense-data, i.e. the use of only *sensed* sensibilia, to construct "physical objects...an impossible programme" (MPD 79). I wish to make all this very plain because Alan Richardson once attributed to Alberto Coffa the view that the 1914 Russell was an ontological idealist.[6]

As in logic and mathematics, Russell makes propositions basic. In this case they are the laws of physics. These laws, along with an assumed continuity of appearances, provide the backbone identity conditions for our talk of physical things. Thus Russell says, "*Things are those series of aspects which obey the laws of physics*" (KEW 88). Thus physics essentially consists of propositions and sensibilia. Physical objects, like all classes, are shaved by Occam's razor (KEW 86–89; see PL 47–48, AMA 319, 325).

The *locus classicus* of Russell's conception of correlational fictitious existence as identifiability is his 1918 "The Philosophy of Logical Atomism." Russell states this conception with great explicitness and clarity. Concerning what is real, Russell says that particulars, or sense-data, "have the most complete and absolute and perfect reality that anything can have" (PLA 274). Thus phantoms, which we call unreal, are real. But chairs and desks, which we call real, are unreal. Russell says, "The distinction between what some people would call real existence, and existence in people's imagination or in my subjective activity, that distinction,…is entirely one of correlation" (PLA 258). Russell says, "When you see a 'real' man, the immediate object that you see is one of a whole system of particulars, all of which belong together and make up collectively the various 'appearances' of the man to himself and others" (PLA 258). Once again, to have correlative existence is to be informatively identifiable. Russell's best statement of theory (5) is:

> In the case of matter,…'What do I mean by saying that this desk that I am looking at now is the same as the one I was looking at a week ago?'…Now the essential point is this: What is the empirical reason that makes you call a number of appearances, appearances of the same desk? What makes you say on successive occasions, I am seeing the same desk?…There is something given in experience which makes you call it the same desk, and having once grasped that fact, you can go on and say, it is that something (whatever it is) that makes you call it the same desk which shall be defined as constituting it the same desk, and there shall be no assumption of a metaphysical entity which is identical throughout. (PLA 272–73)

Eli Hirsch makes his theory of bodies "fairly close to" Russell's theory (5) (Hirsch 1982: 134). Hirsch is well aware that theory (5) is a 'no entity without identity' theory, if not that Russell is a 'no entity without identity' ontologist in general (Hirsch 1982: 7–8). Russell proceeds to his best statement of theory (6):

> What is it that makes you say, when you meet your friend Jones, 'Why, this is Jones'? It is clearly not the persistence of a metaphysical entity inside Jones somewhere, because even if there be such an entity, it certainly is not what you see when you see Jones coming along the street…Therefore plainly there is something in the empirical appearances which he presents to you, which enables you to collect all these together and say, "These are what I call the appearances of one person'…It does not matter…what exactly is the given empirical relation between two experiences that makes us say, 'These are two experiences of the same person'….because the mere fact that you can know that two experiences belong to the same person proves that there is such an empirical relation to be ascertained by analysis. Let us call the relation R. We shall say that when two experiences have to each other the relation R, then they are said to be experiences of the same person. That is a definition of what I mean by 'experiences of the same person'. (PLA 276–77)

Sydney Shoemaker is well aware that theory (6) is a 'no entity without identity' theory, if not that Russell is a 'no entity without identity' ontologist in general (Shoemaker 1974: 147–48). Russell deems theories (5) and (6) strictly parallel to theory (4):

> We proceed here just in the same way as when we are defining numbers. We first define what is meant by saying that two classes 'have the same number', and then define what a number is. (PLA 277)

Knowledge of bodies and minds (or persons) is wholly empirical, just as knowledge of the actual world was for Leibniz. Russell urges elsewhere against Peano that even knowledge of numbers comes from the experience of counting similar series (POM 124–27; IMP 9–10; HK 237). Note how factually informative identity is equally constitutive of fictitious "existence" in every case.

While the 1914–18 Russell's bodies are nothing, they are for all that what Leibniz would call *bene fundata*, i.e. fictions that are well-founded in sensed and unsensed sensibilia. A train may be a logical fiction, but in ordinary terms one does well not to stand on the tracks in front of it. Again, there seems to be some tension in that while a temporal series of classes may be strictly nothing, it will correspond to a complex relational fact—and facts very much real.

Russell's 1921 *The Analysis of Mind* shows that Russell's notion of correlational reality is not confined to realist subject-act-object theories, but applies to neutral monism as well. Russell now rejects sense-data (objects) for a distinction between psychological sensations and noticed data. Yet Russell clearly retains correlative reality. So that Russell's analysis of, e.g., matter, is virtually the same as in 1914. Thus Russell still uses logical constructions. In fact, the identity conditions for matter are even more fully examined. Russell's earlier tendency toward neutral monism comes to fruition here literally as a matter of mix-and-match identity conditions using events. Identifiability in 1921 is even more constitutive of the secondary fictionalist 'reality' of bodies and minds than it was in 1918, since in 1921 he holds that even one's own mind is so constituted. Now all bodies, all minds, all numbers, and all classes are so constituted and so quantifiable over. Russell's 1921 neutral monism is the zenith of his logical fictionalism and the zenith of his fictionalist being *qua* identity.

4. General Relativity Theory

No doubt due to his new-found scientific realism, in 1927 Russell asks a new question: Can any existence-identity connection be extended beyond constructions to any inferred existents besides unsensed sensibilia? His answer is "Yes." A science such as physics is 'true' just in case there is an interpretation for it, that is, in case there are logical structures or particulars which satisfy its hypotheses. That physics is largely true in this sense, where the logical structures or particulars exist independently of our existence, is called "the realist hypothesis." This is as opposed to phenomenalism and to solipsism, on which the only genuine entities are percepts. In physics we may have to assume entities we cannot perceive, such as electrons and units of space and time. Such a realism is broadly representational, since physical structures can cause us to sense sense-data which, as representations, may be very remote from physical reality (AMA 15–16, 27; see HK 7, 220–22, 456).

Russell's most important discussions of such existence-identity connections in scientific theories concern general relativity theory and quantum mechanics. Concerning relativity theory Russell says, "Relativity physics, like all physics, assumes the realistic hypothesis, that there are occurrences which different people can observe" (AMA 48). And a common-sense principle assumed even in relativity is "that when different observers are doing what is called 'observing the same phenomenon,' those respects in which their observations differ do not belong to the phenomenon, but only those respects in which their observations agree" (AMA 48). Russell explains how considerations of relativity of motion make the old notions of identity of temporal length, identity of spatial distance, and identity of material continuants obsolete:

> It is natural to think of motion as following a path in space which is there before and after the motion: a tram moves along pre-existing tramlines. This view of motion, however, is no longer tenable. A moving point is a series of positions in space-time; a later moving point cannot pursue the "same" course, since its time coordinate is different, which means that, in another equally legitimate system of coordinates, its space coordinates will also be different. We think of a tram as performing the same journey every day because we think of the earth as fixed; but from the sun's point of view, the tram never repeats a former journey. 'We cannot step twice into the same river', as Heraclitus says. (AMA 61–62)

Thus relativity theory in effect denies the existence of times and distances due to their lack of identity across frames of reference. This implies a 'no entity without identity' connection for the realist hypothesis. But Russell is also concerned to find an assay of bodies which does preserve their identity across frames of reference:

> There is one matter of great theoretical importance, which is not very clear in the usual accounts of relativity. How do we know whether two events are to be regarded as happening to the same piece of matter? An electron or a proton is supposed to preserve its identity throughout time; but our fundamental continuum is a continuum of events. One

must therefore suppose that one unit of matter is a series of events, or a series of sets of events. It is not clear what is the theoretical criterion for determining whether two events belong to one such series....The decision must depend on intermediate history—i.e. upon the existence of some series of intermediate events (or sets of events) following each other according to some law....[T]here are such laws, but their importance in this connection is not emphasized, because it has hardly been realized that there is a problem owing to the substitution of events for bits of matter as the fundamental stuff of physics. (AMA 80–81)

This passage states theory (10) as a modification of theory (5). Clearly, Russell rejects the old pieces of matter because identity conditions can no longer be maintained for them. Equally clearly, he admits the new serial sort of matter because identity conditions can be maintained for it. These two facts conjoined imply 'entity if and only if identity'. Similarly for Russell's rejection of times and distances and admission of intervals. Russell's account closely follows Albert Einstein's. Far from making all things relative, relativity theory "is wholly concerned to exclude what is relative and arrive at a statement of physical laws that shall in no way depend upon the circumstances of the observer." Thus "relativity theory" is wrongly named with respect to realism *versus* relativity. It would be better named "realism theory." First, the identity of events and observers is assumed. In the special theory a special space-time interval is assumed, and the laws are formulated using Lorentz transformations. "The interval is the same for all observers and represents a genuine physical relation between the two events, which the time and the distance do not." For Russell an interval is a "physical fact." In general relativity we assume the identity of events and observers as before. We also assume that there are intervals of a general form, but not that we know how to measure them. They are based on a Gaussian system of assigning neighboring coordinates to neighboring events. The system is like a large rubber map which, no matter how you twist it, keeps the same events at the same coordinates. Einstein uses Riemann's development of Gauss's system into a non-Euclidian geometry of positive curvature, of course, but the general existence-identity connection of isomorphism remains Gaussian. The predictive and explanatory success of the theory presumably vindicates our calling general intervals probable general physical facts (Russell 1958: 16, 18, 23, 38–40, 58, 68, 73–77, 83). This is theory (10).[7]

Theory (10) leads us directly to theory (21), which concerns laws of nature in general:

Physics is intended to give information about what really occurs in the physical world, and not only about the private perceptions of separate observers. Physics must, therefore, be concerned with those features which a physical process has in common for all observers, since such features alone can be regarded as belonging to the physical occurrence itself. This requires that the laws of phenomena should be the same whether the phenomena are described as they appear to one observer or as they appear to another. This single principle is the generating motive of the whole theory of relativity. (AMA 213)

Russell then gives the following general requirement for the identity of laws:

We want to express physical laws in such a way that it shall be obvious when we are expressing the same law by reference to two different systems of coordinates, so that we shall not be misled into supposing we have different laws when we only have one law in different words. (AMA 114)

The special theory of relativity makes laws of motion the same for all systems of reference in uniform relative motion. The general theory of relativity makes laws of motion the same for all systems of reference in any sort of relative motion, including acceleration. Thus gravity is included, since gravity is an acceleration of one body towards another. In preserving the identity of laws of motion, Einstein's theories probably describe the real physical facts of motion. Theory (21), in generalizing Einstein's aim in theory (10), asserts an identity-existence connection for objective natural laws, and for general physical facts, that could not be much clearer or more fundamental for philosophy of science.

5. Quantum Mechanics

Russell discusses identity conditions in quantum mechanics in several works. In the 1929 edition of *Our Knowledge of the External World*, Russell says:

Permanent things, even as a logical construction, are no longer quite adequate to the needs of physics....After a quantum change in an atom, according to Heisenberg, we can no longer identify a given electron with a definite one of those existing before the change. (KEW 90)

Here Russell takes existence-identity connections to their ultimate conclusion: Without identity conditions forthcoming from physics, not only literal material continuants, but even constructive simulations of them, are to be abandoned. Russell also quotes Heisenberg as saying, "It is...in principle impossible to identify again a particular corpuscle among a series of similar corpuscles" (AMA 46). In the quotation indented above, Russell finally rejects his own 1914–21 constructions of bodies ("permanent things") as useless in quantum theory. In quantum theory electrons are no longer like little bodies at all, since they have no identity conditions as continuants over time. For a 'no entity without identity' theorist like Russell, the situation is therefore far more desperate in quantum mechanics than it is in general relativity theory. The question is, Can Russell sketch any construction which preserves identity conditions for quantum phenomena, if even constructing them as fictitious continuants is impossible?

Russell says concerning waves that "there are identities in physics which are not material. A wave has a certain identity; if this were not the case, our visual perceptions would not have the intimate connection they in fact do have with physical objects" (AMA 82). Therefore, Russell once again upholds an existence-identity connection, admitting waves. Perhaps one may wish to suggest that wave-identities are the best solution here. But a new identity problem arises. Heisenberg asks, "How could it be that the same radiation that produces interference patterns, and therefore must consist of waves, also produces the photoelectric effect, and therefore must consist of moving particles?" (Heisenberg 1962: 35) Bohr's principle of the complementarity of the two descriptions led to the Copenhagen interpretation of quantum mechanics. On Russell's view, Heisenberg's Copenhagen interpretation is not known to be true, since a better and more classical theory may come along. But if it is true and its nonclassical features are physically fundamental, it may still be roughly accommodated by Russell's theory of events. A triple distinction between steady events, rhythms, and transactions is the basis of this accommodation. This is Russell's basic new division of types of physical occurrences. Planck's constant h in particular "represents something of fundamental importance in the physical world, which, in turn, involves the conclusion that periodicity is an element in physical laws, and that one period of a periodic process must be treated as in some sense, a *unit*" (AMA 365–66, italics mine).

The 'elements' which we admit here and which have identity conditions are neither particles nor waves, but events. Russell devotes chapters 33–34 of *The Analysis of Matter* to the interpretation of both particle and wave phenomena as logical structures of events. In keeping with Occam's razor, they may have more physical reality than that, but we cannot know if they do. In any case, if the interpretation proves adequate, such structures may be presumed to have smooth, if artificial, logical identities. Russell attempts to accommodate both discontinuity and potential action. Now, interpreting quantum phenomena in terms of events may seem less elegant than interpreting events in terms of quantum phenomena, which is what the scientists, after all, developed quantum theory to do. Such an inversion of the natural order of scientific explanation may seem to fit only Russell's general program of Occamistic epistemic caution. But here Russell is interpreting quantum phenomena in terms of sub-atomic events, and ordinary events in terms of quantum phenomena, closely following the physicists (Russell 1968: 138–39). In fact, whether he does so is the test of whether he has abandoned (neutral monist) constructionism for probabilistic realism, i.e., the realist hypothesis. There is no doubt he should pass the test, since he expressly assumes the hypothesis (AMA 215–17; see 200–14). And his view that we can know only the abstract structure of matter implies that matter is beyond experience; it would make no sense if he constructed electrons out of sensible events (AMA 215, 227). While an ordinary thing's "biography" includes percepts (AMA 213), and an electron in my head probably includes percepts as member-events (AMA 320), the three basic kinds of physical occurrences (steady events, rhythms, and transactions) are not sensible. Note that steady events are "devoid of physical structure," while any percept lasting "about a second" can "be analyzed into a structure of events" (AMA 287, 356). Some passages in *The Analysis of Matter* suggest that only structure is important to physics, so that the book can present a constructivist or at least transitional appearance; but other passages show that Russell does move to a probabilistic physical realism (compare AMA 9, 199, 205, 215–17, 244, 276–77, 285–86, 319–20, 325, 347, 352, 400–2).

Russell's best statements of theory (11) reflect the fact that the identity of a series depends on the identity of its members. Russell says that Heisenbergian atoms are "systems of wave-motions, or radiations" (KEW 83; again, this is the 1938 edition). Russell's own theory is much the same: "Electrons and protons are not events, according to my theory; they are series of groups of events." More conservatively, "it is prudent, in physics, to regard an electron as a group of events connected together in a certain way" (AMA 246–47; see 246n and Russell 1989a: 685, 701).

Russell's treatment of relativity theory and quantum mechanics is strictly parallel. In each case, an existence-identity connection is threatened. It is specifically threatened in that there seem to be existents which lack identity conditions. Faced with the dilemma of rejecting the existents or rejecting the connection, Russell upholds the connection by offering new interpretations of the scientific theories, interpretations in which the connection is retained. Specifically, relativity theory is interpreted in terms of events and intervals instead of bodies, times, and distances, and quantum phenomena are interpreted in terms of events and invariants instead of particles or waves. This is just the kind of application we would expect of a basic principle of probabilistic realism that to be probably real is to be identifiable across observers.

The 1913 Russell's theory of causation as mere regularity admits some simple regularities, but also admits that regularities are almost never simple. "The principle 'same cause, same effect', which philosophers imagine to be vital to science, is therefore utterly otiose" (ONC 182). Russell explains:

> There is no question of repetitions of the 'same' cause producing the 'same' effect; it is not in any sameness of causes and effects that the constancy of scientific law consists in, but in sameness of relations.

And even 'sameness of relations' is too simple a phrase; 'sameness of differential equations' is the only correct phrase. (ONC 188)

Of course, if we assign constant values to all but one variable in a more or less closed system of interacting variables, then we have a more or less simple if-then causal relationship. And the 1911 Russell finds the converse of 'same cause, same effect' basic to our knowledge of the external world (RUP 121).

Russell is anxious to preserve 'no entity without identity' for real things in real space as well:

> [A]ccording to the general principles which must govern any correspon-
> dence of real things with objects of perception, any principle which
> introduces diversity among objects of perception must introduce a
> corresponding diversity among real things. I am not now concerned to
> argue as to what grounds exist for assuming a correspondence, but, if
> there is such a correspondence, it must be supposed that diversity in the
> effects—i.e., the perceived objects—implies diversity in the caus-
> es—i.e., the real objects. Hence if I perceive two objects in the field
> of vision, we must suppose that at least two real objects are concerned
> in causing my perception. (RUP 121; see MPD 147)

Thus theory (23) implies theory (24). Russell affirms this 'different effect, different cause' principle four times in *The Analysis of Matter* and explains it as a many-one correlational "extension of the notion of similarity" (AMA 224, 226, 255, 282; see HK 206, 331–32).

6. Common Sense Recognition

In *Principles*, "all knowledge must be recognition" (POM 451). Primitive ideas "can be intrinsically distinguished, as yellow and blue are distinguished," and "must be simply recognized" (POM 126). There must be simple terms; and in fact we know many of them (POM 145, 147). Recognition in *Principles* seems to be virtually what Russell later calls acquaintance, and virtually what he still later calls noticing. It is not clear to me that acquaintance or noticing should be simply identified with *Principles*' knowledge as recognition, however. For one's first acquaintance with a certain shade of red is acquaintance, but can hardly be recognition. For recognition implies memory of some past acquain-tance of that shade, or at least a "habit of association" with past acquaintances, whether remembered or not. So not all acquaintance (1905–18) or noticing (post-1921) involves recognition. But surely all recognition involves acquain-tance or noticing.

In *The Analysis of Mind*, Russell distinguishes two senses of recognition: knowing what something is when we see it, and knowing we have seen it before. These respectively concern what I called essential and memorial identifiability in chapter 1. The first "does not necessarily involve more than a habit of association." The second is never literally correct, since past events are not literally present; in the present there is an image at most. The second sense concerns perceptual similarity (AMI 169–72). Russell develops his notion of recognition in 1921–48. I shall now briefly describe that further development.

The common-sense world is based on recognition. Recognition implies memory. Recognition is a process that actually occurs. Recognition involves similarity, may be mental or physiological, and is shown by behavior. Even where recognition involves events which we notice, i.e., data, identity is not involved for the reason that you will not have the same datum twice. Identity is strict identity, or absence of difference. But similarity of data may be mistaken for identity of data. Two people can see the same body only in the sense of having similar, perspectively related data. Nor can we distinguish in perception between exact and approximate similarity. But science has ways to achieve precise concepts based on vague percepts. We can easily define exact similarity in terms of similarity and then define identity as exact similarity. Identity, like similarity, goes beyond the present percept and involves memory, and therefore has no high degree of certainty. But identity has more "logical smoothness" than similarity, insofar as identity involves articulate definitions. Some philosophers take the reverse approach by defining similarity as identity in some respect. But similarity cannot be reduced to identity of quality in the epistemological order of things. For similarities are data and ultimately uninferred.[8]

The definition of identity as exact similarity in the epistemic and scientific order of things is compatible with the status of identity as primary in the ontological order of things, in which exact similarity itself needs an identity in order to exist. But such a definition in the epistemic order is better called an explanation in Frege's sense, since ontology is prior to epistemology.

Recognition antedates language. For instance, a dog can recognize its master. Thus even animals construct a common-sense correlational reality in a crude recognitional manner, and even animals have in their perceptions the raw materials for sophisticated scientific construction. But construction by animals and children is different from logical or scientific construction in some ways. The latter is too hard for most people, let alone animals, to understand. The latter attempts to follow a logical order, while the former constitutes the natural epistemological (or psychological) order of things (IMT 290–91; HK 186–88, 431–32).

Construction of the common-sense world largely involves nondeliberate or even unconscious corrections and interpretation. It is not clear to what degree it is learned or innate. Humans must learn correlations of sight and touch. But chickens make them as soon as they are hatched (HK 7, 218). The common-sense world is largely a delusive construction. Physical things "probably" have no color or odor. Nothing is understood beyond their structure. (This is why I called the 1927–59 Russell a representational realist.) Common-sense natural kinds comprise a passing phase. The basic natural kinds are kinds of subatomic events. And even these are probably not ultimate, but have further structure: electrons have the smooth properties that smack of constructions, and quantum mechanics casts doubt on them; but they *may* be what is real. Compresence, the earlier-than relation, and only a few other things may be called the scientific residue of naive realism, or of our common-sense construction of the external world (AMA 319; HK 7, 230, 321–23, 443–44).

Logically smooth properties define identity conditions for constructions. Russell says, "Matter, traditionally, has two of those 'neat' properties which are the mark of a logical construction; first, that two pieces of matter cannot be at the same place at the same time; secondly, that one piece of matter cannot be in two places at the same time" (Russell 1971a: 329; see POM xi; MAL 87).

The common-sense world is based on an existence-recognition connection, and the scientific world is based on an existence-identity connection. The difference is one of method. The scientific world develops from more deliberately logical constructions and inferences. At bottom this is a matter of degree. Therefore, the root of all identity-existence connections seems prehuman and innate. That there is such a root, namely the existence-recognition connection, is theory (16).

7. Inference of Events

While accepting as fundamental the Cartesian conception of knowledge as beginning with the individual's private world, Russell assumes that the scientific conception of knowledge is largely correct and seeks mainly to analyze that conception. It is not a precise conception, and it admits degrees of certainty (IMT 12–16, 131, 143–44; HK 96–98, 154–63, 496, 498; MPD 99).

The scientific world is a mixture of inference and construction. Physics cannot be construction alone. It must rely on inferences that go beyond what we experience and construct out of experience. Inference is the preliminary and more important part of physics, though it should be minimized in formulating our theories. The constructions in our later theories, such as structural definitions of copper and gold in terms of atomic structure, actually conceal our earlier inferences. And while protons and electrons are very remote constructions, they may be what actually exists (HK xiv, 7, 90, 139, 143, 268, 283).

If we are to go beyond immediate experience, then we need nondeductive principles of inference which are not known to be true empirically. The only legitimate nondeductive inferences concerning physical things are structural. For we have no reason at all to assume that the qualities with which we are acquainted belong to physical things. Russell's postulates of nondeductive inference are epistemological, not logical. Russell holds that while there may be more fundamental principles, these five are what our knowledge-claims about the external world are more or less based on. These five postulates maintain an existence-identity connection for all inferred existents. Together they seem sufficient to maintain that connection (HK 230, 494–95; MPD 149). The postulates are completely indifferent as to whether directly identified events are sense-data, bundles of qualities, or even Continental-style three-dimensional intentional objects. The postulates are as follows:

(1) The Postulate of Quasi-Permanence is:

Given any event A, it happens very frequently that, at any neighboring time, there is at some neighboring place an event very similar to A. (HK 488)

This postulate applies to both subjective and objective events. For the former it resembles Hume's psychological law of association due to similarity. For the latter it construes physical things as series of similar events. The postulate does not tell us, however, where one thing ends and the next thing begins, for instance, drops of water in the sea. Thus the postulate describes how organisms, using similarity alone, and not identity or even recognition, might infer with probability a certain very primitive world (HK 488).

(2) The Postulate of Separable Causal Lines is:

It is frequently possible to form a series of events such that from one or two members of the series something can be inferred as to all the other members. (HK 489)

A causal line is Russell's version of a Minkowskian world-line. It is "a string of events having a certain kind of causal connection with each other" (HK 458; AMA 135). The postulate allows us to recognize one billiard ball among others in a game due to the probable progressive changes of visual appearance of shape, color, and position. Similarly, the postulate allows us to infer from several visual sensations that we are seeing a plurality of stars, each of which we recognize and distinguish from the rest. In this way Postulate 2 underwrites theory (23) and its implication of theory (24) (HK 489).

(3) The Postulate of Spatio-Temporal Continuity is:

[W]hen there is a causal connection between two events that are not contiguous, there must be intermediate links in the chain such that each is contiguous to the next, or (alternatively) such that there is a process which is continuous in the mathematical sense. (HK 490–91)

Thus there is no action at a distance. (Russell follows Einstein on gravity.) Postulate (3) does not express a likelihood, but a requirement. If things are series of events, this postulate is necessary if we are to recognize things on discontinuous perceptual occasions. If you put the billiard balls away in a box and take them out later, your recognition of them is based on discontinuous perceptions. The intermediate events are the balls existing while they are not perceived. As Russell says, this greatly increases the domain of common-sense recognition.

It is with Postulate (3) that we pass beyond similarity and recognition to identity. Postulate (3) concerns identity in two ways. First, where phenomena can be interpreted as "things" preserving identity through regular changes, we may speak of inferences of identity as based on "intrinsic" causal laws, that is, laws which concern series of events which are more or less causally closed to the rest of the world (HK 489). A series' being a continuous causal line is then a sufficient condition of ordinary thing-identity:

> When "substance" is abandoned, the identity, for common sense, of a thing or person at different times must be explained as consisting in what may be called a "causal line." We normally recognize a thing or person by qualitative similarity to a former appearance, but it is not this that defines "identity." When a friend returns from years in a Japanese prison, we may say, "I should never have known you." Suppose you know two twins whom you cannot tell apart; suppose one of them, in battle, loses an eye, an arm, and a leg. He will then seem much less like his former self than the other twin is, but we nevertheless identify him, not the other twin, with his former self, because of a certain kind of causal continuity. (HK 458)

And ordinary thing-identity is a sufficient condition of a causal line's continuity:

> If you know two twins, A and B, whom you cannot tell apart, and you see one on one occasion and one on another, you cannot assume that a continuous chain connects the two appearances until you have satisfied yourself that it was the same twin on both occasions. (HK 491)

That a continuous causal line is a necessary and sufficient condition of an ordinary thing's identity is theory (17). Theory (17) modifies theory (10), which in turn modifies theory (5).

The second way Postulate (3) is concerned with identity is that it is the basis for inferring with Postulate (4) that several people are seeing the same event, since each of their percepts must be causally connected by "continuous processes in intervening space" to this probable event (HK 491). This event must be in the causal line of each person's percept.

(4) The Structural Postulate is:

When a number of structurally similar complex events are ranged about a center in regions not widely separated, it is usually the case that all belong to causal lines having their origin in an event of the same structure at the center. (HK 492)

Like Postulates (1) and (2), Postulate (4) expresses a likelihood. According to it, if several people describe their perceptions of a tree, or if several photographs are taken from various angles and compared, then by the laws of perspective it may be inferred that a physical tree having a certain structure probably exists in a certain location. Postulate (4) is theory (18).

(5) The Postulate of Analogy is:

Given two classes of events A and B, and given that, whenever both A and B can be observed, there is reason to believe that A causes B, then if, in a given case, A is observed, but there is no way of observing whether B occurs or not, it is probable that B occurs; and similarly if B is observed, but the presence or absence of A cannot be observed. (HK 493)

Postulate (5) allows us to infer the probable existence of other minds, without whom we cannot infer anything about a public external world. Theories (17)–(18) are thus revealed to be epistemically prior to publicity and communication. Postulate (5) seems to be related to the simpler theory (7).

Postulates (1)–(5) are epistemologically fundamental. They may or may not be logically fundamental. They may be, as a group, not even logically necessary for justifying elementary science. But as a group they should be epistemologically sufficient for justifying elementary science (HK 494–95). They are also jointly sufficient for giving corresponding pairs of existence and identity assertions about any possible unobserved event the same probability of truth.

Nothing epitomizes Russell's development of 'no entity without identity' throughout his long career so much as the vast difference between his simple formal descriptivist account of informative identity in "On Denoting" and his complicated causal line account of informative identity in *Human Knowledge*. With a fine sense of irony, Russell chooses Frege's famous Evening Star and Morning Star as his illustration. Russell's account of Hesper and Phosphor is a four-step account. "[G]iving the name 'Venus'" to Hesper and Phosphor involves assuming that (1) "Our visual sensations...have external causes," and that (2) "These causes...persist when they are not causing visual sensations." Steps (3) and (4) concern astronomical laws (HK 479–82). Indeed, theory (18) is a communal 'no *probable* entity without multiple causal line identity' theory of denotation. Among name theorists, descriptivists who champion Russell and causal-communal use theorists who attack Russell seem equally unaware of this causal chain account, even though it is obviously a major revision. The later Russell's theory of names, which integrates descriptivism with a community of causal lines, even transcends Richard Fumerton's fine critique of causal theories of reference.[9]

8. Space, Time, and Events

In *Principles*, the ontological status of spatial points is puzzling. They are terms with self-identities. But they are not actual existents, since they are not empirically knowable and have no causal properties. Nor are they nonexistent entities such as the Homeric gods. Nor are they mathematical existents. Russell's program is to reduce mathematics to logic, and geometry is part of mathematics. But Russell distinguishes ideal points, defined as sheaves in that program, from what he calls "actual points" or "real points." While ideal points have only mathematical existence, real points are simples with "absolute and metaphysical validity." Therefore I am inclined to argue that real points have a special fifth kind of ontological status which is more specific than mere being, but is neither empirical existence, mathematical existence, nor nonexistent being. I call the status "spatiotemporal reality." Real temporal instants have it too. Spatiotemporal reals are analogous to actual existents in two important respects. First, they are particulars. Second, while real points are not empirically distinguishable from each other individually, collectively they constitute Euclidian space, which the 1903 Russell holds is the space which physics empirically confirms as actual. From his 1897 *An Essay on the Foundations of Geometry* to his 1948 *Human Knowledge*, Russell has distinguished between many possible geometries and one actual geometry which is empirically better suited to physics than the others. Note that Russell's material points are not individually distinguishable any more than his spatial points or instants are, and seem equally eternal, thanks to the principle of conservation of mass. The main differences are that material points are mobile and stand in causal relations. With all these different categories of different entities, it is a wonder that the 1903 Russell allowed the reduction of mathematical entities to logical entities at all. Recall that the 1903 jungle realist Moore's epigram in *Principia Ethica* is Butler's maxim, "Every thing is what it is, and not another thing." Russell is largely following Moore's turn to Butlerian 'no entity without identity' here.

Russell's theory of space and time in *External World* begins with Russell's acceptance of Alfred North Whitehead's method of providing identity conditions for spatial or temporal points in terms of classes of 'overlapping' events. The points are mere logical constructions. Russell uses Whitehead's method in *External World*, lecture 4. The method assumes the identity of at least some overlapping events as given. The relations of compresence and earlier-than are dependently given "among events" (KEW 93). This is theory (8). Times, distances, and motions are then constructed from the points.

In Russell's general relativity theory in *The Analysis of Matter*, points are still constructed using overlapping events. Russell then tries to construct intervals. Russell makes intervals (probable) physical facts in *The ABC of Relativity*, as we saw in section 3.

Leibniz admits the static world of Zeno. Russell mainly follows Leibniz's endorsement of Zeno.[10] In *External World*, Russell describes an analysis of motion in terms of series of continuous events which thoroughly honors Zeno. Motion is thus a mere logical construction. The identity of at least some events is assumed as given. This is theory (9).

But the 1914–48 Russell also admits the appearance of motion (KEW 110–114; IMT 34–36; HK 210–11, 219–20, 260–61). And for Russell, appearances are as real as anything can be. This presents two related dilemmas. First, he seems to be either admitting a neo-Heraclitean flux as real, or inviting a return to substances identical over time. In *The Analysis of Matter* Russell says that "a quick movement can be apprehended as a whole"—and then says later that "the conception of motion depends upon that of persistent...substances" (AMA 254, 355). The second dilemma is that since he believes that presented changes exist and have presented identities, theory (20)—that sensed items have presented identities—conflicts with and presumably overrules theory (9) that changes are series of static events. That might seem reasonable; theory (20) is about the sense-data from which the series of physical events of theory (9) are inferred. But this dilemma is about the percepts themselves. Thus it cannot be solved by distinguishing real percepts of change from a "staccato" *underlying* Zenonian physical reality conforming to theory (9). Either a change-percept *is* a change or it is not. That is, either it is a flux or it is a continuant, since it is not presented as a series of static events.

Russell is well aware of both dilemmas and attempts to extricate himself by comparing presented changes to Poincaré's indistinguishable but different color patches. "The analogy with the case of the colours arises through the existence, in each case, of a series in which differences of neighbouring terms are imperceptible while those of different terms are perceptible. And it elicits the important principle that a percept may have parts which are not percepts, so that the structure of a percept may be only discoverable by inference" (AMA 281). Percepts also have imperceptible parts when "[t]wo indistinguishable percepts are found to be followed by different results....[W]e argue: 'Different effects, different causes'" (AMA 282). (This is theory (22) again.) Thus Russell's resolution of the second dilemma seems to be that *percepts themselves* have hidden parts. This unified resolution of the Poincaré-Zeno difficulties in *The Analysis of Matter* seems already implicit in *External World*. The parts for Poincaré presumably are events composing color-wavelength structures.

Interestingly enough, Russell never says that we completely know sense-data with which we are acquainted, but only that we "have a...complete understanding of the name" (PLA 202). In fact he says we *never* fully know the data with which we are acquainted; what we lack is full propositional knowledge of facts about them (KEW 110–14). This may explain why we can only theoretically distinguish interpretation in a datum from its sensation-core (KEW 58; IMT 119, 124; HK 167–79). But it does not help here. What are these propositions we do not know about our data—that they have indistinguishable but different parts? Russell's solution is to admit nonmental parts of mental percepts (AMA 282; see HK 201–3), or at least parts one can notice later (HK 302).

None of this affects Russell's cognitively rigid trans-world identities of sense-data, since acquaintance yields the complete meanings of genuine names, and knowing meanings alone seems enough to guarantee rigid designation. Since the meaning of a logically proper name *is* its denotation, to change the name's denotation in any possible world is to change its very meaning in that world, so that it would no longer be the same name. If we can fully know the meaning of a name without fully knowing its denotation due to hidden structure, where meaning and denotation are nonetheless identical, that is best glossed as just an inference failure in a context of Russellian epistemic (or better, cognitive) propositional attitude, i.e. of referential opacity. This is theory (20).

But the first dilemma remains. If a structure is a complex relation, then an instantiated structure of imperceptible parts is a complex fact. (If it underlies change over time, it can scarcely be a "complex of compresence.") What is the difference between such a structure and a literal continuant? Even substances need not be absolutely homogeneous monoliths. Aristotle's ordinary bodies are composed of atoms; natural trees and artificial boxes have varying degrees of structural cohesion. That we are talking about percepts does not detract from this point. Far from being unknowable substrata, Aristotle's material substances are not understood if not taken as *perceptible* things remaining the same through change (Wiggins 1980: 4–5). That Russell's changes occur within a specious present is a another difference that makes no difference. Descartes' piece of wax changes every sensible quality when heated, and yet is judged to remain the same piece of wax. Surely we must judge Russell's brief percept of a waving hand, which changes only in location, to remain the same percept. And as Russell admits, no change can be presented if there is not *something that changes*, something judged to be the same (AMA 254, 355). Perhaps Russell's imperceptible parts might not be continuants, but his hidden instantiated structures cannot avoid underlying changes. Even if Russell *defines* a percept of motion as a temporal series of classes of imperceptible static parts, those very same parts will instantiate a complex and real relational fact which underlies the change, which fact is his *analysis* of that percept. This is also a problem for his theories of general relativity and quantum mechanics.

Russell seems to try to avoid commitment to the view that "the whole [percept] W can preserve its identity throughout the [temporal] process of analysis" (IMT 334), but seems to affirm it in the end (IMT 336; see HK 297–307 on complexes of compresence). One might argue that a temporal whole is not a literal continuant because we apprehend it only temporal part by temporal part. But that vitiates Russell's whole claim that we perceive wholes *as* wholes which change in the specious present (IMT 336). Even worse, it seems clear that a bundle of qualities as such cannot accommodate changes because to change a quality is to change the bundle (Loux 1970: 191). And that implies that Russell has hidden instantiated structures in *addition* to bundles, which seems most unparsimonious. But could perhaps changes just *be* qualities in bundles?

Russell seems to wish to say a change *is* a quality. But qualities—even particular qualities—are not changes. They come into being and pass away from being. If the motion of a waving hand is a quality, then it is not a change. Apples change from green to red. Green does not change to red, nor is red a change. Still hands change to waving hands. Motionlessness does not change to motion, nor is a quality of motion a change. We casually say, "This *is* a change," pointing to the apple's new color. But if the apple has a new color, then the change was already completed.

In the *Inquiry*, Russell treats Poincaré's problem as an instance of a problem of vagueness afflicting "all empirical concepts" (IMT 105). He finds "inexactness essential" to "the fundamental empirical concept of indistinguishability" (IMT 106). Later he explains a vague perception as one that "does not allow so many inferences as some other perception would allow" (IMT 158). The Poincaré problem is indeed one of inability to infer. But the first dilemma is only swept under the rug. For what is this inference problem about but what the three sense-data really are? And can the problem of change be resolved by saying that a waving hand is a vague perception of a precise staccato reality? If that is correct, the staccato physical structure is again a complex substance that underlies our vague perceptions of change. Indeed, this is not really another way out. What is the difference between lack of full propositional knowledge about our sense-data and lack of full inferential knowledge about our perceptions? Indeed, we already discussed the inferential discovery of structure (AMA 281).

Russell offers three theories of events. (i) The 1912 Russell assays recurrent events, which scientific laws concern, as universals. His examples are striking a match and dropping a penny (ONC 180). Observe that "striking" and "dropping" are the gerundial forms of the verbs "strikes" and "drops." Such verbs indicate type 1 order 0 universal relations among individuals in Russell's quantificational logic. (ii) The 1914–27 Russell assays nonrecurrent events as sensed or unsensed particulars (KEW 165, AMA 286). (iii) The 1940–59 Russell assays nonrecurrent events as unique bundles of qualities, but allows that whole bundles theoretically can recur (IMT 103, HK 82–83, MPD 122).

Russell's theories of events differ from Davidson's and Quine's theories of events in at least three ways. First, Russell shows no interest in quantifying over events to explain the use of adverbs to modify verbs. But since the 1912 Russell holds that verbs express universals, and that events are universals, it seems that he would hold by direct parity of reason that adverbs express universals, and that empirical adverbs express events or modifications of events (PP 93; verbal nouns, adjectives, and prepositions also stand for universals). Second, Russell defines spatiotemporal regions, lines, and points in terms of physical events (sense-data and unsensed sensibilia, to use the lexicon of his 1914 articles). But Davidson and Quine reverse this and individuate events, and indeed physical objects, in terms of spatiotemporal regions. I shall be mainly concerned with the second difference. But first I shall note a third difference between Russell and Davidson.

It is hard to develop any adequate theory about the nature of change without discussing the views of Parmenides and Zeno. But Davidson does not even mention Parmenides or Zeno in his book *Essays on Actions and Events* (1985). For Davidson, "Many events are changes in a substance" (Davidson 1985: 173). Whether or not Davidson is right, *Essays on Actions and Events* is shallow for its ignoring of Zeno. Even Quine at least briefly discusses Zeno. In contrast, Russell fully acknowledges the power of Zeno's arguments and discusses them in detail.

The problem with the second difference is this. 'No entity without identity' applies to whatever one quantifies over. This includes events and physical objects. It also includes spatiotemporal regions. Now Russell can reasonably take the individuation of sensed physical events as phenomenologically given along with the existence of such events. But how are Davidson and Quine going to individuate spatiotemporal regions? How can one identify regions, after all, except in terms of events? Regions of the same size and shape are, as Russell well knows, empirically indistinguishable. They are not empirically given at all. But Davidson and Quine cannot use events or physical objects to individuate regions without introducing a gross circularity into their philosophies. For they already use regions to individuate events. The problem is primarily logico-metaphysical, secondarily cognitive, and only then epistemic.

The problem is familiar. Russell makes a similar criticism of Carnap; Michael Dummett of Michael Ayers; Michael Loux of Strawson; and David Wiggins of a proposed account. Wesley Salmon and Hugh McCann claim that a locational identity criterion for events presupposes either an untenable 'substantivalist' theory of space-time or the individuation of events. "Substantivalist" is too strong a word. They forget Frege's distinction between what is real and what is objective. Space and time are only objective, not real, for Frege. For Davidson and Quine, space-time need only be objective to individuate events and physical objects. But the real problem is not whether regions are substantival or merely objective. It is whether regions have individual identities in any independent sense at all.[11]

It is circular of Quine to define the identity of physical objects in terms of spatiotemporal regions in "Things and Their Place in Theories," since he already defines the identity of spatiotemporal regions in terms of physical objects (particle-events) in *Word and Object*. Quine's three ways of defining space-time regions in terms of particle-events differ from the Whitehead-Russell way using overlapping events. But the differences make no difference as to the circularity (TT 12–13, 16–18; WO 255–56).

Loux suggests a way out: "one might argue that the notion of circularity is inappropriate here. The identification of [physical objects], on the one hand, and spaces and times, on the other, are so intimately related that it is simply impossible to examine one in isolation from the other" (Loux 1970: 203). This is the way out Quine seems to take. In "Events and Reification," Quine says "our conceptual apparatus of space, time, and physical objects is all of a piece." Yet in that same article Quine rejects Davidson's earlier definition of events in terms of causal relations, as well as a definition of events in terms of class membership, for circularly assuming the individuation of events. And one might reasonably claim that our conceptual apparatus of events and causes "is all of a piece," or that our conceptual apparatus of events and classes "is all of a piece." So that Quine should either reject his own definition of events as guilty of the same circularity, or should exonerate Davidson's two definitions of events on the same ground on which he exonerates his own. Quine's living in Neurath's ship, which can be rebuilt at sea only using parts of itself, is no way out of such a circularity of definition either. Is such a simple and direct circular definition of events in terms of regions and regions in terms of events what Neurath's ship metaphor is all about (WO 3)? Now we can accept Davidson's causal definition, the class membership definition, and Quine's space-time definition of events as equally all of a piece, equally Neurathian, or both. But surely it is better to reject all three definitions as equally circular (see Quine 1985: 166, 168).[12]

Quine's definitions of region and physical object need fixing up, but I see no serious problem of circularity. Since both Einstein and Russell find they must take some observed events' identities as given to make general relativity theory work, a principle of charity suggests that Quine too would take some initially posited physical objects as having given identities within our scientific theory (WO 4–5). As a last resort, we can even go all the way back to sensory stimulus patterns as having given qualitative identities and differences (WO 83).

More seriously, an indexical existence-identity connection seems needed, and this is hard to reconcile with Quine's nonindexical physical realism (PQ 227). The problem is that since Quine's science is totally objective in describing dates, places, and observers, it cannot tell us where or when anything is, which observers we are, who posits which posits as being where and when, or even who has which neural stimulus patterns where and when. Thus indexicals such as "this," "here," "now," or "my" are an ineliminable vocabulary belonging to or associated with any actually usable natural science. This criticism is Russellian (HK 89–93). Russell's own sense-data or noticed events are, of course, "egocentric" physically real particulars nameable 'this' and 'that'.

If a metal ball is both warming and spinning, are these two events or one? Davidson says "it seems natural to say that two different changes [Davidson's events] can come over the whole of a substance at the same time" (Davidson 1985: 178). In contrast, for Davidson the death of Scott is the same event as the death of the author of Waverley, yielding one event denoted by two definite descriptions. But Quine would assay the ball's warming and spinning as one event under two descriptions or "general terms." For Quine this event would be a change; Quine admits changes. Quine also admits acts, such as walking and chewing gum; these are the same act if done by the same person at the same time. Quine assays events and acts as physical objects, and so accommodates "Davidson's logic of adverbs." Davidson's "Reply to Quine on Events" is unclear. Davidson neither endorses nor rejects Quine's accommodation, but only discusses it (Davidson 1985a: 178; 1985b: 175–76; TT 11–12; PQ 115).

How would Russell individuate events in a warming, spinning ball? Russell says in *Principles*:

> In the Grundlagen der Arithmetik, other possible theories of number are discussed and dismissed. Numbers cannot be asserted of objects, because the same set of objects may have different numbers assigned to them...; for example, one army is so many regiments and such another number of soldiers. This seems to me to involve too physical a view of objects: I do not consider the army to be the same object as the regiments. (POM 519)

This is theory (2). Russell includes among "objects" both terms (including classes as one) and classes as many (POM 55n). *The* army is a class as one, its regiments are a class as many, and its soldiers are a different class as many (POM 513). These classes have different descriptive properties. Their members are different. They are different in number. The number of soldiers may even fluctuate over time while the number of regiments remains the same. As Thomas Reid observed, a famous regiment would not have any of the soldiers it had a hundred years ago. Though Russell banishes all classes in *Principia*, the very same problem of identity confronts the 1914–21 Russell. For one constructed army is many constructed soldiers. The regiments occupy the same space-time region as the army, but are not the same construction as the army. Also, Russell is mistaken about Frege. Classes are objects for Frege as well. Frege would not consider an army, its regiments, and its soldiers to be "the same set of objects" any more than Russell does. But for Frege, a class is one and its extension can be many.

Imitating the spinning ball, if an army is ordered to wheel about under a hot sun, it is strictly speaking the soldiers who are warming as the army is moving. We would ordinarily say, "The army is getting warmer," but we would mean the soldiers as many, not the army as one. Conversely, the army as one is spinning about in place. But the soldiers as many are not spinning about in place. Indeed, not one of the soldiers is spinning about in place, much less the whole lot of them. Each soldier is instead marching in a circle about the army-as-one's axis of spinning. To think they are spinning about is to commit the fallacy of division.

One may object that the army's wheeling about is an action, while each soldier's warming is an event. I reply at once that this proves my point. For the warming and the wheeling about can hardly be the same event if the wheeling about is not even an event! Still, one may wish to distinguish wheeling about as an ordered action from spinning about as a physical event. But then I have already been describing our example in terms of spinning. And perhaps a purely physical example will make the objector happy. I select classical statistical mechanics for pedagogical convenience. A warming and spinning ball consists of, besides (two at most) macro-events of warming and spinning, many thousands of molecular events roughly describable as complex curvings or revolvings about an axis by molecules. (The Earth is frame of reference.) None of these micro-events is itself a warming or a spinning. Now, in *Principles* an actual motion, be it complex curvilinear or not, may be analyzed into component vectors, one being 'part' of the ball's spinning and the other being 'part' of the ball's warming, only as a doubly fictitious analysis. For motions are fictions, and their component vectors are not even motions (POM 474). Thus each micro-event would seem to be one event under two descriptions. Thus the class of micro-events-causing-macro-warmness as many and the class of micro-events-causing-macro-spinning as many are identical (have the same members). But that class as many remains a different object from the ball as one. And the complex-curve revolving of the class as many remains a different object from the ball's warming and even from the ball's spinning, which is not a complex curving about an axis but a simple circular motion. There is not even the same number of events, though the very same spatiotemporal region is occupied. To be sure, I have shifted Davidson's example. I have not shown either that the warming and the spinning of the ball-as-one are two events or that they are one event. Due to the fallacy of composition, the latter alternative does not follow from the fact that a single class of many molecular motions is concerned. But I have shown that different events, or in the respective senses of Frege and Russell, different objects, can occupy the same spatiotemporal region. And that was the issue.

We can enforce an adjudication of differences of properties if we judge that two things are one (Butchvarov 1979: 37, 66–68). But in judging the spinning as one and the complex curvings as many, we have judged that their identity does not obtain. In *External World*, Russell no longer accepts classes as many or classes as one. All classes are now fictions. But Russell still says, "Two general terms, such as 'man' and 'featherless biped', which are applicable to the same collection of objects, will obviously have the same number of instances; thus the number depends upon the class, not upon the selection of this or that general term to describe it" (KEW 157). So the micro-events are still not one macro-event, though occupying the very same spatiotemporal region. Quine would not hesitate for a moment to individuate each single micro-event from the others and also from the macro-event on the basis of different regions. But this is not the problem. The problem is that the class of micro-events occupies the same region as the macro-event. Or perhaps the problem is that a class of events is not itself an event. Indeed, the natural objection to my ball example is that I may have shown that the complexly curving micro-events are not the same object as the spinning ball, in Frege's sense of "object" as well as in Russell's, but I have not shown that they are not the same event in Davidson's sense of "event." My brief reply is that Davidson does not even address this matter, so far as I know.

Now for Quine, all physical objects, including events, are their own unit classes. In fact, every thing is its own unit class. Quine quantifies over "real classes." Physical objects, including events, are real classes. He quantifies over them. And Quine says on the first page of the Introduction to his *Set Theory and Its Logic*, "the [class] of say seven given pairs of shoes is not to be identified with the [class] of those fourteen shoes, nor yet with that of the twenty-eight soles and uppers." Now, those three classes occupy the same spatiotemporal region, but they are not the same physical object. Presumably they are not even physical objects, since they are not unit classes. But then the class-of-many micro-events and the class-of-one macro-event are different classes. And only the latter is an event in Quine's sense of "event." This how Quine solves the puzzle. For Quine there is no one event that satisfies two open sentences which two different classes determine: 'x is a micro-event of complex motion', and 'x is a spinning ball'. The class of micro-events of complex motion, and the macro-event of spinning, as a unit class of itself, are different classes occupying the same spatiotemporal region. For their memberships are different, and are not even of the same number. The former class has thousands of members, and the unit class by definition has only one. Quine's solution is artificial, as he well knows. After all, is a molecule or a ball really a unit class of itself? But Quine may be right that his artifice is in many ways harmless. And we can easily rescue Quine by just forgetting about unit classes and observing that no physical event is identical with even a real class having thousands of members (Quine 1980: 1, 19–20, 28–29, 47, 74–75).[13]

But are the warming and the spinning two events or one? For the 1914–18 Russell, each would be a series of classes of sensed and unsensed sensibilia. These series would be different. For their members would be different. Not all sensibilia of warming would be sensibilia of spinning, and not all sensibilia of spinning would be sensibilia of warming. For the 1948 Russell, they would be two events as well. For Russell's Postulate 3 of Spatio-Temporal Continuity is an anticipation of Davidson's definition of events in terms of their causes and effects. The warming and the spinning would be different segments of different causal lines. Russell can even say that if there *were* no sun, the ball *would* not be warming as it spins. That he would view such subjunctive conditionals reductively as formal implications does not detract from this point (see chapter 4, section 4). But this Russellian solution of the warming-spinning problem does reveal the main weakness in Russell's assay of ordinary things as causal lines. Namely, several very different causal lines may intersect in one ordinary thing. Russell's definition of a causal line as "a string of events having a certain kind of causal connection to each other" (HK 458) might be neither too broad nor too narrow, but it is either question-begging or vague concerning the meaning of "kind," as Russell seems well aware (KEW 88; AMA 135).

It is only fair to consider how a major contemporary event theorist would evaluate Russell in return. James D. McCauley attacks Russell in his "Actions and Events Despite Bertrand Russell" (McCauley 1985). Unfortunately McCauley has not read Russell, and so attacks a caricature of Russell. Among Russell's works, McCauley cites "On Denoting" alone. This is disingenuous, since Russell does not even discuss actions or events in that paper. Equally unfortunately, McCauley's criticisms are not criticisms of actions and events as such, but are more general in scope. McCauley drops the pretense when he discusses dogs and unicorns at the end of his article, as if Russell would have considered dogs actions or unicorns events. But due to that general scope, discussing McCauley will be instructive concerning Russell's general conception of 'no entity without identity'.

First, McCauley criticizes Russell for disallowing "overlapping particulars" which are "distinct" but not "disjoint": in my terms, conceptually distinct but not really distinct. This preposterous claim ignores Russell's army-soldiers example and whole-part theory in *Principles*. It ignores Russell's bundle of qualities theory and attendant whole-part theory of logical deduction in the *Inquiry*. It ignores Russell's 1914–18 constructionism, where minds overlap perceived bodies. It ignores his 1921 neutral monism, where even one's own mind overlaps one's own body. I cannot imagine who has more overlapping particulars than Russell. Russell even uses the word "overlap" four times in his theory of instants as classes of overlapping events (KEW 94–95).

Second, McCauley finds "a better instance of spatiotemporal identity between distinct events [in] Austinian locutionary and illocutionary acts," e.g. Fred's act of saying "I apologize" and Fred's act of apologizing. McCauley might be shocked to learn that Russell made this distinction in *Human Knowledge*: "A man may express sorrow...by saying 'Alas!' or 'Woe is me!' He may communicate...by saying, 'Look.' Expression and communication are not necessarily separated; if you say, 'Look' because you see a ghost, you may say it in a tone that expresses horror" (HK 59).

Third, McCauley criticizes Russell for disallowing fuzzy sets and "fuzzy spatiotemporal extent." McCauley overlooks Russell's many writings on vagueness from 1914 to 1948. In fact, endorsing vagueness is one of the few constants persisting through Russell's many changes in philosophy. Russell has a rich and sophisticated theory of vagueness with three levels. On the metaphysical level, vagueness is as real as anything can be. For sense-data or percepts are vague, and they are as real as anything can be. On the epistemological level, all data are vague (MAL 88; the notion of a datum is epistemic). All three bases of knowledge are vague: "(1) faint perception, (2) uncertain memory, (3) dim awareness of logical connection" (HK 393–94). Understanding vagueness is basic to understanding inductive logic (HK 335–44, 380–98). On the level of logical analysis, Russell says, "All ostensive definitions, and therefore all definitions, are somewhat vague" (HK 424). Logical analysis in science and philosophy is devoted to diminishing vagueness as much as possible (HK 424). Russell offers a formal method for deriving exact concepts from vague data (IMT 103–7). Russell's term for sharp identity conditions is "logical smoothness." Logical smoothness belongs not to real events, but to logical constructions. Russell makes all this abundantly clear (MAL 87–88; PLA 179–81; AMA 319; POM xi; IMT 57, 98, 103–7, 119, 315; HK 61–63, 67, 86, 98, 146–48, 186–88, 225–26, 238, 260–61, 393–95, 424, 497; LK 329, 338). Russell even wrote a paper entitled "On Vagueness" (1988a). As for spatiotemporal extent, Russell admits "quasi-equality" and "quasi-transitiveness" as fuzzy relations in *The Analysis of Matter*, in the chapter entitled "Measurement."

Bart Kosko hails Russell as a major precursor of fuzzy logic. I entirely agree with Kosko's portrait of Russell's views on vagueness as double-aspected. That fuzzy logic is an applied logic and not a formal logic fits nicely into Kosko's double-aspected portrait. Russell's black-and-white formal logic tries to eliminate fuzziness from the world (Kosko 1993: 288). But as to the real world and our knowledge of it, Russell insists, "Everything is vague…" (PLA 180; quoted by Kosko 1993: 121). Russell says "all words outside logic and mathematics are vague: there are objects to which they are definitely applicable, and objects to which they are definitely inapplicable, but there are (or at least may be) intermediate objects concerning which we are uncertain whether they are applicable or not" (HK 497; see 146–48, 424). In fact, vague statements need have no truth-value (IMT 320). "Russell used the term 'vagueness' to describe multivalence" (Kosko 1993: 19). "Charles Peirce and Bertrand Russell and other logicians had used [the term "vague"] to describe what we now call 'fuzzy'" (Kosko 1993: 137). Thus the inventor of fuzzy sets, Lotfi Zadeh, "called 'fuzzy' what Bertrand Russell and Jan Łukasiewicz and Max Black and others had called 'vague' or 'multivalued'" (Kosko 1993: 143; see 148). Again, Russell finds three-valued logic both "possible" and extremely interesting

(Russell 1989a: 681–82). Indeed, Russell says, "I do not think there is anything wrong with two-valued logic, nor yet with three-valued logic. Each is appropriate for its own class of problems" (Russell 1969: 135). If Russell did not endorse Zadeh's fuzzy logic as well, surely that is because Zadeh invented it when Russell was in his mid-nineties and had long ago stopped following the latest developments in logic. Also, Zadeh's logic was not well-received until several years after Russell's death.[14]

Kosko's portrait of Russell as double-aspected on vagueness and sharpness is confirmed by Russell himself: "This problem derives its difficulty from the attempt to accommodate to the roughness and vagueness of the real world some system possessing the logical clearness and exactitude of pure mathematics" (MAL 87). This is Russell's modernization of the two-tiered Platonic world of flux and forms, which modernized in turn the older Heraclitean world of fire and law. Formal systems recall law and forms. For Russell, fuzzy logic would cope more directly with fire or flux. Just as with Plato, if not also Heraclitus, sharp and stable identity conditions belong to the world of form, while rough identity conditions belong to the world of fleeting and vague particulars.

Fourth, McCauley criticizes Russell for failing to admit the arbitrariness of many sharp identity conditions and the importance of pragmatics in fixing sharp conditions. But who is more aware of this than Russell? Russell's whole project is inventing logically smooth artificial constructions! And it is McCauley who fails to understand pragmatics. For McCauley says that the inference, presumed valid for Russell:

> The place where Fred lives is New York City.
> <u>Manhattan is not identical with New York City.</u>
> Therefore, the place where Fred lives is not Manhattan.

is invalid, but not simply invalid: it fails to reflect "discourse pragmatics," or what in David Lewis's "scorekeeping" would be called "the setting and changing of values for a set of parameters ('the score') that affect the possibilities for using and interpreting sentences in the given discourse." But "discourse pragmatics" is merely new jargon. Any ancient logician could have told you that this syllogism commits the fallacy of four terms, "place where Fred lives" being the equivocal term. And only a singularly ungenerous interpretation of Russell would accuse him of not concurring with that ancient diagnosis.

Now we come to the nadir of McCauley's critique. McCauley says that Russell cannot accommodate sentences like "The dog was barking at another dog." That is McCauley's sentence (11b). McCauley says, "The Russellian formula for (11b) is self-contradictory (the 'uniqueness term' for the dog implies that there isn't any such thing as 'another dog'..." McCauley's solution is to admit a "conceptual domain" which fixes reference even to unicorns which do not exist, in addition to a universe of discourse of Russell's sort which "supplies the values for ordinary bound variables." The real problem is that McCauley fails to allow Russell any charity in paraphrasing ordinary language sentences into his canonical notation, as Quine would put it. No first year student of neo-Russellian predicate logic would dream of making (11b) self-contradictory by translating (11b) as McCauley suggests: $(\exists x)[x$ is a dog & $(y)($if y is a dog then $((y = x)$ & $(\exists z)((z$ is a dog & $\neg(z = x))$ & x is barking at z at time $t)))]$. Surely Russell admits different dogs, and would describe them differently. Even if dogs are logical fictions and therefore nothing, and even if two different things cannot both be nothing, the sensed and unsensed sensibilia which logically compose dogs are as real as anything can be, and wholly differ from dog to dog.

The problems of paraphrase include overlapping particulars, vagueness, pragmatics, and plain common sense—as in translating (11b)—alike. McCauley no doubt would translate the ordinary definite description "the charlady who ain't never done no harm to no one" as 'the charlady who in at least one moment injured the entire human race'. But Russell's famous reply to Strawson makes it clear that Russell would find that literal translation as ludicrous as McCauley's translation of (11b). Indeed, Russell gives the charlady example precisely as a parody of McCauleyan logicians with no common sense. The message of the charlady example is that "My theory of descriptions was never intended as an analysis of the state of mind of those who utter sentences containing descriptions....I was concerned to find a more accurate and analyzed thought to replace the somewhat confused thoughts which most people at most times have in their heads" (MPD 179).

6

The Ancient Realist Basis
of Conceptual Relativity

Some discuss conceptual relativity as if it were first discovered by analytic philosophers. Conceptual relativity is often said to be a recent or even a contemporary discovery. For example, Stephen Barker, in his 1967 "Number," says:

> Frege insisted on an elemental point that earlier philosophers had not recognized. Having a number...is not a feature of individual things or heaps of things...but pertains rather to concepts or sets. (Barker 1967: 5/529)

For a second example, Hilary Putnam says in his 1987 *The Many Faces of Realism*:

> That there are ways of describing what are (in some way) the 'same facts' which are (in some way) 'equivalent' but also (in some way) 'incompatible' is a strikingly non-classical phenomenon. (Putnam 1987: 29–30)

Indeed, members of the analytic tradition have often portrayed themselves as radically breaking from traditional philosophy. Roughly, the break consists of making the study of language prior to the study of the nonlinguistic world. The study of the nonlinguistic world becomes indirect at best. At worst, it becomes totally relative to choice of language, even meaningless apart from choice of language. Traditional realism is viewed as outdated. But in these last two chapters, I shall argue that on the fundamental level of ontology, there was no radical break.

Traditional modified realism is the ancient foundation of conceptual relativity. Conceptual relativity is a strikingly classical phenomenon if there ever was one. Conceptual relativity was suggested by Plato and formulated by Aristotle. That identities, numbers, and even kinds of being "shift" as sortal concepts, terms, or ideas "shift" became deeply embedded in the substance tradition. This way of grounding the legitimacy of conceptual relativity ruled out radical relativity for a good reason. Most Western philosophers adopted the ontology of modified realism to allow conceptual relativity to have something real *to* slice into conceptual beings. *Pace* Putnam, real things are what make conceptual relativity possible at all.

The ontology of 'no entity without identity' was implicit in many ancient views. The basic problem of ancient philosophy was to determine what remains the same through change. The Milesian philosophers were concerned with identifying what 'stuff' remains the same through natural changes. Even though Heraclitus denied that there is anything that remains the same (his view that all is fire paradoxically means not that fire is the basic substance, but that fluctuation itself is the basic reality of nature), his denial of substance was stated as or based on a denial of identity: "You cannot step into the same river twice." Parmenides is traditionally revered as showing that whatever is is one and that the rational is the real (that what we speak or think of cannot be nothing). The Sophists, turning from nature to humanity, found the same problem at the bottom of ethics and morality: What remains the same in values through all the changes from culture to culture, from person to person (Windelband 1979: 73)? And for Plato, what remains the same in nature and in ethics alike is precisely what is most real: forms. Plato explicitly saw his theory of forms as modified realist. It is "not a paradox but a truism" that wood and stones are both one and many, while the forms are "absolutely many" (*Parmenides* 129). Forms are objective and supremely real, while sensible objects are relative and scarcely real at all (*Republic* 437–38, 479, 602).

The ancients knew identity as a relation in informative identity statements. Plato notes that if Socrates is the person we see at a distance, and if we know Socrates, it does not follow that we know whom we are seeing at a distance (*Theaetetus* 191). Aristotle attributes to the Sophists a similar problem concerning Coriscus in the Agora and Coriscus in the Lyceum. Aristotle uses formulae to solve the problem much in the manner of Frege's senses: Coriscus in the Agora and Coriscus in the Lyceum are one in substance but distinct in formula (*Physics* 219*b*). So are teaching and learning, and "the road from Thebes to Athens and that from Athens to Thebes" (*Physics* 202*b*). Eubulides raises the problem of The Hooded Man (I both know and do not know my brother), but, unlike Aristotle, offers no solution. For Aristotle every informative identity statement about Coriscus, e.g., "The person sitting in the Lyceum is Coriscus," is either true or false. And if Coriscus exists, then indefinitely many identity statements about him are true. As Hippocrates G. Apostle says, "Socrates and the gadfly of Athens and the philosopher of Athens who drank the hemlock are numerically one and have just one substance" (in Aristotle 1973: 340). Similarly for any entity in any category. For instance, the teaching relation is the learning relation, and the road from Athens to Thebes is the road from Thebes to Athens. Aristotle's theory of informative identity is basic to the history of conceptual relativity. Formulae apply both to real beings in the category of substance and to conceptual beings in the other categories. Coriscus is one human being but many in formula. Teaching is one relational activity, but is many in formula. Indeed, the notion of a formula is simply a broadening of the notion of a form.[1] You can "shift" formulae and unities will "shift" along with them (one actual race track length, two merely potential half-lengths). Yet one formula (race track) may be incomparably more reflective of reality than another (half-length). Thus identity and, by extension, unity involve far than just the law "A = A."

Unity and being are multivocal transcendentals for Aristotle. They apply to everything in all of Aristotle's categories. One category, substance, is the category of *per se* unity and being. Beings in any other category have unity and being only relative to *per se* being in some way. This should be enough to make it clear that Aristotle was a modified realist. The foremost scholars concur on this. Francis M. Cornford, in *Plato and Parmenides*, says:

> The distinction between numerical and conceptual (formal, specific, εἴδει) sameness or difference is frequently stated by Aristotle as familiar. This distinction, like many others, was probably first formulated in those discussions at the Academy in which Aristotle had taken part as Plato's pupil and colleague and which the *Parmenides* itself must have done much to provoke and encourage. (Cornford 1939: 160–61)[2]

W. D. Ross, in *Aristotle*, says:

> There is one kind of being which is in the strictest and fullest sense—viz. substance;...And what is true of being is true of unity; whatever is is one, and whatever is one is, and unity has different though connected meanings according as it is unity of substance, of quality, of quantity, etc. 'Being' and 'unity' are terms standing above the distinction of categories and applicable in every category. (Ross 1960: 153–54)

Ignacio Angelelli, in *Gottlob Frege and Traditional Philosophy*, says:

Aristotle mentions in the *Physics* (and of course in the corresponding series of commentaries one may find the same idea) that a subject may be "one numerically" though "two in form"; he applies this idea to the analysis of movement. (Angelelli 1967: 44)

Angelelli is referring to Aristotle's solution of Zeno's "divided line" paradoxes of motion by distinguishing among one actual length, two potential half-lengths, four potential quarter-lengths, and so on. Apostle, in *Aristotle's Philosophy of Mathematics*, says:

> Since that which is one is a being and that which is a being is one, and since a unit *qua* part is potentially one, that which is a unit would fall under as many genera as there are of being. The unit would then be either a substance, or a quality, or a quantity, or any of the rest, and the number would be a number of substances, or a number of colors, or a number of lines, etc. And to say that the one or the unit is either a substance, or a quality, or a quantity would be…to give the nature of that which is one or a unit….Hence, the term "unit" is not univocal *qua* nature but has many senses, as in the case of "one" and of "being."
>
> Just as in other things there is that which is primary and prior and that which is secondary and posterior, so in units there is that which is primarily a unit and that which is secondarily a unit….Hence, substance comes first, because *qua* substance, it is indivisible with respect to quantity… (Apostle 1952: 85–89)[3]

I conclude that Aristotle is a paradigm of modified realism.

Where only substances, in the category of substance, are really distinct in sense (1), all other distinctions for Aristotle might be very broadly called distinctions in reason. However, this must not obscure the great variety of distinctions Aristotle makes.[4]

According to G. E. M. Anscombe and P. T. Geach in their *Three Philosophers* (1961), Aristotle accepts Geachian relative identity. This confirms my view in chapter 1 that Geachian relative identity and ontological real identity are compatible. At least, Anscombe and Geach report no conflict, and Geach is the chief propounder of relative identity. However, their interpretation of Aristotle as accepting Geachian relative identity is debatable.[5]

There is the Occamite interpretation of Aristotle's categories as primarily linguistic. I follow the mainstream in viewing the categories as primarily conceptual (Ross 1960: 31).[6] In any case, Aristotle is no radical realist. For in my lexicon, radical realism holds that all identities said to be true, other than real identities, are fictitious. This does not fit Aristotle. In Aristotle's modified realism, all identities said to be true in language, other than real identities, are true in a qualified manner. As Apostle puts it, "[I]f we call two unequal squares the same, they would be so with a qualification, namely, with respect to the definition of a square but not the quantity of surface" (in Aristotle 1973: 369). Likewise, you and your neighbor are numerically two substances, but are one with respect to formula , i.e. humanity (*Metaphysics* 1054*b*15–20).

1. Does Aristotle Have an Ontology?

I have just described what I consider to be Aristotle's ontology. Joseph Owens, Charles H. Kahn, Jaakko Hintikka, and Leila Haaparanta have recently questioned whether Aristotle has an ontology. I proceed to consider the main objections they raise.

Joseph Owens finds Aristotle's science of being *qua* being very different from ontology. Ontology as developed by Christian Wolff is the study of being, where being is the most general, abstract, and empty entity. Evidently Aristotle discusses no such being. His study of being *qua* being is not the study of an abstract or general entity named "being" or "existence." It is the study of a particular divine being: "separate substance," i.e., the "unmoved mover." The study has import for all beings. For the being of all other beings can be understood only in relation to the being of separate substance. Aristotle views the being of things other than separate substance in a *pros hen* way. Humans are healthy in the literal sense. But food, climate, and complexion are said to be healthy only insofar as they are related to health. Thus health is said in many ways. Likewise, the unmoved mover has being in the literal sense. Other things are said to have being only insofar as they are related to the unmoved mover. So that Aristotle has no ontology, but instead a *theology*. Thus Paul Natorp was wrong in imposing a Wolffian conception of ontology on Aristotle. We would be equally wrong in imposing any contemporary analytic version of Wolffian ontology, such as the Frege-Russell conception of existence as a second-level concept, on Aristotle. Also, Owens notes, for Aristotle being cannot be a genus to which all things belong. For a species must not only belong to a genus. It must also have differentia to which the genus is inapplicable. However, all differentia must have being in order to differentiate things. Therefore there can be no species of being. For being, as their genus, would be applicable to all their respective differentia (Owens 1982: 33–59; Owens 1963: ch. 7).

My reply to Owens is this. First, we philosophers are in the business of finding resemblances. And while we may say that a thing resembles itself out of logical courtesy, resemblances are mainly studied between different things. Indeed, the more different things are, the deeper and more illuminating their resemblances tend to be. Thus it ironically benefits my purpose if Aristotle differs so much from Wolff and Frege-Russell concerning being. Thanks to Owens, our analogical comparison that Aristotelian being is to Aristotelian unity as Frege-Russell existence is to Frege-Russell identity becomes all the more illuminating of Aristotle and Frege-Russell alike. Second, I defined "ontology" itself in a *pros hen* sense in chapter 1. And Aristotle's theory of being *qua* being as a particular divine being, with its attendant *pros hen* way of saying being in many ways related to the primary way, is ontological on my *pros hen* definition. For it is a theory that concerns the existential use of the word "is." It is a theory concerning what it is to say that something exists. That is, it addresses standard ontological issues. And all my definition of ontology requires is a theory of the use of the word "is" which is ontologically interesting. Similarly for Aristotle's denial that being is an abstract genus, an ontological theory if there ever was one. Third, being, most deeply for Aristotle, simply *is* the divine being, and not empty Wolffian being. Or else being in the literal sense is what only the unmoved mover *has*. Thus all Owens shows is that Aristotle has a theocentric ontology as opposed to a Wolffian ontology. More accurately, Aristotle has a *pros hen* ontology. Frege and Russell have yet a third sort of ontology. They admit no divine being, and they deride anything like Wolffian being.

Kahn's objection may seem deeper. Kahn seems to deny that Aristotle uses the word "is" in an existential sense at all. Thus it seems that on Kahn's view, even my broad definition of "ontology" is too narrow to apply to Aristotle's science of being *qua* being.

Kahn says, "When Aristotle applies his scheme of categories to show how Being (*it is*) 'is said in many ways', we may prefer to describe his various modes of being as so many different kinds of existence, or even as so many different senses of 'exists'. But Aristotle does not speak in such terms, and he regularly illustrates his categorial distinctions by copula uses of *to be*." Kahn suggests that the copulative use of "is" is "fundamental" to Parmenides, Plato, and Aristotle. Closely related to the copulative use of "is" is the noncopulative use called veridical. This use is the next most important one. The existential use is a distant third. Its pure use is so "rare" in ancient Greek that "[t]he Greeks are...untroubled by the modern puzzle of negative existentials." Plato and Aristotle "both...systematically subordinate the notion of existence to predication; and both tend to express the former by means of the latter. In their view *to be* is always to be a definite kind of thing....[I]t was another use of *to be* that gave Parmenides and Plato their philosophical starting point: the veridical use of *esti* and on for 'the facts' that a true statement must convey" (Kahn 1986: 3, 5–14, 21–22; Kahn 1982: 7–17).

My reply to Kahn is also simple. My definition of ontology applies to the ancient use of "is" Kahn describes. Kahn does not deny the ancient existential use of "is." *Au contraire*. Kahn says, "My suggestion is that for understanding the early philosophical usage,...the veridical notion...turns out to be more important than the idea of existence, although both notions are present." Kahn finds existence often "implied" where it is not "asserted" or "expressed." He speaks of "a copula construction overlaid with the existential function" or as

"acquiring 'existential' connotations." Kahn says, "The notion of existence...
must be included in our account of Parmenides' argument." Kahn makes further
concessions in several notes. Kahn admits that the arguments of Parmenides,
Plato, and Aristotle are concerned with existence, and cannot be understood
apart from the notion of existence (Kahn 1986: 10–14; n.45, n.46, n.49).

I have twelve further comments on Owens and Kahn.

(1) Owens admits that great scholars differ on whether Aristotle has an
ontology.

(2) The contention that Aristotle has no general notion of being because he
denies that being is a genus is a *non sequitur*. The primary and tertiary senses
of "exists" described in chapter 4 are general notions of being, but are not
genera. Instead, they are what Anscombe and Geach would call transcendental
or topic-neutral notions, following Gilbert Ryle (Anscombe 1961: 73).

(3) Indeed, Aristotle's very pairing of being and unity equimultivocally and
isomorphically across categories suggests a general notion of being: to be is to
be one. This general notion is not generic, but transcendental or topic-neutral.
If this general notion illuminated Aristotle, but were something Aristotle himself
did not explicitly assert, then it would be precisely what excellent philosophical
scholarship consists of. But in fact Aristotle does assert it. Aristotle says, "That
'unity' has in some sense the same meaning as that of 'being' is clear"
(*Metaphysics* 1054a10–15). Furthermore, Owens says that for Aristotle, being
is a "concept," i.e., common predicate. Thus this general notion of being as
unity may not be a genus, but at least it is a concept (Owens 1963: 456 n.1).

(4) It is not clear that Frege or Russell attributes to Aristotle or to the other
ancients an entity named "being" or even a purely existential sense of "is."
Frege does not discuss the ancients. Russell attributes to Parmenides not absolute
being, but an entity called "the One." Russell's discussions of both Plato and
Aristotle use the word "exists," but with no concern for an entity, Being, or for
a purely existential sense of "is." Russell criticizes Plato on existence, but his
criticism concerns the logical type-level of "is," considered *insofar* as "is" is
existentially understood. When Russell makes the same criticism of Aristotle,
he criticizes not Aristotle's theory of being *qua* being, but Aristotle's logic
concerning "some" and "all," for being in "purely formal error." Russell says
of Aristotle's categories not that they concern different senses of "exists," but
that the word "category" represents "no clear idea," He discusses Aristotle's
categories under the heading "Aristotle's Logic," not under the heading
"Aristotle's Metaphysics." Russell criticizes Aristotelian substance as due to
taking Indo-European grammar too seriously. But this does not concern the
existential use of "is." Russell has subject-predicate structure in mind instead.
In fact, Russell's discussion of existence in Aristotle concerns only the problem
of universals: whether particulars or universals can exist without each other. No
pure general sense of existence is involved. All this is open to view in Russell's
obviously most relevant work, *A History of Western Philosophy*, in the obviously

most relevant chapters, which Owens and Kahn (and Hintikka and Haaparanta) overlook. Russell may not be a great Aristotle scholar. But Russell does avoid saying about Aristotle what Owens, Kahn, Hintikka, and Haaparanta think is wrong, and it is unfair to Russell that not one of them acknowledges as much.

(5) Frege and Russell do not really care at all about whether the word "is" (or *ist*) has one use or one hundred in English or in German, let alone in ancient Greek. Frege and Russell are not ordinary language philosophers, but ideal language philosophers. The ambiguity of the ordinary "is" is an item of incidental interest discovered only after the important theories and arguments have been given. Like McCauley and Strawson, Kahn is unaware that Russell is not in the business of *reporting* lexical usage, but of *replacing* our vague thoughts with clearer ones. See chapter 5, section 8 on Russell's charlady who "ain't never done no harm to no one" (MPD 179).

(6) A conceptual penalty for forgetting the ideal language philosophy of Frege and Russell is that Kahn forgets that philosophy's most natural theory of translation itself. Quine suggests that the regimentation of quantification is best for translating foreign languages only insofar as it promotes referential clarity. Aristotle quantified is Aristotle referentially clarified. The "Aims and Claims of Regimentation" are more modest than Kahn seems to think. And Aristotle need not use *esti* always in the same sense or always purely in one or other of the four Frege-Russell ways, in order for us to find those four ways implicit in Aristotle. What matters is whether Aristotle can be illuminated by paraphrase into canonical notation, and whether the existential quantifier, the identity sign, and the class-inclusion sign (there is no copula sign) would be appropriate to paraphrasing Aristotle at all. We would not be concerned with whether Aristotle expressly acknowledges the Frege-Russell distinction (BG 5–7, BL 1–25, PM 1–3, MPD 170–75, 178–79; see WO 157–66, 242–43, FLPV 106–7, PT 27–28, and Ayer 1972: 57).

(7) *Pace* Kahn, Quine's test of ontological commitment in any language, ancient or not, is not the existential use of "is." It is the use of pronouns. It is in Aristotle's use of pronouns that we find Aristotle's ontological commitment to items in all categories. Quine stated this test in *Word and Object*, thirteen years before Kahn published his book, *The Verb 'Be' in Ancient Greek*. It is our guide to paraphrase by existential quantifier.[7]

(8) *Pace* Kahn, the existential sense of "is" is not connoted by the existential quantifier for Russell. What Russell would deem to have "absolute and metaphysical validity" for Aristotle would be Aristotle's most ultimate entities, substances. Yet substances would be only a very small part of what Russell would quantify over in paraphrasing Aristotle. As I argued in chapter 5, Russell's quantifier means 'not always true' and has no ontic commitment. This 'is not always *true*' is, on the face of it, a form of Kahn's *veridical* use of "is." And this veridical use of "is" is prior to the existential use for both Frege and Russell, insofar as both hold context principles on which the significance of

sentences is prior to the denoting or reference of names. (Russell's context principle is manifested in several texts.)[8] Where is the great difference between Frege-Russell and Aristotle on the priority of the veridical use of "is" to the existential use?

(9) To be is to be determinate for Frege and Russell, since they accept the law of excluded middle. And their existential quantifiers cannot be used except as predicating instantiations of properties: "There exists an *F* such that..." Again, existential quantification is *posterior* to the predicative use of "is." For Frege, existence is an essentially predicative concept predicated of essentially predicative concepts. For Russell, existence is a predicative propositional function predicated of predicative propositional functions. For both, existence can be asserted only of an *F*. Where is the great difference between Frege-Russell and Aristotle on the priority of predication to existential assertion? Where is their great difference on whether to be is to be *F*?

(10) Kahn suggests "against linguistic relativism" that the veridical use is "so essential to the basic descriptive or informative use of language that it is bound to be in some sense a linguistic universal." Kahn says that this is unlike the existential use of "is." For that use is functionally entwined with other uses in a way "rarely [found] in languages outside of Indo-European" (Kahn 1986 21–22). But once again, Kahn has no conception of ideal language philosophy or of its most natural theory of translation. Consider Quine's fine defense of quantification against the charge of Indo-European "parochiality" (PT 27–28). To put Quine's point in my own way, if we cannot paraphrase a language into a canonical notation, then the language may be a fine language, but we cannot understand it as saying anything about anything. Further, Kahn's charge must not be confused with the very different and more plausible charge Russell often makes that Indo-European grammar singularly encourages traditional substance metaphysics (LK 254–55, 330; AMI 192; AMA 151–52; HWP 201–2; HK 73, 293). I do not even know whether Kahn uses "linguistic relativism" to mean extreme linguisticism in our sense. He never explains his use of the term. His use seems to concern the fact that some languages lack some word uses.

(11) Perhaps the ancients were "untroubled" by the specific puzzle of negative existentials: How do you say "This does not exist" truly of what is not? But they were sorely vexed by the general puzzle underlying it: How do you say anything at all of what is not? Both puzzles present the very same problem: evidently, you are not saying anything *about* anything. And the general puzzle of Parmenides is ontological, on my definition of "ontological" in chapter 1. Certainly it is an ontological issue.

(12) The puzzle of negative existentials is a genuine, deep philosophical puzzle. Thus if Aristotle is untroubled by that puzzle, thanks to his ancient language's innocence of any "pure" sense of "exists" (Kahn 1986: 12, 23 n.10; Kahn 1982: 8; J. Hintikka 1986: 81–84), then Frege and Russell are right to think that they have made some progress over Aristotle.

In light of the foregoing comments, I proceed to my two major criticisms of Kahn, and by extension, of Hintikka and Haaparanta.

2. Meanings or Uses? Aristotle, Frege, Russell

Kahn states the whole problem of applying the Frege-Russell theory of "is" to Aristotle in terms of a basic dichotomy between senses or meanings on the one hand and uses on the other. Kahn speaks of a recent "trend away from the Mill-Russell view that 'is' has different senses." Kahn's basic position is to affirm Aristotle's existential use of "is," but to deny that "is," so used, has an existential sense. But Kahn is aware of his hairsplitting between "use" and "sense." He admits a "general reluctance to decide when a different use becomes a different sense." He admits that "the question whether 'is' has different meanings or only different uses cannot be answered without confronting certain very deep problems in the theory of meaning..." He concludes, "Whether this diversity [of functions of "is"] is...a case of ambiguity of *meaning* is a question on which I do not propose to take a stand" (Kahn 1986: 4, 9, 23 n.10).

Hintikka heartily endorses Kahn without any of Kahn's reservations about the dichotomy between meaning (or sense) and use. Hintikka says, "...Aristotle never officially acknowledges the Frege-Russell distinction ["between the *is* of identity, the *is* of predication, the *is* of existence, and the *is* of generic implication (class inclusion")) even as a difference between several uses, let alone as a difference between logically different meanings [or] senses of *esti*....More accurately speaking, he does acknowledge some differences between the relevant uses,...but he does not co-ordinate them into a three-part [or] four-part distinction." Hintikka proceeds to argue for a "purely existential use" of *esti*. Hintikka says of *Posterior Analytics* B89*b*33, "How could Aristotle possibly have explained more clearly by the means at his disposal that he was presupposing a purely existential use of εἰ ἔστι?" He adds, "In the same way as the Aristotelian *esti* sometimes has existential force and sometimes does not,... it can sometimes have the force of identity and sometimes does not....[But] this difference in use does not mean that Aristotle is thinking of *esti* as having different senses or meanings." (J. Hintikka 1986: 82–83, 84, 89, 93).[9]

My first major criticism is this. There is no dichotomy between sense (or meaning) and use. Kahn and Hintikka have not even attempted to make one clear in their accounts. And there is no sense-use dichotomy in Frege and Russell either. I am unable to imagine what Kahn and Hintikka may think they are doing when they postulate some bizarre sense-use dichotomy of their own, never even attempt to explain it, and then attribute to Frege and Russell the theory that the word "is" (*ist* for Frege) has several senses as *opposed* to several uses, as if Frege or Russell ever admitted such an absurd dichotomy. For Frege or Russell, what could be the difference between an existential use and an existential sense? How could a word have an existential use but no existential sense, or an existential sense but no existential use? Indeed, how could any word have a use but no sense (in any sense)? How could any word have a sense but no use (in any sense)?

Hintikka's article and one of Kahn's are included in Simo Knuuttila's and Hintikka's anthology, *The Logic of Being* (1986). The anthology's mission is to attack any imposition of the Frege-Russell senses of "is" where only uses of "is" can be found. Yet remarkably, not a single author in the whole anthology offers any explanation whatsoever of the difference between a sense and a use, either in general or for Frege or Russell. As we saw, Kahn even concedes a "general reluctance" about the distinction. Kahn does not "propose to take a stand."

For Frege, senses are (or roughly are) linguistic meanings (Dummett 1993: 40, 64–66. Frege admits different senses, of course, for the existential quantifier and the identity-name in his formal notation. (There is no copula-name in his notation.) But Frege never explains what senses are, as I said in chapter 2. And Dummett emphasizes that (1) Frege never discusses the relation between senses and uses of words, and that (2) nonetheless Frege's whole philosophy of language is virtually unintelligible unless we suppose that the sense of a word is virtually identical with its semantic use or role, i.e. contribution to the determination of the truth-values of sentences in which it can occur. Dummett says, "It is because a theory of meaning is...a theory of the practice of using a language that the notion of sense...is not a psychological one....It is this conception, which is part...of what the later Wittgenstein intended by his slogan 'Meaning is use', to which Frege came so close but never actually formulated..." (Dummett 1981: 682; see 360, 415, 427, 679; Dummett 1981a: 45–47, 53–58, 104–5, 109–14, 132, 250–51). And as we saw, Dummett does not go as far as Kluge, Sluga, and I go. For Kluge, Sluga, and I identify Frege's saturation theory, which applies to senses as well as to references, with Frege's context principle that words have meanings only if they can have uses in sentences (chapter 2, note 13). As Geach says, "uses of names simply are what Frege meant by senses of names" (Geach 1978: 205). Frege himself says, "[T]he name 'Nausicaa'...behaves as if it names a girl, and it is thus assured of a sense" (PW 122; see SR 58). Thus it seems that senses are timeless, abstract use-types.

For Russell, the meaning of a logically proper name is its bearer *qua* acquaintance, but a description or propositional function has "meaning in use" (PM 30, 66, 67, 71, 162). Which of these two kinds of meaning applies when Russell says in *Introduction to Mathematical Philosophy*, "The *is* of 'Socrates is human' expresses the relation of subject and predicate; the is of 'Socrates is a man' expresses identity. It is a disgrace to the human race that it has chosen to employ the same word 'is' for these two entirely different ideas..."? It can only be meaning in use. For the "is" of identity is a propositional function, and the copulative relation would be a propositional function if Russell admitted it. Existence, a property of propositional functions, is a propositional function as well. Observe that identity, predication, and existence are scarcely given as acquaintances. Russell says that "we must not define [such incomplete symbols], but must define the *uses* of [such symbols]" (PM 67).

Russell does distinguish uses from meanings in that most people know how to use words without knowing how to state their meanings. But Russell makes meanings the very explanations of use people ordinarily find hard to state. He says a word's "meaning is only to be discovered by observing its use: the use comes first, and the meaning is distilled out of it" (LK 300; compare AMI 198–99). That "is" could be 'existentially used' without *having* an existential meaning would be absurd. For propositional functions such as identity and existence, Russell admits meanings in use from *Principia* on.

So where is the great sense-use dichotomy which Kahn and Hintikka make so much of? Is it in Frege or Russell? No. Is it in Kahn and Hintikka? Yes, but only as unexplained jargon. The problem is not one of a few indeterminate cases in a sort of "no man's land" between two large groups of clear or paradigmatic cases. Grice and Strawson cannot come to Kahn's and Hintikka's rescue here (Grice 1956). The problem is that there is *not one* case of a Fregean sense or of a Russellian meaning of "is" which would not be a use for Frege or a meaning in use for Russell. And there is *not one* case of a use of "is" which would not be a sense for Frege or a meaning in use for Russell.

Thus when Hintikka finds a "purely existential use" of *esti* in Aristotle, this is just what Frege would call a purely existential sense, and just what Russell would call a purely existential meaning in use. When Kahn finds "a copula construction *overlaid* with the existential function," this is just what Frege would call a copula construction overlaid with the existential *sense*. After all, for Frege every significant sentence Aristotle wrote expresses a thought. Indeed, for him even ordinary language sentences express thoughts. That certain 'ideas' or 'notions' or 'functions' or 'uses' or 'connotations' (to use the jungle talk of Kahn) or 'senses' (to use the desert lexicon of Frege) are primary and others are subordinate makes no difference at all to the ontological status of such senses. Similarly, Russell would replace Kahn's jungle talk with his own desert talk of meanings in use. Thus Kahn and Hintikka themselves unwittingly prove that so far as Frege and the 1910–70 Russell are concerned, Aristotle's of *esti* expresses an existential sense.

I wholly grant a *prima facie* case that uses and meanings are different. In ordinary language, the words "use" and "meaning" are used differently, have different lexical meanings, and are not intersubstitutable *salva veritate*. ("'Red' means red" is true, but "'Red' uses red" is false, if it has a truth-value at all.) But when we investigate what meanings and uses are, or even only what their distinction amounts to, we find that they are distinct only in reason. The *prima facie* distinction merely amounts to the fact that "meaning" and "use" are not interdefinable by means of explicit definitions. Contextual definition would be more appropriate. But even contextual definition is not necessary. For our purposes, it is enough that there can *be* no verbal meaning without verbal use, and no verbal use without verbal meaning. For this is definitive of distinctions in reason. The context principle, "Words have meaning if and only if they can be used in sentences," makes this point more precise. The principle need not be definitional or analytic to be true. Yet used as a definition, it contextually defines meaning in terms of use. Indeed, all four great analysts uphold the context principle, and some of them affirm even wider 'meaning holisms' than that. All four connect meaning and use, despite *Investigations* #43's apparent qualification. The meaning-use connection is what the linguistic turn is all about. It is what all the great analysts affirm as basic to analysis.

It is arbitrary to associate meanings with word-types and uses with word-tokens, as if meanings were fairly fixed, stable, longstanding, and independent of the flux of contextual nuances of actual occasions of word use. Are Kahn and Hintikka basing their dramatic charges on a mere arbitrary regimentation? There is no reason why we cannot speak of use-types or meaning-tokens. Indeed, there is reason why we must, if we speak of meaning-types and use-tokens: meanings and uses are distinct only in reason.

George Pitcher's point that we can know how to use "Q.E.D." without knowing the meaning of the Latin it abbreviates is irrelevant (Pitcher 1964: 252). That use of "Q.E.D." is not as a phrase, but as a mark to indicate the end of a proof, roughly in the way we use a period to indicate the end of a sentence. And "Q.E.D.," so used, does have a sense or meaning to us. But that use, like Frege's use of the judgment-stroke to indicate assertoric force, has only a tenuous bearing on the specific sense-use dichotomy problem confronting us. That problem is to explain the difference between the 'existential sense' and the 'existential use' of the word "is," which is not used as punctuation. Nor does "is" abbreviate some obscure old Latin phrase whose meaning we need not know.

And insofar as Aristotle bases his metaphysics on his logico-grammatical categories, he too bases reference on linguistic use (*Categories* 1a–4b).

3. The Meanings of "Is": Aristotle, Frege, Russell

I proceed to my second major criticism.

For Kahn and Hintikka, the heart of the matter is that Aristotle largely mixes or blends together what Frege and Russell would sharply separate. Kahn speaks of the "logical overlap" of some types of use of *einai*. In one use it is "overlaid with a secondary function." In another use, it is "a copula construction *overlaid* with [an] existential function [emphasis Kahn's]." Kahn speaks of "how veridical and existential values can intersect in a single occurrence." He says there is a "pretty clearly existential" use which, however, retains "a veridical undertone." Kahn concludes that while *esti* "*can* mean 'exists'[,] the verb performs so many other functions, and its copula role is so prominent, that there is rarely any systematic reliance upon the fixed sense of the verb as 'exists'....[F]or Parmenides, as for Plato and Aristotle..., existence is a subordinate and not a primary component in the concept of being." Both Plato and Aristotle "systematically subordinate the notion of existence to predication." Hintikka cites *Metaphysics* 1003*b*22–32, where Aristotle says "*[One] man* and *a man that is* and *a man* are the same thing," as showing that Aristotle's "purely existential use" of *esti* "is not different from the identity sense of *esti*," and that "the predicative sense" in "'he is a man' will be a further synonym..." Hintikka finds the "irredeemable ambiguity between predication and identity" in Frege and Russell absent in Aristotle, whose formulations "express *ipso facto both* something's being such-and-such *and* its being identical with some one entity." Hintikka adds that terms in an Aristotelian syllogism "must carry...both a predicative sense and the existential one." And "in the last Aristotelian analysis, essential predications are in a sense identities." To sum up, "No longer does it make any sense to ask which of the several distinctions Aristotle 'really' means, for they are all inextricably intertwined." Thus there is an "absence in Aristotle of any real distinction between the *is* of predication, which expresses the obtaining of facts[,] and the *is* of existence" (Kahn 1986: 11, 13, 14, 21; J. Hintikka 1986: 84–85, 89, 95, 103, 105).

My second major criticism is this. Yes, existence, identity, predication, and class inclusion are sharply distinguished by Frege and Russell, who have the merit of clearly fixing the uses of their formal expressions concerning those notions. But the notions remain at least as "inextricably intertwined" for Frege and Russell as they are for Aristotle. Indeed, I have devoted this book to showing how only *two* uses of "is," the existential and the identitative, are inextricably intertwined for Frege and Russell. I should have thought that anybody who read Frege and Russell would see how the four notions intertwine in their logical systems. It is the most characteristic feature of their systems.

In *Word and Object*, Quine attributes the identity of indiscernibles to Frege, and follows Peano in tracing that principle back through Leibniz and Aquinas to Aristotle (WO 116–17). But Kahn and Hintikka ignore *Topics* 151*b*–153*a*5, in which Aristotle affirms the identity of indiscernibles. Evidently Kahn and Hintikka have not heard of Frege's explanation of identity as indiscernibility, or of Frege's *Basic Laws* (BL I 29) on sufficient conditions of names denoting in terms of conformance to the law of excluded middle. For Frege, conformance to the identity of indiscernibles, conformance to the law of excluded middle, self-identity, and being identical with some item that exists are *not different concepts*. The concept-names express different *senses*, but refer to the same *concept*, representatively speaking. There is no "real distinction" between existence, identity, and predication here.

Further, Frege requires for any predication that the logical subject-term of the sentence in question have a reference. And for that Frege requires in turn that we have "a criterion for deciding in all cases whether b is the same as a." And Frege requires for any assertion of existence a concept under which (or within which) the item in question is said to fall. Again, for Frege the "is" of existence *is an essentially predicative concept predicated of essentially predicative concepts*. See comment (9) on the systematic subordination of existence to predication in Frege and Russell. The "is" of identity is essentially predicative as well. This is not to mention the conditions of propertial determinacy and of identitative identifiability for an object–name to denote, *Basic Laws* I 29. How much more "inextricably intertwined" can predication, existence, and identity be? Where is the great difference between Frege and Aristotle on 'inextricable intertwining'? If anything, Hintikka has got it backwards. These notions are more clearly and necessarily intertwined in Frege and Russell than in Aristotle.

Quine says, "John Bacon has noted a nice parallel here: just as 'a eats' is short for 'a eats something', so 'a is' is short for 'a is something'....Predication and quantification are, indeed, intimately linked; for a predicate is simply any expression that yields...an open sentence, when adjoined to one or more quantifiable variables" (OR 94–95). Frege and Russell created this intimate link, and in so doing created the nice Aristotelian parallel Bacon noted.

Quine says, "Within extensional theories we can continue...to subordinate reference to predication in the manner of unregenerate Fregeans" (PQ 115). There could not be a clearer statement that Frege subordinates reference to predication. Similarly for Russell, insofar as Russell champions extensionalism.

I turn now to what I believe are the most relevant aspects of Aristotle's logical writings. We should not confine our search for Aristotle's identitative sense or existential sense to his uses of "is" or *einai*. In fact we would do better to look primarily at the quantifier "some" in Aristotle's logic, and his treatment of identicals as indiscernible and symmetrical in *Topics* 152*a*30–*b*. These are what most closely correspond to Frege and Russell on existence and identity. And the 'intertwining' in Aristotle we should look at is his deductions and conversions of sentences in logic. Here there is no question but that existence, identity, singular predication, and class inclusion are formally different but logically related in inference patterns, and are quite close to the Frege-Russell notions—though also liable to the Frege-Russell criticisms. This is not an 'oversimplified analysis' of Aristotle (J. Hintikka 1986: 110), but a highly selective critique by Frege-Russell.

Hintikka does discuss Aristotle's logic. He supports his view by saying, "Aristotle's logic is more like ordinary language (or many-sorted *Sprachlogik*) than it is like the Frege-Russell logic." But Hintikka overlooks that the

Frege-Russell logic systematically duplicates every Aristotelian inference. The beauty of the Frege-Russell logic lies not in falsifying Aristotelian logic, but in subsuming it as a limited branch, much as general relativity theory subsumes classical physics as valid for local space-time. Irving M. Copi's *Introduction to Logic* clarifies this elementary point. As Copi says, the existential import of "some" is the same in both Aristotelian and modern logic. But to derive the Aristotelian "all," existential import must be *added* to the modern logicians' "all" (Copi 1978: 187–89). Thus Hintikka has things backwards again. Instead of expressing too little existential import, Aristotle expresses too *much*! Needless to say, Aristotle would use both "all" and "some" with existential import, i.e. ontological commitment, across all his categories. Hintikka's many sorts, which are virtually Aristotle's many categories, and which are revealed by many uses of relative pronouns (J. Hintikka 1986: 96–99), concern Aristotle's categorial metaphysics more than his quantificational logic.

Kahn's Russell scholarship in his magnum opus, *The Verb 'Be' in Ancient Greek*, is even more careless. Kahn (1973: 4) quotes Russell's *Principles*:

> The word *is* is terribly ambiguous, and great care is necessary in order not to confound its various meanings. We have (1) the sense in which it asserts Being, as in "A is"; (2) the sense of identity; (3) the sense of predication, in "A is human"; (4) the sense of "A is a-man"...which is very like identity. In addition to these there are less common uses....Doubtless there are further meanings which have not occurred to me. (POM 64n)

(Note how Russell indiscriminately wanders from meanings to senses to uses and back to meanings again in this, his fullest statement of the distinctions. I see no great distinction among meanings, senses, and uses here!) Kahn proceeds to quote the "disgrace to the human race" text from *Introduction to Mathematical Philosophy* about how people use the word "is" for such "entirely different ideas" (IMP 172). Kahn praises Leśniewski for showing "how all or most of the uses of be in Indo-European languages can be derived from three basic notions: truth, predication for singular subjects, and existence for singular subjects." Kahn then praises Quine's theory of ontological commitment for achieving the same reduction to "the three fundamental notions of existence, predication, and truth." (Kahn overlooks the veridical "not always false" in "On Denoting" and *Principia Mathematica*.) Kahn concludes:

> This brief glance at Leśniewski's Ontology is designed to provide some counter-weight to the dominant tendency in the Mill-Russell-Carnap tradition which insists upon the *diversity* of meanings and functions for *be*. The spokesmen for this tradition often assume, for example, that because the "is" of the copula and the "is" (or "there is") of existence

are distinct in meaning and in grammar, there can be no wider conceptual system that relates them to one another. Thus they overlook the possibility that, even if the system of *be* cannot be reduced to a single unambiguous meaning, it may nevertheless exhibit *some* conceptual unity.

The ontology of Lesniewski, and perhaps also that of Quine, suggests how the various uses and senses of be need not be taken as sheerly univocal (as the dominant tradition tends to suppose), but that they may be recognized as distinct and nonetheless related to one another in a systematic way. (Kahn 1973: 6)

But in the very work Kahn quotes to show how independent of one another the meanings of "is" are for Russell, Russell proclaims the opposite:

The whole theory of definition, of identity, of classes, of symbolism, and of the variable is wrapped up in the theory of denoting. (POM 54)

Russell makes all his uses of "is" systematically interdependent in both of his great logical works, *Principles* and *Principia*. So does Frege in *Begriffsschrift* and *The Basic Laws of Arithmetic*.

Kahn remarks that Mohan Matthen's logical equivalence between "Socrates is healthy" and "The healthy Socrates exists" "captures something quite deep, and quite strange to us, in the use of *einai* by the Greek philosophers" (Kahn 1986: 27 n.46). But as we have just seen, this would not be strange to Frege or Russell at all. In the Frege-Russell logic, "*s* is *H*" is logically equivalent to "There exists an *x* which is *H* and which is identical with *s*." I suspect that the real problem is simple: Kahn studied the ancient Greeks in great detail for many years, but did not study Frege and Russell closely at all. Hintikka adopted Kahn's quick way with Frege and Russell, and Haaparanta followed suit.[10]

7

The Ontology of the Analytic Tradition

I shall argue that Frege, Russell, Wittgenstein, and Quine are best viewed as modified realists. This undermines contemporary debates on relativity on two scores. First, the great analysts are realists. Second, their ordinary conceptual relativity, which would be the basis of their radical relativity if they were radical relativists, serves only to modify their realism. The analogy is to Aristotle's modified realism. One may substitute ordinary linguistic relativity for ordinary conceptual relativity and extreme linguisticism for radical relativity in discussing Wittgenstein and Quine. In that case the analogical argument is to Aristotle's modified realism on the Occamite interpretation of all Aristotle's categories save that of substance as merely nominal.

I give seven criteria of modified realism. Meeting any one of these criteria implies modified realism as defined in chapter 1. My principal argument is that the analysts meet these criteria as easily as Aristotle does. I show this for each analyst in the sections to follow. For each analyst: Private language arguments entail mind-independent, language-independent realism. Objects' "shifting" (a metaphor) as sortal terms or concepts "shift" modifies the realism. The realism and the sortal relativity are compatible and co-exist. "Really distinct" is reformulated as *wholly* distinct. Further, in intimate analogy to traditional metaphysical systems, each analyst in some sense treats some categories as more real than others.

The seven criteria are:

(1) *Metaphysical Modified Realism.* The thinker attributes some or all of the characteristics of substance to some but not to all things:

a. Being mind-independent
b. Having a changeless form (essence, nature, kind)
c. Being an ultimate subject of predication
d. Being logically independent (of other substances)
e. Being recognizable realities
f. Having an identity which persists through changes
g. Having real (numerical, literal) identity (unity).

This is the list of seven Aristotelian themes with which this book began.

(2) *Substance Analogue Modified Realism.* The thinker admits substance analogues or substitutes as some but not all things, as typically indicated by expressions such as "subsistent," "real," "ultimate," "rock bottom," "what is the case," and so on.

(3) *Explanatory Modified Realism.* The thinker gives a fundamental objective role or status in explaining (grounding, accounting for) the world to some but not all things. Scientific realism is one kind of explanatory realism. Criterion (3) is Aristotelian. Aristotle's substances have a fundamental role in grounding items in the other categories. Aristotle's metaphysic is scientific realism. His substances are posits of the most advanced natural science of his time.

(4) *Methodological Modified Realism.* The thinker gives a fundamental objective role in analysis (definition, description, reduction, elimination) to some but not all things. If analysis is explanation, then methodological realism is explanatory realism. If analysis arrives at simple entities, this is simplist realism. If it arrives at wholes which are logically prior to their parts, this is holist realism. Holist realism is a kind of simplist realism. Criterion (4) is Aristotelian. Aristotle has a scientific method of definition by division, but says that we must start with items that are not defined. Insofar as Aristotle's substances are hylomorphic compounds of form and matter, Aristotle is a holist realist. Criterion (4) is not met either by Rudolf Carnap's methodological phenomenalism or by his later methodological physicalism, since these disavow ontological commitments.

(5) *Phenomenological Modified Realism.* The thinker holds that some but not all things are presented (perceived, given) as real. Criterion (5) is Aristotelian in that Aristotle's substances comprise a perceptually "common sense" world. If the world is explained or analyzed in terms of ultimately real presented items, then phenomenological realism is also explanatory or methodological realism.

(6) *Epistemic Modified Realism.* The thinker holds that we can have some knowledge or evidence that some but not all things are real. Criterion (6) is Aristotelian in that substances are recognizable.[1]

(7) *Linguistic Modified Realism.* The thinker holds that when we name or describe in language, we sometimes but not always denote or refer to entities whose nature and existence is independent of the nature and existence of

language. Criterion (7) is Aristotelian in that items in all Aristotle's categories can be referred to in language.

I omit one traditional theme which is not a helpful criterion: being an eternal or a durable thing. For even momentary things—Hume's impressions and Russell's particulars—can be substantival.[2]

Criterion (1) is both traditional and paradigmatic. Criterion (2) covers all theories sufficiently similar to paradigmatic theories. Criteria (3)–(4) are next; phenomenologically or epistemically real things seem less real than things which explain or compose them. As G. W. F. Hegel suggests in his *Phenomenology of Mind*, the given is real, but it is the least real (Hegel 1967: 149). There is no need to order the last three criteria for my purposes. That criteria (1)–(7) are indeed criteria of realism may be ensured by using Butchvarov's definition of "real" to define the sort of realism criteria (1)–(7) concern. Butchvarov's definition was given in chapter 1.

My principal argument is an analogical argument, a comparison of the great analysts to Aristotle, with one *caveat*. Analogical arguments are traditionally understood as inductive; by definition they are never formally valid. Thus *omnis analogia claudiat* (every analogy limps). However, in many cases my criteria would seem logically sufficient to establish modified realism. Perhaps then my arguments are more criterial than analogical. However, analogy may still appear behind the scenes as the question to what extent my criteria really apply. And I do question the traditional division of arguments. My use of "analogical" is broader and more contemporary than usual. For instance, suppose there are several shades which are norms or paradigms of red. In some cases a new shade may so closely resemble the norms that it cannot fail to be red. Now, looking within the substance tradition itself, surely the substances of Descartes, Spinoza, and Locke so closely resemble Aristotelian substances that they cannot fail to be substances too. Would anyone say, for instance, that Descartes might not admit any substances? I am merely adding that my seven criteria articulate seven different but overlapping norms of modified realism, such that many of my arguments in the sections to come may be logically sufficient to show that the analysts are modified realists.

I wish to modify the view of Brentano (chapter 1, section 2) and Russell (chapter 5, section 2) that real things cannot be composed of real things. A modified realist may admit items as real on different levels of the world's structure if (i) different senses of "real" are used, so that one real being is not composed of other real beings in the same sense of "real"; and (ii) some items are admitted as real and others as real in a muted sense. The muted items need not be among those said to be real in different senses. For instance a modified realist may admit percepts as phenomenologically real, muons as scientifically real, and as more real than percepts, and classes as real in a muted sense. Condition (ii) defines modified realism; and condition (i) is compatible with condition (ii). The different senses of "real" may be very close. We might say a chain is nearly as real as its links, or a wall is nearly as real as its bricks and mortar, or a heap of sand is nearly as real as its grains, or a body nearly as real as its micro-states.

Indeed, this suggests a second modification of Brentano and Russell. To say that a whole is *not* real in a certain sense because its parts *are* real in that sense seems a kind of inverse fallacy of composition. Physical reality is a case in point. Consider again the chain, the brick wall, the heap of sand, and the body composed of micro-states. Conversely, to say that parts are not real in a certain sense because a whole is real in that sense seems a kind of inverse fallacy of division.

These two modifications explain what is wrong with the two arguments for radical relativity described at the end of chapter 1. Insofar as that in one sense a whole is logically prior to its parts, while in another sense its parts are logically prior to it, my second modification of Brentano reduces to my first. For even if a chain and one of its links are equally physically real, each is logically prior to the other in a different sense. And that alone makes each more real than the other in a different sense.

The more general explanation is this. The arguments for radical relativity sought to establish that since a thing could be both one thing and many things, the ontological *locus* of identity is always in concepts (or language, viewing extreme linguisticism as a form of radical relativity). The radical relativist resolves and explains the problem of relativity, i.e., the problem of one and many, by saying in effect that the seeming contradictions of one and many are entirely in our different ways of thinking or talking about things. The modified realist says that there is a better way to resolve and explain the problem. Namely, some objectual identities are real—perhaps in different senses of "real"—and others are merely conceptual, or even merely linguistic. For a one-many contradiction would exist in reality only if one and many are said of the same thing in the same sense of "real." The pratfalls of radical relativity are avoided, and far greater common-sense plausibility and flexibility in describing the world's structure are achieved, or at least made possible. Logical priority alone can avoid the problem of one and many. Or one term may prove prior in the order of explanation, and be logically prior in that sense. Even where a so-called "family circle" of terms is interdefinable, rough real distinctions may still be drawn in the domain of discourse (compare Grice 1956). Or the whole family circle may concern a domain really distinct from those of other family circles. All the real work of sorting everything out lies ahead. But at least it is not foreclosed by the radical relativist. For my part, I must finish the scholarly task of this book, and then leave the adventure of philosophy to the reader.

1. Frege's Modified Realism

Frege's version of number shifting may seem like radical relativity. His examples in *Foundations* involve objects such as copses and trees, cards and card decks, the foliage and the leaves of a tree, boots and boot pairs, heaps and grains of sand or wheat. He does not admit substances or even a distinction between real distinction and distinction in reason. Granted, Frege's objects are objective in the sense that they are public and mind-independent. Some are even real in Frege's sense of causal action or capacity. But it seems hard to tell which of them have real identities. Are trees real and copses mutedly real? Or is it the other way around? Or do trees and the copses they compose both have real identities?

Does Frege admit any substance analogues? Is he a modified realist? I say yes on both counts for eight reasons.

First, Frege accepts selves as real bearers of ideas. It would be incredible if he held that selves are not really distinct, although he does not explicitly say so. And we know that he rejects "homeless" ideas, i.e., ideas which can exist independently of minds. Thus ideas are distinct only in reason from minds. This alone is enough to make Frege a modified realist. This is not to mention that mental ideas or sensations are real in their own right, if they have causal effects or capacities, or that some ideas or sensations are doubtless complex and thus distinct only in reason from their constituent ideas or sensations.

Second, Frege's concrete objects, including at least bodies, are more real than his abstract objects. Many concrete objects are really distinct from each other, while many abstract objects are distinct in reason from each other. In particular, Frege's numbers are interdefinable.

Third, thanks to the possibility of mere hypothetical supposition of a thought without any judgment that it is true, it seems that denotations could exist even if forces such as assertion, question, or command did not. But surely forces could not exist if thoughts did not; what would they be forces *of*? And many denotations will be really distinct; and many forces will be really distinct. Similarly for (emotive or expressive) tones.

Fourth, Frege deeply endorses the notion of essence or nature in describing his basic categories; this supports traditional real identity.[3]

Fifth, Frege infers no idealism from the fact that numbers and objects "shift" as concepts "shift." His private language arguments establish an objectivity that applies to objects (including numbers) and concepts alike.

Sixth, Frege says "the physical phenomenon" is what may be divided into different objects. Such physical phenomena seem to be phenomenologically real objects with given real identities, when perceived (FA 32–33; 32 n.2).

Seventh, Frege admits "physical difference" (FA 42). And some physical differences would be real differences among "individual objects" (FA 42).

Eighth and decisively, Frege openly endorses real identity in *Foundations*:

> We cannot succeed in making different things identical simply by dint
> of operations with concepts. But even if we did, we should then no
> longer have things in the plural, but only one thing; for, as DES-
> CARTES says, the number (or better, the plurality) in things arises
> from their diversity. And as E. SCHRÖDER justly observes: "That
> things should be numbered is a reasonable demand only where the
> objects submitted appear clearly distinguishable from one another...and
> isolated in contrast with one another."...W. S. JEVONS makes this
> point with unusual force: "Number is but another name for diversi-
> ty..." (FA 46)[4]

Frege is telling us he belongs to the pluralist branch of realism, and that if he
did not, *he would choose belonging to its monist branch over accepting radical
relativity.*

I therefore interpret Frege as follows. Frege says in *The Basic Laws of
Arithmetic* that what is real is what can act on the senses, and says in "The
Thought" that what is real is what acts and is acted upon. Frege, then, makes
real distinctions among wholly distinct concrete objects, which are real in both
of these senses, and makes distinctions in reason between all other entities. That
is my principal interpretation. I also suggest as a secondary interpretation that
Frege makes real distinctions among those concrete objects which he deems
phenomena. I do not wish to make the molehill of Frege's use of the word
"phenomenon" into a mountain of Fregean phenomenology. But on the face of
it, Frege's modified realism is most closely analogous to phenomenological
realism. Compare the following text to similar texts in Husserl, Heidegger, and
Sartre:

> The more the internal contrasts within a thing fade into insignificance
> by comparison with the contrasts between it and its environment, and
> the more the internal connexions among its elements overshadow its
> connexions with its environment, the more natural it becomes for us to
> regard it as a distinct object. For a thing to be "united" means that it
> has a property which causes us, when we think of it, to sever it from
> its environment and consider it on its own. (FA 42)

Are not "contrasts" much like Heidegger's 'differences'? Are not "elements"
much like Husserl's 'primary objects'? Does not Frege in effect accept Sartre's
observation that any synthetic unity presupposes that there are elements to unite
into things? On pain of vicious regress of conceptual identities, must not Frege's
contrasts, elements, and properties be given as already having identities?[5]

As a perceived object itself has a property which causes us to consider it as
severed from its environment, is not that object really distinct from its

environment? Are not its presented elements distinct in reason from it? Indeed, this text is a ninth excellent reason for holding that Frege is a modified realist.

One might object that real things are being composed of real things. A card deck is as really distinct from its environment as each of its cards is from its own respective environment. My reply is that phenomenological real distinctions shift over time. At one time, a property of the card deck causes us to sever the card deck, when we think of it, from its environment. At another time, a property of one of its cards causes us to sever that card, when we think of it, from its environment. That is part and parcel of phenomenological realism. There is no inconsistency, since presentations are always at some time, and the times are different. A second reply is to apply our second modification of Brentano's view that real things cannot be composed of real things. Physically real ("concrete") objects can be composed of physically real objects; and phenomenologically real objects are merely perceived concrete objects. Card decks and cards are physically real, and can be phenomenologically real.

Since Frege speaks of visible and tangible phenomena (FA 32, 33), it seems likely that Frege would count all and only perceptible physical objects as phenomena. Frege says that a horse in Germany and a horse in America cannot count together as one phenomenon, though either horse by itself "could be so described" (FA 32 n.2; Frege writes before the present time of astronauts and spy satellites). My gloss is merely that a physical object O perceived as distinct from its environment by person P at time T is phenomenologically real to P at T. This is all I mean by "phenomenologically real" in Frege's case. In effect the environment counts as a second phenomenologically real object, O^*, from which O is wholly distinct, even if P's attention at T is primarily on O. Now, two phenomenologically real objects $O1$ and $O2$ which P perceives at T to be wholly distinct, are really distinct in my first sense of "really distinct" (chapter 1). But cards remain phenomena, i.e., perceptible, at all times; and so do card decks if they are not split up too far apart with respect to P. What about card decks and cards when nobody is actually perceiving them? Which objects are really distinct from which then?

Much clarification is needed. What is the proper analysis of a phenomenon for Frege? In what sense or senses are phenomena really distinct?

Frege never explains or analyzes what phenomena are. But surely a Fregean phenomenon is in some sense a physical object given in sense-perception, and individuated by a property in a way over which the observer has no control, and of which the observer may not even be conscious. If we were conscious of the property (i.e. concept), then presumably we would be free to shift the concept, and so to shift the objects and their identities, as we pleased. Consider the last sentence of the last indented quotation. The property's causing us to sever the thing from its environment implies that we have no control over the severance. The severance occurs just when we single out the thing in perception. Nor need we be conscious of the causal relation. All three occurrences of the word "it" in that sentence refer to the thing, not to its property. We need be conscious only of the thing. We need not be conscious of the property at all, much less conscious of its causal impact. Observe that this is just the sort of causal impact that a card deck might have on us at one time, and one of its cards might have at another. Observe also that this account allows dogs to single out phenomena as easily as humans can, just as Frege would want (FA 42).

Frege's phenomena seem best interpreted using Frege's notions of concrete object, sense-impression, sortal concept (property), and self. My interpretation is that a phenomenon is a concrete object presented *via* a sense-impression in connection with a sortal concept to a self, the concept not being freely chosen by that self, but instead causing the self to consider the object as united, whether the self is aware of the causation or is even aware of the concept as such. All phenomena are not only preconceptually but prehumanly perceivable.[6]

Our interpretation of phenomena is supported by what Frege says about perception and concept-development in "On the Scientific Justification of a Conceptual Notation," published two years before *Foundations*. We humans start with sense-impressions, as do animals. Frege writes, "The perception of a thing can gather about itself a group of memory-images...." (CN 83). But for a lasting perception of the thing, we must "produce" a symbol that gives "a firm, new focus about which ideas gather" (CN 83–84). Frege continues:

> [W]ithout symbols we would scarcely lift ourselves to conceptual thinking. Thus, in applying the same symbol to different but similar things, we...no longer symbolize the individual thing, but rather what [the similar things] have in common: the concept. This concept is first gained by symbolizing it; for since it is, in itself, imperceptible, it requires a perceptible representative in order to appear to us. (CN 84)

Frege is saying that there is a plurality of "different but similar" perceptible objects which are not only preconceptually but prehumanly perceptible. These objects are just what Frege calls phenomena. Frege says that the symbolization of different things must precede any awareness of concepts. Since concepts are imperceptible, and since perceptible symbols, as well as the perceptible objects to which we apply them, must be individuated by perception alone, i.e., without the aid of concepts, neither such symbols nor such objects can possibly involve even ordinary (nonontological) conceptual shifting of identities. Their identities can only be presented real identities, on pain of our never acquiring concepts at all. Shifting of concepts yields an objectual slicing we intellectually do *to* phenomena; and for that we must first intellectually grasp some concepts.

Granted, we need not be aware at every moment of every concept in our conceptual framework. The point is that the concept individuating a phenomenon is literally embedded in the phenomenon itself as its property, independently of any conceptual framework we have, and independently of our awareness of any concepts at all.

This phenomenological interpretation of Frege is not based just on some obscure early article. Frege says right in *Foundations*:

> Can...a dog staring at the moon...have an idea...of what we signify by the word "one"? This is hardly credible—and yet it certainly distinguishes individual objects [*einzelne Gegenstände*]: another dog, its master, a stone it is playing with, these certainly appear to the dog every bit as isolated, as self-contained, as undivided, as they do to us. (FA 41–42)

The dog cannot have any awareness of concepts, since dogs are prelinguistic. Yet dogs distinguish perceptible objects (phenomena) as well as we do. Frege distinguishes the present metaphysical sense of "unity," in which all objects have unity, from the arithmetical sense of "unity" which is "connected with [the number] 'one'," in which it is ill-formed to say that an object is one (FA 42–43). The two senses must not be confused. The first sense concerns the integrity of objects *qua* objects, some of which can be preconceptually apprehended. It is Aristotle's theme (7). The second sense concerns the predication of numbers, notably the number one, of concepts. Identity itself is an imperceptible concept, specifically the relation between names of denoting the same denotation. Clearly the concept of identity cannot be intellectually grasped before we learn some language. Yet metaphysical unity is best glossed as embedded in an object itself, regardless of whether languages, humans, or even dogs exist.

In light of all this, it would be incredible to depict Fregean phenomena as Strawsonian observable regions of space into which we "feature-place" our predicates (*pace* Dummett 1991: 162–63). Frege is telling us in the plainest terms that the first phenomena we perceive are at least temporally prior to any concept acquisition, and therefore at least temporally prior to any feature-placing. This is not to mention that regions of space are imperceptible abstract objects for Frege. Thus awareness of regions of space must be posterior to names of phenomena, hence post-linguistic.

There is no reason for Frege to have ever changed his mind on the priority of names of phenomena, not even when he later split contents into senses and references. Frege does not address this issue. But since Frege's argument that names of phenomena are prior to concept acquisitions is based on the imperceptibility of concepts, names of phenomena are also prior to any grasping of senses. For at least on my view, every sense is intimately associated with some concept. More directly, Frege's key principle is that the naming of phenomena is prior to the grasping of *any* imperceptible entities. And that includes senses, since senses are just as imperceptible as concepts. Thus when Howard Wettstein proclaims the standard view that "direct reference" or "reference without sense" is "unthinkable" or "impossible" for Frege (Wettstein 1990: 115–17), he ignores Frege's theory of how we first name phenomena, not to mention Frege's theory of concept acquisition. Indeed, these direct references to phenomena at the beginning of language acquisition make Frege a haecceitist whose phenomena have trans-world identities, *pace* David Kaplan (1975) and Leila Haaparanta (1986: 283). The alternative is to hold that we somehow use senses without intellectually grasping them. But since all thoughts are senses, this is equivalent to saying that we can use thoughts without thinking them, which is absurd.[7]

My conclusion is that Frege meets criterion (5) of modified realism. But if that is incorrect, only my secondary interpretation of Frege is defeated. There remains my primary interpretation of Frege, on which he is a modified realist in accordance with criterion (1g), the most basic criterion. That is, there is a sense in which Frege accepts both real distinctions among real concrete objects and also many distinctions in reason. It is as follows.

Frege replaces substances with a wider category, concrete objects. In so doing, he has replaced real distinction in sense (1) with real distinction in sense (2). (See chapter 1, section 2 for my four senses of "real distinction.") In sense (2), many of what used to be collections of substances, such as card decks or heaps of sand, are for Frege concrete objects which are really distinct from each other, just as much as leaves or grains of sand are really distinct from each other. By "collection" I mean not classes, which are abstract objects, but their extensions. Not all collections are really distinct from each other; some collections overlap. Of course, collections are only distinct in reason from their members. Thus Frege, in widening the old category of substance into the new category of concrete objects, widens the scope of real distinction. And insofar as any former parts of substances are really distinct concrete objects for Frege, for instance Smith's arm or a flower's petal, Frege widens the scope of real distinction once again. What Frege reveals by widening the scope of real distinction in these two ways is just this: Insofar as conceptual distinction had been traditionally applied to all *collections* of substances and to all *parts* of substances, in many cases this was due not to clause (1) but to clause (2) of the first sense of "real distinction." That is, such collections and parts were considered to be not really distinct from each other not only because they cannot exist independently of each other, but also because they are not substances. Frege makes all such distinctions in reason into real distinctions. He can do this because his concrete objects include such collections and parts. Yet there remain many distinctions in reason among Frege's concrete objects. For instance, Smith's arm remains distinct in reason from Smith's body. A card deck remains distinct in reason from its own cards. The collection of card decks remains distinct in reason from the collection of cards.

Indeed, this is a perfectly intelligible way to explain my second modification of Brentano's view that real things cannot be composed of other real things: Real distinction applies to *pairs* of objects, yet different pairs can overlap in various ways as just described. Or, if you please, real distinctions obtain among *groups* of objects which can be regimented into levels of the world's structure. Thus there can be really distinct objects at every level of the world's structure. To realists who admit a real world of real things, that picture should look right.

Now, real identity is a precondition of real distinction. For real identity cannot exist apart from real distinction unless only one real being exists. And Frege is no monist. Thus real identity, in the sense most natural to apply to Frege's concrete objects, allows real things to be composed of other real things. Similarly for Russell's army, Wittgenstein's chessboard, and Quine's rabbits. With all these the most appropriate sense of "real distinction" to apply is sense (1), where to be a real thing is to be mind- and language-independent.

For Frege, some objects, such as the Sun, are more real than others, such as the number two. But real distinction in sense (2) concerns only whether things are logically independent of each other. Thus in sense (2) of real distinction, some of Frege's *abstract* objects are really distinct from others. For instance, the axis of the Earth is really distinct from the axis of Jupiter. For either planet could cease to rotate and the other continue to rotate. Thus either axis could continue to exist in the absence of the other. Recall that "abstract" means not 'timeless', but 'without causal impacts' ("The Thought") or 'without causal capacities' (BL 16).

That abstract entities which are not really distinct from each other can be grasped only by abstraction or by definition suggests that they are conceptual beings, where conceptual beings are not nothing, but instead genuine objects. In the case of numbers, they are logical objects.

One might go on to ask whether Frege admits real distinctions in sense (3), the *per impossibile* sense, between abstract objects. Perhaps wholly distinct units of space would be really distinct from each other in this sense, while numbers and classes of classes would not be really distinct from each other. But even if this is so, we have left Frege too far behind to claim very seriously that we are interpreting him.

But we can revive sense (1) of real distinction in two ways. First, conjunct (2) of sense (1) could require that both entities be real in the sense of being concrete objects. Second, conjunct (2) could require more specifically that both entities be phenomena. Way (1) is best from the scholarly point of view. For all concrete objects are equally real in Frege's ontology. Phenomena are not more real than other concrete objects. Notice also that concrete objects in general are the natural analogues to Aristotle's substances. Not all concrete objects are perceptible to us. Some may be too small or even too big, e.g. a Cosmic Man within whom our galaxy might be like an atom. But they might be perceptible to ants or to Cosmic Women. More decisively, electrons are imperceptible for theoretical reasons.

Frege's concrete objects are mind-independent (1a), essentially saturated (1b), ultimate logical subjects (1c), often logically independent of each other

(1d), both intelligible and recognizable as the same again (1e), persisting through changes (FA 59) (1f), and often really distinct in sense (2), if not also really distinct in sense (1) the revived sense just described, as well as in a phenomenological modified realism (1g). Thus criterion (1) is fulfilled in detail.

Thus Frege is a metaphysical modified realist. Also, Frege is a methodological modified realist, since for him, analyses end with simple existents.

2. Russell's Modified Realism

Russell, in *Principles of Mathematics*, may seem to be a radical relativist. I quote this text again:

> Numbers cannot be asserted of objects, because the same set of objects may have different numbers assigned to them...; for example, one army is so many regiments and such another number of soldiers. This view seems to me to involve too physical a view of objects: I do not consider the army to be the same object as the regiments. (POM 519)

Alternatively, in that every application of a concept 'presupposes numerical diversity', in that every entity has its own immediate identity, *Principles* suggests a radical realism. The one thing *Principles* seems to not to be is modified realism, since Russell expressly denies the distinction between real distinction and conceptual distinction (POM 466). But this denial seems quite disingenuous in light of his own distinction between empirical (or actual) existence and mathematical (or logical) existence.

Surely the truth is that *Principles* indulges in a rich and complex modified realism. Spatial, temporal, and material points are kinds of terms which differ only immediately. Material points are not even classes as one, but real individuals. Material points seem really distinct in sense (1) for Russell. Armies and regiments are classes as many. Soldiers are classes as one of material points. Classes are intensional "objects denoted by concepts" (POM 66). Thus it seems classes as many and classes as one are conceptual beings, while material points are real beings. Surely classes as one and classes as many are distinct only in reason. Of course, classes as one, such as tables and chairs, have empirical existence. Like material points, they exist only at certain times, have causal capabilities, and are individuals. Nonetheless, they are analyzed as composed of material points. This suggests both criterion (3) and criterion (4): explanatory and methodological modified realism. Surely material points can exist even if tables and chairs do not, and surely the reverse is not the case. Also, surely minds are really distinct in sense (1) for the 1903 Russell, while the "psychic existents" in a mind are dependent on that mind's existence. As Frege would say, there are no "homeless ideas." Thus criterion (1g) would seem fulfilled for bodies and minds several times over, despite Russell's official rejection of it.

Consider also Russell's distinction in *Principles* between actual existence, logical existence, and mere nonexistent being, in order of progressively muted substance substitutes. Empirical existents are much like Frege's concrete objects, Logical existents are much like Frege's abstract objects. Logical existents seem less real than empirical existents, but more real than nonexistent beings. Spatiotemporal reals (points and instants) seem to be in between empirical existents and logical existents, since empirical evidence determines the geometry of the actual world. Being is the general status of which the foregoing are kinds. Objects roughly include both terms and classes as many (POM 55n). Terms are simply beings. Classes as many have mathematical existence, or better, logical existence. Properties and relations are probably hybrid classifications, since some are empirically given and others are logico-mathematical. Possibly there are similar gradations of ontological status among nonexistent chairs, nonexistent material points, nonexistent colors, and so on, though possibly they are all just nonexistent entities. Russell does not address that question.

We saw that Frege distinguishes the metaphysical sense of unity from the numerical sense, making the former prior to the latter. Russell seems to make the same distinction. In *Principles*, every term, *qua* logical subject, is one (PM 43–44). This echoes Russell's more fully stated view in his 1898 "An Analysis of Mathematical Reasoning" that

> every logical subject is *one*. That this is a significant judgment, not a tautology, and that *one* does not mean the same as *logical subject*, appears, if not otherwise evident, by the fact that *one* is opposed to many, while *subject* is opposed to predicate....Moreover, the converse is true, that only a logical subject can be *one*; this follows at once from the fact that *one* is a predicate. (Russell 1898: 167–68)

In *Principles*, "[n]umerical identity and diversity [of terms] are the source of unity and plurality" (PM 44). In "An Analysis" Russell says, "The conceptions of *one* and *all*...are prerequisites for the assertion of number....the subject must be one, and must be non-numerical[ly one]" (Russell 1898: 196–97). Numerical relativity enters only with the relativity of the unit we select as a precondition of assigning a number (Russell 1898: 197, 210–11). Arithmetical units, being one in number, and the metaphysical unity of a logical subject are three different kinds of unity for the 1898 Russell. So far as I can see, Russell later always distinguishes metaphysical unity from merely applying the number one, despite the sloppy language just quoted from *Principles* on "[n]*umerical* identity and diversity [of terms]" (PM 44, italics mine). Many writers casually use "numerically one" to refer to what is more accurately called metaphysical unity.

Russell rejects substances and essences in the traditional sense. But he admits six sorts of beings or substances, or substance substitutes: (1) All entities, including both being and existence, have timeless being in 1903. (2) Universals have being in 1912. (3) Being is general timelessness in 1914. (4) Being is logical atoms in 1918. (5) Being is object words in 1940. (6) Being is qualities (particulars, not universals) in 1940–59. I described these six sorts of being in my *Erkenntnis* paper (Dejnožka 1990). In addition, Russell admits two substitutes for material substances: (7) Ordinary physical things are causal lines in 1927–59 (AMA 285; HK 453–60, 489–90; MPD 146–47). "Thus the persistence of substance is replaced by the persistence of causal laws" (AMA 285). (8) Space-time structures are what are probably real in 1927–59 (AMA 249–57; HK 250–66, 460–75, 491–92; MPD 147–48). Russell speaks of "substantial structures" which replace "pieces of matter" and also of structures of events (HK 461). Of course, (7) and (8) overlap; a causal line is an instantiated structure.

In his 1914-18 philosophy of logical fictions, in which particulars (sense-data) or perhaps simples are alone real, Russell may seem a *radical* realist. Bodies, numbers, and minds (except one's own mind) are logical fictions with fictitious identities. And "there is no such thing as a fiction" (PLA 189). In 1919 this virtually becomes Hume's neutral monist distinction between impressions and fictions. Like Hume's impressions, Russell's particulars are real beings. Each can logically happen to be the whole universe. But instead of admitting distinctions of reason within lone sense-data, as Hume does within impressions, Russell admits "parts" which, if you attend to them, become "new" data (new real beings) in their own right (PLA 203; see RUP 114 and IMT 334). Much as with Frege, this is a shifting of phenomenological real identities over time *sans* any shifting of concepts. Russell assigns particulars the "logical position" of substances (PLA 204). Particulars are mind-independent (1a), essentially complete (1b), ultimate logical subjects of predication (1c), logically independent (1d), given in acquaintance (1e), the unchanging building blocks in the logical construction of changes (1f), and have phenomenologically real identities as opposed to the conceptual identities of logical fictions (1g). Criterion (1) seems fulfilled—but for *radical* realism, since logical fictions are said to exist only in a purely nominal sense.

Nonetheless, I classify the 1914-18 Russell as a modified realist. For there is that exception to logical fictions, one's own mind, which ought to be in some sense more substantival than sense-data, despite everything Russell says about sense-data as being as real as anything can be. Only the 1921 Russell's neutral monism, in which even one's own mind is a construction, seems a truly radical realism. It is also worth noting that as series of classes of sensibilia, two constructed bodies are really distinct in sense (2) just in case they have no sensibilium in common.

The 1914–21 Russell's constructionism (this includes neutral monism), in positing unsensed sensibilia to account for perception and physical lawfulness, is a scientific explanatory realism. It is also a phenomenological realism in that sense-data are physically real events. And third, it is a methodological realism. Analyses end with sensed entities, if not with entities known to be simple.

Russell's 1927–59 representational realism meets criterion (3) of explanatory modified realism. It is a kind of scientific realism. In *The Analysis of Matter*, Russell defends realism against radical reductionism. He says, "There are many possible ways of turning some things hitherto regarded as 'real' into mere laws concerning the other things. Obviously there must be a limit to this process, or else all the things in the world will merely be each other's washing" (AMA 325). Russell says, "We must find some reality for the electron, or else the physical world will run through our fingers like a jelly-fish" (AMA 319). Thus physical structures such as electrons are not mere logical fictions. Indeed, two electrons are really distinct in sense (2) if they have no constituent event in common (AMA 288). Yet Russell reserves metaphysical status for the events which compose electrons, and ultimately for whatever entities may comprise the final interpretation of physics (AMA 2, 9). This suggests a modified realism in which instantiated physical structures are real facts, but are less real than any ultimate, i.e. simple, constituents they may have.

3. Wittgenstein's Modified Realism

Ludwig Wittgenstein, in his *Tractatus Logico-Philosophicus*, may seem to be a radical relativist for five reasons. First, "There are no privileged numbers" (T 5.453). Second, "To perceive a complex means to perceive that its constituents are related in such and such a way," and there are different possible ways to do this (T 5.5423). Third, objects are simple substances (T 2.02, T 2.021), but there seems to be no number of them at all (T 4.1272). Fourth, numbers are the exponents of operations on propositions (T 6.021). Numbers vary as we transit by operations from one proposition to another (T 6.01). Fifth, an elementary state of affairs may be both one elementary state of affairs and, let us suppose, two objects.

The first and third reasons collapse because Wittgenstein holds only that objects cannot be *said* to exist, to have a certain number, or to be identical or different (T 4.1272, T 4.243, T 6.2322). Wittgenstein himself openly speaks of the identity and difference of objects (T 2.0233, T 5.53), and even of the "totality of objects" T 5.5561). He later says only that such statements must be "transcended" (T 6.54). It seems that objects exist, have identities, and have a definite number, but that we must be silent about this in language. Recall that even for Frege and Russell, it is ill-formed to predicate existence or number of objects. Elementary states of affairs seem to have a definite number as well. For there is a "totality of elementary propositions" (T 4.52, T 5.5262, T 5.5561).

As to the second reason, Julius R. Weinberg observes that in the *Tractatus*, language does not determine states of affairs, but quite the reverse. States of affairs completely and univocally fix the truth and meaning of every statement (Weinberg 1936: 56–57). That is the whole point of the picture theory of language in the *Tractatus*. As for language and states of affairs, so for perception and facts. Indeed, T 5.5423's perceptual relativity is assessed as concerning "two different facts." That is, there is not one complex fact (truth-functional combination of elementary states of affairs) being viewed in two ways. There are two different complex facts. Indeed, the picture theory would lead to radical realism, were it not for distinctions of reason among objects within an elementary state of affairs, and among elementary states of affairs and the complex facts they combinatively constitute.

The fourth and fifth reasons seem to be Tractarian versions of ordinary conceptual relativity at most.

I shall now argue that Wittgenstein meets criterion (1g) of metaphysical modified realism. Elementary states of affairs are really distinct, while objects in an elementary state of affairs are distinct in reason. "[Elementary s]tates of affairs are independent of one another," but objects "fit into one another like the links of a chain" (T 2.061, T 2.03). Facts, all of which are either existent elementary states of affairs or combinations of them, are what is real (T 1–T 2, T 2.06–T 2.063). This best fits a modified realism in which elementary states of affairs have real identity, combinations of elementary states of affairs have conceptual identities, and the objects in an elementary state of affairs also have conceptual identities. Facts would be the most real states of affairs.

But Wittgenstein's terminology is unfortunate. He calls objects both the substance and the form of the world (T 2.021–T 2.0271). This meets criterion (2), and suggests a second interpretation on which objects have the real identities.

Only the first interpretation is acceptable. How can objects have real identities when "[i]n a state of affairs objects fit into one another like the links of a chain" (T 2.03)? Wittgenstein says that "the form of independence of [objects] is a form of connexion with states of affairs, a form of dependence" (T 2.0122). In contrast, elementary states of affairs meet criterion (1d), which outweighs the parasitic criterion (2). Thus I agree with Urmson that while "it would seem that Wittgenstein's objects are very like the Aristotelian first substance as it appears in the *Categories*[,]...Wittgenstein took the fact as the basic entity" (Urmson 1966: 57–59). But Urmson should have said "elementary state of affairs," since Wittgenstein seems to restrict "fact" to existent states of affairs, while elementary states of affairs may be existent or nonexistent (R. Bradley 1992: xx).

Bradley argues that there is a great actualist-nonactualist difference between Russell and the early Wittgenstein in that Wittgenstein admits alien objects in the *Tractatus* (R. Bradley 1992: 38–40). (Alien objects are what David Lewis calls objects that are only in possible worlds other than the actual world.) I think that Bradley has got things backwards.

As to Russell, alien objects can be *known by description*. Even simple entities can be described in all sorts of ways. Here "simple" may mean only 'really undivided' (compare R. Bradley 1992: 69). And I have abundantly shown the ways in which Russell can extend talk of the ways the actual world might have been, so as to allow talk of alien objects without according alien objects any ontological status (Dejnožka 1990: 391–93).

As to Wittgenstein, there can be no alien objects because every object is in every possible world. "If all objects are given, then at the same time all *possible* states of affairs are also given" (T 2.0124). "Objects contain the possibility of all situations" (T 2.014). "It is obvious that an imagined world, however different it may be from the real one, must have *something*—a form—in common with it. Objects are just what constitute this unalterable form" (T 2.022, T 2.023).

Wittgenstein's transcendental Parmenideanism is stronger than Russell's. In Kripkean terms, a Russellian logically proper name is a rigid designator in the sense that it has the same denotation in every possible world in which the denoted particular occurs. Its meaning is its denotation, and to change its meaning is to change it as a name. Since the existence of a particular is logically contingent, no Russellian particular can occur in every possible world. Each of Russell's particulars "might happen to be the whole universe" (PLA 202). But Wittgenstein's object-names name the same object in every possible world. That is because not only is the meaning of an object-name its denotation as with Russell (Pitcher 1964: 49; T 3.203; I assume that to be is not to be nothing), but objects subsist, i.e., have necessary existence (T 2.024); they constitute the "substance" (T 2.021) and "form" (T 2.023) of the world (see Black 1970: 9, 58–61).

Both Russell and the early Wittgenstein follow Leibniz and ultimately Parmenides in holding that *ens et unum convertuntur*. Both hold that composite things are not real beings (chapter 5, section 2; Black 1970: 58–61). But they have rather different interpretations of *ens et unum convertuntur*. Namely, the early Wittgenstein requires that an entity be a logically necessary being, while Russell does not. Wittgenstein's view seems closer to Parmenides than Russell's does.

For Wittgenstein, the world is defined by what is *not* the case in it as much as by what is (T 1.11, T 1.12, T 2.0121, T 2.04, T 2.05, T 2.06, T 2.063.) "The existence and non-existence of states of affairs is reality" (T 2.06). "The sum-total of reality is the world" (T 2.063). Granted, the totality of existing states of affairs determines the totality of nonexisting states of affairs (T 2.05). But the converse is true as well.

All these considerations outweigh Bradley's arguments, which I shall not address in this book.

This presents a paradox for the first interpretation. How can elementary states of affairs be what is real if many of them are nonexistent, while in contrast, Tractarian objects are always actual? The solution is to realize that at least in the paradoxical *Tractatus*, the real–less real distinction is not the simple–complex distinction, and is not even the actual–nonactual distinction. Elementary states of affairs are what constitute reality because a mere listing of objects does not tell us what the world is like. To describe reality is to describe how objects fit together into existent states of affairs (T 1.2, 2.04, 2.063).

Objects contribute content to the reality of states of affairs. The Hintikkas show this well in *Investigating Wittgenstein*. Evidence external to the *Tractatus* suggests that Tractarian objects are Moorean or Russellian objects of acquaintance (IW 51–52), and perhaps also their properties and relations. (In fact, I note, their properties and relations must be included, since if all objects were sensible particulars, they would not hang together like links of a chain. Even whole-part series of particulars would provide only one-way linking.) Thus in the *Tractatus*, language is primarily phenomenological (IW 58–61). The Hintikkas see this as reinforcing the transcendental Parmenideanism of names' always being names of something. Namely, objects of acquaintance must be actual, and cannot be nothing (IW 62), much as with Russell (IW 71–86). "Russellian objects of acquaintance are introduced by displaying them and pointing to them, that is, by 'showing' them. This is a fine explanation of Wittgenstein's mystical-sounding doctrine of *showing* in contradistinction to *saying*" (IW 64). The logico-phenomenological fundamentality of objects is why logic and phenomenology "are one" for the early Wittgenstein (IW 61). But while objects are sense-data, they have no "particular subjective (mind-dependent) status" (IW 66–67). This too follows Russell and Moore, and shows in what sense the *Tractatus* is a realist work.[8] In fact the *Tractatus* is largely Russellian constructionism. The Hintikkas say that structure itself is a construction of the forms of objects (IW 66).[9] This may seem to support the interpretation that objects have the real identities. But thanks to the fact that objects stick together "like the links of a chain" (T 2.03), it does not.

The Hintikkas miss three basic similarities between Russell's particulars and Wittgenstein's objects. First, they see that Tractarian objects are substances (IW 68–70), but not that Russell's particulars are substance substitutes. Second, they see that Tractarian objects are the basis of a combinatorial modal logic of possible worlds, but not that Russell's particulars are such a basis (see IW 72, 110–11, 117–18 and my 1990). Third, they miss the main reason why these things are so. Again, both Russell and the early Wittgenstein follow Leibniz and ultimately Parmenides in holding that *ens et unum convertuntur*. Both hold that composite things are not real beings (chapter 5, section 2; Black 1970: 58–61). These three similarities deepen the Hintikkas' already strong case.

The Hintikkas also miss three basic dissimilarities. First, Tractarian objects hang together like links of a chain (T 2.03). But each of Russell's particulars "might happen to be the whole universe" (PLA 202). Second, Wittgenstein's transcendental Parmenideanism is stronger than Russell's. In Kripkean terms, a Russellian logically proper name is a rigid designator in the sense that it has the same denotation in every possible world in which the denoted particular occurs. Its meaning is its denotation, and to change its meaning is to change it as a name. Since the existence of a particular is logically contingent, no Russellian particular occurs in every possible world. But Wittgenstein's object-names name the same object in every possible world. That is because not only is the meaning of an object-name its denotation as with Russell (Pitcher 1964: 49; T 3.203; I assume that to be is not to be nothing), but objects subsist (have necessary existence); they constitute the "substance" (T 2.021) and "form" (T 2.023) of the world (see Black 1970: 9, 58–61). Third, the main reason for these two differences is different interpretations of *ens et unum convertuntur.* Again, the early Wittgenstein requires that an entity be a logically necessary being, while Russell does not.

The Hintikkas and I could be wrong. Bradley recounts the history of *Tractatus* interpretations as follows. At first, Tractarian objects were widely believed to be "phenomenal" because people tended to associate the *Tractatus* historically with Russell and the logical positivists. Then in 1959, G. E. M. Anscombe observed that the main content of the book is metaphysical, not epistemological, and that there is very little, if any, internal evidence as to what objects are. Then in 1986, the Hintikkas revived the first view by citing external evidence from Wittgenstein's other writings. Last, in 1992 Bradley himself tried to show that the external evidence indicates that objects are never phenomenal, and arguably include Hertzian material points (R. Bradley 1992: 74–79). (I note that not all of them can be material points, or they will not hang together like links on a chain.) Material points, of course, would be excellent really distinct real things. I shall content myself with observing that any of these interpretations is compatible with my view that it is elementary states of affairs which are the really distinct real "things" in a modified realist *Tractatus.*

Note also that "all the propositions of our everyday language, just as they stand, are in perfect logical order" (T 5.5563). This includes ordinary language identity statements, existence assertions, and even assertions of real distinctions and distinctions in reason, e.g., "Either the Earth or the Moon could conceivably vanish and the other continue to exist." That such assertions greatly disguise their real logical forms, e.g. that in "Hesperus is the same planet as Phosphorus," the subject-terms are not even names of objects (planets are not ontological simples), does not detract from this point (T 4.002, T 4.0031). Wittgenstein would simply be providing us with his eliminative analyses of real distinctions and informative identities among ordinary things. Of course, analogues to real distinctions and distinctions in reason among objects and states of affairs remain more fundamental in any case.

Eight facts suggest that Wittgenstein is a radical relativist in *Philosophical Investigations.*

First, Wittgenstein attacks the logical atomism of Frege, Russell, and his own *Tractatus* even more than he attacks traditional substances. Thus he rejects even the substance substitutes of Frege, Russell, and his own *Tractatus*.

Second, the example of the duck-rabbit shows the multiplicity of aspects of an object of perception. One diagram may be interpreted as one box or three boards (PI 193). Köhler's one figure may be seen as two interpenetrating hexagons (PI 203-204). Another figure may be seen either as a single octagon with concave and convex aspects or as a two dimensional cross on an octagonal background (PI 207). The attendant remarks on aspects and organization (PI 196, 208) are suggestive of radical relativity.

Third, Saul Kripke, in *Wittgenstein on Rules and Private Language*, brings out a radical skepticism based on the fact that linguistic rules can always be reinterpreted, and finds it to be very close to what Quine calls his ontological relativity (Kripke 1982: 55–58).

Fourth, Wittgenstein gives four cases of conceptual relativity much like the ones we have seen: a chair, a tree, a chessboard (PI #47), and a broom (PI #60). Wittgenstein finds no absolutely simple elements in any of these. And 'simplicity', 'compositeness', and 'identity' themselves shift in like manner (PI #47, #215).

Fifth, there are various "grammatical" kinds of being. These latter are determined by language. Wittgenstein almost calls them grammatical fictions, and does speak of grammatical illusions (PI #97, #110, #307). Our bewitchment by metaphysics is due to our considering grammatical categories as actual "queer" kinds of being, owing to a misleading picture of all words as referring. The bewitchment of ontology is to consider being itself a queer kind of being, owing to the same misleading picture (PI #116). This picture is that all words are names. The picture seems to be shared by realists, idealists, solipsists, phenomenologists, and nominalists alike (PI #383, #402, #436). This suggests a deep irrealism indeed.

Sixth, Wittgenstein criticizes the notion of essence as part of his view that words do not have single essential meanings. The notion is of something that is "metaphysical" or hidden. It leads to preconceptions or illusions (PI #65, #89, #97, #113, #116, #173, #176, #371–#373, #547). Wittgenstein also seems to know the weakness of the analytic-synthetic distinction in science (PI #79). This militates against essences in a Duhemian-Quinean way.

Seventh, Wittgenstein, in *Remarks on the Foundations of Mathematics*, holds that numbers are properties of concepts (RFM 186/V #35).

Eighth, the Hintikkas argue that the later Wittgenstein makes a strong connection between verificationism and linguistic relativity. The link is that only those people who share the same ways of verifying sentences can belong to the same linguistic community. The very notion of an object cannot be understood independently of our use of language (see chapter 2, section 3 on 'language as a universal medium'). Wittgenstein seems to draw an analogy to Einstein's neo-verificationist theory of relativity (IW 21-22).

The account just given may seem convincing. But fifteen facts suggest that the later Wittgenstein is a modified realist.

First, Wittgenstein distinguishes phenomena from concepts (PI #383, 199).[10] He says "the will is not a phenomenon" because a concept is involved (PI #176). I say I experience things which are not in fact phenomena only because "when I reflect on what I experience in such a case I look at it through the medium of the concept" (PI #177). It seems phenomena are not grammatically queer kinds of being. Since Wittgenstein studied Frege carefully, it seems only natural that he would use Frege's word "phenomenon" (both use both *Phänomenon* and *Erscheinung*) for a public item which is not the result of an application of some concept (both use *Begriff*) (FA 32-33; PI #176-#177, #383, 199).

Second, Wittgenstein distinguishes perception from 'seeing as' (PI 197). He says:

If you put the 'organization' of a visual impression on a level with colours and shapes, you are proceeding from the idea of the visual impression as an inner object. Of course this makes the object into a chimera; a queerly shifting construction. (PI 196)

Evidently a perceived color or shape is not a chimerical construction. Facts (1) and (2) both suggest phenomenological modified realism.

Third, Wittgenstein distinguishes interpretations of rules from "a way of grasping a rule which is *not an interpretation*" (PI #201).

Fourth, he distinguishes looking and seeing how words are used from being bewitched by a picture of what words mean (PI #66, #115, #122).

Fifth, he opposes natural science to grammar (PI #85, #392, #441, 230).

All five distinctions suggest criterion (1g) of metaphysical modified realism. Phenomena, perceived colors, the noninterpretational way of grasping some-thing, looking and seeing, and natural science suggest real identity. Looking at something through the medium of a concept, seeing as, picture bewitchment, interpretation, and grammar suggest conceptual identity or linguistic identity.

Sixth, Wittgenstein says, "The fundamental fact is that we lay down rules, a technique, for a game, and when we follow the rules, things do not turn out as we assumed" (PI #125). Thus he admits a "fundamental fact." He admits "things" which do not correspond to our conceptions. He says, "The language games are...set up as *objects of comparison*....We can avoid ineptness...only by presenting the model *as what it is* [my italics], an object of comparison" (PI #131). "Philosophy may in no way interfere with the *actual use* [my italics] of language....It leaves everything *as it is* [my italics]" (PI #124). "*What has to be accepted, the given* [my italics] is...*forms of life*" (PI 226; see #241). He says that "we ought to look at what happens as a proto-phenomenon. That is, where we ought to have said: *this language-game is played*" (PI #654). Thus it is language-games that are fundamental and real. He says:

> Look on the language-game as the *primary* thing. And look on the feelings, etc., as you look on a way of regarding the language-game, as interpretation. (PI #656)

Language-games are substantival in their primacy as 'fundamental facts'. Ways of regarding them, interpretations of them, seem less than fully real. This is not to mention coming to the "bedrock" on rules and interpretations: This is simply what we do. Here rules, identity, and "bedrock" are "interwoven" (PI #217, #219, #222–#227, #230). Criterion (2) of substance analogue modified realism is met by "bedrock," "*primary* thing," "fundamental fact," "as what it is," "as it is," and "What has to be accepted, the given." Perhaps "Look on" means only "as if," as if this too were a bewitching picture, specifically, a ladder we cast away after we climb it to transcend all the other bewitching pictures. But *Investigations* does not condemn itself as bewitching; it promotes itself as therapeutic. The ladder metaphor belongs to the bewitching *Tractatus* picture of language which *Investigations* rejects. The *Investigations* therapy seems to be based on sayable, thinkable facts about language use.

Seventh, Wittgenstein actually has two notions of essence. As we saw, the first sort is rejected as 'metaphysically hidden'. But the second sort applies to things as they are, to what Wittgenstein takes to be really the case (PI #92, #140, #141, #272, #396). Essence in this second sense is open to view, but might not be noticed (#89, #92). This meets criterion (1b), and amplifies fact (7).

Eighth, primary language-games seem to be hypothetical metaphysical posits to solve the problem of logically multiple interpretation. That is explanatory realism. Thus the very important criterion (3) is met. The positing of language-games is explanatory modified realism. In fact, the later Wittgenstein is an explanatory modified realist in two ways. First, the games themselves are posited holist units or patterns of physical behavior, many of which are independent from each other. Second, each game is a method of verification which concerns mind-independent, really distinct physical things. This is modified realism with a twist. Primary language-games, as holistic units of physical behavior, are logically prior to physical things, and not mere emergent relations of groups of physical things. This reverses the ordinary way of looking at physical structure. But in another sense, physical things, *qua* verifiers (my gloss) of various statements in various language-games in various situations, must be logically independent of, i.e., really distinct from, the language of our games in order to provide genuine verification at all. For instance, suppose a mountain community which has only rocks to talk about, and a forest nation which has only trees to talk about. The two groups and their respective language-games would seem just as really distinct from each other in sense (2) as are the rocks and trees themselves. But in sense (1) of real identity, the groups and their language-games would be holistically more real, yet analytically less real, than the persons, trees and rocks that enter into them. As to our uses of the word "real," these ontological games are played!

Ninth, Nicholas Gier, in his *Wittgenstein and Phenomenology* (1981), makes a good case for whole languages or forms of life as more basic than specific language-games in *Investigations*. Such a holist realism would introduce a deeper layer of methodological modified realism and probably also explanatory modified realism. This amplifies fact (8).

Tenth, I can find no link between Wittgenstein's verificationism and any sort of linguistic relativity, *pace* the Hintikkas. Verificationism and linguistic relativity do not imply each other either formally or intuitively. Methods of verification can be and often are nonlinguistic. Examples include watching an expression, dipping a litmus paper, flipping a switch, or striking a match. In fact, methods of verification imply realism. They imply that there is something independent of any assertion which can totally verify (strong form) or at least be evidence for (weak form) its truth or falsehood. Methods of verification do not imply radical relativity. They do not imply linguistic or conceptual identity as opposed to real identity, except in the trivial sense that if you verify that a card belongs to a certain card deck, you verify that it is distinct in reason from that deck. And even a dog can verify things, such as where a bone is buried.

In fact (8) for the other side, Einstein is misunderstood. Einstein uses his verificationist theory of meaning to arrive at a theory of motion which is objective and wholly independent of all conceptual frameworks of motion, and which assumes the identities of objectively given observers and events. Thus Wittgenstein's analogy really connects verificationism with language-independent realism, as I assume he is well aware (see chapter 5, section 3 on Einstein).

Wittgenstein held two kinds of verificationism, both realist. First, early Tractarian verificationism is based on phenomenological realism. Wittgenstein describes it as follows. In the 1929 ms. 107, a phenomenon "is the reality" and "is itself what verifies the sentence" (IW 141). On page 1 of ms. 107 he says, "The visual space has its independent reality as it is," and "can be described immediately" in a phenomenological language (IW 163). Second, *Investigations*' public verificationism is the basis of Wittgenstein's physical realism.

Eleventh, Wittgenstein's private language argument commits him to modified realism. The argument stops *radically* skeptical regresses of concepts,

rules, or interpretations. And it legitimizes *limited* conceptual relativity by giving
us public things to slice and public concepts or terms to slice them with. The
private language argument is the true power behind criterion (1g)'s fulfillment
in Frege, Russell, Wittgenstein, and Quine alike. Hilary Putnam finds the
private language argument in *Investigations* realist even on Kripke's interpretation: "The relativist cannot, in the end, make any sense of the distinction
between *being right* and *thinking* he is right; and that means that there is, in the
end, no difference between *asserting* or *thinking*, on the one hand, and *making
noises* (or *producing mental images*) on the other....[Thus one would be] not a
thinker at all but a *mere* animal....[And this is] mental suicide" (quoted in
Passmore 1985: 107). Putnam's point is excellent. His point is about #202,
Kripke's key to understanding the private language argument in *Investigations*.

It seems to me that Wittgenstein's private language argument is a dance of
two veils. The first veil is the verificationist PI #272 discussed by the first
generation of *Investigations* scholars, notably Alfred Jules Ayer. The second,
inner veil is the de-epistemicized, purely semantic 'justificationist' interpretation
of Kripke, modified by the Hintikkas. Stripped of both veils, Frege's realist
private language argument seems revealed as the dancer.

The core Fregean argument and the first veil occur together in this famous
section:

> The essential thing about private experiences is really not that each
> person possesses his own exemplar, but that nobody knows (*weiss*)
> whether other people also have *this* or something else. The assumption
> would thus be possible—though unverifiable (*nicht verifizierbar*)— that
> one section of mankind had one sensation of red and another section
> another (PI #272).

The basic problem is metaphysical: mental ideas cannot be literally compared
across persons (or across time). Take away the epistemic aspect of #272, and
the argument is Frege's. The very example of color inversion using red is an
homage to Frege (FA 36; Frege 1956). The Fregean argument is realist. So are
both veils, on facts (6)–(10). Thus everything works together for realism on all
three levels of Wittgenstein's private language argument. Note that Frege is
never attacked in *Investigations*, and that Russell never attacks *Investigations*,
concerning private language arguments. For all three analysts use such
arguments to establish their realisms.

The virtue of the first-veil scholars is to be faithful to the consequent
epistemico-verificationist problem Wittgenstein raises in #272. Wittgenstein
admits a verification principle in #353: "Asking whether and how a proposition
can be verified (*Verifikation*) is only a particular way of asking 'How d'you
mean'?" The first-veil epistemic problem remains grave; Kripke and the
Hintikkas are wrong to discount it. For the Cartesian evil genius may well

deceive us on semantics, on verificationism, and on private language arguments, in short, on the very theories Kripke and the Hintikkas advance against Cartesian doubt. Thus Kripke and the Hintikkas beg the question. This fallacy bedeviled O. K. Bouwsma's "Descartes' Evil Genius" over forty years ago; Kripke and the Hintikkas repeat Bouwsma's error (Bouwsma 1949: 141–51).

The gossamer second veil—Kripke and the Hintikkas see it as the argument itself—comes from Wittgenstein's Semantic PLA of October 1929 (IW 165). The 1929 PLA, which I shall call A, is:

1. Verification requires comparing a proposition with a reality which is independent of that proposition.
2. "Language itself [spoken or written] is a part of the physical world" (IW 165).
3. What is compared (juxtaposed) to part of the physical world must itself be part of that same world.
4. The meaning of a statement is its verification (IW 77).
5. Therefore, language must be primarily physicalistic, that is, primarily physicalistic in meaning, that is, primarily about physical things.

The Hintikkas say, "If Wittgenstein has a rock-bottom 'private language argument',...it is his discussion of rule-following in PI, secs. 143-242" (IW 243). They construe Wittgenstein's 1944 Semantic PLA, which I shall call B, as:

1. Language-games must be logically prior to rules or ostensions, due to a problem of logically multiple interpretations of rules or ostensions.
2. And language-games are either public or parasitic on public language-games.
3. Therefore rules are public or parasitic on public language-games.
4. "[A]nd hence...'obeying a rule' is a practice. And to think one is obeying a rule is not to obey a rule. Hence it is not possible to obey a rule 'privately'..." (PI #202; IW 243).

The Hintikkas recount: Wittgenstein's conversion from phenomenological realism to a nondescript physicalism (mere nonmentalism) due to public verificationism; his consequent need to change verification from strong to weak, and also his rejection of ostendings and rules as criteria of meaning due to a problem of multiple interpretation; and his final acceptance of language-games as logically prior to rules and as providing the contexts which fix the meanings of ostendings and rules appropriately. My comment is this: The conversion to physicalism is not only historically prior to the acceptance of language-games, but logically prior. Language-games may be logically prior to rules and ostensions, but they are not logically prior to the physicalism. But the Hintikkas would disagree with me, as I shall now explain.

The Hintikkas assert that Wittgenstein's conversion to physicalism in 1929 rests on "weak" and "inadequate" grounds: 'language as a universal medium', and interpersonal, independent verification or comparability. They say that the first ground has no logical connection with publicity or privacy. And they say that the second ground begs the question of reference to private experiences. For a private language speaker can be convicted of speaking a language which cannot be related to ours, "but not yet of bad philosophy of language" (IW 262). The Hintikkas then claim that "Wittgenstein was...[only] in 1944 able to justify the step he took in October 1929" (IW 264). Namely, he went beyond the issue of interpersonal verification or comparison to a totally different issue, namely, the issue of the nature of reference or name-object relations *as such*, regardless of whether they occur in public or private languages. And he found that the problem of logically multiple interpretation required language-games to be logically prior to ostensions or rules, and to be constitutive of reference relations. Only then did he find that language-games must have an "inevitably public character" (IW 264). That is why the Hintikkas would disagree with me.

But the interpersonal comparability requirement is logically prior to the need for language-games. For what are language-games but a device to handle the problem of logically multiple interpretations of ostensions and rules? And how can that problem arise unless private ostension, or direct phenomenological verification, has already been ruled out? There simply is no issue of the nature of reference or name-object relations as such, which gives rise to a problem of logically multiple interpretations of what I am referring to, unless incorrigible private ostension and reference have been already ruled out. For private singling out is of what seems to me to be the case, and I cannot be mistaken about that. Whether the 1929 Wittgenstein's conversion to physicalism rested on "inadequate" grounds or not (this is criticism, not scholarship), Wittgenstein had to be committed to the conclusion of argument A before there could be any point to argument B.

Argument (A) already provides a realism in which things are really distinct from their names—both are physical—as well as from each other. This precludes radical relativity.

Twelfth, as the Hintikkas explain beautifully, a primary language-game is not a linguistic barrier between us and the world, but a vehicle by which we can grasp reality. "Language-games do not *replace* naming relations according to later Wittgenstein: they *constitute* them" (IW 193–94). Thus argument (B) establishes reference to physical things. It is easy to find among physical things many which are really distinct. Multiple interpretations emerge as mere common sense linguistic relativity.

Thirteenth, any attempt to absorb the words "really distinct" within some contextualistic language-games seems self-defeating. What would the games be?

One would be: Take two sticks and burn one. Try to make the sticks depend on each other's existence by altering your language or your conceptual framework. Try speaking Hopi. Adopt a theory of internal relations. Or reject quantum mechanics. If, despite your best efforts, the burning stick is destroyed but the other continues to exist, then assuming the same result had you burned the other stick instead, they may be said to have been really distinct from each other. The game is limited by the facts, not the facts by the game. Could you honestly say the other stick survived because you simply did not try hard enough, or just did not come across the right framework in time?

Fourteenth, while Wittgenstein rejects identity understood as uninformative self-identity, he admits criteria for factually informative identifications in various situations. And factually informative identifications are objective facts.

Fifteenth, only modified realism is compatible with all twenty-three facts presented here for either side. In this way, Wittgenstein meets criterion (7) of linguistic modified realism.

I omit Michael J. Loux's suggestion that really distinct items in *Investigations* include the recurrent features which variously belong to language-games, e.g., to what we ordinarily call "games" (Loux 1970: 12–13). Loux is rejecting Renford Bambrough's suggestion that Wittgenstein would treat "feature" the same way he treats "game" (Loux 1970: 12 n.14; Bambrough 1970: 114). This issue of interpretation may be unresolvable; my compliments to Bambrough and Loux on raising it.

Both primary language-games (physical behavior patterns) and the ordinary things involved in them are: mind-independent (1a), each possessed of character or essence in the sense in which Wittgenstein accepts essences (1b), ultimate subjects of predication (1c), largely independent of each other (1d), largely recognizable (1e), ordinarily describable as undergoing changes (1f), and, thanks to Wittgenstein's explanatory realism, special bearers of real identity (1g). Thus criterion (1) of metaphysical modified realism is quite substantially met.

It might seem that in view of Wittgenstein's construal of queer kinds of being as grammatical illusions, Wittgenstein seems to be a radical realist. But radical realism is in a sense an extreme limit of modified realism. And, more importantly, his modified realism is constituted by his holist realism of language-games as physical patterns of behavior which contain physical objects.

4. Quine's Modified Realism

I shall give eight arguments that Quine is a modified realist.

First, if Quine were a radical relativist, no modified realist would be impressed by his examples in "Ontological Relativity." A modified realist would *expect* rabbits to be distinct in reason from undetached rabbit parts and from temporal stages of rabbits. Rabbits are really distinct not from rabbit parts, but from cows and cow parts. And on Quine's own definition of physical objects in terms of their spatiotemporal regions (see my chapter 5, section 8), the rabbit portion of the world is wholly distinct, hence really distinct, from the bovine portion of the world. Lo! a modified realist. Even translating "rabbit" as 'place 100 miles north of a rabbit' concerns only a distinction in reason. This is in sharp contrast to pointing to a gauge to refer to gasoline, which Quine calls "deferred ostension." Deferred ostension involves real distinction. The gauge is really distinct from the gasoline.

That is, if Quine were a radical relativist, then besides the two conditions he gives in "Ontological Relativity" for translational indeterminacy:

(i) Each of the translations is "accommodated by compensating adjustments in the translation of other words" (OR 29); and
(ii) Each agrees "equally well with all observable behavior on the part of speakers of the remote language and speakers of English" (OR 29),

he should also give this third condition:

(iii) They make the same translated words refer to really distinct things, e.g. a rabbit and a cow.

But he never gives condition (iii).

To be sure, Quine's thesis that no statement is immune from theoretical revision entails that we could so contort our overall theory that all three conditions could be met for translating, say, "gauge" as 'gasoline'. But such contortions remind me of Saki's famous automobile, the Envy of Sisyphus, which went uphill quite nicely if you pushed it. Quine is well aware of this.

Second, if Quine were a radical relativist, his argument would be self-defeating. On Quine's own verificationism, the only meaningless language in "Ontological Relativity" is his own systematic reference inversion hypothesis. For there is no empirical way to test for systematic reference inversion across language speakers, if condition (ii) is met! I submit that his full argument must be a *reductio ad absurdum* of any systematic reference inversion, and therefore of the theses of translational indeterminacy and referential inscrutability, which function in the end as ladders to be thrown away, or at least set aside.

These first two arguments also apply to Kripke's Wittgenstein.

The third argument is circumstantial: Quine is a realist both before and after "Ontological Relativity." By "before" I mean in *Word and Object*. By "after" I mean in "Things and Their Place in Theories" and *The Philosophy of W. V. Quine*.

It may seem that Quine is a radical relativist even in *Word and Object*. Quine says there of terms of divided reference, "The contrast lies in the terms and not the stuff they name" (WO 91; see 115). Identity and terms presuppose each other. The discussion of analytical hypotheses is much the same as that in "Ontological Relativity." However, Quine's first words in the Preface paint a different picture:

> Language is a social art. In acquiring it we have to depend entirely on intersubjectively available cues as to what to say and when. Hence there is no justification for collating linguistic meanings, unless in terms of men's dispositions to respond overtly to socially observable stimulations. An effect of recognizing this is that the enterprise of translation is found to be involved in a certain systematic indeterminacy....
>
>   The indeterminacy of translation invests even the question what objects to construe a term as true of. Studies of the semantics of reference consequentially turn out to make sense only when directed upon substantially our language, from within. But we do remain free to reflect, thus parochially, on the development and structure of our own referential apparatus; and this I do in ensuing chapters (WO ix).

This text gives the Hintikkian Wittgenstein's A-B Sorites in microcosm. For sentences (1)–(3) give argument A, the first private language argument, which eliminates private meanings and private references in favor of "socially observable [physical] stimulations." In this case, A is a Social PLA. Sentences (4)–(5) state the problem of logically multiple interpretation, which cannot arise until after argument A has established a physical realism. Sentences (6)–(7) give the solution in terms of our own language community. Argument B is simply that this is the best solution of the problem. I proceed to what Quine says some time after he wrote "Ontological Relativity." In "Things and Their Place in Theories," Quine says:

> The point is not that we ourselves are casting about in vain for a mooring. Staying aboard our own language and not rocking the boat, we are borne smoothly along on it and all is well; 'rabbit' denotes rabbits, and there is no sense in asking 'Rabbits in what sense of "rabbit"?' Reference goes inscrutable [only] if, rocking the boat, we contemplate a permutational mapping of our language on itself, or if we undertake translation. (TT 20)

In "Reply to Paul A. Roth," Quine says, "Within the home language, reference is best seen (I now hold) as unproblematic but trivial, on a par with Tarski's truth paradigm" (PQ 460). The "I now hold" does not refer to a new argument but to a new clarification. In "Reply to Robert Nozick," Quine says, "Ontological relativity...is just an adjunct of translation. To say what objects someone is talking about is to say how we propose to translate his terms: such is the relativity" (PQ 367; compare PT 51–52).

To sum up, the overall impression is that Quine's views have not changed so much as his tone. *Word and Object* is calm. "Ontological Relativity" is more stormy. The debate is seesaw. Sometimes reference briefly seems in doubt. But then Quine calms down again in his later works, as if reassured by a new sense of clarity. Indeed, both the relativity of translation and our genuine ability to refer in our home language now appear trivial to him. At no point does his argument B significantly change. (Quine's alleged improvement of "Ontological Relativity" in "Things and Their Place in Theories" is his setting up the problem using proxy functions instead of translations. But what is a proxy function? A translation manual!) It is too much to believe that Quine, in that single essay, jumps from realism to radical relativity, and then jumps back again to realism, with no major change of argument, and no public explanation, whatsoever. Could he really be that rarest of relapsers, a *double* renegade realist? I hardly think so.

Home reference and translational relativity taken conjointly look like linguistic modified realism. Home reference provides the realism; translation provides ordinary linguistic relativity. More accurately, argument A provides the basic physical realism, while argument B provides ordinary linguistic relativity, as well as home reference to real things, and thus a linguistic modified realism. Thus argument B builds on argument A, much as Aristotle's less than fully real categories build on the category of substances.

In fact, in 1994 Quine almost seems concerned that he made ontological relativity *too* trivial: "It is not…analogous to the relativity of temperature to a scale. It is a more desperate relativity. There is no clear senses in asking whether Edwin's 'rabbit' refers to a rabbit or to a proxy…" (Quine 1994: 498). But Quine blandly continues, "What does make sense is to ask whether a given manual gives 'lapin' as translation of 'rabbit'" (Quine 1994: 498). And just a few pages earlier he wrote, "The thesis, then, is simply that truth-values are unchanged by permutation of ontology" (Quine 1994: 495). Thus the relativity seems more desperate, but not much more. Quine explains:

> The indeterminacy is not surprising in the case of abstract objects, where it was noted by Frege, Russell, and Ramsey. It is nonsense to wonder whether your number seven is identical with mine as long as we use them alike. Shock comes only in the case of gross bodies and substances.…Bare structure, through identity and diversity and quite apart from fleshier traits, is ontology's contribution to our knowledge of the external world. (Quine 1994: 496)

Fourth, in "Ontological Relativity," the issue of ontological relativity is in the spotlight. The article is named accordingly. The thesis is put under the microscope and the argument drawn out. In keeping with that, the tone is dramatic concerning the individual steps of the argument. This may have misled some readers into thinking that Quine was denying there that reference is possible. Quine has been reassuring everyone of his robust realism ever since.

Fifth, the worst Quine says later about the argument in "Ontological Relativity" is not that it is wrong, but that it is "murky," that is, needs clarification (PQ 460). And I take it that the realist later Quine is an honest man who knows what he was trying to say in "Ontological Relativity."

Sixth, "Ontological Relativity" is based on a private language argument which not only establishes an external world, but an external world in which references occur (OR 26–28). And radical relativity would make nonsense of that argument. On a principle of charity in interpretation, Quine's relativity is not so self-destructive as to saw off the branch it is sitting on. The argument, which corresponds to argument A in the Hintikkian sorites, is absolutely essential to "Ontological Relativity." In "Reply to Morton White," Quine says, "Natural science owes its *objectivity* to its intersubjective check-points in observation sentences, but there is no such *rock bottom* for moral judgments" (PQ 664, italics mine). This objectivity is also the rock bottom of the essay "Ontological Relativity." Criterion (2) applies to "rock bottom."

On Kripke's view of Wittgenstein, and in Quine's so-called ontological relativity argument, the elimination of private ostension is a precondition of the problem of multiple interpretation (systematic reference inversion). The adoption of public identity conditions for reference is a precondition of the elimination of private ostension. And the admission of a mind-independent world including perceived real identities is a precondition of the adoption of public identity conditions. This leads to a realist view of both analysts. The realism may seem to be a conclusion concerning home languages or language-games. But the multiple interpretation argument presupposes realism. To be sure, Frege's systematic reference inversion argument in *Foundations* and Wittgenstein's in *Investigations* #272 attempt to show that meanings are not private ideas. Ironically, *that* sort of systematic reference inversion argument can be used to establish the public world of reference that leads to the Kripkean Wittgenstein's and Quine's sort of systematic reference inversion argument for contextualist language-games or home languages as the ontological *loci* of acts of reference.

Seventh, a modified realist interpretation of Quine removes the criticism that his robust realism of physical objects, and his "mathematical Platonism" of abstract objects, i.e. classes, are inconsistent with his relativism (Hugley 1990: 144, 149). As with Wittgenstein, only modified realism seems to account for all the facts about Quine. Quine himself seems to assert a form of modified realism to resolve the conflict (WO 21–25; PQ 315–16, 567–68, 622).

Eighth, I simply invite you to read "Ontological Relativity" carefully. To this end, I edit and highlight the text as follows:

> We *seem* to be maneuvering ourselves into the absurd position that
> there is no difference between...referring to rabbits and referring to
> rabbit parts or stages;...Surely this *is* absurd....Toward *resolving* this
> quandary, begin by picturing us at home in our language....Relative to
> it *can and do talk meaningfully* of rabbits and parts....In this principle
> of relativity lies the *resolution* of our quandary....[T]he situation *sounds*
> desperate, but in fact it *is* little different from questions of position and
> velocity (OR 47–49, italics mine).

Far from destroying reference, our home language is the vehicle by which
determinate reference is achieved, much as Frege's senses, Russell's descriptions, and Wittgenstein's primary language-games are intended to be. Quine says
that truth-seeking or prediction is "what language, science, and philosophy are
for, as eyes are for seeing" (PQ 665). Similarly, reference is what a referential
apparatus is for. Reference is not eliminated, only "cut down to size in
Ontological Relativity" (PQ 367). That is, "immanent" "truth, as Tarski
appreciated, is meaningfully predicated, *rightly or wrongly*, only within the
theory that is operative at the time" (PQ 367, italics mine). So that if we only
do not question our home language (or our currently operative theory), truth,
and reference, can be ours. Even if referring (denoting) terms are but "neutral
nodes" in a theoretical structure which can be variously interpreted (PT 33),
much room remains for references to really distinct rabbits and cities: "'rabbit'
denotes rabbits, whatever *they* are, and 'Boston' designates Boston" (PT 52). All
this seems quite consistent with Quine's holding that if two empirically
equivalent theories have different ontological commitments, then neither can be
meaningfully said to describe how the world really is (PT 101; see Dejnožka
1995a for a critique of Quine on empirical equivalence).

It may be worth comparing Quine with his mentor, Rudolf Carnap.
Probably Carnap is a genuine radical relativist. Weinberg noticed Carnap's
linguistic relativity in 1936. Carnap's most famous statement of radical relativity
is his "Empiricism, Semantics, and Ontology." There metaphysical realism is
rejected as an "external" question. Carnap admits only 'theory-internal'
existence assertions. Thus Carnap is committed to rejecting not only real
identity, but also conceptual identity and linguistic identity. For all ontological
questions about real beings, conceptual beings, and linguistic beings would be
equally external questions about the true *locus* of identity. Again, Carnap's
methodological phenomenalism and methodological physicalism are not forms
of methodological modified realism. Carnap denies that ontological phenomenalism and ontological physicalism are respectively involved (Carnap 1967;
Carnap 1963).

In contrast, Quine sharply rejects Carnap's distinction between external and
internal questions. Quine finds no point at which such a distinction can be drawn
(WO 271; Quine 1976: 178–93). For Quine, although all questions are internal

or immanent, truth and reference are possible in home languages. Thus we can speak of what there is after all (WO 276). Indeed, we can devise an exceptionally clear canonical notation to help us do so.

Carnap does all he can to play down the status even of "internal" questions of existence. For instance, that we quantify over numbers in number theory is a mere manner of speaking for him. For Carnap, science is simply a matter of the most convenient language. But Quine uses the existential quantifier to make genuine ontological commitments. Quine holds that the existential quantifier means 'exists', as opposed, say, to Russell's 'not always false' (WO 242). And Quine's admissions of an "unswerving belief in external things" (TT 21), "robust realism" (TT 21), and "real external objects" are too many to be ignored. Quine lives up to that emphasis on ontological commitment, that interpretation of the existential quantifier, and those admissions of realism with great seriousness in finding those items whose existence he believes he must admit if science is to be workable. (Quine's "robust realism" is meant to recall Russell's robust sense of reality, but Quine misapplies the expression. Quine's robust realism consists of his physical objects; for the 1918–19 robust Russell, physical objects are mere constructions. Russell's robust sense of reality is instead his primary Parmenidean sense of "exists." But this corresponds to Quine's opening statement in "On What There Is": "'What is there?'...'Everything'." Thus Quine's heart is in the right place.)

I have suggested that Quine's home language/translation distinction makes him a linguistic modified realist. But beyond that, what kind of realist is he? Specifically, is he a monist or a pluralist?

Quine's "Two Dogmas of Empiricism" suggests a holism of theory and a holism of collective world experience analogous to monist modified realism. In effect, human experience is one big thing which different theories conceptually slice up in different ways. Two theories that account for experience equally well are certainly analogous to distinctions in reason. And differences between Quine's translation manuals are distinctions in reason: rabbits, undetached rabbit parts, and temporal rabbit stages are a case in point. And if plurality is a mere matter of language ("The contrast lies in the terms and not in the stuff they name," WO 91), may it be that Quine is a monist radical realist?

The argument that Quine is a monist would be this. The reference of any term or sentence is incomplete ("too short for significant translation," OR 37). Further, "our statements about the external world face the tribunal of sense experience not individually but only as a corporate body." Even in 1987, "many scientific sentences inseparably share empirical content" (PQ 619). This means that the relations between the typical sentences in a theory, with respect to that theory's overall connection to experience, are a special sort of *internal relation*. Now the acceptance of internal relations, as Russell makes plain, is a logical basis of Bradleyan and ultimately Hegelian monism. And Quine's monism is a form of physical realism, since for Quine it is the external world as a whole with which theory as a whole connects. Quine admits to "methodological monism," i.e., naturalistic holism (TT 71–72), and to Donald Davidson's "anomalous monism," on which what is mental is only "ways of grouping" physical things (PT 72). But the present argument implies much more than methodological monism or anomalous kind-monism. It implies thing-monism.

However, Quine is not a thing-monist. His picture of the world is best seen not when we rock the boat with a demand for translation, but when we simply use language to talk about what there is. And in our ordinary home language, and even in our scientific theories, our references are normally pluralist.

Quine admits four kinds of pluralist realism.

First, Quine's observation sentences each have an "individual empirical content." They may not be "about" anything except in linguistically more sophisticated retrospect. But in such retrospect, Quine likens them to mass terms. Indeed, Quine assimilates observation terms to Russell's logically proper names, "nearly enough," with respect to Russell's epistemological distinction between knowledge by acquaintance and knowledge by description. This is Quinean transcendental Parmenideanism (see chapter 4, section 4). In the lexicon of Russell's *Inquiry*, Quine's observation terms are primary language object words, with much the same slurring of whether they are terms or assertions.

Second, Quine begins *Word and Object* by positing ordinary physical things. In "Things and Their Place in Theories" Quine asserts a "robust realism" of ordinary things—"people, nerve endings, sticks, stones." And while he goes on to characterize our initial account of the world as revisable in principle, in fact his final account of the world is as physical as our initial one. Sticks and stones, for example, remain physical objects. The only differences are that they are now defined by the regions they occupy, and are in some sense composed of microphysical states.

Third, whole sciences have largely "independent empirical meaning," i.e., are theoretically quite independent of each other.

Fourth and most basic, Quine admits microphysical states. Quine thus "rescues the notion of a matter of fact," which for him is a "distribution of microphysical states and relations." It is in just this sense of "matter of fact" that there is for Quine no fact of the matter as to which of two equally successful translation manuals is right when we leave our home language. (Note that microphysical states allow a Quinean nonmodal combinatorial atomism.)

Thus Quine admits at least four kinds of pluralist realism. His reasons are respectively the need for: (1) empirical content and evidence, (2) an initial frame of reference for science, (3) some reflection of the large theoretical independence of the sciences, and (4) basic building blocks.[11]

Insofar as microphysical states are Quine's basic building blocks of the physical world, they are Quine's substance substitutes at bottom. This is explanatory modified realism. But even Quine's macrophysical objects have real identities. Quine admits real identity in sense (2), if not sense (1), for them. He considers his spatiotemporal identity conditions for physical objects quite clear, if not always verifiable (TT 101). Physical objects are really distinct if and only if the spatiotemporal regions they occupy are wholly distinct. Otherwise they are only distinct in reason. Thus Quine differs little from Frege on real distinctions and distinctions in reason among physical objects. Thus Quine meets criterion (1g) of metaphysical modified realism.

It may seem that Quine does not reconcile his realism and his relativity through modified realism, since he says instead, "Vuellemin senses a tension between my professed realism and my seeming relativism and instrumentalism. The reconciliation is to be sought in my naturalism, which...recognizes no higher truth than what we seek in science" (PQ 622; see 316, 611). But I think we agree: his reconciliation is through a naturalistic modified realism.

Quine's physical objects are mind-independent (1a), ultimate subjects of predication (1c), often mutually independent (1d), and naturalistically recognizable (1e). They lack traditional essences but have lawful structures (1b). They are changes (WO 171; Benardete 1993) which undergo changes (TT 10–12; PQ 115) (1f). Quine admits both wholly distinct and overlapping physical objects, and both definitionally wholly distinct and definitionally overlapping classes, allowing both real distinctions and distinctions in reason (1g). Thus Quine meets criterion (1) of metaphysical modified realism rather fully.

In his 1960 *Word and Object*, Quine is a modified realist in a second way as well. There he admits, in effect, that physical objects are less real than abstract objects (WO 124, 237–38). He lists four reasons why. (i) Physical objects alone have "access to all term positions" (WO 237; see 238). (ii) "In a contest for sheer systematic utility to science, the notion of physical object still leads the field" (WO 238; see 124). (iii) Terms for physical objects "are so basic to our language" (WO 238). (iv) Physical objects "are at the focus of such successful communication" (WO 238). Over twenty years later he says in his 1981 *Theories and Things*: "Bodies...are the things, first and foremost. Beyond them there is a succession of dwindling analogies" (TT 9). This is a remarkable reappearance of Aristotelian *pros hen* theory of being in the last of the great analysts. But in 1987, Quine abandons his long-held degrees of reality ontology for an ontology in which physical objects and abstract objects are equally real. He lists four reasons why. (i) In quantum mechanics, there is no longer any sense to the notion of the identity of physical objects; we can only speak of microstates which are functions of quadruples of numbers giving space-time locations. The functors are physical, but the ontology is "pure sets" (PQ 402):

> I have been dwelling on the ontological contrast between mathematics and nature, and on whether to accommodate it in terms of two grades of existence....But I would now suggest an opposite line of thought....
> Imagine two neighboring electrons, and consider the question whether

some given point event and some later one belong together as moments in the career of the same electron or belong rather to different electrons. Quantum mechanics teaches, I think, that this question will sometimes lack physical meaning....[N]ature is better conceived as a distribution of local states over space-time....The ontological contrast between mathematics and nature lapses. (PQ 401–2)

(ii) There is a genuine difference between mathematics and physics in that only the latter has "terms that can be taught strictly by ostension....Being epistemological, however, this is properly a cleavage not between kinds of objects but between kinds of terms" (PQ 402). (iii) Differences in kinds of reality should be reflected by different sorts of restricted variables; however, it is better to have general variables (PQ 592). (iv) The existential quantifier expresses existence in the same sense for all values of the variables it binds. "To quantify over classes is to assume them as real, I say, and no hedging" (PQ 593). I am filled with admiration of this basic change. The reasons for both the earlier and the later ontology make a great deal of sense in Quine's philosophy. I have only two comments. First, I see nothing wrong with letting the existential quantifier express existence, and letting various predicate letters express more specific kinds of ontological status. This is the most natural way to gloss Frege; his existential quantifier would express objectivity and a predicate letter could express the causal reality of concrete objects. Second, no flaw has been detected in the four reasons for the earlier ontology. And since it remains the case that only physical objects have "access to all term positions," then it would seem that they remain "the things, first and foremost," and that Quine still has a *pros hen* ontology hidden by his quantifier.

Quine's naturalistic epistemology is a kind of epistemic modified realism. It presupposes scientific modified realism. Specifically, it is an epistemological foundationalism of observation sentences, many having really distinct stimulus meanings. (PQ 336, 364, 427–28). Quine says, "I do indeed combine foundationalism with coherentism, as I should think it evident that one must" (Quine 1990: 128). Quine's foundationalism "consists in [his] appreciation...that the checkpoints of beliefs are sensory observations" (Quine 1990: 128).

Quine is also a methodological modified realist. For him, ontological analysis ends in physical microstates and classes. He is also a linguistic modified realist due to his canonical notation.

Quine suggests, citing quantum mechanics, that someday the best world-theories may dispense with outmoded concepts such as existence or existential quantification. Even then, Quine would admit the reality of the physical world beyond our "human apparatus" (PT 101). I suggest that it is our understanding of the domain of quantification that grows subtle. Without a domain, physics would be no longer about anything. I agree with Quine that quantificational logic is only a theory to explain our data about existence and identity, among other data, and that we may find a better theory someday. But we must not confuse theories with the data they explain. Our theory of existence and identity may become outmoded, but not, I think, the intellectual data that first led us to 'no entity without identity' theory. In the meantime, Quine does hold that no theory T can make ontological commitments to things of kind K without providing an extensional criterion of identity for K's. And Quine's own theory seems ontologically committed to a desert (as opposed to jungle) modified realism.

Quine contrasts the reality of the physical world beyond competing empirically equivalent physics with the nonexistence of meanings beyond rival manuals of translation. But his illumination of the "one and the same world" beyond physical theories is, in effect, a "black box" private language argument: "I think of the disparate ways of getting at the diameter of an impenetrable sphere: we may pinion the sphere in calipers or we may girdle it with a tape measure and divide by pi, but there is no getting inside" (PT 101). My criticism is that the diameter analogy seems equally apt for muons and meanings.

For further study of the similarities of the analysts to Aristotle concerning their respective forms of modified realism, this comparison chart may help:

Philosopher	Substantive Categories	Not Fully Real Categories
Aristotle	Substances	Qualities, Relations, Places, Dates
Frege	Phenomena, Concrete Objects, Selves	Functions, including Properties and Relations; Abstract Objects, including Places and Times; Senses
1903 Russell	Actual Existents (Material Points, Bodies, Selves, Psychic Points)	Spatiotemporal Reals (Spatial Points, Instants) Concepts (Properties and Relations), Mathematical Existents and Classes as Many, Nonexistent Beings
1918 Russell	One's Own Mind, Sensibilia, Simples	Properties and Relations, Facts, Logical Fictions
1940 Russell	Qualities, Physical Events	Generic Properties, Relations, Facts, Fictions
Early Witt.	Elementary States of Affairs	Objects, Complex States of Affairs

Later Witt.	Language-Games, i.e.,	Grammatical Categories,
	Physical Patterns of	i.e., Bewitchments of Grammar
	Behavior; Phenomena	
Quine	Physical Objects,	Classes, including extensi-
	Stimulus Patterns,	onal Attributes and Relations
	Initial Posits	

The main anomaly among substantive categories is that the early Wittgenstein's elementary states of affairs are not logical subjects of predication. They cannot be named, only described. This violates criterion (1c). I omit Frege's forces, tones, and ideas because it is unclear whether they are real for Frege, i.e., have causal impacts or capacities. I omit the 1912 Russell because for him, the worlds of existence and being are equally real.

5. Conclusion

The view that the great analysts achieved a radical new break from the realism of the past is an illusion. The pace of change in ontology is glacial. Modified realism has been the theory of preference for two millennia. It is a theory accommodating huge amounts of relativity on a realist base. From its Aristotelian paradigm many versions flow. All the main Western traditions seem mainly modified realist: the ancient and medieval metaphysical tradition (chapters 1 and 6), the early modern epistemological tradition (chapter 1; chapter 1, note 4; chapter 7, note 2), the phenomenological tradition (chapter 7, note 5) and the analytic tradition (chapter 7). In general there is some sort of substance or substance analogue along with some sort of ordinary conceptual relativity on which numbers and identities of items can shift.

The analytic philosophers' ontologies are twice removed from Aristotle's paradigm. Frege seems closer to the phenomenologists. Russell seems closer to Hume. The later Wittgenstein and Quine, in their pragmatic forms of holism, seem closer to Hegel. But the ancient realism of Aristotle remains the dominant archetype of the analysts' own realist foundations of their conceptual relativities.

The differences between Aristotle and the analysts, changes perhaps constituting a genuine progress of philosophy, cannot hide the underlying similarities which make such changes possible as changes and intelligible as progress.

Aristotle's categories, Frege's and Russell's concepts, Wittgenstein's criteria, and Quine's sortal terms make little sense except as ways to slice an already given public real world into different patterns. Also, their philosophies make little sense except as theories in which the individuation of some entities is prior to that of others in the order of theoretical explanation. The prior entities include Aristotle's substances, Frege's simples, Russell's sense-data, Wittgenstein's language-games, and Quine's microstates and classes. Quine is a foundationalist; explanatory foundationalism need not be truth-functional (Quine 1990: 128).

Frege's phenomenological modified realism (phenomena sliced into smaller or larger objects) has certain parallels in Russell (sensed events sliced into bundles of qualities or classes of events), Wittgenstein ("objects" of sight sliced into aspects, including both smaller parts and larger organizations (PI 193), and Quine (initially posited physical things later sliced into smaller microphysical states or larger classes). Thus in their various ways, the great analysts are fairly specifically the heirs of Aristotle's phenomenological modified realism of individual things given in experience. And each is in some sense a physicalist.

Indeed, the specificity is greater than that. At the beginning of this book it seemed that among Aristotle's seven themes of substance, only unity remained in the analytic tradition. I have not asked why these themes ought to hang together, or even why they have hung together for millennia. But I have shown that all seven themes occur together in each great analyst. Thus the stone the great analysts rejected became their foundation. Yet they seem to have so widened the old category of substance that conjunct (2) of sense (1) of "really distinct" drops out. We are left with sense (2) of "really distinct" and the mix-and-match interplay of real distinctions and distinctions in reason I described as Frege's second kind of modified realism. That is perhaps their greatest achievement. It eliminates Brentano's problem of not knowing on which level of the world's structure the substances are. Namely, there are real beings on every level on which there are real distinctions in sense (2). There is no need for ultimate simples, or for a monistic One, merely to ensure that there is something there to be sliced. We may even reinstate conjunct (2) of sense (1) in various ways, using the chart at the end of section 4 for guidance.

Ontological relativity attacks realism. Private language arguments establish realism. Thus they conflict. The seeds of the conflict exist in all four great analysts: Frege, Russell, Wittgenstein, and Quine. Each advances some sort of conceptual relativity in a famous work. Each also gives some sort of private language argument in the very same work. The works are *The Foundations of Arithmetic, The Principles of Mathematics, Philosophical Investigations,* and *Word and Object*—as well as "Ontological Relativity."[12] I suggest that this seeming conflict is best resolved by, and that the analysts resolve it by, modified realism. Far from being radical relativists or extreme linguisticists, if anything they sometimes verge on radical realism. Following Leibniz and Frege, number applies to everything (FA 31); thus ordinary number-shifting applies to everything. In chapter 1 it took three levels of ontology to explain the compatibility of realism and relativity in modified realism. Private language arguments support this explanation by ensuring the objectivity of all three levels of ontology.

The private language arguments of the analytic tradition may be best understood in terms of their historical origins. There are at least eight origins: verificationism, naturalism-pragmatism, materialism, projective geometry, justificationism, realism *versus* nominalism, the thesis that language and thought are identical, and as a second-level overview, 'no entity without identity' theory. Anticipators include Dewey, James, Peirce, Helmholtz, Müller, Hamann, Herder, Humboldt, Marx, Engels, Feuerbach, Hegel, Schelling, Schopenhauer, Tooke, Hobbes, Bonald, Lamettrie, Arnobius, Cicero, and Plato. See my "Origins of the Private Language Argument" (Dejnožka 1995).

As an improvement on Parmenides' connection between the rational and the real, i.e. between word and object, atomistic, i.e. analytical, substance realism is ancient news.

Analysis itself did not begin with the analytic movement. As Sheldon P. Peterfreund and Theodore C. Denise say in their *Contemporary Philosophy and Its Origins* (1967), Socrates, Plato, and Aristotle constantly engage in language analysis. No doubt their kinds of analysis differ greatly from those practiced in this century. But that is another story (Peterfreund 1967: ch. 5).[13]

I very broadly distinguish the analysts' analyses of the logical structure of identity statements from their ontological theories of identity. For Frege, informative identity statements are about names expressing senses. For Russell, at least one of the subject-terms of a true informative identity statement must express a definite description, since if both terms were logically proper names, then the statement would be tautologous (PLA 247). The early Wittgenstein does not even admit an identity sign: "Identity of object I express by identity of sign" (T 5.53); yet numbers shift as we shift "operations" (T. 6.01). For the later Wittgenstein, the subject-terms of a true informative identity statement seem to use different criteria (or language-games) as vehicles for referring to the same item. Quine finds "$a = b$" true and informative just in case "a" and "b" are not stimulus-synonymous, but refer to the same object (WO 55, 117). Thus concerning the logical structure of informative identity statements, all admit some form of linguistic or conceptual mediation between word and thing. Yet these forms of mediation are not barriers between us and the world, but vehicles by which we can speak of things. And all also admit some linguistically and conceptually unmediated connections with things. To "shift" sortal media (these include Wittgenstein's rules and Quine's translations) is to "shift" objectual identities of items. Yet all posit items in the world whose identities can be reflected in language, items some pairs of which surely are really distinct from each other and other pairs of which surely are not. This distinction of linguistic analysis from ontological analysis has roots in Aristotle's "distinct in formula" theory of the logical structure of factually informative identity statements as reflecting ontological identities in all categories. Which analyst comes closest to these Aristotelian roots is as much a question of interpretation of Aristotle as it is a question of interpretation of the analysts.[14]

Notes

I could not improve on Edmund Husserl's dedication of *Logical Investigations*.
All the epigrams are from works cited in the Bibliographical References. The
quotations of Heraclitus and Parmenides are respectively from Kahn, *The art and thought
of Heraclitus* (Kahn 1979: 53/Heraclitus fr. 51), and Kirk, *The Presocratic Philosophers*
(Kirk 1985: 249–51/Parmenides fr. 8).

Chapter 1: Introduction

1. This book is about what the great analysts have in common. Therefore I have
felt it inappropriate to suggest that any of their philosophies is better than the others. My
occasional criticisms are merely "local" or "in-house." This must not be confused with
the fact that the book is mainly about Frege and Russell as the two great neglected 'no
entity without identity' ontologists of the analytic tradition.

2. Stuart Hampshire, in "Identification and Existence," explains the essential sense
as follows: "(1) 'That is Socrates' (2) 'That is a dagger' (3) 'It is yellow'. In (1) and (2)
I am not describing; I am identifying; I am answering the question 'What, or Who, is
that?. In (3) I am describing, not identifying, whatever is referred to by 'that'....
[C]ontemporary empiricists, following Russell's logic, have so closely assimilated (2) and
(3) as scarcely to mark any difference in function between them" (Hampshire 1956: 199).
Hampshire seems to argue that using the essential sense presupposes the criterial sense:
"It is a further requirement that, attached to any substantival phrase which occurs in a
direct identification, there should be some principle of individuation; for in answering
the question 'What is that?', or 'What is that so-and-so?', the speaker must have some
way of marking as a unit the object referred to" (Hampshire 1956: 205). He also seems
to argue that using the essential sense presupposes the memorial sense: "When I identify
an object before me as a man,...I also pick out something which can be constantly
referred to as the same man....And it is a necessity of discourse that I should be able to
pick out and identify recurring things as the continuing subjects of discourse..."
(Hampshire 1956: 207). P. F. Strawson, in "Entity and Identity," seems to hold that all
entities require cognitive or epistemic identifiability (Strawson 1976: 193–94, 219). In
the main body of his essay, Strawson argues that essential identity is not required for
everything we might call an "entity." He discusses colors, sounds, smells, ways of
walking, gestures, literary styles, poems, cargoes, parcels, games, and smiles.

3. Some recent writers suggest that theory of linguistic meaning and epistemology coalesce in Frege's notion of a sense. Leila Haaparanta, in *Frege's Notion of Being*, praises the shift from Dummett's construal of senses as meanings to Sluga's, Currie's, and her own emphases on Frege's 'epistemological project', ironically due in part to Dummett's own stressing of the cognitive nature of senses (Haaparanta 1985: 67–70). Currie is right that Frege's project to show that arithmetic is analytic is epistemological, in that a discussion of it would fit perfectly in, say, chapter 5, "The Truths of Reason," in Roderick M. Chisholm's *Theory of Knowledge*. But this particular branch of epistemology seeks to explain the *a priori* in terms of propositional form. Thus we shift right back from epistemology to language. Currie admits that Frege does not have a theory of knowledge any more than Frege has a philosophy of religion.

Even Dummett's foes, G. P. Baker and P. M. S. Hacker, endorse Dummett's view that the "semantic value" of an expression is "the contribution it makes to determining as true or false sentences in which it occurs" (Baker 1987: 94). Frege says in *Basic Laws* vol. 1 sect. 32, "The names...of which the name of a truth-value consists, contribute to the expression of the thought, and this contribution of the individual [component] is its sense." Thus senses are semantic values on Baker's and Hacker's own endorsement of Dummett's fine definition of "semantic value." It is hard to find any epistemology here.

Whether epistemology and theory of meaning intersect in Frege's senses is of no interest to the question whether Frege's senses make him a radical relativist. Much the same arguments pro and con would apply in any case. The parallel nature of my evaluations of the two great revolts should show this. But for the record, senses always contain modes of presentation. These modes are neither linguistic nor epistemic, but cognitive. As to modes of presentation being cognitive and not epistemic, compare Plato's view that perception is not knowledge, *Theaetetus* 151–95.

4. I speak of tendencies and impacts. Most of the early modern philosophers admit substances or substance substitutes. This is obvious for Descartes, Arnauld, Locke, Berkeley, Hume, Spinoza, and Leibniz. Hume makes sense-impressions substance substitutes (Hume 1973: 24–25, 244). Kant admits things in themselves in *Prolegomena to Any Future Metaphysic* (Kant 1950: sect. 32), and admits noumenal moral agents. Hegel admits an Absolute.

5. But Quine says elsewhere, "Disquotation as such is neutral to truth and reference" (Quine 1976a: 318).

6. Compare Dummett (1981a: 441–42); Quine, TT 21, 180–81). I believe that Michael Devitt makes a point similar to mine somewhere in *Realism and Truth* (1984), or perhaps elsewhere.

7. An anonymous reviewer objects, "But if there are some substances whose identity conditions are absolute, wouldn't there be some true nonrelative identity statements? And doesn't this contradict Geach's claim?" No. The import of my theory of linguistic 'reflection' of real objectual identities is that there need not be any true nonrelative identity statements. Geach's theory about statements might still be true.

Chapter 2: Is Frege a Radical Relativist?

1. Morris says, "No one has suggested, as I have, that [Frege] can be understood [in 'On Sense and Reference'] as continuing to hold a metalinguistic account" (Morris

1984: 50; see 27–34 on Frege). Morris's book was published in 1984; no other works of his are cited in his Bibliography. Bynum gave the name interpretation in 1972 (in Frege 1972: 67–68). And there are my two statements of it (Dejnožka 1979: ch. 3; Dejnožka 1981: 31–41). Bynum and I both antedate Morris by several years. Angelelli, Sluga, and Currie *may* endorse the name interpretation as well, but I am unable to confirm that from reading their books.

2. David Coder claims that Linsky holds that Fregean identity is a relation between objects (Coder 1974: 343 n.1). Coder cites p. 22 in Linsky's *Referring*. I find no evidence there for his claim. The oversight I describe is also fatal to Thomas V. Morris's functionalist theory of identity (Morris 1984).

3. Read Bertrand Russell, POM 64 and 502, lines 1–11 carefully together. And remember I said that Russell only roughly holds the sense interpretation.

That it ought to be Frege's doctrine that "the sense of expression 'A'" can never refer to a sense vitiates Russell's critique of Frege's theory of senses in "On Denoting" that one can never refer to the sense to which one intends to refer. One might object that this only heightens the mystery of the nature of senses (another of Russell's criticisms). But even a partisan of Russell such as Herbert Hochberg allows that primitive terms are not mysterious if we are acquainted with (experience) their references (Hochberg 1978: 179). And on theories like Butchvarov's or mine, which replace Frege's complete senses with objects we experience, the mystery vanishes. To be sure, Russell's critique comes back to life, if we can refer to such objects. But it would be a feeble life. Russell's main argument is that reference to meanings is always misdirected. But Russell is obtusely determined to "want" to refer to meanings in misguided ways. All we need do is redirect our wishes to refer to meanings in natural ways. Even Hochberg (1978: 188) and Russell admit that the meaning of any denoting phrase C can be referred to by the expression

"the meaning of 'C'"

or by using Russell's own convention of inverted commas. But Russell objects in "On Denoting" to these two natural ways as follows: "Now the relation between meaning and denotation is not merely linguistic through the phrase: there must be a logical relation involved, which we express by saying that the meaning denotes the denotation." Certainly Frege would agree, though we should replace the word "denotes" with the Furthian "is a sense of" (Furth 1967: xix), since for Frege it is names that denote. I hold that for Frege there are at least *three* such logical relations. First, there is the Furthian "is a sense of." Second, there is the relation of a mode of presentation to that which it presents, if anything. Third, there is the relation between the sortal concept intimately associated with the sense and the object, if any, that falls under it. All three obtain with logical necessity. Ironically, it is only Russell who makes his own denoting relation "merely linguistic," since in "On Denoting" he assays it in terms of language alone, denying that descriptions have any meaning.

Russell more specifically accused the relation between the meaning of "the meaning of 'C'" and the meaning it denotes, namely, the meaning of "C," of being merely linguistic instead of logical, because "C" occurs in the expression "the meaning of 'C'". But the connection of a denoting phrase to its meaning *ought* to be "merely linguistic." Every good Frege scholar knows that it is arbitrary which senses we assign to which expressions. But once the senses are assigned, the references of the resulting names (including definite descriptions) are not arbitrary. Now, Russell is assuming Frege's program so as to achieve his *reductio*. And in that program, assigning senses is just how we introduce expressions as names we can use. Thus for the sake of the argument, we must grant that a sense has *already* been assigned to "the sense of ( )" or to Russell's convention, as well as to the name "C" in the context of such notations. Hence what Russell and Hochberg deem as merely linguistic is emphatically not so, thanks to the three logically necessary relations I described. Or if "merely linguistic" means 'can be referred to only by means of language', then any linguistic reference to anything is, trivially, merely linguistic. Or if "merely linguistic" means 'can be intended only by means of language, as opposed to through acquaintance or imaging' (Hochberg 1978: 194–97), then the problem Russell raises is not one for meanings alone. It is shared by every item we can know only by description: muons, which for theoretical reasons cannot be imaged even with an electron microscope); the center of mass of the solar system, which point is inadequately imaged as a small dot (OD 48); other minds; numbers. This raises the question, Just what does Russell mean when he accuses the relation *is the meaning of* of being "merely linguistic"? Just what *is* his criticism, anyway? The value of Russell's criticism cannot be assessed if we do not know what the criticism is.

Sadly, Russell never says what he means by "merely linguistic." And Hochberg's explication, if that is what it is, though very sympathetic to Russell's cause, seems to be not a report on Russell, but an amplification of Hochberg's own (Hochberg 1978: 176–78). And when Hochberg says, "What Russell argues in detail is that we are forced to use a merely linguistic denoting phrase, such as 'the meaning of "C"', to denote a meaning, because we cannot use a denoting phrase like 'the meaning of C'" (Hochberg 1978: 181; see 184), this scarcely tells us what "merely linguistic" means.

Nothing depends on using "C" in "the meaning of 'C'". For we can use a definite description instead, say, "the meaning of this mark," *pace* Hochberg, who applauds Russell's demand for misguided referential intentions (Hochberg 1978: 184). Should descriptions of marks count as "merely linguistic"? Do descriptions have no conceptual content?

The main recent literature does not gainsay the points made here: Simon Blackburn and Alan Code (1978: 65–77); Anthony Manser (1985: 269–86); Pawel Turnau (1991). I endorse Geach's reply to Blackburn and Code that Frege's senses are graspable as certain (timelessly understood) uses (Geach 1978: 204–5). Hochberg misses Geach's point (Hochberg 1978: 180, 189). Senses do not uselessly duplicate uses; they *are* uses. At the same time, senses are closer to descriptions than Hochberg thinks, on my view that each sense is intimately associated with a concept. Here useless duplication is avoided by the difference in function between senses and denotations, including concepts. Denoted entities simply do not function as modes of presentation for Frege. Perhaps an entity can have more functions than a Swiss Army knife, but this is not Frege's view. For Frege, an entity's category is tied to its logical function(s) in a fairly conservative way.

Citing John Searle, Geach also cautions us that Russell unduly conflates his own theory of meaning in *Principles* with Frege's theory of senses, and suggests that in "On Denoting," the criticisms Russell directs against Frege are best understood as directed instead against Russell's own earlier theory of meaning in *Principles* (Geach 1972: 27–31). This suggestion helps explain the weakness of Russell's critique of Frege. It would be natural to expect Russell to be mainly impressed by the similarities, not the differences. Also, Russell is a *very* early interpreter of Frege, and scholarship is not Russell's strong point.

However misguidedly, Russell expressly rejects Frege's senses in "On Denoting." But I know of no commentator who has observed that Russell repudiates his critique of Frege and even offers his own neo-Fregean meaning-denotation distinction only six years later (MAL 216–24). Russell retrospectively finds meaning in use implicit in "On Denoting," the very paper in which he rejects the meaning-denotation distinction (MPD 63–65; see LK 70).

4. Dummett claims that in "The Thought," "thoughts and their constituent senses" are objects (Dummett 1991: 225). Every thought has at least one incomplete constituent sense which cannot be a complete object. Even more astonishingly, Dummett says that in *Foundations*, mental ideas are objects (Dummett 1991: 225). In *Foundations* Frege restricts the word "idea" to *subjective* ideas and then classifies objects as *objective* ideas, making it clear that *no* mental ideas are objects (FA 37 n.1). If it seems odd that no objective ideas are mental ideas, remember that for Frege no *thoughts* are mental ideas either.

5. Haaparanta forgets that thanks to the problem of the concept *horse*, "the x which is F and G" refers not to a complex of 'individual properties' but to a course-of-values, i.e. class of ordered pairs of arguments and values, in *Basic Laws*. Frege has no individual properties. His properties are not as individual as the individuals that have them, but universals. For Frege the concept-name "x is red" refers to the same concept no matter which object-name veridically completes it. Perhaps Haaparanta means by her expression "individual properties," individua*ting* (i.e. sortal) properties. These can be universals, but that still does not make them senses. Even if she *defines* a complex of universal properties as the kind of sense expressed by expressions like "x which is F and G", where only one object falls under the concept F *and* G, she is begging the question of whether senses are complexes of properties. Nor does it help when she speaks of 'bundles of properties' (Haaparanta 1986b: 274). Frege's radical bifurcation of complete objects and incomplete properties (or more generally, incomplete functions) makes objects no bundles of properties.

Haaparanta's *Frege's Notion of Being* (1985: 66) echoes some of the mistakes I have found in her interpretation of senses in her 1986b. She admits that it is "curious" that properties of objects should be parts of thoughts, "but it does not cause any problems, after all, for in Frege's view" thoughts are as mind-independent as objects and their properties. But I see two major problems: (i) Frege wrote a 'smoking gun' letter making concepts, i.e. properties, references, not senses; and (ii) senses contain modes of cognition, while surely references do not. Note that Haaparanta equates concepts with properties herself (Haaparanta 1985: 65). Second, she suggests that if senses are complexes of properties, "their names ought to be such as 'being the teacher of Alexander the Great' or 'being the pupil of Plato'." But her proposal faces a dilemma. If such names are complete, then "Smith believes that Aristotle was Greek" becomes "Smith believes that being the pupil of Plato was Greek," which is unintelligible. Contrast Frege's own rendition of one sense expressed by "Aristotle" as 'the teacher of Alexander the Great and the pupil of Plato' (SR 58n). I agree with Dummett that "being F" refers to an incomplete concept (Dummett 1973: 216–18); observe that "being F" is the gerundial form of "is F." By parity of reason, if "being F" named a sense, then it must name an incomplete sense, which could scarcely be a sense expressed by the complete name "Aristotle." Third, Haaparanta says, "Someone might also argue that senses cannot be properties, because, unlike properties, they are complete, or saturated, for Frege. This problem can be solved by recalling the fact that a sense of an object is not just any property whatsoever, but it is a complex of properties which has the ability of identifying the object." Haaparanta fails to explain how her complexes of properties are anything other than incomplete *complex properties*, i.e. logical conjunctions of incomplete simple properties. Complete or saturated complexes of properties seem to be Haaparanta's own invention. There is nothing like them in Frege.

Yet another problem with Haaparanta's identification of senses with complexes of properties is that for Frege, properties (concepts) have extensional identities, while senses have intensional identities.

Haaparanta claims that if "it is not possible for us to consider objects in any other way than...in terms of our concepts," then objects are "bare particulars" (Haaparanta 1985: 100). Haaparanta is so bewitched by this *non sequitur* that she even dismisses Frege's express ridicule of 'natureless things' in "Über die Zahlen des Herrn Schubert" as not ontological in nature (Haaparanta 1986b: 283). Haaparanta also overlooks *Foundations*. When we abstract the concept *cat* from cats and ignore their many colors, "for all that the cats do not become colourless and they remain different precisely as before" (FA 44-45). Frege also cites dogs and stones as examples of objects (FA 42). Are dogs and stones bare particulars? Even if Frege admitted bare particulars, they would not be dogs or stones, but only part of Frege's ontological analysis of such objects, the remainder being their properties. Needless to say, Frege never gives any such analysis. Frege's ridicule of natureless things, ridicule of Husserlian psychological abstraction of bare units from groups of objects (not to be confused with Frege's logical abstraction operator), denial that variables denote objects devoid of properties (for Frege, variables are the only remotely feasible candidates for doing so), and express admission of stones and colored cats as objects, all show that Haaparanta has got it backwards (see FA 44-47; TW 85, 109; and Dummett 1991: 84-85). Frege's objects are best viewed as simply things themselves. Compare Douglas C. Long's critique of bare particulars as opposed to ordinary particulars (Long 1970: 280-82).

It is especially curious that Haaparanta deems objects bare particulars, since in saying that complete senses are complexes of properties, she makes Frege a bundle theorist for complete senses. Thus she attributes to Frege two conflicting solutions of the problem of universals. Yet the same basic problems of individuation arise for both objects and senses. E.g., Can there be two senses which have all their 'properties' in common? Haaparanta offers no explanation of this most curious interpretation.

6. If I am wrong and complete senses are objects, then they are very special abstract objects indeed, but surely not complexes of properties. Rather, they would be translucent objects, like panes of glass through which we view (other) objects, and intimately connected with the concepts under which the (other) objects fall.

The special nature of Fregean representative assertion shows us how Frege could use senses to explain the possibility of informative identity propositions without appealing circularly to a special class of such propositions about senses. For the subject-terms in "The sense of expression '*A*' is identical with the sense of expression '*B*'" refer to themselves, on my view that identity for Frege is a relation between names, and customarily ought to refer to objects which represent the senses in question. This confirms Butchvarov's observation that Frege need not be guilty of such an easy fallacy (Butchvarov 1979: 25).

7. Mistakenly thinking that Frege holds such a view unhappily seems to be the basis of a major criticism of Frege's theory of identity (Butchvarov 1979: 21–24).

8. The explanation Frege gives of identity as indiscernibility was accepted by Frege as a definition earlier (FA 76). Frege changed his mind for a technical reason: on his view, all definitions are identities, so that identity itself must be indefinable (TW 80).

9. The fact that the explanation under discussion is an axiom should provide at least part of the rationale behind Frege's saying that it is of fundamental importance. Frege might possibly also mean in part that identity is in some sense essentially indiscernibility, since the axiom is fundamental philosophically speaking.

10. The relations of identity and of intersubstitutability *salva veritate* always yield the same value for the same ordered set of arguments. But Frege has a technical reason for holding that identity is indefinable. Namely, every definition takes the form of an identity: "*A*" is to mean the same as (or express the same sense as and denote the same denotation as) "*B*." Therefore we must understand the identity relation before we can understand what definition is. This amounts to 'no defined entity without identity'.

11. The progressive distortion of Frege is comparable in Haaparanta's *Frege's Notion of Being*. On p. 74, "a proper name is related to an object via a sense and only via a sense." By p. 88, "the existence of the object to which we aim at referring, is relativized to our conceptual frameworks." Finally, on p. 96, there is no less than a "chasm between objects in themselves and objects as falling under...concepts." Haaparanta does admit that "nonetheless...concepts...guarantee the objectivity of our knowledge" (Haaparanta 1986b: 92). But it never occurs to her that this is self-contradictory. What is objective knowledge of objects but knowledge of objects in themselves? How can objective knowledge of objects be 'relativistic'?

12. Contrast IW 1 and 27 n.1 with Heijenoort (1967: 324–30).

I find Heijenoort's remark, "Semantic relations are unknown" in Frege and Russell, astonishing (Heijenoort 1967: 326). Just what is reference to truth-values for Frege, if not a semantic relation? Just what is 'always true' for Russell, if not a semantic relation?

Among other authors, Baker and Hacker agree with Heijenoort that Frege has no semantics (Baker 1984: 365–77), while Angelelli writes a whole chapter on Frege's semantics (Angelelli 1967). Dummett has the best view. Namely, Frege has a semantics, but does not explicitly call it such (Dummett 1983: 202–3; Dummett 1981: 81–82).

13. Michael D. Resnick says that Frege's context principle "was superseded in 1891 by the theory of unsaturated senses and references" (Resnick 1980: 171). I shall argue that Frege's theory of saturation *is* his context principle, ontologically articulated as basic to realism.

Michael Dummett notes that there is no 'direct clash' between Frege's contextual principle and his realism (Dummett 1981a: 362). To the contrary, the principle is that it is only in the context of a sentence that a word *can* refer to objective things. Moreover, the principle is used to '*license*' the contextual definition of mind-independent objects (Dummett 1981a: 363–66, italics mine), as a "*justification*" of Frege's saying we refer to abstract objects (Dummett 1981a: 399, italics mine). So far, Dummett and I are in complete agreement.

For Dummett, contextual definition goes awry in a way that does not reflect on the context principle itself, and is replaced by mere explicit definition in *Foundations* (Dummett 1981a: 363; Dummett 1991: 117, 118). Dummett is aware of the fact that the context principle is repeatedly stated in the conclusion of *Foundations* (Dummett 1981a: 363, 401). And Dummett admits, "It appears, in the recapitulation, as an essential step in the argument; it leads directly to the need to fix the sense of statements of identity between numbers; and this leads in turn to defining numbers as extensions of concepts" (Dummett 1981a: 401; compare Dummett 1991: 118–19. But Dummett has never made the natural inference that *Foundations'* definition of 'number belonging to *F*' must therefore be in some sense a contextual definition after all. He asks, "But how has it [the context principle] guided it [the definition]?" and cannot find an answer (Dummett 1981a: 401).

I have found Frege's post-*Foundations* context principle to be in effect his theory of saturation. Dummett says that Frege had not "clearly distinguished" those two topics in his 1881 "Booles rechnende Logik," where they overlap only in the case of incomplete expressions, but "disentangled" them in *Foundations* (Dummett 1981a: 370). Dummett then accuses Sluga and Kluge of 'confusing' and 'conflating' the context principle with "the principle of the incompleteness of concepts and relations," saying that the latter principle is "applicable only to predicates and relational expressions," while the former holds "for all expressions" (Dummett 1981a: 373, 377). Dummett's charge of confusing and conflating two principles begs the question. For if Sluga, Kluge, and I are right, then we have confused or conflated nothing. And the context principle is properly speaking the principle of the incompleteness of concepts and relations *and the completeness of objects*. Thus all referring names are included. My argument is that surely the completeness of objects is not so great that objects cannot or need not be complements to incomplete functions. Surely it must be the kind of completeness that must be able to complete all incomplete functions of the appropriate type-level. Such a complementary kind of completeness cannot be understood apart from understanding sentences which involve its use to complete the incomplete functions that logically complement it, any more than the incompleteness of those functions can. Dummett and the Hintikkas overlook this point. Whether Sluga and Kluge are aware of it, I do not know. But the early Wittgenstein shows a fine metaphysical grasp of it:

> It is essential to things that they should be possible constituents of states of affairs. In logic nothing is accidental: if a thing *can* occur in a state of affairs, the possibility of the state of affairs must be written into the thing itself. (T 2.011, T 2.012)

This would include complete particulars as well as incomplete properties and relations, if all these are Tractarian objects—which they might well be.

Here is a second argument. The later Wittgenstein says that "a thing...has not even got a name except in the language-game. This is what Frege meant, too, when he said that a word had meaning only as part of a sentence." (PI #49). Now, Frege's object-names are no exception to Wittgenstein's point. Therefore, the completeness of object-names is just as sentence-contextual for Frege as is the incompleteness of function-names.

Due to the need to account for our understanding new sentences formed from old words, Dummett sees the mature Frege as retaining the context principle "in the background," but as unable to state it for sentences as a "distinct logical category" of language, due to his making sentences a proper subclass of names (Dummett 1981a: 374, 378; see Dummett 1981: 7). Now, Dummett himself seems to recognize that the two theses:

(1) One understands the sense and reference of a word only if one understands how to use that word in sentences.

and

(2) Sentences are a kind of words: proper names of truth-values.

are logically consistent (Dummett 1981a: 378). Indeed, all that is required is that the sense and reference of sentences be understood only if we understand how to use sentences in (larger) sentences (or larger proper names denoting truth-values). And this involves no vicious regress of sentences that must be understood. It involves only our understanding how to construct larger sentences. Really we should speak of a trivial mutual dependence of simple and complex sentences. I wholly grant that children are said to understand words without understanding sentences, and to understand simple sentences without understanding complex sentences. But nobody is rightly said to have a full or adult understanding of words or sentences without satisfying such requirements. Further, the obviously Fregean premisses of the following argument logically entail Frege's context principle, stated as the conclusion:

1. No name's sense or reference can be understood apart from understanding in principle how to use it in all the more complex names in which it can occur.
2. Sentences are a kind of proper name.
3. For any name, there is some sentence in which it can occur.
4. Therefore, no name's sense or reference can be understood apart from understanding in principle how to use it in all the sentences in which it can occur.

Premiss (1) comes from *Basic Laws* I 29. Premiss (2) comes from *Basic Laws* I 2. Premiss (3) is plainly true of *Basic Laws'* formal notation. Thus the context principle is logically implicit in *Basic Laws*.

And we also need to account for our understanding new names formed from old words, which new names do not name truth-values. Surely understanding how "Czechoslovakia" completes "I visited ( ) in 1990," but not how it completes "the capital of ( )," is not fully understanding the role of "Czechoslovakia" in sentences. For what about "I visited the capital of ( ) in 1990"? Thus Frege's including the completion of functions which are not concepts or relations, such as *capital of* ( ), is quite necessary for a context principle which applies to all words in all the sentences in which they may occur. For all the function-names which are not concept-names or relation-names occur in indefinitely many sentences. This is true both in natural languages and in formal notation. Thus, far from making Frege unable to state his context principle, *Basic Laws*

I 29's whole condition of proper names' denoting is a necessary condition of his context principle. This deepens the systematic elegance of *Basic Laws*.

P. M. S. Hacker is as mistaken as Dummett in thinking that Frege did not give a contextual definition of number in *Foundations* (Hacker 1979: 223). But Hacker rightly finds a new version of the context principle in *Basic Laws* I 32: "The names...of which the name of a truth-value consists, contribute to the expression of the thought, and this contribution of the individual [component] is its sense" (Hacker 1979: 225). However, Dummett claims that this statement is merely "in conformity with the context principle," and "is so phrased as not to commit Frege to the context principle" (Dummett 1981a: 380). Dummett gives two reasons for his view.

Dummett's first reason is that Frege "makes no general statement about what the sense of an expression other than a sentence consists in" (Dummett 1981a: 380). Therefore Frege cannot "explain in what the sense of an expression other than a sentence consists only in terms of its contribution to the senses of sentences containing it" (Dummett 1981a: 380). We may say that Dummett sets up here an 'explanation requirement' for a statement's counting as a context principle. But his requirement is a strange one. For when Frege says in *The Foundations of Arithmetic* "never to ask for the meaning of a word in isolation, but only in the context of a proposition" (FA X), Frege makes no general statement in what the *content* of an expression other than a sentence consists. Now what I just quoted from *Foundations* (FA X) is admitted by all and sundry to be Frege's famous context principle. Yet it cannot be a context principle at all according to Dummett's explanation requirement. That is, on Dummett's showing, even the context principle stated in *Foundations* is not a context principle. For there is nothing in *Foundations* that 'explains in what the *content* of an expression other than a sentence consists only in terms of its contribution to the contents of sentences containing it', or in any way at all. Dummett is evidently imposing a philosophical requirement of his own on the adequacy of context principles. That may be good criticism, but it is bad scholarship. Indeed, Frege does not explain what senses are or what contents are anywhere in his writings, either in terms of their contributions to sentential contents or in any other way. This does not mean that he does not hold that words *have* senses or contents only insofar as they can occur in sentences. And insofar as Frege's senses are a special primitive category, Dummett's requirement is not even good criticism. However, we may in retrospect explain senses, if not also contents, as abstract, timeless sorts of uses (Geach 1978: 205). Dummett himself explains senses as criteria of identity (Dummett 1981: 498). If such glosses are philosophically illuminating at all, then they are also illuminating of how Frege would satisfy Dummett's philosophical requirement here.

Dummett's second reason is that "no reason is given why just the same may not be said when the expression occurs as a part of a proper name which is not a name of a truth-value" (Dummett 1981a: 380). But as I already explained, "just the same" can and must be said of proper names such as "the capital of Czechoslovakia," if the context principle is to obtain for all names in all sentences, since indefinitely many sentences contain the proper name "the capital of Czechoslovakia."

The truth is that *Basic Laws* I 29 not only upholds the context principle, but it upholds the *Foundations* requirement that for objects for to be named, a sense for their identity must be fixed—the very requirement Dummett says Frege abandoned in 1884. In *Basic Laws* I 29, sufficient conditions of a name's denoting are given for various kinds of names. The conditions are also necessary conditions, since they are mutually dependent. In every case, names denote if and only if all the more complex names they can help complete denote. To be sure, these more complex names include both sentences and names like "the capital of Czechoslovakia." So far we have only introduced names, including sentences, *as* names. We have *asserted* nothing. (That requires prefixing the vertical judgment-stroke.) However, Frege's three basic functions, judgment (named by the horizontal stroke), negation, and identity, always map their arguments onto truth-values. And including their names in the formal notation logically entails that the section 29 conditions for names' denoting logically entail that names have sense and reference if and only if they do occur in (certain names which are) sentences having sense and reference. And that is just the context principle of *Basic Laws*. Even more strikingly, negation is truth-functionally reducible to the judgment function, and the judgment-function is similarly reducible to identity. Thus identity is the most primitive function of the three. Thus the contextualism implicit in *Basic Laws* I 29 is at bottom a requirement of *fixing the sense and reference of identity statements*. And that is just the requirement for defining number which Dummett says Frege abandoned in *Foundations*. The resemblance between all this and *Foundations* sect. 62 on our having to fix the sense of an identity for numbers *due to* the context principle is all too obvious. If anything, the two reducibilities spell it out even more clearly.

This is not to mention that the whole purpose of *Basic Laws*, stated in the Introduction, is to prove theorems, i.e., the truth of certain sentences, so as to show that arithmetic, which consists entirely of equations, or identity statements for Frege, is reducible to logic. It is also not to mention that *Basic Laws* I 29 fixes the identity of every reference thanks to *Basic Laws* I 20's endorsement of the identity of indiscernibles (Russell's Paradox is criticism, not scholarship). Thus to fix all the properties of an object simply *is* to fix its identity. It is also not to mention that to determine whether each object *a* falls under each concept *C*, as *Basic Laws* I 29 specifically demands, simply is to determine whether $(\exists x)(Fx \ \& \ (x = a))$. Thus we must theoretically fix the identity of object *a* piecemeal, i.e., one property at a time.

In the face of all this, Dummett's remarks seem lame. Dummett says of the three basic functions I mentioned, "As it happens, these functions always take truth-values as values....This fact is not stressed by Frege, however, in his discussion..." (Dummett 1981a: 410; compare Dummett 1991: 213). Not stressed? "As it happens," how well would Frege's logic work *without* them? How many equations could Frege prove without negation? How many could he prove without *identity*? Dummett's next pronouncement is even more incredible: "Moreover, it so happens that Frege is able to reduce the case of the negation function to that of the horizontal, and that of the horizontal in turn to that of identity, so that, in the end, the question comes back to that of deciding whether objects not given as value-ranges, are to be identified with value-ranges, which was all that Frege's first argument [vol. 1, sect. 10] appeared to require" (Dummett 1981a: 410). This proves the very point Dummett denies. The reason why the question comes back to value-ranges in the end is just that for Frege, the sense and reference of every arithmetical identity statement *must* be fixed for every number-name. And that is because names have sense and reference only if *all* identity statements which contain them have sense and reference (see my chapter 3, sect. 1). How could the context principle be more obviously included, short of an explicit statement which Frege probably felt was unnecessary?

Dummett seems right that the difficulty of fixing the sense of a numerical identity is postponed to the level of extensions of concepts (Dummett 1981: 501). But that is criticism, not scholarly evidence that Frege has abandoned the requirement that the sense of a numerical identity be fixed. And Frege did not pick the extensions out of a hat. See chapter 3, section 1.

Dummett's last point is that the general principle Frege does state at the end of *Basic Laws* I 32 (the one I cited Hacker as observing seven paragraphs ago) "is not one specifically concerning identity, or even the context principle in the form in which it is stated in *Grundlagen*, but a generalization of that principle which no longer accords a distinguished role to sentences" (Dummett 1981a: 410; see Dummett 1991: 210-15.) All this shows, as does "This fact is not stressed by Frege," is that Frege has achieved an elegant generalization which *subsumes* the context principle. The context principle is now a Stealth airplane, too hard for scholarly radars trained only on explicit assertions to detect. Dummett has no qualms about digging below the explicit text anywhere else, and often far deeper than their plain logical implications. So why does he wrap himself in the flag of explicit pronouncement now? I have described nothing but the plain logical implications of *Basic Laws* I 20, 29.

Now, the Hintikkas claim Wittgenstein "realized a tacit contradiction which lurks in the contrast Frege drew between saturated and unsaturated symbols and the context principle" (IW 42). The contradiction is supposed to be that only unsaturated symbols conform to the context principle. By definition, saturated symbols have independent meanings. I have already resolved this matter, but let me amplify my earlier remarks. Saturation theory is the later Frege's ontological articulation of the context principle. As such, it need not insist that all references and all senses be unsaturated in order to ensure that all words have meaning only in the context of statements. Saturation theory's basic logico-metaphysical aim is to solve Bradley's Regress (CO 54-55); Frege may not have known the problem of needing relations to relate relations to their relata by Bradley's name. It is not required, in Frege's view, that all references and all senses need completing or saturating to solve that problem. The problem begins as the question: How can we distinguish between an object's having a property and its not having that property? We might say: It is the distinction between that object's and that property's standing in the relation of exemplification and their not standing in that relation, respectively. But then what is the distinction between that object, property, and exemplification relation as being so related as opposed to their not being so related? A vicious regress of relations needed to relate relations ensues, and in the end, nothing is related to anything else. Frege's solution is to admit functions as intrinsically 'relating relations', as the 1903 Russell put it. Objects, and the senses expressed by object-names, are not required to be unsaturated as part of the solution. *Au contraire*. They are required to be the sort of *saturated* existent that *can* saturate unsaturated existents. And this is enough to ensure that object-names, too, have meaning only as expressions that logically *can* occur in the context of statements. For every saturation of a property or relation by an object (or by a lower-level property or relation) is theoretically describable by a statement. And every statement describes some saturation or other, or I should say, expresses a thought involving a saturation of some sort. (For the mature Frege, a statement does not describe a fact but instead names an object, either the True or the False.) With saturation theory governing the senses and the references of all names, Frege *no longer needs* to mention his 1884 context principle on the mere level of names themselves. Such a metaphysical saturation theory is just what *explains* the blank spaces to be filled in by names or variable expressions in Frege's function-names. The saturation of a concept (or property) by an object is *represented* by the placing of an object-name in one or more places occupied by the same variable in a concept-name. Dummett's own fine words on having a logical role to play in sentences as what is basic to all names for Frege (Dummett 1981: 194) surely include object-names as having a logical role in sentences, a role directly based on the *saturated* nature of their senses and references. The contribution an object-name must make to sentences simply is to express and to refer to entities which *can* saturate other entities which are unsaturated in themselves. The Hintikkas seem unaware of all this.

I offer three more comments on Hacker's account of how Frege's context principle survives in an altered form in Frege's later works. First, Hacker agrees with Dummett that Frege gives a noncontextual definition of "number belonging to the concept *F*" in *Foundations* (Hacker 1979: 223). I sharply disagree in chapter 3, section 1. Hacker's point that contextual definitions can have insurmountable problems even if the context principle is true is a good one. But Frege switches to another *kind* of contextual definition which eliminates the problems he found with the first *kind* of contextual definition he tried. Second, Hacker disagrees with Dummett on the reason why Frege first held the context principle in 1884. Dummett sees the reason as the sentence's primacy in speech (in acts of communication). Hacker sees it as the sentence's primacy in deductive inference, including inferences of new sentences with old words in new arrangements. But these reasons are not wholly distinct. Deductive inferences are themselves part of speech, and can always be written as hypothetical ("if-then") sentences. Third, Hacker's view that logical types of expressions are the basis of Frege's later context principle overlooks the real basis. For saturation and the different types of unsaturatedness are what metaphysically underwrite the different logical types of names for Frege.

Dummett raises a seemingly deeper problem for realism even when Frege's context principle is "taken simultaneously as a principle concerning sense and reference," (Dummett 1981a: 457. The problem is that since "words have no function" outside of sentences, "their semantic features [notably reference] are abstracted from the semantic features of sentences" (Dummett 1981a: 457; Donald Davidson gives the argument in "Reality Without Reference" (Davidson 1986a: 220). The argument, of course, is a *non sequitur*. Specifically, it commits the fallacy of division. And even if Dummett and Davidson are right that reference is a mere abstraction, our sentences still have objective truth-conditions. Realist semantics continues.

That Davidson's argument is invalid may be easily seen by using the Hintikkas' fine analogy in *Investigating Wittgenstein* between references and poles used to test river bottoms (IW 50–51). Suppose that poles have no function outside of testing for river bottoms. Perhaps poles always magically vanish when we try to use them for anything else. Still, the capacity of poles to test river bottoms is no mere abstraction of the sentential fact that some river bottoms are tested by us. Their capacity is based on their size, shape, and material. And while abstractions can be made at will, one cannot infer at will even that a pole was used to test a river bottom, just because that river bottom was tested. One might have dropped anchor, used sonar, dived in, or diverted the river. Here poles might be likened to Fregean senses, and the other means of testing river bottoms might be likened to other semantic vehicles such as indefinite description, definite description attributively used, or names connected to their referents by causal chains. Which vehicle is used is not a matter of abstraction, but of one's theory of generally available vehicles (Fregean senses, Russellian acquaintance, Russellian causal lines), and of one's view as to which vehicle is actually used on which actual occasion of use of the name in question. Even knowing the truth-conditions for all the sentences in which the name (or definite description) occurs does not begin to tell us that. We must look instead to things like context and speakers' intentions.

Perhaps Dummett is right that truth and reference must be understood in terms of each other, due to the internal relations between new sentences, the old words needed to construct them, and the need of even our first words to be able to play a role in sentences (Dummett 1981a: 460–61). But there is also a need to characterize reference cognitively, at least in part. Plainly, singling out and the reference relation are not the same relation. But reference is not wholly distinct from, and ultimately cannot be understood apart from, the more primitive relation of singling out on which it is based, and which David Wiggins rightly considers the most basic and direct notion of identification we have. "[O]ne may well refer to *x* in our primary sense without singling out *x* at all. (Though, if there were no singling out of anything by anyone at any time, it seems there could be no referring)" (Wiggins 1980: 5; 1971: 315–17).

In fact, Davidson has things backwards. It is the truth-conditions of a sentence which we must construct from the references of its constituent terms. This is consistent with the context principle and with (what amounts to the same thing) the principle of the logical priority of propositional unity. These principles demand only that words have references only as possibly occurring in sentences. They do not demand that words' references be mere abstractions of the truth-conditions of the sentences in which they occur. A modified realist can consistently hold that Fido is a real being, that the fact that Fido barks at Felix is a conceptual being (a construction that cannot exist without Fido), that the word "Fido" cannot name Fido unless that word can occur in sentences, that the propositional unity of the possible sentence "Fido barks at Felix" is logically prior to the mere set of words ("Fido," "Felix," "barks at"), that the fact that Fido barks at Felix is the truth-condition of "Fido barks at Felix," that when Jones says "Fido barks at Felix," she is saying something about Fido by means of a causal chain—and that her referring to Fido by a causal chain is not an abstraction or construction from either the nature of the sentence or its truth-condition, or even from the fact that that sentence has that truth-condition. For Smith might use the same sentence, with the very same truth-condition, to say something about Felix (or about barking), using his responsiveness to a question just asked, instead of Jones's reliance on conventional grammatical subject, as indicator of his logical subject-term, and using a definite description attributively as his tacitly intended semantic relation between that term and Felix (or barking).

The distinction between referential and attributive use is due to Keith Donnellan. As early as 1966, Donnellan established a referential use of language which Davidson and Quine have ignored. Donnellan says, "In general, whether or not a definite description is used referentially is a function of the speaker's intentions in a particular case. This, I think, means that the view...that sentences can be divided up into predicates, logical operators, and referring expressions is not generally true" (Donnellan 1972: 67–68). Donnellan notes that while speakers' intentions can vary on different occasions of use of "The murderer of Smith is insane," one speaker using "The murderer of Smith" referentially and another speaker not, sentential grammar and semantics remain exactly the same. Donnellan is ignored in Quine's major works and in Davidson's *Truth and Interpretation*. But Frege's notion of explication anticipates Donnellan so strongly that explication might be called "referential explication." Russell noted against Strawson that names of sensed events are referential (MPD 175–78). Surely Wittgenstein early and late would admit referential uses of names if the question were put to him. Here Quine seems the odd analyst out.

Donnellanian referential use is not destroyed by Quine's argument for referential inscrutability based on empirically equivalent interpretations. First, any reasonable determination that a term is referentially, as opposed to attributively, used is based on some empirical *in*equivalence concerning the speaker's intention. Second, there are ordinary language paradigms supporting Donnellan's distinction. Far from being inscrutable, the distinction is easy to understand. Third, any such destruction would depend on what, if anything, Quine's argument shows. I argue in chapter 7 that Quine's argument allows reference in one's home language. Far from destroying Donnellan, this might be used to support him.

Saul Kripke tries to rescue Davidson and Quine from Donnellan. Kripke sees Donnellan as discussing not semantics but speech acts, as if assertions were not speech acts. Kripke introduces the notion of a "semantic referent" as that which attributively satisfies the description in a referentially used definite description. He says that this semantic referent need not be the actual referent of the referentially used definite description. He then proceeds to ignore the actual referent in favor of the semantic referent. Kripke adds, "If…a more cautious substitute [definite description] is available, it is really the substitute which fixes the reference in the sense intended in the text." He means the intent of referring to the semantic referent, i.e. the intent of referring by a veridical description. Kripke's argument is that when the descriptive error is detected, we reject the erroneous description. I have three criticisms. First, there is no difference between the actual referent of an expression and the referent of that expression. Thus there are no semantic referents in addition to actual referents. Thus semantic referents are a false and gratuitous postulation. At most they are possible referents which are sometimes actual referents. Second, Kripke says "it is really the substitute which fixes the reference." This is not always so. Kripke overlooks not only the intended referents of many descriptions already known to be incorrect, but also the deliberately retained referents of many descriptions subsequently discovered to be incorrect. The speakers' intentions may be sarcastic, ironic, humorous, polite, politic, official, analogico-illuminative, or even time-saving. Thus reference is not always fixed by veridical description, nor always intended to be so fixed. Third, the very possibility of discarding an erroneous description because of finding a veridical substitute description presupposes the successful reference of the erroneous description in the first place. How else could we identify the referent so as to correct or even detect the error? Thus Kripke's argument is self-defeating. Indeed, the very notion of semantic reference is parasitic on that of reference. Semantic reference is merely a species of the genus reference, where veridical description is the differentia.

14. Hill's account of Frege contains some surprising errors. On her interpretation of Frege's theory of informative identity, "$a = b$" may be true "extensionally" but false "intensionally" and on the "level" of signs. Hence $(a = b)$ & $(a \neq b)$. Hence a must belong to some class to which b does not, which "begins to look like" Russell's Paradox (Hill 1991: 3, 50–51, 169). The resemblance is superficial and the argument is bizarre.

Any real resemblance would be found instead in the sense expressed by "senses impredicable of themselves," which Frege's simple theory of sense-types eliminates as ill-formed. On Hill's interpretation, see section 1. Also *pace* Hill, Frege's theory that "the concept *C*" refers not to the concept but to its extension does not lead to Russell's Paradox. Concepts do not yield the paradox, since the concept *concepts impredicable of themselves* is ill-formed on Frege's simple theory of concept-types. Only certain extensions are paradoxical. Indeed, if Frege utterly rejected the theory that "the concept *C*" refers not to the concept but to its extension, and insisted that "the concept *C*" refers to the concept itself, Russell's Paradox would arise concerning exactly the same extensions it did before. Hill takes Frege's metaphoric talk of converting concepts into objects literally (CO 46; Hill 1991: 119–20), not seeming to realize that Frege's theory of types precludes literal conversion. Even if "the sole difference between concept and extension...is the difference of *saturation*" (Furth 1967: xxxix, xlii), this is an irreducible categorial difference (CO 43). Indeed, it is this very chasm between objects and concepts which *leads* to the problem of the concept *horse*. Hill seems unaware of Frege's representation function or its role in the mutual *representation* of concepts and objects. (Even Furth forgets to include the representation function; the "sole" prefixing of an empty level 0 argument-place, *sans* representation function, to a course-of-values-name scarcely yields a first-level concept-name, or even a well-formed expression.) Hill even claims that Frege had to "blur" the first-level relation of objectual identity and the second-level relation of concept-equality (Hill 1991: 44–46, 120, 150, 168–69). Hill wildly says of *Foundations* sect. 65, "If two objects are equal in a certain way then, [Frege] has reasoned, for all intents and purposes they are equal in all ways" (Hill 1991: 46). But even in Hill's own examples, Frege is saying that if certain objects are similar in some respect, say, two lines are parallel, then certain *other* objects, in this case the *directions* of those lines, are identical (FA 76). Similarly for the second-level *equality* of concepts and the first-level *identity* of the numbers belonging to them. The only blur of type-levels is Hill's. The only way Frege would call objects equal is to speak of numbers as equal. And to say numbers are equal is to say they are identical. Numbers cannot be equal in one "way" and unequal in another. Either they are equal or they are not.

Hill goes so far as to say that "Frege's analyses...led to gross problems with substitution (notably that from...'Socrates is wise' and 'Tully is wise' we can conclude that Socrates is Tully)" (Hill 1991: 120). Hill seems to mean that Frege would allow the inference from Socrates = wise and Tully = wise that Socrates = Tully (Hill 1991: 151). But even a casual reading of "On Concept and Object" reveals that Frege would have regarded Hill's inference as ill-formed due to mixing up type-levels. Again, the only 'gross problem' of mixing up type-levels is Hill's.

Hill's revisionist account of Frege also includes misidentifying the unsaturated with the indeterminate (Hill 1991: 93), despite Frege's requirement that all entities, including unsaturated entities, be determinate (BL I 29).

Hill offers trendy suggestions of Fregean "points of view" (Hill 1991: 46) such that "reference is always perspectival" (Hill 1991: 158). But as Hill herself says elsewhere, concepts are "guarantors of objectivity" (Hill 1991: 130).

Chapter 3: Existence Defined as Identifiability

1. This one is in Frege, "The Thought" (Frege 1956: 299–302). The other eleven are: three in *Foundations* (FA 35, 36, and 37); two in *Basic Laws* (BL 15–16, 23); two in *Translations* (TW 79, 120–21); two in *Posthumous Writings* (PW 133–34; 269–70); one in *Philosophical and Mathematical Correspondence* (Frege 1980: 80); and one in "On the Scientific Justification of a Conceptual Notation," (CN 83–86).

2. For splitting up and related metaphors, see FA 34, 43, 73–74, 100–1. See CO 49 on the analysis of thoughts. Compare BL 92–94.

3. The second-level relation of equivalence, (A) $(x)(\phi x = \psi x)$, would be mutually represented by the first-level relation (B) $(x)[(x \cap \xi) \cap ((x \cap \zeta) \cap \dot{\alpha}\dot{\epsilon}(\epsilon = \alpha))]$. But (B) can be rewritten as (C) $\xi \cap (\zeta \cap \dot{\alpha}\dot{\epsilon}(\epsilon = \alpha))$, and (C) can be rewritten as (D) $\xi = \zeta$. I use "ϕ", "ψ", "ξ", and "ζ" to mark the argument-places (see BL 94–95).

4. On the extensionality thesis, Frege's definitional program in *Basic Laws* I 29, (BL 84) states, for each of several sorts of function-names, a logically sufficient condition of their denoting functions. In each case the condition boils down to their mapping values onto arguments in a logically determinate (i.e. exhaustive) manner. But in every case, the very condition of their denoting is also a sufficient condition of representative identifiability of the functions denoted. That is because a function is represented precisely by its own course-of-values. (This is the representative aspect of the identity of indiscernibles.) Also, the truth of "The concept F is representatively identifiable" is a sufficient condition of the existence of $F(\ )$ itself, since it must exist to be represented identifiably by the object denoted by "the concept F."

5. This is why for Frege there is no "Hegelian deduction" of the existence of the existence of Herr Krug's pen from its (mere) self-identity or even from the axiom $(x)(x = x)$, *pace* Benardete (1989: 20–24). *Basic Laws* I 29 makes this plain.

6. On forces, see BL 37–38, and "The Thought" (Frege 1956: 293–95). On senses and tones, see chapter 2, section 1.

7. The correspondences in the *Tractatus* might include: ethical or aesthetic act—ethical or aesthetic pleasure or displeasure (T 147); God—the world (T 143, 149); causation—constant conjunction (T 143); the thinking subject—the human being (T 119).

Chapter 4: Russell's Robust Sense of Reality

1. Ivor Grattan-Guinness, in a very kind note to me dated August 16, 1990, distinguishes five formal senses of "exists" in Russell: $(\exists x)$, $E!(\iota x)\iota x$, $\exists_\alpha^\phi$, $\exists!\alpha$, and $\exists \alpha$ (Grattan-Guinness 1990; see Grattan-Guinness 1973: 10, 15–16, 33–35, 66–74). The more Russellian senses of "exists," the merrier. See the *Principia* List of Definitions for further variations.

2. Often it is objects that exist only in the primary sense which are deemed weak or shadowy beings; but that puts the cart before the horse. I suspect that the mythological chimera is nothing, not even a "linguistic being." But our concern is with objects of acquaintance, the primary "building blocks" of Russell's constructive world.

There is a timeless sense of satisfaction in which a propositional function's satisfaction cannot be gained or lost. This seems in fact to be Russell's sense (PM 41n). But that does not affect my point.

3. It is not logically necessary that particulars be informatively identifiable, since the meanings of logically proper names for them are completely given in acquaintance (PLA 202), and "[e]ach might happen to be the whole universe" (PLA 202). Russell says "it will be generally implied that" we are not acquainted with things we know by description, but allows that it is possible (PP 53). "This is the fifth patch below the green patch in my visual field" can easily be an informative identity for me. The explanation is that we do not always know all the properties and relations of a sense-datum when we are acquainted with it (KEW 110–14).

4. The idea that Parmenides was the first purely logical philosopher dates back at least to Hegel. Hegel says, "With Parmenides, philosophising proper began" (quoted in Russell 1985a: 373n).

5. The later Wittgenstein accepts language-games and forms of life. Quine accepts theories. The later Russell has a holistic theory of knowledge, if not of truth or meaning.

6. Thomas Magnell (1991) asks two basic questions. First, if Russell has a modal logic, where may we find it in his writings? In *Principia*, though not announced as such. The modal logic I call "MDL" is the key to reinterpreting *Principia* as functioning as a modal logic. Why expect poor Russell to rewrite *Principia* when he can explain how to reinterpret it in a few brief lines?

Second, if Russell has a modal logic, what is its S1–S5 strength? MDL is the basis of Russell's modal logic. But we cannot look directly to MDL for the answer. MDL predicates 'necessity' of propositional functions, not of propositions. MDL says only that $F(x)$ is necessary with respect to x just in case $F(x)$ is always true. Now, a fully generalized statement which is always true with respect to every one of its variables is necessary without qualification. This, Russell says, is how he intends to analyze logical truths (1994a; the unpublished ms. transcript is cited as c. 1903–5). But he later adds that a logical truth is true in virtue of its logical form, since he comes to realize that full generalization alone is not a sufficient condition of logical truth. Call this new modal logic "FG–MDL*". MDL is just a stepping-stone to FG–MDL*. Now, logical form is timeless and unchanging. Thus in FG–MDL*, whatever is possible is necessarily possible. And that is the distinctive axiom of S5. Thus Russell has the strongest of the S1–S5 logics without admitting any modal entities or even modal notions; 'always true' is a veridical notion. In fact, FG–MDL* is stronger than S5. Insofar as Russell admits $(x)(x = x)$ as a logical truth (see PM *24.01; PLA 245–46), FG–MDL* is S5 + I, where I is $\Box(x)(x = x)$. Of course, Russell did not intend that FG–MDL* have a specific S-strength, since he developed FG–MDL* while unaware of C. I. Lewis's S-logics.

7. Gaskin dislikes Russell's "curious doctrine of the 'two-fold nature' of verbs" and notes that Russell himself admits he does "'not know how to give a precise account of the distinction' [POM 50]. Russell's pessimism is well placed: the moral of Frege's paradox is indeed that nothing can play both the roles which Frege assigns to verbs [i.e. logical subject over which one may quantify, and incomplete logical predicate which stops Bradley's Regress]." (Gaskin 1995: 167). Gaskin's own resolution of Bradley's Regress is that the mere copula, i.e., the predicative "is," binds logical predicate to logical subject(s) can refer to a relation of "predicative being" which philosophers can talk about, yet generate only a harmless version of the regress: instantiations of instantiations, which Gaskin compares to iterations of "trues" ("Sentence S is true"). Gaskin concludes that we must "distinguish, in every predicate, a strictly predicative element (the copula), and a strictly non-predicative conceptual component (available to

be quantified over)" (Gaskin 1995: 177). E.g., in "is red" only the "is" is predicative; the "red" is a complete proper name of a color.

I have several comments. First, the 1903 Russell is no pessimist, and his solution seems as clear as it need be. Gaskin overlooks Russell's explanation of the dual nature of verbs as a relation considered in itself as opposed to actually relating something (POM 84, 100). That is a fairly simple distinction of reason, not much harder to understand than considering a hammer in itself as opposed to actually hammering a nail with it. What compares to hammering a nail is simply asserting a proposition.

Second, Gaskin has a rather narrow conception of ontologically committal quantification because he connects reference with being nameable by a proper name. In effect, Gaskin is willing to quantify over properties only if we regard them as second-level *objects* (Gaskin 1995: 173). Now, some may require that all entities be complete as Russell does in *Principia*. But I see no reason why Frege cannot admit essentially incomplete concepts (i.e. properties) and allow them to be denoted by incomplete concept-names, and even quantified over by second-level quantification. The real question is whether incomplete entities are entities. It seems to me that the main arguments will be by analogy to various incomplete things. Such arguments will be inconclusive even if they are not question-begging. (If wars exist, then judging that a nearly complete war is a war would presuppose that some incomplete entities are entities.)

Third and most interestingly, Gaskin says nothing about what Russell—or Frege—would or could do with the copula, i.e., the predicative "is." It strikes me that they might not be so different from Gaskin's mentor Wiggins, who stops Bradley's Regress by making the copula a syncategorematic (i.e. nondenoting) tie that binds, or even from Gaskin himself. My own gloss of Frege and Russell is that incomplete predicative expressions subsume the copula precisely as their incompleteness. In fact, Russell makes much the same distinction within a predicate between a nondenotative connective predicative element and a denotative conceptual element Gaskin does. The 1903 Russell finds a constant element and at least one variable in every propositional function (see POM 49, 107). The 1911 Russell says that every propositional function has a determinate constituent and at least one undetermined constituent, the latter indicated by a variable (MAL 165). I submit that the argument-place(s) variables mark are both ties that bind and syncategorematic copulas, since they are the *loci* of a predicate's incompleteness. I would gloss Frege much the same way. And while that is what I think Frege and Russell actually do, instead they *could* have admitted the predicative relation as a relation with no more difficulty than Gaskin does. I agree that they do not because they want to stop Bradley's Regress; but even aside from that, it would be inelegant not to use Occam's razor where such a relation need not be assumed. Gaskin demands that there exist an entity, a predicative relation, so that philosophers have something to talk about when they discuss the predicative "is" (Gaskin 1995: 175). This argument is too easy. Why not demand round squares so that philosophers have something to talk about when they discuss "round square"? Why not demand God and angels so that philosophers have something to talk about when they discuss "God" and "angels"?

8. Thus the problem described in the previous note disappears in the 1918 Russell. Predicates and relations no longer have a dual-aspected nature. Gaskin would still have a problem with Russell's solution of using semantic ascent to "'Red' is a predicate" to be able to talk about red (PLA 205). Namely, "remaining at the level of language is not a posture which can be indefinitely sustained. At some point we will have to acknow-

ledge that language is connected to the world....Instead of saying that the paradox is not genuine because we can always shift from the ontological to the linguistic level, where it does not arise, one might as well say that the fact that we can always shift from the linguistic level, to the ontological, where it does arise, shows that it is genuine" (Gaskin 1995: 166). I find this argument too general. With a little charity to the 1918 Russell, the ontological level consists precisely of talking about red by using sentences such as "This is red." We might also appeal to "Being red is something I can understand" (see chapter 3, section 3), or even "Green is grass." Green grow the rushes, ho! This is not to mention my third comment on Gaskin in note 7.

Chapter 5: Russell's Forty-four 'No Entity without Identity' Theories

1. Both (i) "the class of classes not members of themselves" (POM 101–7) and (ii) "the null class" (POM 75) must be nondenoting. Russell says (iii) the phrase "is 30. per cent. healthier" is nondenoting (POM 176). (iv) The phrase "the particularized relation" (i.e. "the relation which is a particular") is nondenoting (POM 211). (v) Russell rejects Frege's view that certain function-expressions denote functions (POM 508–10). (vi) All motions are fictions (POM 473). (vii) A component vector of a motion "is doubly a fiction," not even being a motion (POM 474). (viii) Infinitesimal rational or real numbers are rejected as impossible (POM 335). (ix) Infinitesimal magnitudes as orders of functions are rejected as impossible (POM 336–37).

2. That Russell's notion of a term is a modification of Moore's notion of a concept (POM 44n) does not make the notion of being in *Principles* 'merely conceptual'. For Moore, concepts are universals that have mind-independent being. Russell cites Moore (1899); see Moore (1899: 179, 192) and Moore (1966c: 383). The early Moore and early Russell are famous for their close agreement on a jungle realism of mind-independent beings.

3. Simo Knuuttila says, "Scotus seems to think that the possibility of being identified as something is the most primary constituent of the positive nature of whatever is and, as such, is the real basis for the univocal metaphysical concept of being....In the metaphysical sense *ens* [for Scotus] is a univocal word which can be truly applied to anything which can be thought of as identified and which is therefore something positive and distinct from the nothingness of impossible things." (Knuuttila 1986: 208). This comes closest, among Russell's many metaphysical phases, to his neo-Meinongian realism in *Principles* (Russell misconstrues Meinong as holding that nonexistents have being).

4. See IMT 97, 102–3, 130; HK 83. Russell flatly asserts that the identity of indiscernibles is analytic on his view (IMT 103). The deepest ground of the analyticity is obviously the metaphysical nature of bundles itself. A thing is a bundle of qualities with certain properties, including relational properties. D. M. Armstrong, Albert Casullo, and Michael Loux question these two elementary points and assert that the identity of indiscernibles is not definitely a necessary truth for Russell. See Michael Bradley for a good reply (M. Bradley 1986: 325–33). For now it is enough to observe that Armstrong, Casullo, and Loux are suggesting in effect that for Russell, analytic truths are not necessary truths. Russell does weaken the analytic-synthetic distinction in 1948, and there is a strong anticipation of that in the introduction to the second edition of *Principles* (POM ix), and even in *Principia* (PM 59). The trio's best line would be

that Russell says that it is "the principle merit of the [bundle theory] that it makes the identity of indiscernibles analytic" (IMT 103), as if another theory might not *make* it analytic. Russell calls the bundle theory "tentative" (Russell 1989a: 685). And he argues in 1948 that constructions 'conceal' inferences (HK 139)—and the bundle theory certainly was inferred by arguments. All this makes the *Inquiry* view that the identity of indiscernibles is analytic a mere construction that conceals our tentative inference of the bundle theory. But by the same token, this also shows that *on* the *Inquiry* theory, the identity of indiscernibles *is* analytic, hence tautologous, hence necessarily true. Also, Russell makes the analyticity of that principle virtually a *criterion* of the correctness of the bundle theory (IMT 103).

Casullo interprets Russell's qualities as universals. Casullo dismisses Russell's later statements on the subject as unreliable reporting since Russell is in general a notoriously unreliable reporter of his views, and dismisses other possibly relevant statements as statements of a manifestly new theory. The result is that Casullo rests his case on the *Inquiry* itself. One such later statement is in "Reply to Criticisms": "Like most other people, Mr. Weitz has failed to understand the tentative theory, set forth in the *Inquiry*, according to which a given shade of colour is a particular, not a universal" (Russell 1989a: 685). Russell even repeats the point: "According to my theory in the *Inquiry*,....My view is that a particular shade of colour (or any other precisely defined quality) is a particular, not a universal" (Russell 1989a: 714). Casullo's rejection of it would seem to presuppose some sort of probability argument counting all the sentences in which Russell describes his past views and finding that the vast majority of them are false. But it seems to me that these two statements are so definite that the burden is on those who consider them a misreport based on such a remote general probability argument. Just how likely is it that when Russell twice reports a major revision of theory in his *Inquiry* only four years after he wrote it, namely, that in that book he held for the first time ever that sensible qualities are particulars and not universals, that both reports were deluded ravings, there was no such major revision, and he really held in that book exactly the opposite, that sensible qualities are universals and not particulars? Has anyone made a statistical survey of all of Russell's reports of earlier views?

Now let us turn to the *Inquiry* itself. Russell says, "A 'universal' may be defined as 'the meaning (if any) of a relation-word'" (IMT 343). Thus it would seem that qualities are not universals, since only relations can be universals by definition. But in a kind note to me dated January 9, 1991, Casullo notes that Russell says on the same page, "Sentences...require words other than names. Such words, generically, we call 'relation-words', including predicates as words for monadic relations" (Casullo 1991). Casullo argues: "For Russell predicates are monadic relations. Hence his conclusions regarding relations apply also to qualities" (Casullo 1991). Casullo supposes that quality-words are predicates, in particular, words for monadic relations. Casullo is right that Russell accepts monadic universals. Namely, Russell accepts as monadic universals the abstract monadic universals such as "colour, sound, taste, etc." which Russell accepts in *My Philosophical Development* (MPD 127). But the very passage Casullo quotes proves that qualities are not monadic universals. For in that passage, words for monadic relations (i.e. monadic universals) are predicates, and predicates are words other than names. And Russell flatly says that a quality-word is "a name, not a predicate." Russell says this in chapter 6, entitled "Proper Names":

I wish to suggest that, wherever there is, for common sense, a "thing" having the quality C, we should say, instead, that C itself exists in that place, and that the "thing" is to be replaced by the collection of qualities existing in the place in question. Thus "C" becomes a name, not a predicate. (IMT 98)

Russell states the point even more plainly a second time, speaking of his "theory developed in the chapter on proper names, according to which 'hotness'...is a proper name, not a universal of which there is one instance in A and another in B" IMT 227). Russell makes plain that he upholds that theory in *Inquiry* (IMT 230–31).

There is also the consideration of the structure of logic itself in *Inquiry*. Namely, qualities are now ultimate subjects of predication. This is the whole point of Russell's rejection of instances of qualities. Now to suggest that these type 0 order 0 logically proper names of qualities are names of universals is to destroy *Principia* logic completely. For in *Principia* logic, type 0 order 0 names denoting ultimate subjects of predication are complete and denote individuals. It is predicates which are incomplete and, at most, indicate concepts (i.e., universals with which we are acquainted). Names complete the lowest type-level of predicates. In this, names reflect the fact that individuals exemplify universals. Now no scholar has ever suggested that Russell abandons *Principia* logic in the *Inquiry*, much less gives a theory in *Inquiry* totally incompatible with the *Principia* theory of logico-metaphysical types. But Casullo is committed to holding that Russell either is making bottom level proper names incomplete for the first time, or else is keeping them complete but making them name universals. But Russell gives every indication of conforming to *Principia* logic as always (IMT 194–203). And the plain implication is that qualities are Russell's new individuals, individuals that exemplify relation-universals, including monadic abstract universals. The only evidence that qualities are universals in *Inquiry* is that (i) Russell used to hold that view, and (ii) Russell allows in *Inquiry* that qualities can recur. But *pace* (i), the *Inquiry* itself, as I just explained, shows that Russell changed his mind. And *pace* (ii), water, sand, and gold, and many other things not normally considered universals, can be in many places at once, even if *Inquiry*'s qualities are not scattered particulars in Quine's sense. In the *Inquiry* the whole of water, understood as all the puddles and lakes (and so on) there are, does not recur to the right of itself (not in the world as it is); but the whole of a shade of red can and often does (IMT 100–3).

I grant Casullo that there is a philosophical tension between the *Inquiry* doctrine that qualities are particulars and the *Inquiry* view that qualities can be in many places at once. Indeed, it might seem that the latter is precisely the identity condition that constitutes universality. But predicative identity also seems to constitute universality. Russell might be showing sensitivity to this when he says in "Logic and Ontology," "Finally, the question 'Are there universals?' is ambiguous" (MPD 175). Now, the ambiguity is equally about the word "individual." There is the Frege-Russell objectual sense in which individuals are ultimate instances of predication. And there is the spatial sense in which individuals are items that can be in only one place at a time. But the general objectual sense is surely deeper than the specifically spatial sense, and Russell is surely aware of that. Thus the tension resolves in favor of my view.

Finally, Casullo says "you couldn't make sense of what Russell regards as the primary obstacle to getting rid of 'things' [the old mere instances]" unless qualities were universals. The obstacle in question is defining "place" (IMT 98–99). But that makes sense to Russell as the main obstacle precisely because qualities *are* recurring particulars (IMT 100–3).

5. C. F. Presley erroneously speaks of Russell and Quine almost in the same breath concerning ontic import (Presley 1967: 7/54). So does A. J. Ayer (1972: 54). Even Grattan-Guinness makes his first Russellian sense of "exists," existential quantification for individuals, ontological as opposed to conventional (Grattan-Guinness 1973: 71).

On the ontological commitment of Quine's existential quantifier, see OR 94–99; WO 176, 184, 242; PQ 533–34. Compare Wang on Frege's influence on Quine (Wang 1987: 634).

I suggest that the *Principles* distinction between classes-as-many and classes-as-one passes over in *Principia* to that between class existence and individual quantification for apparent individuals. On *24.03, hallucinated rats would "exist" as classes(-as-many) of wild particulars with at least one member. But hallucinated rats would not "exist" as apparent individuals (classes-as-one), since they would not have enough lawfully correlated members to "exist" in the secondary sense. See POM 523. On my gloss, Russell demotes classes-as-one from individuals to groups of correlated particulars, in keeping with the not-always-false individual quantifier as used to quantify truly over logical fictions.

Russell's *Principia* 'not always false' existential quantifier must not be confused with substitutional quantification, either in the current sense of quantification over names as opposed to objects or in the sense in which Russell endorsed it in 1906. But there are some resemblances. See Hylton (1980: 1–31) and Landini (1987: 171–200).

6. Alan Richardson cites Coffa (1985: 145–46). Actually Coffa discusses neutral monism, which is not idealism. The whole point of neutral monism is that its building blocks are neutral. If Richardson has access to unpublished Coffa papers stating that Russell's 1914–18 constructionism is ontological idealism, I have not seen them. But Richardson himself was certainly caught red-handed (Richardson 1989). He graciously acknowledged he had not done his Russell homework, and now agrees that the 1914 Russell, unlike the *Aufbau* Carnap, is a realist (Richardson 1990: 8).

In 1914 Russell construes his view as realist. He follows Moore in making sensed sense-data mind-independent and even physical (MAL 144, 146). Russell also admits unsensed sensibilia, which are the same kind of event, though nobody has sensed them. Unsensed sensibilia are very obviously mind-independent. He does admit that this is not traditional realism. See MAL 115–18, 120, 123, 125ff. 144–47; PP 14 on the sensation/sense-datum distinction, and PP 41–42 on the act-object distinction. By 1918 sensed particulars (sense-data) are "completely self-subsistent….Each one might happen to be the whole universe" (PLA 201–2). Obviously, the existence of minds is not necessary even for the existence of *sensed* particulars; they need not have been sensed. Last, see MPD 79 on 1914.

7. Though simultaneity is relative to observers' frames of reference, Russell may keep his relation of compresence of events, insofar as it applies to neighboring local events in the private perspective of a single observer. See Russell (1958: 39, 47–48) and AMA 385. Compare Einstein (1961: 31–32; see 95 on "physical existence").

8. Thus Russell already had an answer to the 'current' problem of how vague objects can have identity. On vagueness, see PLA 179–81; AMA 319; POM xi; IMT 57, 98, 103–7, 119, 315; HK 61–63, 67, 86, 98, 146–48, 186–88, 225–26, 238, 260–61, 393–95, 424, 497; MPD 152; LK 329, 338; and Russell 1988a.

9. Reference theorists seem unaware that Russell offers a sophisticated causal theory of names involving social use, habits, training, reflexes, and laws of association in *The Analysis of Mind*, chapter 10, *An Outline of Philosophy*, part 1, chapter 4, and *Human Knowledge*, part 2, chapters 1–3. Obviously Russell now wants a much fuller theory of how ordinary names denote than his old descriptivist theory of 1905–18. Causal chain reference theorists are unaware of Russell's anticipation of their theory: "The community that speaks a language has learnt it, and modified it by processes almost all of which are not deliberate, but the results of causes operating according to more or less ascertainable laws. If we trace Indo-European languages back far enough, we arrive hypothetically...at the stage when language consisted only of the roots out of which subsequent words have grown" (AMI 190). Putnam's suggestion that names refer to whatever a community of experts would refer to by them, and the suggestion that names refer to whatever the 'linguistic community' at large refers to by them, are anticipated by Russell's encyclopedia and geography book examples (HK 79, 102). These suggestions are noted in Fumerton, "Russelling Causal Theories of Reference" (Fumerton 1989: 111, 114), whose very title ignores Russell's own causal theory of reference. Fumerton is unaware that his own theory that a name I use refers to the individual I think of, "whose being called by some name resulted in this use of the name" (Fumerton 1989: 115) was anticipated in *Human Knowledge*: "when you speak of Mrs. B., you may be mentally defining her as 'the lady whose name is "Mrs. B."'" (HK 87). Again, adults "will naturally suppose that the French have a way of naming bread" (HK 64). Russell adds, "When we mean to think about Napoleon, we substitute the description 'the man whose name was "Napoleon"'" (HK 89). And there is 'purely verbal' knowledge: "When I believe 'William the Conqueror, 1066', what I am really believing (as a rule) is: 'The words "William the Conqueror, 1066" are true'" (HK 96–97). Even (noncausal) description-cluster theorists, who analyze names as vaguely defined disjuncts of definite descriptions, are anticipated by HK 79. And the 1911 Russell anticipates the mentalistic Fumerton and the cluster theorists in one fell swoop: "When we, who did not know Bismarck, make a judgment about him, the description in our minds will probably be some more or less vague mass of historical knowledge—far more, in most cases, than is required to identify him" (MAL 209).

In result, not only does Fumerton make the fine point that any causal theory can be 'Russelled' by rewriting it as a definite description, but the point is more Russellian than Fumerton thinks. When Russell made the point himself 41 years before Fumerton, he did not 'Russell' causal theory, since it was his own theory. Rather, he integrated his definite-description-and-causal theory. The definiteness of the definite descriptions, of course, superimposes a 'no entity without identity' requirement on Russell's causal theory of names' reference.

Fumerton also misses that causal theorists can return the favor and recast any use of a definite description as the last link in a causal chain. And Fumerton's descriptive thoughts of individuals are fair game to be such last causal links—as much as written or spoken descriptions are. (For the 1919–40 Russell such thoughts would be image-propositions or word-propositions, perhaps along with some habitual expectations.) Thus Fumerton does not achieve victory for descriptive theories, but a hopeless stalemate instead. But Russell is in fine shape with his integrative theory.

That causal chains and descriptions can be always recast as each other does not affect my point, chapter 2, note 13, last paragraphs on the Davidsonian problem, that in practice some references are more naturally described as made by causal chains, and others by definite descriptions. Such a flexibility is of course also open to Russell, and is in fact exuberantly practiced by him, as we can see in the first paragraph of this note.

Fumerton is only following the crowd. For instance, Leonard Linky expounds Russell without a clue as to Russell's embracing of cluster theory or causal theory, and even suggests Russell would be much improved by adding aspects of those theories! (L. Linsky 1977: 93–111). Hilary Putnam says in praise of Devitt's *Designation*, "In recent years a new 'causal' theory of reference and meaning, based on the works of Saul Kripke, Hilary Putnam, and Keith Donnellan, has taken a position of prominence in the philosophy of language. The first serious effort to work out...the details of the new theory, Michael Devitt's book provides a theory of...'designation'—and shows the bearing of this relationship on the meanings of various simple and complex expressions" (Putnam 1981). Putnam is merely pretending, as many do, that Russell died in 1918. Putnam's praise better describes *Human Knowledge*, the *Inquiry*, which appeared over forty years before Devitt's book, or *The Analysis of Matter*, which already connected Jones by multiple causal lines to users of "Jones" in 1927 (AMA 154, 203, 217, 314), or even *The Analysis of Mind*, written sixty years before Devitt's book.

Kripke is perhaps the most famous critic of Russell who seems unaware that Russell holds a causal theory of reference not that far from his own (Kripke 1980).

That Russell has a Humean analysis of causation does not detract from anything I have said in the present note.

10. See Hager (1987: 3–10) on Russell's vagaries on Zeno.

11. The Whitehead-Russell way of defining points and regions is given in KEW 91–102; AMA 290–312. Russell criticizes Carnap's approach (HK 74–78). Russell says that Carnap in effect makes regions neo-Cartesian–Democritean substances, i.e., substrata. Thus like Salmon and McCann, he makes the right criticism but rather overstates it. Susan Hale very kindly sent me a copy of her "A Defense of Giving Identity Conditions for Events in Purely Spatiotemporal Terms," citing Wesley Salmon (1969: 95–97), and McCann (unpublished ms.) For an abstract of Hale's paper, see Hale (1989: 63). Dummett observes that we cannot know an event's location in or path through space unless we can already identify the event (*pace* Michael Ayers), and that we cannot know an event's causes or effects unless we can already identify the event, *pace* Davidson (Dummett 1991: 113). On Loux, Strawson, and Wiggins see (Loux 1970: 202–3; 203 n.7; Wiggins 1970: 310–12). See also POM 452; IMT 96–97; HK 292.

12. Davidson's earlier definition was given in Davidson (1985a: 179); Davidson rejects it in Davidson (1985b: 175). Loux and Wiggins suggest various ways out of the circularity which I shall not discuss (Loux 1970: 203; Wiggins 1970: 312–16ff.).

13. Davidson's criterion of events' identity in terms of their causes and effects may be circular. Yet the indiscernibility of identicals may well mandate that the warming and spinning of the ball be different events, if they have different causes and effects. Davidson himself suggests that events are distinguished by "our predicates" (Davidson 1985b: 176). But only certain component vectors of the micro-complex curves would have the same causes and effects as the macro-spinning. Other component vectors would have the same causes and effects as the macro-warming. And component vectors are "doubly" analytic fictions, not even being motions, where all motions are fictions (POM 473–74).

14. Russell does not say so, but I suspect that universals with which we are acquainted through the senses are virtually as vague as the sense-data (particulars) that instantiate them. Recall that colors and shapes are themselves sense-data (PP 12, 46, 101), and that all sense-data are vague (MAL 88). We learn to become acquainted with sensible universals through a fairly direct process of abstraction (PP 101–3). Universals with logically sharp identity conditions require much higher abstractions. All our logical and mathematical knowledge is of abstract universals (PP 103–9; OD 41). Such knowledge involves what we might gloss as intellectual acquaintance (see MAL 154–55). Recall that the principle of acquaintance applies to all propositions (MAL 159, 167; PP 58). Universals are the determinate constituents of all propositional functions (see MAL 165). Thus it seems that 'no vague entity without vague identity' applies to real particulars, sensible universals, and to any vague abstract universals which may exist in the primary sense of "exists." (Surely the logical woods are full of vague abstract universals.) And 'no sharp entity without sharp identity' applies to constructions in the secondary sense of "exists"—but applies to sharp abstract universals in the primary sense of "exists." For universals are entities, not logical constructions.

Chapter 6: The Ancient Realist Basis of Conceptual Relativity

1. On "formula" see Owens (1963: 351 n.18) and Apostle's glossary in *Aristotle's Metaphysics* (Aristotle 1973: 460). Compare *Posterior Analytics* 71*a–b* on "qualified knowledge."

Physics 202*b* has other examples as well. Angelelli mentions several examples from Aristotle and directly compares Frege (Angelelli 1967: 52–54, 80 n.25. On Eubulides, see Kneale (1964: 114). Jean Buridan mentions Choriscus and the one coming in *Questions on Aristotle's Metaphysics*, Book 4, Question 8 (Hyman 1973: 713). Inference failure of identity statements in epistemic contexts was described by Walter Burleigh (Weidemann 1980: 32ff.). Ivan Boh very kindly sent me Weidemann's article on Burleigh. See also Boh (1993).

2. While saying that Cornford may be right about the Platonic background, Owens cautions that Plato does not use the word "equivocal" exactly as Aristotle does (Owens 1963: 109–10).

3. See also Apostle's notes in *Aristotle's Metaphysics* (Aristotle 1973: 266 n.43; 279 n.25, n.31; 282 n.9; 305 n.10; 311 n.6, n.7).

4. W. G. de Burgh brings out the broad similarity of the relations of the category of substance to the other categories (Burgh 1967: 462–63). Conversely, G. E. M. Anscombe and P. T. Geach note that one may wish to distinguish an even greater variety of kinds of categories than Aristotle does (Anscombe 1961: 11–12, 14–16).

5. Anscombe and Geach give different formulations of relative identity, not equivalent and not always linguistic (Anscombe 1961: 8, 10, 21–22). Anscombe and Geach draw the metaphysical conclusion from their theory that featureless being or matter cannot exist—as if "This is the same *featureless being* as that" did not perfectly conform to relative identity. They proceed to infer that Aristotle cannot have admitted such a being on the strength of their interpretation. They forget the primacy of Aristotelian things and their identity over concepts and words (Owens 1963: 126–29). For the primacy of things and their identity over any intellectual activity of ours, and

over our determination of their essences by the lengthy process of division see Ross (1960: 52–55); see even Suárez (1947: 16–18, 22). Ross describes all that is required to arrive at the essence which Anscombe and Geach claim Aristotle needs to identify a thing (Ross 1960: 52–55). Without any prior knowledge of the identity of things, even the first step in the process cannot be taken; even the first provisional concept cannot be applied to things. Also note that Aristotle expressly makes primary matter featureless (*Metaphysics* 1029a19–26). Though primary matter is relative and merely potential, it is surely not nothing. Aristotle is well aware of Parmenides.

6. Owens deems Aristotle's universals or universal predicates "concepts," and also makes multivocal being a "concept" (Owens 1963: 423). Thus Aristotle's categories are concepts. (This does not make Aristotle's substances a category of mere conceptual beings in the sense explained in my chapter 1.)

7. Jaakko Hintikka is well aware of relative pronouns as the crucial test of ontological commitment (J. Hintikka 1986: 98). Quine stresses relative pronouns (PQ 184–85, 533). Pronouns in general are stressed in *Word and Object* and in *Pursuit of Truth*. Frege can easily use this test, though the post-*Principles* Russell abandoned it (MPD 118, 173, 175). See chapter 5, section 2.

8. Russell, too, upholds a context principle. As Quine says, "Russell gave contextual definition its fullest exploitation in technical logic" (Quine 1981c: 26). The 1903 Russell might seem to reject the context principle: "[E]very word occurring in a sentence must have some [*independent*] meaning..." (POM 42). This is the view the later Russell came to reject in favor of ascribing only "meaning in use" to all words except logically proper names (POM x). But in *Principles*, every term is a logical subject, i.e., a propositional part (POM 44), and a proposition is prior in unity to its parts (POM 139). Propositions are "more fundamental than...classes [or propositional functions]" (POM 13, 31). What is more, Charles Kahn's order of priority for uses of "is" (first copulative, then veridical, then existential) mirrors the 1903 Russell's: "The notion of denoting may be obtained by a kind of logical genesis from subject-predicate propositions, upon which it seems...dependent" (POM 54). And when it comes to defining numbers, Russell makes it essential to be able to tell when "two classes have the same number" (POM 113). Thus numerical identity propositions are prior to numbers. Russell disclaims originality for his propositional contextualism; he attributes it to Hugh MacColl (POM 12).

Russell's contextualism in *Principles* refutes Dummett's fears that contextualism goes against realism. *Principles* is a work of extreme Platonic and even neo-Meinongian realism. Perhaps Hans Sluga, who views Frege's *Foundations* and Wittgenstein's *Tractatus* as Kantian objective idealism due to their contextualist views, would care to interpret Russell's *Principles* as Kantian objective idealism. Sluga's reading of *Foundations*, by the way, is selective. Frege says there, "Astronomy is concerned, not with ideas of the planets, but with the planets themselves" (FA 37). Sluga founders on that rock, not to say planet, of *Foundations* interpretation (Sluga 1980: 54–55, 94-95, 120, 123–24, 133–34, 182).

In *Principia*, propositions are incomplete symbols; but the mere judgment that a proposition is true completes it (PM 44). Propositional functions are derived in the manner Frege's functions are, by slicing up sentences. Logically proper names have "independent meanings," but this only means that they denote individuals. They must still be capable of sentential use, if they are to be admitted as names at all. For they must serve to represent the determination of variables (PM 4–5). In "The Philosophy of

Logical Atomism," not only are propositional functions incomplete, and nothing apart from sentences, but even 'self-subsistent' particulars are defined as "terms of relations in atomic facts" (PLA 199), where "fact" is 'explained' in turn as "the kind of thing that makes a proposition true or false" (PLA 182; see 183). The 1921 Russell agrees with the psychologist Théodule Ribot that "'the concept is the result of judgment'" (AMI 223). In the *Inquiry*, object words are sentential assertions in their own right (IMT 26, 29). Yet Russell is undogmatic enough to poke fun at overblown contextualism (OP 54). Again, Russell is a realist admitting some mind-independent items in each of these works.

9. Hintikka speaks of "the identity sense of *esti*" (J. Hintikka 1986: 84), and speaks three times of "a predicative sense" (J. Hintikka 1986: 84, 86, 89). He speaks of "the predicative sense and the existential one" (J. Hintikka 1986: 89). But the whole thesis of his article is that there are no such senses in Aristotle, only uses! Thus Hintikka blurs his own sense-use distinction.

The important 'purely existential use' text to which Hintikka rightly draws our attention is, "for some objects of inquiry we have a different kind of question to ask, such as whether there is or is not a centaur or a god. (By 'is or is not' I mean 'is or is not, without further qualification'; as opposed to 'is or is not (e.g.) white'.)," *Posterior Analytics* 68*b*30–35, quoted by J. Hintikka (1986: 89). This makes Aristotle's existential *use* of "is" as sharply distinct from his copulative (predicative) *use* as the corresponding *senses* are for Frege, and as the corresponding *meanings in use* are for Russell.

10. Haaparanta admits that Frege is an 'ideal language' philosopher (Haaparanta 1985: 47, 68). Thus she may not target Frege and Russell themselves at all. Haaparanta targets Hermann and Maier (Haaparanta 1985: 48, 58). Hintikka targets Maier, Cornford, Ross, Guthrie, Cherniss, Vlastos, Ryle, Moravcsik, Kirwan, Weidemann, and Gomez-Lobo (J. Hintikka 1986: 81). But the tone of Kahn's, Hintikka's, and Haaparanta's critiques is such that Frege and Russell themselves appear as chief instigators. The tone of opprobrium against Frege and Russell is so great that if Kahn, Hintikka, and Haaparanta hold that Frege and Russell are innocent of misinterpreting Aristotle, they should have plainly said so. But they never say so. Of course, Frege and Russell, far from imposing their four senses of "is" on Aristotle, in effect criticize him on the score of difficulties and limitations.

Haaparanta says that Aristotle has a 'focal meaning' (*pros hen*) theory of being, while Frege's is merely multivocal (Haaparanta 1985: 49, 57). But I have suggested that the "is" of identity is basic for Frege in my chapters 1–3. Thus identity is the focus. Haaparanta herself admits that Frege's four senses of "is" are 'connected' (Haaparanta 1985: 57). Her talk of common components, elements, or ingredients which these senses have in common, without specifying what these components are, is obscure. But she does admit that "In Frege's view, an identity statement like 'That is Saturn' can be transformed into the [predicative] sentence 'That is no other than Saturn,' and can only exclaim, "Surprisingly enough, this remark implies that there is no difference between identity and predication, which view is, however, clearly rejected by Frege in his formula language" (Haaparanta 1985: 56). It does not occur to Haaparanta that while the "is" of identity may not strictly be the "is" of predication, Frege's famous doctrine that 'a thought can be split up in many ways' (CO 49) applies to the thoughts her Saturn statements express as well as to any other thoughts. That is, Frege's four senses of "is" are different, but not wholly distinct. Indeed, they are distinct only in reason.

Haaparanta curiously calls Frege's four senses of "is" 'forms of being', as if some Fregean items enjoyed predicative being, others enjoyed identitative being, still others enjoyed class-inclusive being, while only a select few had genuine existential being (Haaparanta 1985: twice on 50). She gives no reason for her unusual view. Later on she calls the four senses "so many different functions" (Haaparanta 1985: 57). Now her only mistake, besides implying that functions are 'forms of being', is forgetting that the "is" of predication refers to no function. The ordinary language copula is syncategorematic for Frege.

Haaparanta 1986 adds little or nothing to her 1985 work.

Owing to the fundamentality of identity, and to some degree of analogy between identity, predication, and class inclusion (identity is perfect coincidence, while predication and class inclusion are partial coincidence or overlapping, respectively of objects and their properties, and of membership), I gloss Frege and Russell as offering a *pros hen* theory of senses (or meanings in use) of words like "is." But the analogy is not so great that predication and class inclusion are modes or kinds of being (existence) or identity. That would be unFregean, unRussellian, and obscurantist.

Chapter 7: The Ontology of the Analytic Tradition

1. See Ross on Aristotle on phenomenological or perceptual realism (Ross 1960: 51, 57–58, 212–13), on epistemic realism (Ross 1960: 51–52), and on methodological realism (Ross 1960: 54–58). See Wiggins on the knowability and Kenny on the perceptibility of substances (Wiggins 1980: 4–5; Kenny 1980: 35).

2. Hume makes impressions fairly explicit substance substitutes (Hume 1973: 244). This meets criterion (2) of substance analogue modified realism. Hume also distinguishes real distinction from distinction in reason (Hume 1973: 24–25). This meets the crucial criterion (1g) of metaphysical modified realism. Compare PLA 201–2 and IMP 142.

3. One of Frege's most basic views is that the difference between objects and functions, and the differences between the different types of functions, are essential and absolute (CO 47n; compare PM 39). No doubt such essential natures extend to senses and also to forces. Frege says in "The Thought," "[O]ne is inclined to distinguish between essential and inessential properties [concerning thoughts]..." (Klemke 1968: 524). No doubt selves and ideas have categorial natures too.

Therefore, since number concerns all things (FA 31), as does numbers' shifting as concepts shift, it seems that Frege must hold a view much like my theory of reflection of essences (chapter 1). I suggest that for Frege, some concepts are essences. For to fall under a concept and to have a property are one for Frege. I also suggest that the senses of concept-names may be said to reflect their references, some of which will be essences of objects. Here reflection is what Furth calls the relation of being a sense "of" a denotation (Furth 1967: xix). It follows from these suggestions that some senses reflect essences.

Surely the concepts *concrete* and *abstract* are at least part of the essences of concrete and abstract objects respectively. The old litmus test of essence is that objects cannot change their essences. And I can hardly see how a concrete object such as a tree could become an abstract object such as a number. Note that a modality, causal capacity, defines Frege's notion of a concrete or real object in *Basic Laws* (BL 16). Finally, among abstract objects, each number has its own "special character" and unique numerical properties (FA 15, 20).

4. Frege says that objects are "self-subsistent" (FA 67), and conceives numbers "substantivally" (FA 116). Frege intends only to say that objects are individuals or ultimate logical subjects, not that they are substances (FA 72). But even that is enough to meet criteria (1c) and (2) of modified realism.

5. In *Logical Investigations*, Husserl describes a modified realism in terms of wholes and parts:

> Categorial forms do not glue, tie or put parts together, so that a real sensuously perceivable whole emerges. They do not form in the sense in which the potter forms....Categorial forms leave primary objects untouched: they can do nothing to them, cannot change them in their own being, since the result would otherwise be a new object in the primary, real sense. (Husserl 1982: 820)

See also Husserl on "the difference...between categorial unities in the objective sense, and real unities..." (Husserl 1982: 436–39, 476–78, 696, 754–55, 819).

In *Identity and Difference*, Heidegger says:

> [T]his thing that is called difference, we encounter it everywhere and always in the matter of thinking, in beings as such—encounter it so unquestioningly that we do not even notice this encounter itself. Nor does anything compel us to notice it. Our thinking is free either to pass over the difference without a thought or to think of it specifically as such. But this freedom does not apply in every case. (Heidegger 1974: 63)

Compare Heidegger on thinking as "re-presentation," including "analytical synthesis" (Heidegger 1961: 100).

In *Being and Nothingness*, Sartre seems to synthesize Husserlian modified realism with Heideggerian differences:

> If there are three men talking opposite me, it is not as I apprehend them first as a "group in conversation" that I count them; and the fact of counting them as three leave the concrete unity of their group perfectly intact.... [W]e can see that what Husserl calls categories (unity-multiplicity-relation of the whole to the part—...one, two, three, etc.—...)—these are only the ideal mixings of things which leaves them wholly intact, without either enriching or impoverishing them one iota; they merely indicate the infinite diversity of ways in which the freedom of the for-itself can realize the indifference of being. (Sartre 1956: 191–92)

Note that in *Foundations*, Frege says the power of a concept to unite exceeds that of Kant's synthetic unity of apperception, since the concept *inhabitant of Germany* unites more people than anybody could perceive (FA 61). Thus Frege subsumes Kantian-Husserlian-Sartrean synthetic unities as local cases of his own unification by sortal concept, much as Einstein subsumes Newton as valid in local space-time.

In their comparisons of Frege with Husserl, Dummett (1993), Hill (1991), and Mohanty (1982) all overlook this most basic point of resemblance. Hill, whose book compares Husserl, Frege, and Russell, also ignores Russell's view that one object of presentation can become many (RUP 114–15); see Russell's discussion of perceiving *Gestalt* wholes and their parts (IMT 330-40).

6. Frege needs no private mental "proto-concepts/senses," i.e., superimpositions of imagery on already individuated phenomena, to 'assist' his theory of perception, *pace* Dummett (1993: 121–24).

7. I agree with Kaplan that whether every object has essential attributes "is an issue posterior to whether things have trans-world being" (Kaplan 1975: 723). At least, I agree if trans-world being can be just a way of talking. In any case, I have five ideas about Frege. (i) For Frege, dogs individuate objects without using concepts, or in Kaplan's words, "without reference to common attributes and behavior." (ii) This is not to mention Frege's mental ideas, for which Frege might well admit that haecceitist private names are possible. (iii) Frege's phenomena may and, Frege insists, must be named prior to our grasping any concepts or senses. (iv) Concerning abstract objects, the name "1 + 1," expressing its customary sense, could hardly fail to refer to the abstract object 2 in all possible worlds, any more than 2 could fail to be in all possible worlds, were we to impose possible-worlds-talk on Frege. If that name did not express the same sense in all the possible worlds in which it occurs, then it simply would not be the same name in all of them. (v) Frege collapses the denotation-reference distinction altogether, since modes of presentation are both attributive and cognitive. In the ideal language, every object would be rigidly designated.

I note again that every object is essentially complete. And every number has a "special character" (FA 20). Frege's robust essentialism is the metaphysical ground of the logical roles of expressions in sentences.

8. Calling the *Tractatus* a work of phenomenological realism is misleading in one important way. The great analysts are not Continental phenomenologists like Heidegger. It is enough for my purposes that Tractarian objects are neo-Russellian sense-data (and their properties and relations). Similarly for my imputations of phenomenological realism of somewhat different kinds to Frege and Russell. See Harry P. Reeder, "Wittgenstein Never Was a Phenomenologist" (Reeder 1989: 257–76). Still, Frege and Husserl shared a common vocabulary, and Russell studied Husserl and Meinong in some detail. And Nicholas F. Gier wrote a whole book comparing Wittgenstein and the phenomenologists (Gier 1981).

9. The Hintikkas say that this view of Wittgenstein's led Russell to abandon any thought of publishing his 1913 *Theory of Knowledge* ms. But Russell evidently returns in 1918 to his 1913 view that we must be acquainted with structure or complexity (PLA 196–97).

10. The Hintikkas view phenomena in *Investigations* as private sensations. I disagree. See PI #273–#276 and #436 for some indirect evidence. This is not to mention the manifest import of PI #272, *pace* the Hintikkas' esoteric efforts to explain it away.

11. On the four kinds of pluralism, see: WO 1–5, 21–25, 31–46, 91–92; FLPV 44–46; OR 31; TT 12–22, 71–72, 181; PQ 317, 364, 427–29, 533, 566–67, 619–20; Quine (1984: 16). On the ultimate nature of physical microstates, see PQ 429–31.

12. For the conceptual relativity, see: FA 28–29, 33; POM 519; many familiar passages in PI; WO 68–79; OR 32–33, 45, 48, 55. For the private language arguments,

see: FA 35–38; POM 451; PI #243ff.; WO ix, 7, 45, 79; OR 26–27, 28–29, 47; see also PQ 74, 664; PT 61.

13. Eileen Sweeney warns against the view that all kinds of analysis are the same (Sweeney 1991: 80). But the greater the disparities, the deeper the analogies and the *pros hen* relationships we may hope to find. And the principal argument of this book is that if something is enough like a substance—if it looks, swims, waddles, and quacks like a substance—then no matter what kind of linguistic analysis or conceptual supervenience you dress it up in, it is a substance. Or, if you prefer a weaker conclusion, it is very likely a substance, fundamentally like a substance, and best counted as a substance.

14. Compare Lynne Spellman, "Referential Opacity in Aristotle" (Spellman 1990: 17–31).

Bibliography

These are abbreviations for selected works. Citations are below.

Frege:
BG   *Begriffsschrift* (1879)
BL   *The Basic Laws of Arithmetic* (vol. 1, 1893; vol. 2, 1903).
CN   *Conceptual Notation and Related Articles* (various)
CO   "On Concept and Object" (1892)
FA   *The Foundations of Arithmetic* (1884)
FG   *On the Foundations of Geometry and Formal Theories of Arithmetic* (various)
KS   *Kleine Schriften* (various)
PW   *Posthumous Writings* (various)
SR   "On Sense and Reference" (1892)
TW   *Translations from the Philosophical Writings of Gottlob Frege* (various)

Quine:
FLPV   *From a Logical Point of View* (1953)
OR   *Ontological Relativity and Other Essays* (1969)
PT   *Pursuit of Truth*, (1991, rev. 1992)
TT   *Theories and Things* (1981)
WO   *Word and Object* (1960)

Russell:
AMA   *The Analysis of Matter* (1921)
AMI   *The Analysis of Mind* (1927)
HK   *Human Knowledge: Its Scope and Limits* (1948)
HWP   *A History of Western Philosophy* (1945)
IMP   *Introduction to Mathematical Philosophy* (1919)
IMT   *An Inquiry into Meaning and Truth* (1940)
KEW   *Our Knowledge of the External World* (1914, rev. 1929)
LK   *Logic and Knowledge* (1971)
MAL   *Mysticism and Logic* (1918)
MPD   *My Philosophical Development* (1959)
OD   "On Denoting" (1905)

ONC   "On the Notion of Cause" (1913)
OP   *An Outline of Philosophy* (1927)
PE   *Philosophical Essays* (1910)
PL   *A Critical Exposition of the Philosophy of Leibniz* (1900)
PLA   "The Philosophy of Logical Atomism" (1918)
PM   *Principia Mathematica* (vol. 1, 1910) (with A. N. Whitehead)
POM   *Principles of Mathematics* (1903)
RUP   "On the Relations of Universals and Particulars" (read in 1911)

Wittgenstein:
BB   *The Blue and Brown Books* (1933–35)
PI   *Philosophical Investigations* (completed 1945–49)
RFM   *Remarks on the Foundations of Mathematics* (1937–44)
T   *Tractatus Logico-Philosophicus* (1921)
Z   *Zettel* (1928-48)

Other:
IW   Merrill B. Hintikka and Jaakko Hintikka, *Investigating Wittgenstein*
       (1986)
PQ   L. E. Hahn and P. A. Schilpp, eds., *The Philosophy of W. V. Quine*
       (1987)

The works of Plato are cited by Stephens' pagination; the works of Aristotle are
cited by Bekker's pagination.

Alanen, Lilli: 1986, "On Descartes's Argument for Dualism and the Distinction
    Between Different Kinds of Beings." In Knuuttila and Hintikka, eds., *The
    Logic of Being.*
Allaire, Edwin B.: 1970, "Another Look at Bare Particulars." In Loux, ed.,
    Universals and Particulars.
——. 1970a, "Bare Particulars." In Loux, ed., *Universals and Particulars.*
Alston, William P., and Bennett, Jonathan: 1984, "Identity and Cardinality:
    Geach and Frege." *The Philosophical Review* 93/4.
Ammerman, Robert R., ed.: 1965, *Classics of Analytic Philosophy.* New York:
    McGraw-Hill.
Angelelli, Ignacio: 1967, *Gottlob Frege and Traditional Philosophy.* Dordrecht,
    Holland: D. Reidel.
Anscombe, G. E. M. and Geach, Peter T.: 1961, *Three Philosophers.* Oxford:
    Basil Blackwell.
Apostle, Hippocrates George: 1952, *Aristotle's Philosophy of Mathematics*
    Chicago: The University of Chicago Press.
Aquinas, St. Thomas: 1969, *Summa Theologiae.* Vol. 1, part 1. General editor:
    Thomas Gilby. Garden City, N.Y.: Image Books.

Aristotle: 1980, *Physics*. Trans. by Hippocrates G. Apostle. Grinnell, Iowa: Peripatetic Press.

———. 1973, *Aristotle's Metaphysics*. Trans. by Hippocrates G. Apostle. Bloomington: Indiana University Press.

———. 1968, *The Basic Works of Aristotle*. Ed. by Richard McKeon. New York: Random House.

———. 1968a, *Categories*. Trans. by E. M. Edghill. In *The Basic Works of Aristotle*.

———. 1968b, *Posterior Analytics*. Trans. by G. R. G. Mure. In *The Basic Works of Aristotle*.

———. 1968c, *Topics*. Trans. by W. A. Pickard-Cambridge. In *The Basic Works of Aristotle*.

Arnauld, Antoine: 1964, *The Art of Thinking*. Trans. by James Dickoff and Patricia James. Indianapolis, Ind.: Bobbs-Merrill.

Ayer, Alfred Jules: 1972, *Bertrand Russell*. New York: Viking Press.

———. 1971, *Russell and Moore*. Cambridge, Mass.: Harvard University Press.

———. 1959, "Editor's Introduction." In Ayer, ed., *Logical Positivism*.

———, ed.: 1959a, *Logical Positivism*. New York: The Free Press.

———. 1952, *Language, Truth and Logic*. 2d ed. New York: Dover.

Baker, Gordon P.: 1988, *Wittgenstein, Frege and the Vienna Circle*. Oxford: Basil Blackwell.

———, and Hacker, Peter M. S.: 1987, "Dummett's Dig: Looking-Glass Archaeology." *The Philosophical Quarterly* 37/146.

———, and Hacker, Peter M. S.: 1984, *Frege: Logical Excavations*. New York: Oxford University Press.

Baldwin, James Mark, ed.: 1901, *Dictionary of Philosophy and Psychology*. New York: Macmillan.

Bambrough, Renford: 1970, "Universals and Family Resemblances." In Loux, ed., *Universals and Particulars*.

Barker, Stephen: 1967, "Number." In Edwards, ed., *The Encyclopedia of Philosophy*.

Barrett, Robert B. and Gibson, Roger F., eds.: 1990, *Perspectives on Quine*. Oxford: Basil Blackwell.

Barwick, Daniel: 1994, *Intentional Implications: The Impact of a Reduction of Mind on Philosophy*. Lanham, Md.: University Press of America.

Benardete, José: 1993, "Real Definitions: Quine and Aristotle. *Philosophical Studies* 72.

———. 1989, *Metaphysics: The Logical Approach*. Oxford: Clarendon Press.

———. 1964, *Infinity: An Essay in Metaphysics*. Oxford: Clarendon Press.

Bergmann, Gustav: 1971, "The Revolt Against Logical Atomism." In Klemke, ed., *Essays on Russell*. Also in *Meaning and Existence*.

———. 1971a, "Russell on Particulars." In Klemke, ed., *Essays on Russell*.

———. 1968, *Meaning and Existence*. Madison: University of Wisconsin Press.

——. 1967, *The Metaphysics of Logical Positivism.* 2d ed. Madison: University of Wisconsin Press.

——. 1967a, *Realism: A Critique of Brentano and Meinong.* Madison: University of Wisconsin Press.

——. 1964, "Ineffability, Ontology, and Method." In *Logic and Reality.*

——. 1964a, *Logic and Reality.* Madison: University of Wisconsin Press.

——. 1964b, "Ontological Alternatives." In *Logic and Reality.*

——. 1958, "Frege's Hidden Nominalism." *The Philosophical Review* 67. Also in Klemke, ed., *Essays on Frege.*

Berkeley, George: 1965, *Principles, Dialogues, and Correspondence.* Ed. by Colin Murray Turbayne. Indianapolis, Ind.: Bobbs-Merrill.

——. 1965a, *A Treatise Concerning the Principles of Human Knowledge.* In *Principles, Dialogues, and Correspondence.*

——. 1963, *Works on Vision.* Ed. by Colin M. Turbayne. Indianapolis, Ind.: Bobbs-Merrill.

Black, Max: 1970, *A Companion to Wittgenstein's Tractatus.* Ithaca, N.Y.: Cornell University Press.

Blackburn, Simon, ed.: 1975, *Meaning, Reference and Necessity: New Studies in Semantics.* Cambridge, England: Cambridge University Press.

——, and Code, Alan: 1978, "The Power of Russell's Criticism of Frege: 'On Denoting' pp. 48–50." *Analysis* 38/2.

Boh, Ivan: 1993, *Epistemic Logic in the Later Middle Ages.* New York: Routledge.

Bouwsma, O. K.: 1949, "Descartes' Evil Genius." *The Philosophical Review* 58/2.

Bradley, F. H.: 1969, *Appearance and Reality: A Metaphysical Essay.* 2d ed. London: Oxford University Press.

Bradley, Michael: 1986, "Russell and the Identity of Indiscernibles." *History of Philosophy Quarterly* 3/3.

Bradley, Raymond: 1992, *The Nature of All Being.* New York: Oxford University Press.

Brentano, Franz: 1973, *Psychology from an Empirical Standpoint.* 1911 edition. Ed. by Oskar Kraus. English edition ed. by Linda L. McAlister and trans. by Antos C. Rancurello, D. B. Terrell, and Linda L. McAlister. New York: Humanities Press.

——. 1971, Fragment of November 16, 1905. In *The True and the Evident.*

——. 1971a, Letter to Anton Marty, September 2, 1906. In *The True and the Evident.*

——. 1971b, *The True and the Evident.* Ed. by Oskar Kraus. English edition ed. by Roderick M. Chisholm and trans. by Roderick M. Chisholm, Ilse Politzer, and Kurt R. Fischer. New York: Humanities Press.

Burge, Tyler: 1983, "Russell's Problem and Intentional Identity." In Tomberlin, ed., *Agent, Language, and the Structure of the World.*

de Burgh, W. G.: 1967, *The Legacy of the Ancient World*. Baltimore: Penguin.

Buridan, Jean: 1973, "Questions on Aristotle's *Metaphysics*, Book 4, Question 8." In Hyman and Walsh, eds., *Philosophy in the Middle Ages*.

Burkhardt, Hans: 1988, "Modalities in Language, Thought and Reality in Leibniz, Descartes and Crusius." *Synthese* 75/2.

Butchvarov, Panayot: 1994, "The Untruth and the Truth of Skepticism." *Proceedings and Addresses of the American Philosophical Association* 67/4.

———. 1989, *Skepticism in Ethics*. Bloomington: Indiana University Press.

———. 1988, "Russell's Views on Reality." *Grazer Philosophische Studien* 32.

———. 1986, "Our Robust Sense of Reality." *Grazer Philosophische Studien* 26.

———. 1979, *Being Qua Being: A Theory of Identity, Existence, and Predication*. Bloomington: Indiana University Press.

———. 1974, "The Limits of Ontological Analysis." In Gram and Klemke, eds., *The Ontological Turn: Studies in the Philosophy of Gustav Bergmann*.

———. 1970, *The Concept of Knowledge*. Evanston, Ill.: Northwestern University Press.

Carnap, Rudolf: 1967, "Empiricism, Semantics, and Ontology." In Copi and Gould, eds., *Contemporary Readings in Logical Theory*.

———. 1963, "Intellectual Autobiography." In Schilpp, ed., *The Philosophy of Rudolf Carnap*.

Castañeda, Hector-Neri: 1983, "Reply to Plantinga." In Tomberlin, ed., *Agent, Language, and the Structure of the World*.

———. 1974, "Thinking and the Structure of the World." *Philosophia* 4.

Casullo, Albert: 1991, Letter to Dejnožka dated 9 January.

———. 1984, "The Contingent Identity of Particulars and Universals." *Mind* 93.

———. 1982, "Particulars, Substrata, and The Identity of Indiscernibles." *Philosophy of Science* 49.

———. 1981, "Russell on the Reduction of Particulars." *Analysis* 41.

Chisholm, Roderick M.: 1967, "Meinong." In Edwards, ed., *The Encyclopedia of Philosophy*.

———. 1966, *Theory of Knowledge*. Englewood Cliffs, N.J.: Prentice-Hall.

———, ed.: 1960, *Realism and the Background of Phenomenology*. Atascadero, Calif.: Ridgeview Publishing Company.

Coder, David: 1974, "The Opening Passage of Frege's 'Über Sinn und Bedeutung'." *Philosophia* 4/2–3.

Coffa, Alberto: 1985, "Idealism and the Aufbau." In Rescher, ed., *The Heritage of Logical Positivism*.

Copi, Irving: 1978, *Introduction to Logic*. 5th ed. New York: Macmillan.

———, and Gould, James A., eds.: 1967, *Contemporary Readings in Logical Theory*. New York: Macmillan.

Cornford, Francis McDonald: 1939, *Plato and Parmenides*. London: Routledge & Kegan Paul.

Currie, Gregory: 1982, *Frege: An Introduction to His Philosophy*. Sussex,

England: The Harvester Press.

Davidson, Donald: 1986, *Inquiries into Truth and Interpretation.*

——. 1986a, "Reality Without Reference." In *Inquiries into Truth and Interpretation.* Oxford: Clarendon Press.

——. 1985, *Essays on Actions and Events.* Oxford: Clarendon Press.

——. 1985a, "The Individuation of Events." In Davidson, *Essays on Actions and Events.*

——. 1985b, "Reply to Quine on Events." In LePore and McLaughlin, eds., *Actions and Events: Perspectives on the Philosophy of Donald Davidson.*

Davson-Galle, Peter: 1991, "Self-Refuting Propositions and Relativism." *Metaphilosophy* 22/1-2.

Dejnožka, Jan: 1995, "Origins of the Private Language Argument." *Diálogos* 66.

——. 1995a, "Quine: Whither Empirical Equivalence?" *South African Journal of Philosophy* 14/4.

——. 1991, "Russell's Seventeen Private-Language Arguments." *Russell* n.s. 11/1.

——. 1990, "The Ontological Foundation of Russell's Theory of Modality." *Erkenntnis* 32.

——. 1989, "Zeno's Paradoxes and the Cosmological Argument." *International Journal for Philosophy of Religion* 25.

——. 1988, "Reply to Butchvarov's 'Russell's Views on Reality'." *Grazer Philosophische Studien* 32.

——. 1988a, "Reply to Umphrey's 'The Meinongian-Antimeinongian Dispute Reviewed'." *Grazer Philosophische Studien* 32.

——. 1988b, "Russell's Robust Sense of Reality: A Reply to Butchvarov." *Grazer Philosophische Studien* 32.

——. 1982, "Frege: Existence Defined as Identifiability." *International Studies in Philosophy* 14.

——. 1981, "Frege on Identity." *International Studies in Philosophy* 13.

——. 1979, *Frege: Existence and Identity.* Ph.D. diss. Ann Arbor, MI: University Microfilms International.

Descartes, René: 1969, *The Philosophical Works of Descartes.* Trans. by Elizabeth S. Haldane and G. R. T. Ross. Cambridge, England: Cambridge University Press.

——. 1969a, *The Principles of Philosophy.* In *The Philosophical Works of Descartes.*

Devitt, Michael: 1984, *Realism and Truth.* Oxford: Basil Blackwell.

Donagan, Alan: 1970, "Universals and Metaphysical Realism." In Loux, ed., *Universals and Particulars.*

Donnellan, Keith: 1990, "Genuine Names and Knowledge by Acquaintance." *Dialectica* 44.

——. 1972, "Reference and Definite Descriptions." In Feigl, Sellars, and

Lehrer, eds., *New Readings in Philosophical Analysis.*

Ducasse, Curt J.: 1968, "Moore's Refutation of Idealism." In Schilpp, ed., *The Philosophy of G. E. Moore.*

Dummett, Michael: 1993, *Origins of Analytical Philosophy.* London: Duckworth.

———. 1991, *Frege: Philosophy of Mathematics.* Cambridge, Mass.: Harvard University Press.

———. 1983, "An Unsuccessful Dig." In Wright, ed., *Frege: Tradition & Influence.*

———. 1981, *Frege: Philosophy of Language.* 2d ed. Cambridge, Mass.: Harvard University Press.

———. 1981a, *The Interpretation of Frege's Philosophy.* Cambridge, Mass.: Harvard University Press.

———. 1973, *Frege: Philosophy of Language.* New York: Harper and Row.

———. 1967, "Frege." In Edwards, ed., *The Encyclopedia of Philosophy.*

———. 1955, "Frege on Functions: A Reply." *The Philosophical Review* 64.

Edwards, Paul, ed.: 1967, *The Encyclopedia of Philosophy.* New York: Macmillan and The Free Press.

Einstein, Albert: 1961, *Relativity: The Special and the General Theory.* Trans. by Robert W. Lawson. New York: Bonanza.

Evans, Gareth: 1982, *The Varieties of Reference.* Ed. by John McDowell. Oxford: Clarendon Press.

Fales, Evan: 1990: *Causation and Universals.* London: Routledge.

Feigl, Herbert, Sellars, Wilfrid, and Lehrer, Keith: 1972, *New Readings in Philosophical Analysis.* New York: Appleton-Century-Crofts.

Feinberg, Barry and Kasrils, Ronald: 1969: *Dear Bertrand Russell: A selection of his correspondence with the general public, 1950-1968.* London: George Allen & Unwin.

Field, Hartry: 1972, "Tarski's Theory of Truth." *Journal of Philosophy* 69/13.

Findlay, J. N.: 1963, *Meinong's Theory of Objects and Values.* 2d ed. Oxford: Clarendon Press.

Frege, Friedrich Ludwig Gottlob: 1980, *Philosophical and Mathematical Correspondence.* Trans. by Hans Kaal. Oxford: Basil Blackwell.

———. 1979, "Dialogue with Pünjer on Existence." In *Posthumous Writings.*

———. 1979a, *Posthumous Writings.* Trans. by Peter Long and Roger White, and ed. by Hans Hermes, Friedrich Kambartel, and Friedrich Kaulbach. Chicago: The University of Chicago Press.

———. 1974, *The Foundations of Arithmetic.* 2d rev. ed. Trans. by J. L. Austin. Evanston, Ill.: Northwestern University Press.

———. 1972, *Conceptual Notation and Related Articles.* Trans. and ed. by Terrell Ward Bynum. Oxford: Clarendon Press.

———. 1971a, Letter from Frege to Husserl dated 24 May 1891. In *On the Foundations of Geometry and Formal Theories of Arithmetic.*

——. 1971b, "On the Foundations of Geometry" (1903). In *On the Foundations of Geometry and Formal Theories of Arithmetic.*

——. 1971c, "On the Foundations of Geometry" (1906). In *On the Foundations of Geometry and Formal Theories of Arithmetic.*

——. 1971d, *On the Foundations of Geometry and Formal Theories of Arithmetic.* Ed. by Eike-Henner W. Kluge. New Haven, Conn.: Yale University Press.

——. 1971e, "On the Scientific Justification of a Conceptual Notation." In *Conceptual Notation and Related Articles.*

——. 1970, "A Critical Elucidation of Some Points in E. Schroeder's *Vorlesungen Ueber die Algebra der Logik.*" In *Translations from the Philosophical Writings of Gottlob Frege.*

——. 1970a, "Function and Concept." In *Translations from the Philosophical Writings of Gottlob Frege.*

——. 1970b, *Grundgesetze der Arithmetik.* Vols. 1 and 2. In *Translations from the Philosophical Writings of Gottlob Frege.*

——. 1970c, Illustrative extracts from Frege's review of Husserl's *Philosophie der Arithmetik.* In *Translations from the Philosophical Writings of Gottlob Frege.*

——. 1970d, "Negation." In *Translations from the Philosophical Writings of Gottlob Frege.*

——. 1970e, "On Concept and Object." In *Translations from the Philosophical Writings of Gottlob Frege.*

——. 1970f, "On Sense and Reference." In *Translations from the Philosophical Writings of Gottlob Frege.*

——. 1970g, *Translations from the Philosophical Writings of Gottlob Frege.* Ed. by Peter Geach and Max Black. Oxford: Basil Blackwell.

——. 1970h, "What is a Function?" In *Translations from the Philosophical Writings of Gottlob Frege.*

——. 1967, *The Basic Laws of Arithmetic: Exposition of the System.* Trans. and ed. by Montgomery Furth. Berkeley: University of California Press.

——. 1967a, *Begriffsschrift, a formula language, modeled upon that of arithmetic, for pure thought.* In Heijenoort, ed., *From Frege to Gödel.*

——. 1967b, *Kleine Schriften.* Ed. by Ignacio Angelelli. Hildesheim: Georg Olm Verlagsbuchhandlung.

——. 1967c, "Rezension von: E. G. Husserl, *Philosophie der Arithmetik* k.I." In *Kleine Schriften.*

——. 1956, "The Thought." Trans. by Anthony Quinton and Marcelle Quinton. *Mind* 65. Also in Klemke, ed., *Essays on Frege.*

Fumerton, Richard A.: 1989, "Russelling Causal Theories of Reference." In Savage and Anderson, eds., *Rereading Russell: Essays in Bertrand Russell's Metaphysics and Epistemology.*

Furth, Montgomery: 1968, "Two Types of Denotation." In Rescher, ed.,

Studies in Logical Theory.

———. 1967, "Editor's Introduction" to Frege, *The Basic Laws of Arithmetic.*

Gaskin, Richard: 1995, "Bradley's Regress, The Copula and the Unity of the Proposition." *The Philosophical Quarterly* 45/179.

Geach, Peter T.: 1991, "Replies." In H. A. Lewis, ed., *Peter Geach: Philosophical Encounters.*

———. 1980, *Reference and Generality.* 3d ed. Ithaca, N.Y.: Cornell University Press.

———. 1978, "Russell on Denoting." *Analysis* 38.

———. 1973, "Ontological Relativity and Relative Identity." In Munitz, ed., *Logic and Ontology.*

———. 1972, *Logic Matters.* Berkeley: University of California Press.

———. 1969, *God and the Soul.* London: Routledge and Kegan Paul.

Gier, Nicholas F.: 1981, *Wittgenstein and Phenomenology: A Comparative Study of the later Wittgenstein, Husserl, Heidegger, and Merleau-Ponty.* Albany: State University of New York Press.

Gram, Moltke S., and Klemke, E. D., eds.: 1974, *The Ontological Turn: Studies in the Philosophy of Gustav Bergmann.* Iowa City: University of Iowa Press.

Grattan-Guinness, Ivor: 1990, Note to Dejnožka dated August 16.

———. 1985–86, "Russell's logicism versus Oxbridge logics, 1890–1925." *Russell* 5/2.

———. 1973, *Dear Russell-Dear Jourdain: A commentary on Russell's logic, based on his correspondence with Philip Jourdain.* New York: Columbia University Press.

Greenberg, William F.: 1985, *Aspects of a Theory of Singular Reference.* New York: Garland.

Grice, H. P., and Strawson, P. F.: 1956, "In Defense of a Dogma." *The Philosophical Review* 65/2. Also in Ammerman, ed., *Classics of Analytic Philosophy.*

Griffin, Nicholas: 1995, electronic mail to Dejnožka dated May 9.

———. 1993, "Terms, Relations, Complexes." In Irvine and Wedeking, eds., *Russell and Analytic Philosophy.*

———. 1992–93, "The Legacy of Russell's Idealism for his Later Philosophy: The Problem of Substance." *Russell* 12.

———, ed.: 1992, *The Selected Letters of Bertrand Russell,* vol 1. Allen Lane, England: Penguin.

———. 1991, *Russell's Idealist Apprenticeship.* Oxford: Clarendon Press.

Grossmann, Reinhardt: 1969, *Reflections on Frege's Philosophy.* Evanston, Ill.: Northwestern University Press.

Haaparanta, Leila: 1986, "Frege on Existence." In Haaparanta and Hintikka, eds., *Frege Synthesized.*

———, and Hintikka, Jaakko, eds.: 1986a, *Frege Synthesized.* Dordrecht,

Holland: D. Reidel.

———. 1986b, "On Frege's Concept of Being." In Knuuttila and Hintikka, eds., *The Logic of Being.*

———. 1985, *Frege's Notion of Being.* Helsinki: Acta Philosophica Fennica, vol. 39.

Hacker, Peter: 1979, "Semantic Holism: Frege and Wittgenstein." In Luckhardt, ed., *Wittgenstein: Sources and Perspectives.*

———. 1972, "Frege and the Private Language Argument." *Idealistic Studies* 2/3.

Hager, Paul: 1987, "Russell and Zeno's Arrow Paradox." *Russell* 7/1.

Hahn, L. E., and Schilpp, P. A., eds.: 1987, *The Philosophy of W. V. Quine.* La Salle, Ill.: Open Court.

Hale, Susan: 1989, "A Defense of Giving Identity Conditions for Events in Purely Spatiotemporal Terms." Manuscript; see *Proceedings and Addresses of the American Philosophical Association,* vol. 63/2.

Hamlyn, D. W.: 1984, *Metaphysics.* Cambridge, England: Cambridge University Press.

Hampshire, Stuart: 1956, "Identification and Existence." In Lewis, ed., *Contemporary British Philosophy: Personal Statements,* 3d ser.

Heath, P. L.: 1967, "Nothing." In Edwards, ed., *The Encyclopedia of Philosophy.*

Hegel, G. W. F.: 1967, *The Phenomenology of Mind.* Trans. by J. B. Baillie. New York: Harper and Row.

Heidegger, Martin: 1974, *Identity and Difference.* Trans. by Joan Stambaugh. New York: Harper & Row.

———. 1961, *An Introduction to Metaphysics.* Trans. Ralph Mannheim. New York: Doubleday.

van Heijenoort, Jean, ed.: 1967, *From Frege to Gödel.* Cambridge, Mass.: Harvard University Press.

———. 1967, "Logic as Calculus and Logic as Language." *Synthese* 17.

Heisenberg, Werner: 1962, *Physics and Philosophy.* New York: Harper & Row.

Hill, Claire Ortiz: 1991, *Word and Object in Husserl, Frege, and Russell.* Athens: Ohio University Press.

Hintikka, Jaakko: 1986, "The Varieties of Being in Aristotle." In Knuuttila and Hintikka, eds., *The Logic of Being.*

Hintikka, Merrill B., and Hintikka, Jaakko: 1986, *Investigating Wittgenstein.* Oxford: Basil Blackwell.

Hirsch, Eli: 1982, *The Concept of Identity.* New York: Oxford University Press.

Hochberg, Herbert: 1978, *Thought, Fact, and Reference: The Origins and Ontology of Logical Atomism.* Minneapolis: University of Minnesota Press.

———. 1971, "Things and Descriptions." In Klemke, ed., *Essays on Russell.*

Hugley, Philip, and Sayward, Charles: 1990, "Quine's Relativism." *Ratio* n.s. 3/2.

Hume, David: 1973, *A Treatise of Human Nature*. Ed. L. A. Selby-Bigge. Oxford: Clarendon Press.

Husserl, Edmund: 1982, *Logical Investigations*. Second German edition. Trans. J. N. Findlay. London: Routledge & Kegan Paul.

Hylton, Peter: 1980, "Russell's Substitutional Theory." *Synthese* 45.

Hyman, Arthur, and Walsh, James J., eds.: 1973, *Philosophy in the Middle Ages*. Indianapolis, Ind.: Hackett.

Irvine, A. D. and Wedeking, G. A., eds.: 1993, *Russell and Analytic Philosophy*. Toronto: University of Toronto Press.

Jackson, Howard: 1960, "Frege's Ontology." *The Philosophical Review* 69. Also in Klemke, ed., *Essays on Frege*.

Jager, Ronald: 1972, *The Development of Bertrand Russell's Philosophy*. London: George Allen & Unwin.

Kahn, Charles H.: 1986, "Retrospect on the Verb 'To Be' and the Concept of Being." In Knuuttila and Hintikka, eds., *The Logic of Being*.

———. 1982, "Why Existence Does Not Emerge as a Distinct Concept in Greek Philosophy." In Morewedge, ed., *Philosophies of Existence: Ancient and Medieval*.

———. 1979, *The Art and Thought of Heraclitus: An edition of the fragments with translation and commentary*. Cambridge, England: Cambridge University Press.

———. 1973, *The Verb 'Be' in Ancient Greek*. Vol. 6 in John W. M. Verhaar, ed., *The Verb 'Be' and Its Synonyms: Philosophical and Grammatical Studies*. Dordrecht, Holland: D. Reidel.

Kant, Immanuel: 1982, *The Critique of Judgment*. Part 2. Trans. by James Creed Meredith. Oxford: Clarendon Press.

———. 1950, *Prolegomena to any Future Metaphysics*. Ed. by Lewis White Beck. Indianapolis, Ind.: Bobbs-Merrill.

Kaplan, David: 1975, "How to Russell a Frege-Church." *The Journal of Philosophy* 72.

Kenny, Anthony: 1980, *Aquinas*. New York: Hill and Wang.

Kirk, G. S., Raven, J. E., and Schofield, M.: 1985, *The Presocratic Philosophers*. 2d ed. Cambridge, England: Cambridge University Press.

Klemke, E. D., ed.: 1971, *Essays on Bertrand Russell*. Urbana: University of Illinois Press.

———. 1971a, "Logic and Ontology in Russell's Philosophy." In *Essays on Russell*.

———, ed.: 1968, *Essays on Frege*. Urbana: University of Illinois Press.

Kluge, Eike-Henner W.: 1980, *The Metaphysics of Gottlob Frege: An Essay in Ontological Reconstruction*. The Hague: Martinus Nijhoff.

———. 1971, "Introduction." In Frege, *On the Foundations of Geometry and Formal Theories of Arithmetic*.

Kneale, William, and Kneale, Martha: 1964, *The Development of Logic*.

Oxford: Clarendon Press.

Knuuttila, Simo, 1986, "Being Qua Being in Thomas Aquinas and John Duns Scotus." In Knuuttila and Hintikka, eds., *The Logic of Being*.

——, and Hintikka, Jaakko, eds.: 1986a, *The Logic of Being: Historical Studies*. Dordrecht, Holland: D. Reidel.

Koehler, O.: 1956, "The Ability of Birds to 'Count'." In Newman, ed., *The World of Mathematics*.

Kosko, Bart: 1993, *Fuzzy Thinking: The New Science of Fuzzy Logic*. New York: Hyperion.

Kripke, Saul A.: 1982, *Wittgenstein on Rules and Private Language*. Cambridge, Mass.: Harvard University Press.

——. 1980, *Naming and Necessity*. Cambridge, Mass.: Harvard University Press.

Lackey, Douglas: 1974–75, "Russell's Anticipation of Quine's Criterion." *Russell* 16.

——. 1973, editor's commentary. In Russell, *Essays in Analysis*.

Landini, Gregory: 1995, electronic mail to Dejnožka dated January 11, February 24, February 28, March 6, March 7, March 8, and March 10.

——. 1993, "Notes on Dejnožka's Manuscript."

——. 1993a, "Reconciling *PM*'s Ramified Type Theory with the Doctrine of the Unrestricted Variables of the *Principles*." In Irvine and Wedeking, eds., *Russell and Analytic Philosophy*.

——. 1987, "Russell's Substitutional Theory of Classes and Relations." *History and Philosophy of Logic* 8.

LePore, Ernest, and McLaughlin, Brian P., eds.: 1985, *Actions and Events: Perspectives on the Philosophy of Donald Davidson*. Oxford: Basil Blackwell.

Lewis, H. D., ed.: 1976, *Contemporary British Philosophy: Personal Statements*. 4th ser. London: Allen & Unwin.

——, ed.: 1956, *Contemporary British Philosophy: Personal Statements*. 3d ser. London: George Allen & Unwin.

Lewis, Harry A., ed.: 1991, *Peter Geach: Philosophical Encounters*. Dordrecht, Holland: Kluwer.

Linsky, Bernard: 1993, "Why Russell Abandoned Russellian Propositions." In Irvine and Wedeking, eds., *Russell and Analytic Philosophy*.

Linsky, Leonard: 1977, *Names and Descriptions*. Chicago: The University of Chicago Press.

——. 1967, *Referring*. London: Routledge and Kegan Paul.

Long, Douglas C.: 1970, "Particulars and Their Qualities." In Loux, ed., *Universals and Particulars*.

Loux, Michael J.: 1970, "Particulars and Their Individuation." In *Universals and Particulars*.

——, ed.: 1970a, *Universals and Particulars: Readings in Ontology*. Doubleday:

Garden City, N.Y.

Lowe, E. Jonathan: 1989, *Kinds of Being: A Study of Individuation, Identity and the Logic of Sortal Terms*. Oxford: Basil Blackwell (Aristotelian Society Series, vol. 10).

Luckhardt, C. G., ed.: 1979, *Wittgenstein: Sources and Perspectives*. Ithaca, N.Y.: Cornell University Press.

Magnell, Thomas: 1991, "The Extent of Russell's Modal Views." *Erkenntnis* 34.

Mandelbaum, Maurice, and Freeman, Eugene, eds.: 1975, *Spinoza: Essays in Interpretation*. La Salle, Ill.: Open Court.

Manser, Anthony: 1985, "Russell's Criticism of Frege." *Philosophical Investigations* 8/4.

Margolis, Joseph, ed.: 1991, *The Truth About Relativism*. Oxford: Basil Blackwell.

———. 1969, *Fact and Existence*. Toronto: University of Toronto Press.

Marshall, William: 1956, "Sense and Reference: A Reply." In *The Philosophical Review* 65, and in Klemke, ed., *Essays on Frege*.

McCann, Hugh J.: n.d., "Event and Identity." Unpublished ms. cited in Hale, "A Defense of Giving Identity Conditions for Events in Purely Spatio-temporal Terms."

McCauley, James: 1985, "Actions and Events Despite Bertrand Russell." In LePore and McLaughlin, eds., *Actions and Events: Perspectives on the Philosophy of Donald Davidson*.

McDonough, Richard M.: 1986, *The Argument of the Tractatus: Its Relevance to Contemporary Theories of Logic, Language, Mind, and Philosophical Truth*. Albany: State University of New York Press.

Measor, Nicholas: 1978, "Frege, Dummett, and the Philistines." In *Analysis* 38/1.

Meinong, Alexius: 1960, "Theory of Objects." Trans. Isaac Levi, D. B. Terrell, and Roderick M. Chisholm. In Chisholm, ed., *Realism and the Background of Phenomenology*.

Mohanty, J. N.: 1982, *Husserl & Frege*. Bloomington: Indiana University Press.

Moore, Gerald E.: 1989, "Russell's 'Theory of Descriptions'." In Schilpp, ed., *The Philosophy of Bertrand Russell*.

———. 1971, *Principia Ethica*. London: Cambridge University Press.

———. 1968, "A Reply to My Critics." In Schilpp, ed., *The Philosophy of G. E. Moore*.

———. 1966, "Imaginary Objects." In *Philosophical Papers*.

———. 1966a, "Is Existence a Predicate?" In *Philosophical Papers*.

———. 1966b, *Philosophical Papers*. New York: Collier.

———. 1966c, *Some Main Problems of Philosophy*. London: George Allen & Unwin.

——. 1901, "Identity." *Proceedings of the Aristotelian Society* n.s. 1.

——. 1899, "The Nature of Judgment." *Mind* n.s. 8.

Morewedge, Parviz, ed.: 1982, *Philosophies of Existence: Ancient and Medieval*. New York: Fordham Press.

Morris, Thomas V.: 1984, *Understanding Identity Statements*. Scots Philosophical Monographs Number Five. Aberdeen, Scotland: Aberdeen University Press.

Mourelatos, Alexander P. D.: 1974, *The Pre-Socratics*. Garden City, N.Y.: Doubleday.

Müller, Anselm W.: 1991, "Conceptual Surroundings of Absolute Identity." In Harry. A. Lewis, ed., *Peter Geach: Philosophical Encounters*.

Mulvaney, Robert J. and Zeltner, Philip M., eds.: 1981, *Pragmatism: Its Sources and Prospects*. Columbia: University of South Carolina Press.

Munitz, Milton K., ed.: 1973, *Logic and Ontology*. New York: New York University Press.

Nagel, Ernest: 1979, *The Structure of Science*. Indianapolis, Ind.: Hackett.

——. 1956, *Logic Without Metaphysics*. Glencoe, Ill.: The Free Press.

Nakhnikian, George, ed.: 1974, *Bertrand Russell's Philosophy*. London: Duckworth.

Newman, James R., ed.: 1956, *The World of Mathematics*. Vol. 1. New York: Simon and Schuster.

Noonan, Harold W.: 1980, *Objects and Identity: An Examination of the Relative Identity Thesis and its Consequences*. The Hague, Netherlands: Nijhoff.

Notturno, Mark Amadeus: 1985, *Objectivity, Rationality, and the Third Realm: Justification and the Grounds of Psychologism*. Dordrecht, Holland: Martinus Nijhoff.

Owen, G. E. L.: 1974, "Plato and Parmenides on the Timeless Present." In Mourelatos, ed., *The Pre-Socratics*.

Owens, Joseph: 1982, "The Doctrine of Being in the Aristotelian Metaphysics —Revisited." In Morewedge, ed., *Philosophies of Existence: Ancient and Medieval*.

——. 1963, *The Doctrine of Being in the Aristotelian Metaphysics*. 2d ed. Toronto: Pontifical Institute of Mediaeval Studies.

Pap, Arthur: 1966, *Semantics and Necessary Truth*. New Haven, Conn.: Yale University Press.

Passmore, John: 1985, *Recent Philosophers*. La Salle, Ill.: Open Court.

Peacocke, Christopher: 1975, "Proper Names, Reference, and Rigid Designation." In Blackburn, ed., *Meaning, Reference and Necessity*.

Peirce, Charles Sanders: 1901, "Modality." In Baldwin, ed., *Dictionary of Philosophy and Psychology*.

Pelletier, Francis Jeffry: 1990, *Parmenides, Plato, and the Semantics of Not-Being*. Chicago: The University of Chicago Press.

Perry, John: 1978, "Relative Identity and Number." *Canadian Journal of*

Philosophy 8.

Peterfreund, Sheldon P., and Denise, Theodore C.: 1967, *Contemporary Philosophy and Its Origins*. Princeton: D. Van Nostrand.

Pitcher, George: 1964, *The Philosophy of Wittgenstein*. Englewood Cliffs, N.J.: Prentice-Hall.

Plato: 1937, *The Dialogues of Plato*. Trans. B. Jowett. New York: Random House.

——. 1937a, *Parmenides*. In *The Dialogues of Plato*.

——. 1937b, *Republic*. In *The Dialogues of Plato*.

——. 1937c, *Sophist*. In *The Dialogues of Plato*.

——. 1937d, *Theaetetus*. In *The Dialogues of Plato*.

Pols, Edward: 1992, *Radical Realism: Direct Knowing in Science and Philosophy*. Ithaca, N.Y.: Cornell University Press.

Presley, C. F.: 1967, "Quine." In Edwards, ed., *The Encyclopedia of Philosophy*.

Putnam, Hilary: 1991, "Does the Disquotational Theory of Truth Really Solve all Philosophical Problems." *Metaphilosophy* 22/1–2.

——. 1987, *The Many Faces of Realism*. La Salle, Ill.: Open Court.

——. 1981, blurb on dust jacket of Hanfling, *Logical Positivism*.

Quine, Willard Van Orman: 1995, Letter to Dejnožka dated June 27.

——. 1994, "Responses." *Inquiry* 37/4.

——. 1992, *Pursuit of Truth*. Rev. ed. Cambridge, Mass.: Harvard University Press.

——. 1990, "Comment on Haack." In Barrett and Gibson, eds., *Perspectives on Quine*.

——. 1990a, "Comment on Lauener." In Barrett and Gibson, eds., *Perspectives on Quine*.

——. 1990b, Letter to Dejnožka dated October 23.

——. 1987, "Identity." In *Quiddities*.

——. 1987a, *Quiddities: An Intermittently Philosophical Dictionary*. Cambridge, Mass.: The Belknap Press/Harvard University Press.

——. 1987b, "Reply to Dagfinn Føllesdal." In Hahn and Schilpp, eds., *The Philosophy of W. V. Quine*.

——. 1987c, "Reply to David Kaplan." In Hahn and Schilpp, eds., *The Philosophy of W. V. Quine*.

——. 1987d, "Reply to Harold N. Lee." In Hahn and Schilpp, eds., *The Philosophy of W. V. Quine*.

——. 1987e, "Reply to P. F. Strawson." In Hahn and Schilpp, eds., *The Philosophy of W. V. Quine*.

——. 1985, "Events and Reification." In LePore and McLaughlin, eds., *Actions and Events: Perspectives on the Philosophy of Donald Davidson*.

——. 1984, "Sticks and Stones; or, the Ins and Outs of Existence." In Rouner, ed., *On Nature*.

——. 1983, *Mathematical Logic*. Rev. ed. Cambridge, Mass.: Harvard University Press.

——. 1981, "Five Milestones of Empiricism." In *Theories and Things*.

——. 1981a, "Goodman's Ways of Worldmaking." In *Theories and Things*.

——. 1981b, "On the Individuation of Attributes." In *Theories and Things*.

——. 1981c, "The Pragmatists' Place in Empiricism." In Mulvaney and Zeltner, eds., *Pragmatism: Its Sources and Prospects*.

——. 1981d, *Theories and Things*. Cambridge, Mass.: The Belknap Press.

——. 1981e, "Things and Their Place in Theories." In *Theories and Things*.

——. 1980, *Set Theory and Its Logic*. Rev. ed. Cambridge, Mass.: The Belknap Press/Harvard University Press.

——. 1976, "On Carnap's Views on Ontology." in *The Ways of Paradox and Other Essays*.

——. 1976a, "Truth and Disquotation." In *The Ways of Paradox and Other Essays*.

——. 1976b, *The Ways of Paradox and Other Essays*. Rev. and enlarged ed. Cambridge, Mass.: Harvard University Press.

——. 1975, *Word and Object*. Cambridge, Mass.: The M.I.T. Press.

——. 1973, *The Roots of Reference*. La Salle, Ill.: Open Court.

——. 1971, "Russell's Ontological Development." In Klemke, ed., *Essays on Bertrand Russell*.

——. 1970, *Philosophy of Logic*. Engelwood Cliffs, N.J.: Prentice-Hall.

——. 1969, "Epistemology Naturalized." In *Ontological Relativity and Other Essays*.

——. 1969a, "Existence and Quantification." In *Ontological Relativity and Other Essays*.

——. 1969b, "Ontological Relativity." In *Ontological Relativity and Other Essays*.

——. 1969c, *Ontological Relativity and Other Essays*. New York: Columbia University Press.

——. 1966, *Selected Logic Papers*. New York: Random House.

——. 1966a, "Variables Explained Away." In *Selected Logic Papers*.

——. 1961, "Identity, Ostension, and Hypostasis." In *From a Logical Point of View*.

——. 1961a, *From a Logical Point of View*. 2d ed., rev. Cambridge, Mass.: Harvard University Press.

——. 1961b, "Logic and the Reification of Universals." In *From a Logical Point of View*.

——. 1961c, "New Foundations for Mathematical Logic." In *From a Logical Point of View*.

——. 1961d, "On What There is." In *From a Logical Point of View*.

——. 1961e, "Reference and Modality." In *From a Logical Point of View*.

——. 1961f, "Two Dogmas of Empiricism." In *From a Logical Point of View*.

——. 1959, *Methods of Logic*. Rev. ed. New York: Holt, Rinehart and Winston.

Ray, Robert: 1977, "Frege's Difficulties with Identity." *Philosophical Studies* 31.

Recanati, François: 1993, *Direct Reference: From Language to Thought*. Oxford: Blackwell.

Reeder, Harry P.: 1989, "Wittgenstein Never Was a Phenomenologist." *Journal of the British Society for Phenomenology* 20/3.

Reid, Thomas: 1969, *Essays on the Intellectual Powers of Man*. Cambridge, Mass.: The M.I.T. Press.

Resnick, Michael D.: 1980, *Frege and the Philosophy of Mathematics*. Ithaca, N.Y.: Cornell University Press.

Richardson, Allen: 1990, "How not to Russell Carnap's *Aufbau*." *PSA* (*Philosophy of Science Association*) 1.

——. 1989, "Idealisms and the *Aufbau*." Read at Carnap and Wittgenstein Colloquium, American Philosophical Association Eastern Division Meeting, Atlanta, 30 December.

Roberts, George W., ed.: 1979, *Bertrand Russell Memorial Volume*. London: George Allen & Unwin.

Romanos, George D.: 1983, *Quine and Analytic Philosophy*. Cambridge, Mass.: The M.I.T. Press.

Rorty, Richard, ed.: 1967, *The Linguistic Turn*. Chicago: The University of Chicago Press.

Ross, W. D.: 1960, *Aristotle: a complete exposition of his works and thought*. 5th ed. New York: Meridian.

Rouner, Leroy S., ed.: 1984, *On Nature*. South Bend, Ind.: University of Notre Dame Press.

Russell, Bertrand, ed. Alasdair Urquhart: 1994, *Foundations of Logic 1903–05*. London: Routledge. *The Collected Papers of Bertrand Russell*, vol. 4.

——. 1994a, "Necessity and Possibility." In *Foundations of Logic*. The Ms. version is cited as c. 1903-5.

——, gen. ed. John Passmore, ed. Nicholas Griffin and Albert C. Lewis: 1990, *Philosophical Papers 1896-99*. London: Unwin Hyman. *The Collected Papers of Bertrand Russell*, vol. 2.

——. 1989, "Addendum to my 'Reply to Criticisms.'" In Schilpp, ed., *The Philosophy of Bertrand Russell*.

——. 1989a, "Reply to Criticisms." In Schilpp, ed., *The Philosophy of Bertrand Russell*.

——, gen. ed. John Passmore, ed. John G. Slater: 1988, *Essays on Language, Mind and Matter 1919-26*. London: Unwin Hyman. *The Collected Papers of Bertrand Russell*, vol. 9.

——. 1988a, "Vagueness." In *Essays on Language, Mind and Matter*.

——, ed. John G. Slater: 1986, *The Philosophy of Logical Atomism and Other*

Essays 1914–19. London: George Allen & Unwin. *The Collected Papers of Bertrand Russell*, vol. 8. (References to PLA are keyed to 1971h.)

———. 1985, *An Inquiry into Meaning and Truth*. London: Unwin Paperbacks.

———, ed. Richard A. Rempel, Andrew Brink, and Margaret Moran: 1985a, *Contemplation and Action 1902–14*. London: George Allen & Unwin. *The Collected Papers of Bertrand Russell*, vol. 12.

———. 1985b, "Logic and Ontology." In *My Philosophical Development*.

———. 1985c, "Mr. Strawson on Referring." In *My Philosophical Development*.

———. 1985d, *My Philosophical Development*. London: Unwin.

———. 1976, *Human Knowledge: Its Scope and Limits*. New York: Simon and Schuster.

———. 1975, *Autobiography*. London: Unwin Paperbacks.

———. 1974, *An Outline of Philosophy*, New York: Meridian.

———. 1974a, *The Problems of Philosophy*. London: Oxford University Press.

———, ed. Douglas Lackey: 1973, *Essays in Analysis*. London: George Allen & Unwin.

———. 1973a, Letter to Philip Jourdain dated January 1, 1906. In Grattan-Guinness, *Dear Russell-Dear Jourdain*.

———. 1973b, "On 'Insolubilia' and Their Solution by Symbolic Logic" (first published in 1906 as "Les Paradoxes de la Logique"). In *Essays on Analysis*.

———. 1971, *Logic and Knowledge*. Ed. by Robert. C. Marsh. New York: Capricorn Books.

———. 1971a, "Logical Atomism." In *Logic and Knowledge*.

———. 1971b, "Logical Positivism." In *Logic and Knowledge*.

———. 1971c, "Mathematical Logic as Based on the Theory of Types." In *Logic and Knowledge*.

———. 1971d, "On Denoting." In *Logic and Knowledge*.

———. 1971e, "On the Nature of Acquaintance." In *Logic and Knowledge*.

———. 1971f, "On Propositions: What They Are and How They Mean." In *Logic and Knowledge*.

———. 1971g, "On the Relations of Universals and Particulars." In *Logic and Knowledge*.

———. 1971h, "The Philosophy of Logical Atomism." In *Logic and Knowledge*.

———. 1969, letter to Dr. Angel dated May 10, 1958. In Feinberg and Kasrils, eds., *Dear Bertrand Russell*.

———. 1968, *Religion and Science*. London: Oxford University Press.

———. 1966, "The Elements of Ethics." In *Philosophical Essays*.

———. 1966a, "The Monistic Theory of Truth." In *Philosophical Essays*.

———. 1966b, *Philosophical Essays*. New York: Simon and Schuster.

———. 1964, *Principles of Mathematics*. 2d ed. New York: W. W. Norton.

———. 1962, *Human Society in Ethics and Politics*. New York: Mentor.

———. 1960, *Our Knowledge of the External World as a Field for Scientific*

Method in Philosophy. 2d ed. New York: Mentor.

———. 1958, *The ABC of Relativity*. Rev. ed. New York: Mentor.

———. 1957, "Knowledge by Acquaintance and Knowledge by Description." In *Mysticism and Logic*.

———. 1957a, "Mathematics and the Metaphysicians." In *Mysticism and Logic*.

———. 1957b, "Mysticism and Logic." In *Mysticism and Logic*.

———. 1957c, *Mysticism and Logic*. Garden City, New York: Doubleday Anchor Books.

———. 1957d, "On the Notion of Cause." In *Mysticism and Logic*.

———. 1957e, "On Scientific Method in Philosophy." In *Mysticism and Logic*.

———. 1957f, "The Relation of Sense-data to Physics." In *Mysticism and Logic*.

———. 1957g, "The Study of Mathematics." In *Mysticism and Logic*.

———. 1957h, "The Ultimate Constituents of Matter." In *Mysticism and Logic*.

———. 1954, *The Analysis of Matter*. New York: Dover.

———. 1954a, "The Metaphysician's Nightmare: Retro Me Satanas." In *Nightmares of Eminent Persons*.

———. 1954b, *Nightmares of Eminent Persons*. London: George Allen & Unwin.

———, and Alfred North Whitehead: 1950, *Principia Mathematica*. 2d ed. London: Cambridge University Press. *Principia Mathematica to #56* (London: Cambridge University Press, 1978) is the same from p. 1 to p. 326.

———. 1945, *A History of Western Philosophy*. New York: Simon and Schuster (16th pbk. reprint).

———. 1937, *A Critical Exposition of the Philosophy of Leibniz*. New ed. London: George Allen & Unwin.

———. 1933, *The Analysis of Mind*. London: George Allen & Unwin.

———. 1919, *Introduction to Mathematical Philosophy*. London: George Allen & Unwin.

———. 1914, Letter to Ottoline Morrell dated January 18 (#972). In *Contemplation and Action*, p. 347 (excerpt).

———. c. 1903-5, "Necessity and Possibility." Hamilton, Ontario, Canada: The Bertrand Russell Archives Ms. #220.010860.

———. 1904, "Meinong's Theory of Complexes and Assumptions." *Mind* 29.

———. 1898, "An Analysis of Mathematical Reasoning." In *Philosophical Papers 1896-99*.

Sainsbury, R. M.: 1993, "Russell on Names and Communication." In Irvine and Wedeking, eds., *Russell and Analytic Philosophy*.

Salmon, Nathan: 1986, *Frege's Puzzle*. Cambridge, Mass.: The M.I.T. Press.

Salmon, Wesley: 1969, "Comment." In Joseph Margolis, ed., *Fact and Existence*.

Sartre, Jean Paul: 1956, *Being and Nothingness: An Essay on Phenomenological Ontology*. Trans. Hazel E. Barnes. New York: Philosophical Library.

Savage, C. Wade, and Anderson, C. Anthony, eds.: 1989, *Rereading Russell:*

Essays in Bertrand Russell's Metaphysics and Epistemology. Minneapolis: University of Minnesota Press. *Minnesota Studies in the Philosophy of Science*, vol. 12.

Schilpp, Paul A., ed.: 1989, 5th ed., *The Philosophy of Bertrand Russell*. La Salle, Ill.: Open Court.

———, and Hahn, Lewis Edwin, eds.: 1987, *The Philosophy of W. V. Quine*. La Salle, Ill.: Open Court.

———. 1968, 3d ed., *The Philosophy of G. E. Moore*. La Salle, Ill.: Open Court.

———. 1963, *The Philosophy of Rudolf Carnap*. La Salle, Ill.: Open Court.

Sellars, Wilfrid: 1974, "Ontology and the Philosophy of Mind in Bertrand Russell." In Nakhnikian, ed., *Bertrand Russell's Philosophy*.

Shoemaker, Sydney: 1974, *Self-Knowledge and Self-Identity*. Ithaca, N.Y.: Cornell University Press.

Sluga, Hans: 1980, *Gottlob Frege*. London: Routledge & Kegan Paul.

Spellman, Lynne: 1990, "Referential Opacity in Aristotle." *History of Philosophy Quarterly* 7/1.

Sprigge, Timothy: 1979, "Russell and Bradley on Relations." In Roberts, ed., *Bertrand Russell Memorial Volume*.

Strawson, Peter F.: 1976, "Entity and Identity." In Lewis, ed., *Contemporary British Philosophy: Personal Statements*. 4th ser.

Suárez, Francis(co): 1947, *On the Various Kinds of Distinctions (Disputationes Metaphysicae, Disputatio VII, de variis distinctionum generibus)*, Trans. Cyril Vollert. Milwaukee, Wis.: Marquette University Press.

Sweeney, Eileen: 1991, abstract of "'Analyzing' Analysis: Its Different Prototypes in Ancient, Medieval, and Early Modern Thought." *Proceedings and Addresses of the American Philosophical Association* 64/6.

Tarski, Alfred: 1956, "The Concept of Truth in Formalized Languages." In *Logic, Semantics, Metamathematics*.

———, trans. J. H. Woodger: 1956a, *Logic, Semantics, Metamathematics*. Oxford: Clarendon Press.

Tolkien, J. R. R.: 1974, *The Hobbit or There and Back Again*. Rev. ed. New York: Ballantine.

Tomberlin, James. K., ed.: 1983, *Agent, Language, and the Structure of the World*. Indianapolis, Ind.: Hackett.

Turnau, Paweł: 1991, "Russell's Argument Against Frege's Sense-Reference Distinction." *Russell* n.s. 11/1.

Umphrey, Stewart: 1988, "The Meinongian-Antimeinongian Dispute Reviewed: A Reply to Dejnožka and Butchvarov." *Grazer Philosophische Studien* 32.

Urmson, J. O.: 1966, *Philosophical Analysis: Its Development Between the Two World Wars*. Oxford: Clarendon Press.

Wang, Hao: 1987, "Quine's Logical Ideas in Historical Perspective." In Hahn and Schilpp, eds., *The Philosophy of W. V. Quine*.

———. 1986, *Beyond Analytic Philosophy: Doing Justice to What We Know*.

Cambridge, Mass.: The M.I.T. Press.

Weidemann, Hermann: 1980, "Ansätze zu einer Logik des Wissens bei Walter Burleigh." *Archiv für Geschichte der Philosophie* 61.

Weinberg, Julius R.: 1936, *An Examination of Logical Positivism.* London: Kegan Paul, Trench, Trubner, & Co.

Wells, Rulon S.: 1951, "Frege's Ontology." *The Review of Metaphysics* 4. Also in Klemke, ed., *Essays on Frege.*

Wettstein, Howard: 1990, "Frege-Russell Semantics?" *Dialectica* 44.

White, Alan R.: 1979, "Propositions and Sentences." In Roberts, ed., *Bertrand Russell Memorial Volume.*

Whitehead, Alfred North: 1965, *A Philosopher Looks at Science.* New York: Philosophical Library.

Wienpahl, P. D.: 1950, "Frege's *Sinn und Bedeutung.*" *Mind* 59, and in Klemke, ed., *Essays on Frege.*

Wiggins, David: 1980, *Sameness and Substance.* Cambridge, Mass.: Harvard University Press.

———. 1970, "The Individuation of Things and Places." In Loux, ed., *Universals and Particulars.*

Williams, Bernard: 1967, "Descartes." In Edwards, ed., *The Encyclopedia of Philosophy.*

Windelband, Wilhelm: 1979, *A History of Philosophy.* 2d ed. Trans. James H. Tufts. Westport, Conn.: Greenwood.

Winslade, William J.: 1971, "Russell's Theory of Relations." In Klemke, ed., *Essays on Russell.*

Wittgenstein, Ludwig: 1975, *Zettel.* Trans. by G. E. M. Anscombe and ed. by G. E. M. Anscombe and G. H. von Wright. Berkeley: University of California Press.

———. 1972, *Remarks on the Foundations of Mathematics.* Trans. G. E. M. Anscombe. Cambridge, Mass.: The M.I.T. Press.

———. 1968, *Philosophical Investigations.* 3d ed. Trans. G. E. M. Anscombe. New York: Macmillan.

———. 1965, *The Blue and Brown Books.* 2d ed. New York: Harper and Row.

———. 1961, *Tractatus Logico-Philosophicus.* Trans. D. F. Pears and B. F. McGuinness. London: Routledge & Kegan Paul.

Wright, Crispin, ed.: 1984, *Frege: Tradition & Influence.* Oxford: Basil Blackwell.

———. 1983, *Frege's Conception of Numbers as Objects.* Aberdeen, Scotland: Aberdeen University Press.

von Wright, Georg Henrik: 1957, *Logical Studies.* New York: The Humanities Press.

Index of Names

Index of Subjects

About the Author

Jan Dejnožka (Yon DAY-no-shka) was born on December 20, 1951 in Saratoga Springs, New York to Ladislav and Helen Garrett Dejnožka. He took a B.A. with Honors in philosophy from Syracuse University in 1973, writing his honors thesis on Quine on necessary truth. Dejnožka lived the next six years in Iowa City, earning his M.A. in 1976 and his Ph.D. in 1979 from the University of Iowa. His doctoral dissertation, *Frege: Existence and Identity*, was supervised by Panayot Butchvarov.

From 1981 to 1988, Dejnožka served his country as a U.S. Navy officer. He served on board three ships: USS CANISTEO AO-99, USS AMERICA CV-66, and USS CORONADO AGF-11. On board the aircraft carrier AMERICA for two years, he qualified as Surface Warfare Officer and Officer of the Deck Underway, earning the Navy Expeditionary Medal for service off Beirut and the Sea Service Deployment Ribbon for a six month deployment to the Indian Ocean. On board the command ship CORONADO for a fifteen month complex overhaul in Philadelphia Naval Shipyard, he served as Assistant Department Head and Command Duty Officer in Port. Dejnožka then taught history and philosophy on a three year shore tour in the U.S. Naval Academy as Assistant Professor of Philosophy.

In 1990 Dejnožka visited some fifty relatives and friends in Bohemia, Moravia, and Slovakia after their liberation from Soviet domination. In 1991 he entered the University of Michigan School of Law, but took a two year leave of absence as Visiting Scholar in Philosophy in the Horace H. Rackham School of Graduate Studies, the University of Michigan. In 1992 he married Chung Wha Choi, born in Seoul, South Korea. In 1994 he returned to the law school. In December 1994 their daughter, Julie Josephine Dejnožka, was born. Dejnožka has been a Research Fellow of Union College since 1980.